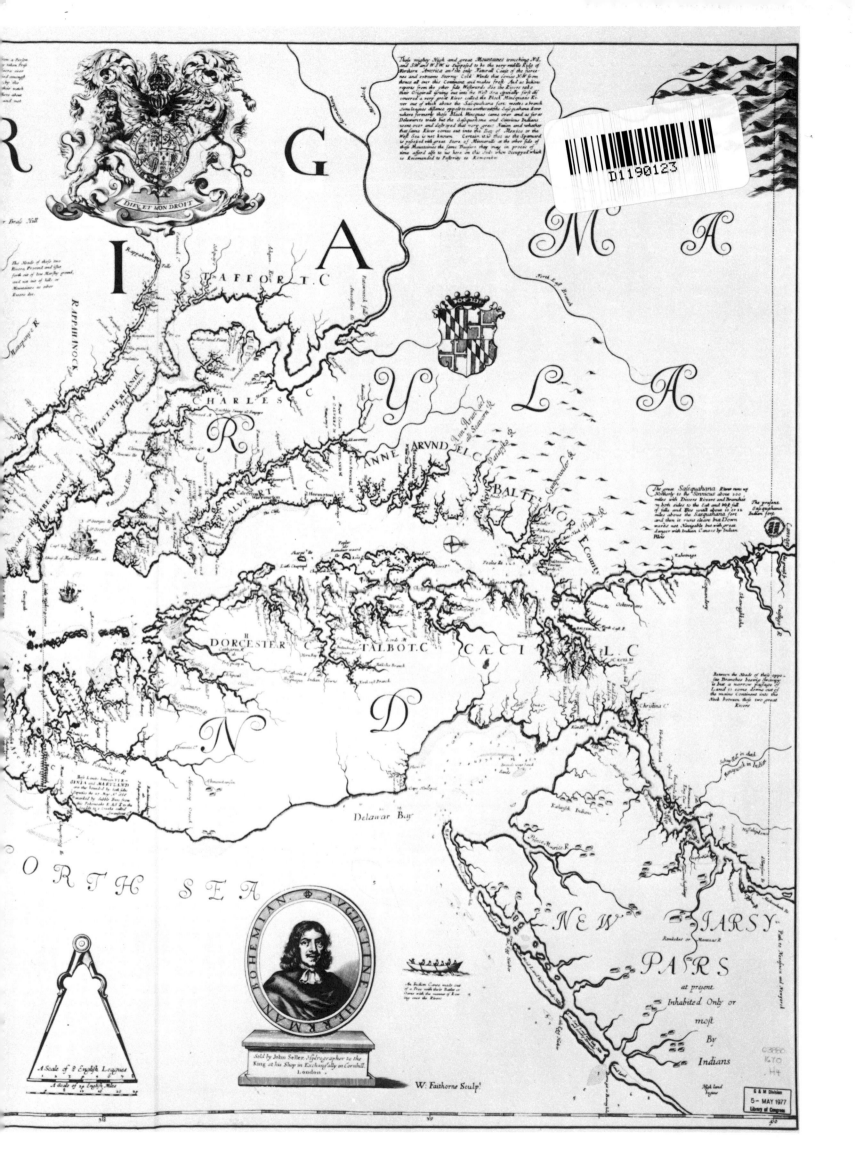

MARYLAND

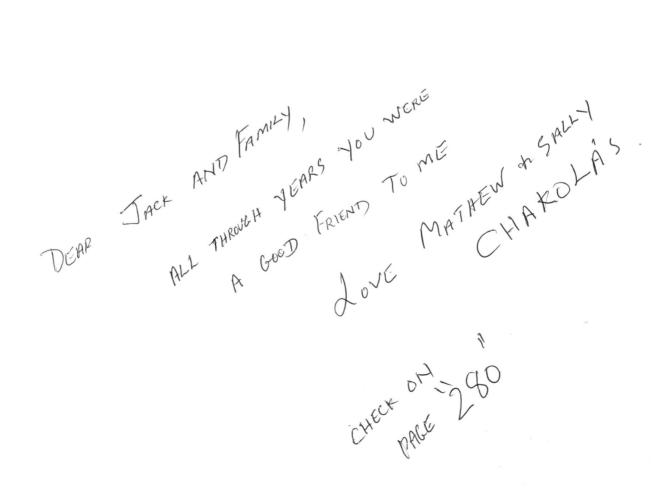

Dear Jack AND Family,
All through years you were
A good Friend to me

Love Mathew & Sally
CHAKOLA'S

check on
Page 280

AMERICAN HISTORICAL PRESS
SUN VALLEY, CALIFORNIA

MARYLAND

OLD LINE TO NEW PROSPERITY

Joseph Arnold
& Anirban Basu

The Pride of Baltimore II *under sail in Baltimore harbor. The Pride sails around the world as a goodwill ambassador for the state of Maryland. Courtesy, Pride, Inc*

Photos attributed to: McKeldin Library,
University of Maryland, College Park
Courtesy, Hughes Company Collection,
Special Collections, University of Maryland Libraries

Library of Congress Catalogue Card Number:
2003096192
ISBN: 1-892724-38-3

Bibliography: p. 358
Includes Index

CONTENTS

INTRODUCTION

For the past three centuries Maryland has been one of the smallest and richest states in the nation. Its strategic location, excellent natural resources, and diverse geography and economy have contributed to its growth and development. The Old Line State (exclusive of the Chesapeake Bay) covers 9,874 square miles, making it nearly the same size as Belgium. Like Belgium, it is also divided into three distinct physiographic regions: a coastal plain, a central plateau region, and a mountainous inland area (Maryland's peaks, however, are about a thousand feet higher than those in Belgium so that the western part of the state has become a major winter sports area). Dramatic contrasts between these three regions have given Maryland the sobriquet "America in miniature."

The core, some say the soul, of Maryland is the great Bay of the Chesapeake and its coastal hinterlands. The Chesapeake is the largest estuary in the United States measuring 190 miles in length and varying in width from four to fifteen miles. It covers more than 4,000 square miles, of which slightly over half lie within Maryland. A dozen major rivers feed into the Chesapeake, but only two of them are of great economic importance—the Potomac and the Patapsco. In 1730 the Patapsco became the location of the city of Baltimore which presently is the second leading port on the East Coast and one of the nation's major metropolitan regions. The Potomac, of course, was selected in the 1790s as the site of the nation's capital—just a few miles upstream from George Washington's home. Today over 80 percent of Maryland's residents live within twenty miles of the bay or the tidewater portions of the Patapsco and Potomac rivers. It is fitting that the ingeniously designed, sleek Chesapeake clipper ships of nineteenth-century fame have become the unofficial symbol of Maryland, for they accurately epitomize this coastal state's innovative and commercial spirit.

After an initial period of difficult "frontier" struggling in the seventeenth century, Maryland emerged as a wealthy and enterprising state; it has remained so ever since. While one does not wish to underestimate the intelligence and the occasional daring of Maryland's business people, there is no getting around the fact that nature has been extremely kind to the state. At every stage in the evolution of America's economic system, Maryland proved to have natural assets upon which its own leaders were able to create new wealth and employment, and these attributes attracted investors. The state's mild climate (the mean winter temperature remains above freezing for all but the mountainous Western region) and its extremely rich, well-watered soil made it one of the most productive agricultural sections of the nation—supporting an urbane aristocracy that figured prominently in American life during the eighteenth and early nineteenth centuries. The wealth of these great planter-traders was tobacco, the first really profitable cash crop in the United States, which grew best in the Chesapeake region. Many of the Marylanders who thrived on this natural resource paved the way for the subsequent commercial and industrial growth of the state. In addition to its excellent climate and soil, Maryland's strategic location, midway between the northern and southern sections of early America, paid great economic dividends. The Old Line State was thus an obvious choice for the site of the national capital.

With the advent of the industrial and transportation revolutions in the years from 1815 to 1860, Maryland's location and resources again placed it in an enviable position. The port city of Baltimore became the premiere shipping point for the entire Chesapeake region, and since it was far closer to the western frontier than either Philadelphia or New York, it emerged rapidly as one of the country's major metropolitan centers. Baltimore's communications with the vast American hinterland was given a further boost when the federal government funded the only major national highway of the nineteenth century—a road which ran from Maryland into Ohio and the Middle West. Today, Interstate 70 extends from the port city to the Pacific slope and is often called "the Main Street of America."

In addition to these contributions, Baltimore played another vital role in American transportation history. A small group of Maryland businessmen early in the nineteenth century took a calculated risk with the new technology of steam power. Their foresight and energy launched the Baltimore and Ohio Railroad, the first regular commercial train line in the United States. Like the B & O, other railroads and early highways assured Baltimore and Maryland of a central place in the nation's economic heartland—a place which it still occupies today. The current transportation network provides overnight access to an area containing seventy million people or 30 percent of all U.S. households, 31 percent of the nation's effective buying power, and 36 percent of its industry.

Beside supremacy in transportation development, the Baltimore area also became one of the nation's early factory, foundry, and chemical centers—again partly because of the easy access to raw materials. The mountain valleys of Western Maryland, never of great value for agriculture, were found to hold some of the highest quality coal anywhere in the world, while adjacent West Virginia and Pennsylvania lands, too, contained enormous deposits of this valuable energy resource. Hauled easily to the port via the B & O Railroad, mineral wealth has fueled Baltimore's industrial plants for 150 years and will continue to do so well into the twenty-first century.

By the 1830s all signs indicated that Maryland would continue to be a naturally strong competitor in the national economy, even though it gradually became one of the nation's smaller states. From the 1830s to the 1940s Maryland experienced a steady expansion of its wealth and population. Yet, beginning in the 1940s it suddenly "took off," welcoming hundreds of thousands of new residents and moving even more rapidly toward the top of the list of the wealthiest states in America. Beside Baltimore's traditional industrial base, Maryland added an enormous high-technology research, development, and professional service sector—much of it located in the burgeoning Washington suburban area. By the mid-1980s the Baltimore and Washington regions were rapidly merging into a single supermetropolis of over five million people—the most highly educated and affluent area in the United States.

Maryland's long ascent from agricultural frontier to high-technology center clearly owes much to natural gifts, but economic success was not automatic or inevitable. Many states and nations possessing great natural assets have squandered them through timid or inept leadership, or perhaps a labor force unable or unwilling to seize opportunities for growth. The Old Line State has achieved its position of wealth because successive generations of Marylanders in both the public and private sectors have taken the greatest advantage of the state's rich resources. In the end the only really crucial asset of any capitalist economy is the quality of its people—bold, astute, and responsible leaders, along with skilled and dedicated workers. This brief history of Maryland's economic development offers a glimpse into the careers of these people, in an endeavor to understand how they created the remarkably prosperous and sophisticated system which today's Marylanders are so fortunate to enjoy.

ACKNOWLEDGMENTS

A number of people were very helpful in providing me with information and advice for this book. The staffs of the economic development commisions in Baltimore City and in the twenty-three Maryland counties supplied me with a great deal of material on the local economic issues. In addition, the librarians of Kuhn Library, University of Maryland Baltimore County, the Central Enoch Pratt Library in Baltimore, the McKeldin Library of the University of Maryland College Park, and the Eisenhower Library of the Johns Hopkins University lcoated many records and document which were difficult to find.

Joseph L. Arnold

My work would not be possible were it not for my father, Tapendu, who taught me how to learn; my wife, Debita; mother, Ruby; sister, Reshmi; and daughter, Kimaya, all of whom teach me how to live each day.

Anirban Basu

Chapter I
THE FOUNDATION:
MARYLAND IN THE SEVENTEENTH CENTURY

The establishment and early growth of the colony of Maryland in the seventeenth century contains few really dramatic events. Its importance lies in revealing to us a major chapter in the epic transformation from the Medieval to the Modern Age. The early decades of Maryland's history offer a classic example of the manner in which the seventeenth century commerce undercut and eventually replaced the static provincial economy and society that had characterized almost all of Europe for a thousand years.

Cecilius Calvert, Lord Baltimore, received a charter from King Charles I of England in 1632 which gave him what amounted to a medieval barony of approximately seven million acres. Calvert and his heirs were to reign as "the true and absolute Lords and Proprietaries" of this land. Devout Roman Catholics, they hoped to create a haven for their peers, gentrified co-religionists who were barred from public office and most other avenues of advancement in Protestant England. Yet, the Calverts also wished to interest Protestants, and the British system of primogeniture, by which the eldest son inherited the entire family estate, spurred a number of younger sons to seek in the new world the lands and position denied them at home. Every gentleman who would bring over five laborers (indentured servants) at his own expense would receive a manor of 2,000 acres. Those paying only their own passage could receive 100 acres. It was hoped that most of the land would be distributed in large estates.

Father Andrew White conducted Maryland's first Catholic Mass on St. Clement's Island on March 25, 1634. Settlers usually stayed on the island until they were able to later move to St. Marys City. From the Maryland Room. Courtesy, Enoch Pratt Free Library. (EPFL)

A large cross was erected on St. Clement's Island by the Maryland Tercentenary Commission in 1934 to commemorate the 300th anniversary of Maryland's founding. From the Maryland Room, EPFL

Manors were to be worked by the indentured servants who, after serving four to seven years, would be freed and be given fifty acres of land for themselves. Annual rents from the manors would cover administrative costs and provide the Calvert family with a large and secure income, augmented perhaps by fur trading with the Indians. In essence, the Calvert plan called for reproducing the society of late medieval England in the lush and wild woodlands surrounding the Chesapeake Bay.

By the time Cecilius Calvert died in 1675, his medieval plan had melted away—replaced by a society of independent tobacco planters pioneering the development of the

great Atlantic economy. It was, of course, the new, vast, expanding commercial network, so well described in the next century by Adam Smith's *Wealth of Nations,* that undid Maryland's manorial society even before it was fully established. Calvert cannot really be blamed for this unexpected turn of events. His ideas of colonization were not as inappropriate as they might at first appear; they had worked well in Europe for many centuries and were given further credence by Calvert's knowledge of the early administrative and land problems at the Jamestown Colony in Virginia, which had almost collapsed in the years from 1607-1620. Nor were the woods of Maryland too wild for these manors. The trees, the bears, the wolves, and the Indians all fell with remarkable ease before the Marylanders' taxes, guns, and diseases. The problem with Calvert's plan was that it represented the best thought of the Middle Ages at the opening of a new era. The history of Maryland, most particularly its economic heritage, represents none other than the origin and flowering of the commercial capitalist system which was to typify the American way of life.

No one understood this mission better than Cecilius' younger brother, Leonard. Embarking on the creation of the modern age with two ships, the *Ark* and *Dove,* he and his crew of 130-140 persons landed at St. Clement's island at the mouth of the Potomac River in March 1634. The most immediate feelings and concerns then took precedence over future aspirations. Prayers of thanksgiving for their survival after a terrifying, storm-tossed, three-month ocean voyage were coupled with fears about hundreds of armed Piscataway Indians who threatened their immediate future. Even smaller matters must have loomed large for those facing a wilderness. The overturning of a small boat meant the loss of a settler's linen which, wrote Father Andrew White, "is no small matter in these parts." White, a saintly and yet practical Jesuit priest who accompanied the settlers, left a remarkable report of the voyage and the establishment of the colony. He recounted how Leonard Calvert, with the aid of an interpreter from Virginia, was able to gain permission from the Piscataway "Emperour" to settle in his land. This agreement was reached largely because the Indians hoped that the English would help protect them from the more powerful Susquehanna tribe who, wrote Father White, "sometimes come upon them, and waste and spoil them and their country." In return for "axes, hoes, cloth and hatchets" Calvert purchased approximately thirty square miles of land around the St. Marys River, a tributary of the Potomac. He then established a town near the center of the tract which, in an adroit mixture of politics and piety, he named St. Marys in honor of both Queen Henrietta Maria of England and the Virgin. The site had been an Indian village; the settlers may have actually used some of the Indian dwellings the first year. This riverside hamlet was to be the capital of Maryland for the next sixty-one years and from it the Marylanders gradually spread out into the whole tidewater region. Tragically, the Piscataways and other Algonquin tribes which befriended the early Marylanders were soon reduced to a pitiful remnant by European diseases, the continued attacks of rival tribes, and Maryland's own expanding frontier. All that remained of them by the end of the seventeenth century were a few scattered clusters of former tribes. However, the names which they had used for their beautiful rivers, Potomac, Patuxent, and Patapsco, as well the name of their bay, the Chesapeake, remain imprinted on the state's maps.

The little colony at St. Marys was the fourth English settlement in what eventually became the continental United States. Jamestown in lower Virginia was now twenty-seven years old and well-established, boasting a population of approximately 4,000 people by the mid-1630s. Massachusetts Bay, filling rapidly with Puritans of the

Bottom, left
Southern Maryland's seventeenth-century tobacco drying barns had steeply pitched roofs and were covered with hand-split unpainted clapboard. A small group of men were able to erect a barn such as this one in several weeks. Courtesy, Historic St. Mary's City

Below
A tobacco planter spent an entire year working his crops. In the spring the tobacco seedlings were sowed. The growing plants were then tended all summer. Fall was the tobacco drying season. During the winter the leaves were stripped and packed into hogsheads for shipment to England. Courtesy, Historic St. Mary's City

"Great Migration," was on the point of overtaking Virginia in numbers. Little Plymouth Colony, south of the Massachusetts Bay settlement, probably held less than 500 persons in 1634, but this still made it three times larger than Maryland.

The Calvert's colony, however, had the advantage of being located in the center of what became the most productive agricultural area of seventeenth-century America—the famed "Tobacco Coast." Even before Marylanders turned to growing the "sotte weed," (as tobacco was often called in that period), the Chesapeake Bay and its surrounding lands were well-known for their natural endowments. The Great Bay of the Chesapeake, the largest estuary on the east coast of North America, is entered by a narrow mouth at Cape Charles across from the modern city of Norfolk. Surrounding the bay, wrote Captain John Smith in 1608:

is a country that may have the prerogative over the most pleasant places of Europe, Asia, Africa or America ... heaven and earth never agreed better to frame a place for man's habitation ... Here are mountains, hills, plains, valleys, rivers and brooks running most pleasantly into a fair bay compassed but for the mouth with fruitful and delightsome land.

Chesapeake Bay is actually the 190-mile estuary of the Susquehanna River running southward into the Atlantic Ocean. The land on each side, called the Eastern and Western shores, is separated by the bay waters which vary in width from three to twenty miles. The bay, itself, is only one half of the regional water system. Its forty-eight principal tributaries, some of which are quite wide at their mouths and navigable for many miles inland, create a combined bay-river shoreline. As one seventeenth-century visitor wrote, these lands "render it so convenient for exporting and importing into any part thereof by water carriage." It was along these shores and the country immediately in back of them that the Marylanders built their colony. Not until the eighteenth century did they begin to settle and exploit the lands beyond this tidewater region.

The "fruitful and delightsome" area, itself, was almost all heavily wooded with enormous oaks, from which heavy timbers 60 feet long could be cut; cypresses sixty to eighty feet high before branching out; and huge tulip trees twenty feet around and ninety feet tall. In addition, there were stands of hickory, ash, chestnut, cedar, pine, and laurel—a vast primeval forest which reminded some Englishmen of what their own land must have been like a thousand years before. John Smith's 1608 "Mappe of Virginia" shows the whole land covered with trees. As Aubrey C. Land notes in his *Colonial Maryland,* these trees were "interspersed with nude Indians and nondescript quadrupeds." The "quadrupeds," in fact, consisted of huge populations of deer, elk, bear, wolves, muskrats, beavers, foxes, and other fur-bearing animals. Also, the woods housed large flocks of wild turkeys, some weighing over fifty pounds. Within and upon the bay and its rivers was one of the world's most abundant and extraordinary collection of fish, oysters, crabs, and waterfowl. The delicately balanced gradient of the Chesapeake's waters, formed by the mixing of the fresh water rivers with the salty bay, provides a perfect environment for hundreds of species of marine life. Herring, shad, rockfish, trout, bass, perch, pike, carp, and sturgeon were only the most prominent of the many types of fish savored by the new settlers. Their size was also impressive. Shad often measured three feet long, and sturgeon varied from three to twelve feet. Even the oysters which the Indians loved and quickly introduced to the Europeans were of heroic dimensions in the seventeenth century, having been variously described as a foot long or as large as a horse's hoof. Most of the early Maryland settlers regarded them as inferior to the more traditional fin fish, but their native born children and grandchildren loved them. The same was true of crabs. This delicious shellfish, which has become the major twentieth-century symbol of Maryland's seafood cuisine, was commonly abundant and of enormous size throughout the middle and lower bay three hundred years ago. Alas, as Arthur P. Middleton noted in his magisterial *Tobacco Coast,* the settlers failed to appreciate its delicate flavor until late in the eighteenth century.

Hundreds of thousands of ducks and geese spent many months of the year in the Chesapeake Bay marshlands, and Marylanders ate unbelievable numbers of them. The Dutch traveler Jasper Danckaerts described in 1680 a massive flock of ducks at the waterfront farm of Richard Adams in Kent County on the Eastern Shore:

I have nowhere seen so many ducks together as were in the creek in the front of this house. The water was so black with them that it seemed when you looked from the land below upon the water, as if it were a mass of filth or turf, and when they flew up there was a rushing and vibrating of the air like a great storm coming through the trees, and even like the rumbling of distant thunder, while the sky over the whole creek was filled with them like a cloud.

The ducks flew when Adams' son fired his gun into the flock, but the boy expressed his disappointment at hitting only three or four "as they are accustomed to shoot from six to twelve." There were many hardships for the early settlers, but the seemingly limitless bounty of Maryland's woods and waters gave these pioneers security against hunger and, within a few years, a reputation for abundant good food at all times of the year.

Maryland's greatest resource in the seventeenth century was the land, itself. The Eastern Shore of the bay was flat, although the land drained well. The Western Shore, on which St. Marys stood, was gently rolling, but like the lands across the bay, was admirably suited to a wide variety of crops. Its woods and marshlands nourished horses, cattle, and hogs. The settlers also raised Indian corn, European wheat, and oats for their own consumption, with some left over for the livestock. Peach trees flourished and from apple trees came excellent cider. The Reverend Hugh Jones, writing to a friend in England from Annapolis, Maryland in 1699, said "Our common drink is syder, which is

very good, and where it is rightly ordered not inferior to the best white wine." The finest tribute to Maryland's culinary resources came from Thomas Lawrence. An Oxford graduate and London-trained attorney of refined tastes, he reluctantly served a term as a Maryland colonial official in the late 1690s. In a private letter to a friend back in London, Lawrence lamented the lack of cultural amenities on the colonial frontier, but found his compensation at the table. The deer, the "large turkeys" and "excellent fish," along with the "variety of good fowl" were praised, but his chief accolades came for the fruits which "excel whatever Art can produce in England." The melons, he wrote, were far better than any grown in his native country and the peaches "are the best in the world; they feed their Hoggs with better than Dutchesses Eat in Hyde Park."

Jones and Thompson, writing from the new capital of Annapolis near the end of the seventeenth century, were enjoying the best of two worlds. The frontier world abounded with wild turkeys, abundant fish, and plentiful game which could still be trapped within site of the kitchen door. The new world prided also itself on well-settled farms and experienced agronomists who could produce fine tobacco, fruits, and other crops, tempting to even the most refined pallet. It should be immediately added, however, that this happy state of affairs did not come easily or quickly. It emerged gradually from the labors of colony's first two or three generations.

The building of Maryland's agrarian economy was accomplished with careful planning, years of hard work, and a fluctuating demand for Chesapeake tobacco. Gloria Main, in her excellent study, *Tobacco Colony: Life in Early Maryland, 1650-1720,* said flatly that tobacco "lies at the heart of Maryland history in the colony's first hundred years." The price of tobacco on the European market influenced almost every aspect of Maryland life—the numbers and types of immigrants entering the colony, the speed with which the frontier grew, the rate at which land was cleared, and the manner in which other crops and occupations were

Above
Cary Carson drew this picture of St. Marys City in 1634. Part of the settlement and the Indian village outside the palisades are shown. From the Robert G. Merrick Archive. Courtesy, St. Mary's City Commission

introduced or expanded. Obviously, tobacco was not the only item raised on local farms, but it was, for almost 150 years, Maryland's major cash crop and the foundation of its great prosperity in the "Golden Age" of the eighteenth century.

Oddly enough, it appears that the Calverts and their colonists did not perceive tobacco to be their major economic enterprise when they established themselves at St. Marys in 1634. This may have been due to some of the leading settlers' aversion to tobacco use, or to the knowledge that the price of Virginia tobacco, which had been very high in the early 1620s, had fallen quite low by 1629. In spite of this initial lack of interest, the settlers began to grow the golden weed almost immediately, probably because tobacco prices had begun to climb again in the 1630s. They started using it as a currency to pay taxes and private debts in 1637, and two years later they exported 100,000 pounds of the leaf. If correct, this figure equaled about 600 pounds for every adult male in the colony. In 1640 Marylanders probably again sent something in excess of 100,000 pounds, while the Virginians shipped approximately 900,000 pounds. By 1663 the two Chesapeake colonies landed almost seven million pounds on the wharves of London, Bristol, and Liverpool. The end of the seventeenth century saw estimated annual shipments of over ten million pounds. Unfortunately for the colo-

nists, the price of tobacco on the British market fluctuated widely from year to year, as the entire trade from the Chesapeake, the Caribbean, and Spain exceeded or fell short of the demand from English and European smokers. Long-term trends from about 1640 to the end of the century indicated gradual downward shifts interspersed with several periods of relatively good prices. The years from 1634 to the 1680s were generally quite profitable for most Chesapeake tobacco planters. As Paul Clemens states in his book, *The Atlantic Economy and Maryland's Eastern Shore,* this extended boom in profits spurred a steady expansion of Maryland settlements up and down the shores of the Chesapeake and its tidewater tributaries. Immigrants, particularly white indentured servants, streamed into the colony at a steadily increasing rate to till newly cleared tobacco fields.

The progression of settlement along the Chesapeake's shores can be seen in the extension of county governments. Settlers around the tidewater portion of the Severn

Center
Archaeologists and historians have recreated Godiah Spray's tobacco plantation in St. Marys City as an example of a seventeenth-century tobacco planter's house and barns. This environment was typical to many early Maryland colonists. Courtesy, Historic St. Mary's City

tually, proprietary rights had been dispensed for areas adjacent to the Anacostia River, Capitol Hill, and what was to become the White House. The unsurveyed frontier lay west of Rock Creek Park.

While settlement continued to expand, the long period of good profits began to decline. In the 1680s the tobacco prices sloped downward with increasing rapidity—below a penny a pound in 1681 and bottoming out in 1688-1689 at 0.7 pence per pound. A reasonable profit now eluded even the more efficient planters. It was, perhaps, not entirely accidental that political change occurred in the "bottom" year of 1689. Maryland's Protestant planters, acting in the wake of England's Revolution of 1688, overthrew the Calvert's proprietary government, ushering in a long period of direct royal administration. At the same time, the long depression suffered by Chesapeake tobacco growers turned prospective settlers, including indentured servants, away from Maryland's fields. As the white labor pool declined, the African slave trade grew. Wealthy landowners began to purchase black slaves in large numbers during the 1680s and 1690s. While no exact figures have survived, there were almost three times as many white servants as slaves in Maryland in 1670, but by 1700 slaves outnumbered servants, jumping from less than 5 percent of the total population to about 20 percent. Finally, the years 1680-1700 witnessed the first diversification of agriculture, as Maryland's farmers attempted to find substitutes for the sluggish tobacco trade.

Long before the tobacco prices tumbled, the Calverts' vision of a manorial economy and society had faded into memory—the victim of Maryland's freewheeling agricultural expansion. The huge estates were too unwieldy to be worked by the small number of indentured servants brought to the colony by petty "barons." In fact, only a handful of the estates were ever established. Labor was the really weak link in the Calvert plan. The period of indenture was usually only four years, after which servants received a small supply of clothing, corn, tools, and fifty acres of land. These generous inducements were successful in attracting

River on the Western Shore were provided in 1650 with a new county named Anne Arundel (in honor of Calvert's wife). Calvert County (1654) and Charles County (1658) solidified their administrative functions in the area lying between the Anne Arundel and St. Marys jurisdictions. The addition of Baltimore County in 1660 completed local government extension on the western side of the bay. Of the Eastern Shore counties, Kent was established in 1658, Talbot in 1662, Somerset in 1666, and Dorchester in 1668. As settlement reached the north, where the Susquehanna River empties into the bay, Cecil County was created in 1674. The Chesapeake was then encircled by a thin line of organized settlements, and the forested shores of the major tributaries were being ascended as the 1690s approached. By 1696 the deepest inland penetration was up the Potomac River. When Prince Georges County was created in that year, patents had been taken on parcels of land along the Potomac as far as the future site of the District of Columbia. Ac-

hands. Over 70 percent of all Maryland immigrants in the seventeenth century were indentured laborers, but after forty-eight months, many became small independent planters. The most successful began to accumulate substantial holdings. Poor Englishmen and women, the great majority of them Protestants, were quite willing to serve four to seven years as servants in Catholic-controlled Maryland in return for free land and the other economic opportunities available on the tobacco coast. By the mid-1640s the ex-servants comprised a clear majority of all freemen. The handful of manorial "barons", who were often Roman Catholic, became a tiny minority compared to the Protestant freeholders farming 100-150 acres of land. In an age when religion and politics were always deeply mixed, this development boded ill for the Calvert family.

Eventually, Maryland's independent planters did away with the entire Calvert proprietorship. The agent of Lord Baltimore's undoing was his own creation—the "assembly of freemen" which Leonard Calvert convened for the first time in 1635. Under the terms of Cecilius Calvert's charter, its purpose was to advise and approve laws suggested by the governor. However, the group also took it upon itself to initiate legislation. The assembly's relationship with the Calverts further worsened as it became larger, met more regularly, and added new representatives from the ever-expanding colony.

Tension between the assemblymen and the proprietary family boiled over into open rebellion in 1688-1689. It began when the Calverts in England sent over, as the new governor, one William Joseph, an English Catholic with a genuinely medieval view of the proprietor's absolute powers in Maryland. The new governor arrived at the little capital of St. Marys on the eve of the overthrow of Britain's pro-Catholic monarch, King James II. Joseph then called the assembly together and harangued it with a speech which historian Aubrey Land says, "surpassed all records for tactless conduct." The governor vigorously reasserted the divine right and absolute power of the Calverts over the colony, berating the Mary-

landers for what he believed was their habitual drunkenness, adultery, and sabbath breaking. As Land laconically states: "Joseph's first Assembly was also his last." Low tobacco prices bred general discontent, but Joseph's speeches actually connected economic woes with the proprietary government. The Protestant leaders decided to remove Governor Joseph, the Calverts, and their Catholic relatives who filled most, but certainly not all, of the high offices and inner councils. An armed, albeit bloodless, coup occurred in July 1869 under the banner of England's new Protestant monarchs, William and Mary.

Royal governors administered the colony until 1715, when it was restored to a grandson of Cecilius Calvert, who had conveniently embraced the Protestant faith. The return of the Calverts to Maryland's government was by this time more form than substance, however. Their influence with the assembly was small, and the Calvert family members in Maryland, who had married into other colonial Catholic families, appeared more interested in tobacco prices, agricultural diversification, and other investments than political issues.

A general overview of Maryland's economic and political development in the seventeenth century is an essential groundwork, but it does little to give one a view of daily economic and social existence of Marylanders in this distant era. Fortunately, a remarkably rich collection of historical records has survived from seventeenth-century Maryland. In the last few years, these documents have been brilliantly researched by a group of historians, including Russell Menard, Lois Green Carr, Lorena S. Walsh, Carville Earle, Allan Kulikoff, and David Jordan. A remarkably clear picture of early Marylanders, their life, and work in the seventeenth-century Chesapeake consequently has emerged.

Between 30,000 and 40,000 men, women, and children immigrated to the colony during the seventeenth century. Over 90 percent were from England with the balance coming from the west coast of Africa. The latter became the core of Maryland's black population. Approximately 70 to 80 percent of white immigrants were indentured servants, men outnumbering women by about three to one. Some of these people were convicts in English prisons, causing an earlier historian to categorize the whole group of servant-immigrants as "rogues, whores, vagabonds, cheats and rabble of all descriptions raked out of the gutter and kicked out of the country." A more careful and exact study of these people by the British historian James Horn shows them to be "a cross-section of the ordinary working men and women of England." For example, emigration records reveal that almost half of those arriving in Maryland from Bristol, England were "yeoman farmers," a quarter were unskilled laborers, and the rest were artisans—weavers, tailors, leather workers, blacksmiths, carpenters, in all representing sixty-six different trades. The women were almost uniformly described as spinsters or widows. They were mostly quite young, averaging close to twenty, with a full third still in their teenage years, hardly the age at which one would expect them to be labelled spinsters. Men were a bit older; twenty to twenty-two was the estimated mean age.

Why did they come? Unfortunately, most of the immigrants were illiterate and therefore left no records. Yet, it is not difficult to guess at the cause for the transoceanic moves. The years from 1630-1670, as described in the monumental *Agrarian History of England and Wales* (Vol. IV), were "the most terrible years through which the country has ever passed." Crop failures and terrible depression combined to destroy the livelihood of thousands of English farmers and artisans—sending them into the towns to find new work or to beg. Younger people who happened to wander into the port cities of Bristol, Liverpool, or London were undoubtedly made aware of the opportunity to gain free passage to Maryland. At the end of a brief period of service there, they could obtain something virtually unattainable to them in England—fifty acres of free land on which to grow a profitable crop. As for the women, none would long remain a spinster. George Alsop, the somewhat ribald former indentured servant who wrote his famous pamphlet "A Character of

the Province of Maryland" in 1666, stated the situation thusly:

The women who go over into this Province as Servants, have the best luck here as in any place of the world besides; for they are no sooner on shoar, but they are courted into a Copulative Matrimony, which some of them (for aught I know) had they not come to such a market with their Virginity, might have kept it by them until it had been mouldy.

Yet, there was another facet to immigration which explains why most of the English poor did not bind themselves to the tobacco coast: life there was primitive and dangerous. Maryland's settlers were scattered in clearings amid dense woods, physically isolated, lacking in most of civilization's amenities—devoting almost every daylight hour to the arduous tasks of wresting a living from raw nature. The death rate was extremely high and the "seasoning" period, usually the first year or two, took a heavy toll on immigrant lives. Relatively few Maryland immigrants (or natives) survived into their fifties and sixties. A lack of wom-

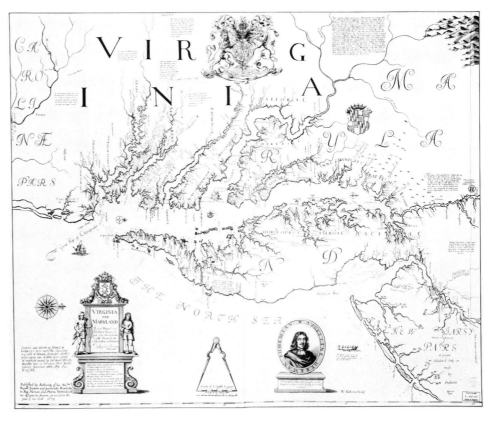

This map of Virginia and Maryland, drawn in 1670 by Augustine Herrman, shows the counties of Maryland, including rivers and plantations. Courtesy, Library of Congress (LC)

en and high mortality made family life difficult and kept the number of children fairly low. By the 1690s the colony still contained less than 30,000 people and the native-born had probably just become the majority.

In spite of these serious difficulties, thousands of indentured servants survived the "seasoning," worked out their indenture, married, and ended their lives as comfortable farmers. Some grew wealthy and became important members of Maryland's government and society. For example, Robert Vaughan probably came to Maryland in 1634 or 1635 as an indentured servant and became a freeman and landowner by 1648. He served as a militia officer, assemblyman, justice of the peace, and member of the governor's council. Zachary Wade rose from servant to planter, and at his death in 1678, held 4,000 acres. Such men were, of course, exceptional. A study of former indentured servants in Charles County, Maryland in the period 1658-1705 showed the more typical servant, after completing his indenture, left the county for the frontier, which was at this time only a few days' journey. Of those who remained, one out of four became landowners and one out of six possessed larger than average farms. The rags-to-riches story applied to very few. Only five men out of the total ex-servant group of 167 ended up with substantial wealth, but these did indeed become rich, owning over 1,000 acres of land along with servants and slaves. A visitor at the end of the century clearly spoke the truth when he said that Maryland "hath been chiefly seated by poor people whose industry hath raised them to great estates."

The life of a typical tobacco planter in seventeenth-century Maryland was one of constant labor during the growing season, but the climate of the Chesapeake region corresponded well to this sort of agriculture. As today, winter lasted only from December through February. By March, when the plants needed to be set out, spring had arrived. The harvesting and drying season was often quite hot, but in October and November, when the tobacco fleets entered the Chesapeake to begin picking up the huge wooden barrels of tobacco (called hogs-

heads), the weather often proved delightful. One adult male could usually grow and harvest somewhere between 1,000 and 1,800 pounds of tobacco in a season on a plot of two or three acres. If the price stayed above a penny a pound, fair profit could be made. Each fall the hogsheads were rolled down to the hundreds of "landings" along the Chesapeake and its tributaries, where they awaited the ships. Rolling Road, a major highway in today's Baltimore County, received its name from the county's tobacco planters who used it in the colonial era to roll their hogsheads down to Elkridge landing on the Patapsco River. During the growing season most small and middling planters purchased necessities from larger farmers who had themselves obtained them from ships coming into the Chesapeake—all on credit. As Thomas Lawrence said in the 1690s, "tho wee have as little money ... yet wee need it not, all the Country lives upon Credit and talk not of payments but in the Tobacco Season." The shipmasters, often acting as traders themselves or having on board a "factor" representing an English purchaser, would buy at a negotiated price, or take the tobacco on consignment to sell in Britain at the current market rate. The ships then off-loaded supplies from Europe: agricultural implements, cooking and eating utensils, window glass, mirrors, cloth and finished clothing, and other light items. Some were sold directly to consumers while wealthier tobacco growers, who ran something akin to general stores on their plantations, would make bulk purchases for resale during the year.

Throughout the whole seventeenth century these ship landings were as close as Maryland came to having regular commercial centers. There simply were no towns. The plantations, as even small farms were called, were scattered along the tidewater areas. Charles Calvert, writing in 1678 from St. Marys City, which was not yet even a village, confessed to the Lords of Trade in London that "wee have none That are called or cann be called Townes ... In most places There are not fifty houses in the space of Thirty Myles." Genuine urban settlements were simply unnecessary to the economy of seventeenth-century Maryland, so none developed. Rather than a sign of economic backwardness, their absence was a tribute to the magnificant water transport system of the tidewater region.

Maryland plantations varied in size from fifty to several thousand acres, but most were under 200 acres and not much more than clearings in the forest. The Reverend Hugh Jones commented in a 1699 letter to England that even in well settled areas where the plantations were "pretty closely seated, yett we cannot see our next neighbor's house for trees." In a remarkable study of All Hallows Parish in Anne Arundel County, Carville Earle found that at the end of the seventeenth century, the eighty-square-mile area was divided into 134 plantations of which 54 percent were under 200 acres, 36 percent were 200-999 acres, and only 10 percent were above 1,000 acres. The top 10 percent of the plantations, however, accounted for over one-third of all the land in the parish.

The poorer, middling, and wealthy planters of Maryland existed on three clearly different standards of living. As the century drew to a close, they became more distant from each other not only in total wealth, but also in more fundamental economic roles. The wealthiest planters were the most innovative and economically sophisticated of the colony's farmers—spearheading the movement toward agricultural diversification, expansion into the production of consumer goods, and use of slave labor. In a deferential society such as seventeenth-century Maryland (and England), these men dominated all the important political and administrative posts in the colony and were regarded as the natural leaders in their respective counties.

The middling planters were the backbone of the colony's propertied electorate, serving in most local offices. Poorer farmers had little material wealth, but they could support themselves and, for those lucky enough to find a wife, their families. The majority of poorer landowners could vote and, therefore, their views and interests could not be ignored. For example, periodic efforts to legally limit tobacco production in the seven-

teenth century were always opposed by the poorer planters who could not afford even a single season without a full crop. As a result, the Calverts never attempted to increase tobacco prices by this method.

The poorer farmer, like everyone else, grew the leaf; but even he did not neglect to cultivate food for the family table. Corn, rather than wheat, was the major crop because it could wait until the late fall when tobacco had already been prepared for shipping. Corn was also easier to grind and store. Self-sufficiency was important, too. Both old- and new-world vegetables grew in small kitchen gardens, but livestock was the great luxury of the seventeenth-century Marylanders. Almost every family possessed several heads of cattle, a larger number of hogs, and one or two horses. This livestock, far in excess of what small farmers in England then owned, was pastured free of charge on the vast areas of wooded land that existed even in the heavily settled counties. In fact, large "wild gangs" of cattle and hogs were numerous enough to require periodic hunting in order to keep them from "resorting among their tame." Animals also were used to pull carts, furnish milk and cheese, and when slaughtered, to furnish meat, fat, and hides. One record from a small farmer in the 1680s showed that over a period of three years, each member of his five-person household was able to consume approximately two pounds of beef or pork per week. Livestock was a vital part of the poorer farmer's sustenance, and the theft of animals was treated with the same seriousness as it was to have on the Great Plains in the 1880s. An act of the Maryland Assembly in the 1660s provided that a hog thief, convicted for a second offense, should be branded with the letter "H".

What sort of houses stood on the plantations? How did the average farmer cook and what material goods did he own? Knowing that death was never far away, wills written by rich, middling, and even poor farmers furnished detailed surveys of possessions. Gloria Main analyzed over 3,000 of these inventories to obtain a vivid picture of the material conditions of life during the seventeenth century.

The average seventeenth-century home contained no more than three rooms. These dwellings were also constructed of unpainted clapboard and usually contained only the essential household goods. Courtesy, Historic St. Mary's City

The average seventeenth-century home contained no more than three rooms. These dwellings were also constructed of unpainted clapboard and usually contained only the essential household goods. Courtesy, Historic St. Mary's City

From these records we now know that plantation homes belonging to the poorer freeholders were one-room, unpainted wooden cottages, varying in size from twelve by twenty to perhaps sixteen by twenty-five feet. Almost 70 percent of all seventeenth-century Maryland houses contained no more than three rooms. Within the dwelling was a small collection of essential household goods and virtually nothing else. While almost every dwelling claimed one or more beds, poorer farmers often slept two to four persons in each. Tables and benches were hand-hewn and few poorer farmers had regular chairs. Personal goods were also limited to necessities. A 1697 estate inventory for a fairly typical small farmer listed as his total possessions: a crosscut saw, four gimlets (for boring holes in wood), wedges, a small assortment of carpentry tools, a tin kettle, a cooking fork, a pair of pothooks for the fireplace, two iron pots, one iron skillet, a brass kettle, an iron pestle, five spoons, a clothes iron, two razors and a hone, two chests, pewterware, an old gun, woodenware, two glass bottles, and three small books.

Middling planters still lived in small two-or-three room houses for the most part, but they possessed a slightly broader range of belongings. In addition to benches, a few had regular chairs. They also could have owned a tablecloth and napkins, candle-

holders, a mirror, some pottery, and perhaps utensils for making cider. Some might have possessed window curtains and even a rug. Their beds were larger and had feather or wool, rather than straw, mattresses. Even these families (the more affluent of which possibly owned several servants) bedded and fed the entire household, family and hands, in the same rooms. The Nicholas Ruxton family of Baltimore County was near the top of the middling class by the end of the seventeenth century. They could afford to keep their servants and slaves in separate buildings, but the entire Ruxton family still slept in three large beds in one room.

Maryland's wealthy elite virtually all lived in the same type of largely unpainted clapboard houses that everyone else inhabited. Apparently, the lack of bricklayers and kilns accounts for the almost total absence of the sort of fine brick plantation houses that were built by this class in the eighteenth century. None of the elite's wooden houses have survived, but the estate inventories describe several of them quite well. They were, for the seventeenth century, large dwellings. Some measured twenty by forty feet and contained six to eight rooms, plus a number of out buildings—summer kitchens, storehouses for food, tobacco barns, and servant/slave quarters. The wealthy owned a few small gold or silver items, numerous chairs, tables, chests, cooking items, mirrors, tools, cloth and clothing, a small library of books, imported wine and brandy, paper and writing instruments, warming pans and chamber pots. They had all the necessities, some comforts and even a few luxuries.

Professor Main's outstanding study of these probated estates notes that the possessions of more affluent Marylanders, which appear so downright palty compared to those owned by moderate income Americans today, were not really lavish by standards of the early colonial period. Nevertheless, Maryland's total per capita wealth, especially for the upper classes, probably exceeded that of the Middle Colonies and New England. Many families could easily have purchased more goods than they did.

Rather than doing this, they tended to reinvest their income in capital goods—property, tools, farming implements, livestock, and servants. One of the earmarks of the wealthy landowner of the 1680s and 1690s was his increasingly heavy investment in slaves and his growing attention to new crops and businesses. Raising cattle for their hides and planting grain for export was mainly pioneered by larger farmers seeking a hedge against the tyranny of tobacco. Middling planters often found slaves too expensive, but they tried new export crops and turned to leather working, carpentry, and other artisan trades—competing with foreign imports through the production of local consumer goods. Such small domestic handcrafts mark the beginnings of Maryland manufacturing. Household inventories in the late seventeenth century show no great increase in these products, but they do reveal a steady use in items like plows and artisan tools for leatherworking, carpentry, blacksmithing, and weaving. All of these capital goods pointed to a diversifying economy.

The 1690s were clearly a decade of fundamental change in Maryland. The half-century rule of the Calverts had come to an end with the overthrow of the Proprietor in 1689. Recessed prices started to force diversification of Maryland's tobacco-dominated agricultural sector, and, as indicated earlier, growers were to rely more heavily on black slaves than white indentured servants. The numbers of Maryland-born men and women were beginning, at last, to burgeon, and the colony probably achieved a native-born majority sometime during the decade. As population grew, the frontier expanded. By the 1690s all the good land in the older counties had been taken and was expensive to rent or purchase. Newly freed servants and the children of small landholders faced an unpleasant choice. They could remain in the fully settled area, where they faced a life as a landless tenant or laborer, or they could move onto the frontier in Prince Georges, Baltimore, or Cecil County. Many opted for the frontier with its virtually free land. The general movement was north and west toward the first rolling hills of the

Piedmont Plateau—farther and farther away from the capital down in St. Marys. By the time the Calverts were overthrown in 1689, there was a strong movement afoot to place the seat of government in a more central location. The population center in the 1690s was probably Anne Arundel County, and the Puritan settlement of "Arundell Towne" was well situated at the mouth of Severn River, close to the narrowest point of the Chesapeake Bay. Francis Nicholson, the gifted and urbane royal governor who moved the seat of government to this site in 1695, skillfully drew the town plan. The capital, soon renamed Annapolis, retains its position to this day. It was described in 1699:

There are in it about fourty dwelling houses, of which seven or eight whereof can afford good lodging and accommodations for stanngers. There is alsoe a statehouse and a free schoole built with bricke which make a great shew among a parscell of wooden houses, and the foundation of a church is laid, the only bricke church in Maryland.

Obviously, this place was still a village rather than a government center, but the brick capital building and the school are clear proofs of improvement. The "bricke church," or at least its foundation, was also a good sign. This latter structure, which remains on what is today called Church Circle, was symbolic of the entire capital and the colony over which it presided; a foundation firmly laid, but yet to be completed. From a quaint enterprise seeking to recast a medieval world on the shores of the Chesapeake, the Calverts' colony entered the eighteenth century. It developed into an aggressive society of commercial farmers poised to channel their hard-earned incomes into a growing variety of enterprises found in the older established counties and on the expanding frontier. Wealthy and educated descendents of seventeenth century pioneers were joined by new waves of bright, forward-looking servants like Daniel Dulaney or immigrant Germans coming down from Pennsylvania. Together they pushed the colony into its Golden Age—a period reaching its apogee in the 1770s.

Chapter II
THE CHESAPEAKE'S GOLDEN AGE:
MARYLAND IN THE 1770s

After a century of economic effort and demographic expansion, Maryland emerged in the mid-eighteenth century as a well-populated, mature, and prosperous society. Its frontier region, which in 1700 stood in the center of the colony not far from the tidewater line, now lay in the mountains of Western Maryland in what would become Washington and Garrett counties. The Central Valley area, located between the mountains and the tidewater, still retained a number of rustic characteristics denoting its more recent settlement, but the scores of farmers and artisans streaming into the area—German immigrants from Pennsylvania and native Americans from the tidewater region—were rapidly domesticating the landscape. Within these broad, fertile valleys comprising the modern counties of Frederick and Carroll, along with the upper portions of Baltimore, Montgomery, Howard, and Harford, Marylanders were creating an economy and society markedly different from that of the older tidewater region.

The spread of Maryland's settlement into the valley and mountain regions in the eighteenth century did not overshadow the historic center of the colony which encompassed the Chesapeake Bay's rich coastal plain. As Table 2.1 shows, the majority of Marylanders still resided in the counties that fronted on the shores of the Chesapeake. The two or three middle decades of the eighteenth century are, in fact, remembered as the tidewater's Golden Age. It was the high noon for the fabulous tobacco coast and its

TABLE 2.1			
POPULATION OF MARYLAND FROM THE CENSUS OF 1782			
COUNTIES	WHITES	BLACKS	TOTAL
Anne Arundel	9,370	8,711	18,081
Baltimore	17,878	5,472	23,350
Calvert	4,012	3,598	7,610
Caroline	6,230	1,698	7,928
Cecil	7,749	2,634	10,383
Charles	9,804	7,920	17,724
Dorchester	8,927	4,575	13,502
Harford	9,377	3,041	12,418
Frederick	20,495	2,262	22,757
Kent	6,165	4,261	10,426
Montgomery	10,011	4,407	14,418
Prince Georges	9,864	8,746	18,610
Queen Annes	7,767	5,953	13,720
St. Marys	8,459	6,246	14,705
Somerset	7,787	5,953	13,740
Talbot	6,744	4,150	10,894
Washington (including Allegany County)	11,448	885	12,333
Worcester	8,561	3,473	12,034
Total	170,648	83,985	254,633

SOURCE: Stella H. Sutherland, *Population Distribution in Colonial America* (New York, New York: AMS Press, Inc. 1966).

planter society. Seizing the opportunities of the politically volatile 1760s and 1770s, the growers removed the last vestiges of the Calverts' power in Maryland and, on the larger stage of American history, played a central role in the Revolution of 1776-1783. The Revolutionary era turned out to be the tobacco barons' final dramatic moment in both the nation and, to a great degree, Maryland. The economy changed, over-planting of tobacco began to wear out the soil, the sot weed went into a long decline, and its chief planters gradually lost their dominant role.

One of the most striking aspects of the Golden Age is the rapidity with which it arose. We in the twentieth century are accustomed to the drastic transformations of our environment by powerful machines, potent chemicals, and lightning communication. One needs some historical reflection to appreciate the ways in which eighteenth-century farmers, merchants, and artisans improved the land and expanded commerce. Through a variety of historic accounts, one can discern the carefully calculated innovations, the painstakingly created networks and institutions, and the shear concentration of time and energy that Marylanders devoted to transforming the simple, rustic frontier society of the 1690s into the complex and sophisticated culture of the 1770s. They achieved all of this with virtually the same level of technology available to those who landed with the *Ark* and the *Dove*: small hand tools and the power generated by horses, oxen, human beings, and a few streams of water for mills. It seems even more astonishing when one remembers the humble origins of most seventeenth-century Marylanders—indentured servants and illiterate yeoman from England's economically depressed villages and towns. This inauspicious beginning was clearly no longer in evidence by 1770 when William Eddis, a newly arrived British official, sent the following account back to a friend in London:

The inhabitants are enterprising and industrious; commerce and agriculture are encouraged; and every circumstance clearly evinces that this colony is making a rapid Progress to wealth, Power and population ... It is worthy of observation that a striking similarity of speech universally Prevails; and it is strictly true that the Pronounciation of the generality of the people has an accuracy and elegance that cannot fail of gratifying the most judicious ear.

Two salient facts emerge from Eddis' observant letter: Maryland's economy had moved from its seventeenth-century concern with survival and moderate security to a new focus on wealth and power. Of equal note, this humble and diverse collection of residents were now amalgamated into a society united by a common and cultured speech. In fact, as Eddis was delighted to discover over the next several years, Marylanders pursued a way of life which even sophisticated Englishmen found utterly enjoyable. The descendants of yeomen and indentured servants had proven themselves astute in the production of wealth. They were equally adept at enjoying it. If one thing has remained constant since the Golden Age, it is the state's pride in calling itself the "land of pleasant living."

The most spectacular change in Maryland between 1700 and the 1770s was the increase in population. The low proportion of females and the relatively high death rate in the seventeenth century had severely retarded population growth. In 1700 Maryland had only 34,000 people, 4,000 of which were black slaves. By 1770 the figures soared to an estimated 202,000. There was no complete enumeration of Maryland's population during the 1770s, but the census of 1782 showed a total of 254,633 inhabitants (170,648 whites and 83,958 blacks).

Immigration from England, Ireland, Africa, and neighboring Pennsylvania accounts for some of the growth. Nevertheless, the major factor was the increasing number of black and white females who married and/or began bearing children quite early, producing much larger families than was usual in Maryland's early decades. Such women were increasingly evident through every strata of society from the hard working and prolific farm girls to the cultured and aristocratic ladies like Henrietta Maria Lloyd, the mistress of Wye House Plantation, whose twelve children and numerous grandchildren established one of the wealthiest and most powerful dynasties on the Eastern Shore. Her epitaph, still visible on a tombstone at Wye Plantation, reads:

*She who now takes her rest within this tomb
Had Rachells face and Leas fruitful womb
Abigails wisdom, Lydeas faithful heart
With Marthas care and Marys better Part*

In an age when human physical labor was the most precious economic capital one could possess and its scarcity was a continual problem, fecund females (both free and slave) were gratefully acknowledged and eagerly sought.

Contrasting with the pattern of demographic growth, there was no fundamental alteration in the socio-economic structure of the colony's population. The hierarchial class structure—from small tenant farmer to great planter—had emerged in the 1680s and 1690s, to persist throughout the eighteenth century. However, several new elements emerging during the Golden Age portended major changes for the future. In 1770 Marylanders were divided into six discernable groups for which the term "classes" seems, in most cases, too rigid a designation. Table 2.2 estimates the approximate size of each group in the 1770s.

The one unbreachable division in Maryland society was racial. Almost one-third of Maryland's residents in 1770 were Afro-Americans; well over 80 percent of them were slaves. This large population had grown primarily through the natural increase of those brought from the west coast of Africa in the previous century. There was still some importation of slaves from across the Atlantic and the West Indies, but the totals were relatively small. The overwhelming majority of black servants were concentrated in the tidewater tobacco counties or the tobacco and wheat farms of the Eastern Shore. In these regions they accounted for 40 to 45 percent of the total population. Farther inland, where tobacco was not an important crop, the slave population dropped to 20 to 25 percent, while the western areas had less than 10 percent. Slaves were valuable. A good field hand was worth fifty to 175 pounds, so relatively few Maryland planters could afford large numbers of them. While the Carrolls, Lloyds, Fitzhughs, Ringolds, Galloways, Taskers, Dulaneys, and the other wealthy families held servants by the hundreds, most slaveholders had only one or two. The majority of tobacco farmers were too poor to buy any. In the 1770s Marylanders generally expressed few moral scruples over the chattel ownership of black Africans and Afro-Americans. The Quakers were the only group to express open disapproval of servitude and largely abstained from purchasing black bondsmen; for the rest, slaves were simply a valuable investment. Because of their high cost and value, most servants were fed and sheltered above the subsistence level. Authorities generally agree that slaves worked harder but were better cared for in the eighteenth century than they had been in the previous hundred years. They were employed not only as field hands, but also as skilled artisans and overseers. Controls on slaves were strict and punishments for the breaking of rules and laws, very severe—clear evidence that eighteenth-century Marylanders never fell victim to the later myth of "happy slaves." The hundreds of advertisements for runaways appearing in the *Maryland Gazette* and the *Journal* testify to the magnitude of the slave's desire for freedom and, most often it appears, their hopes of being reunited with family members who had been sold, leased, inherited, or given to other owners.

The small but growing number of freed blacks were socially and economically circumscribed, but in spite of these great difficulties, some made their way into the middle rank of property holders. Benjamin Brown of Prince Georges County, listed as a "free mallatoe," regularly sold substantial quantities of tobacco through the Glasgow firm of Simpson, Baird and Company. The 1771 debt book of Baltimore County shows one black planter by the name of "Jehu" who owned 131 acres of land—a farm sizable enough to produce a very comfortable living. These cases indicate that men of purpose and skill could achieve economic success even against the enormous pressures of eighteenth-century racial exclusiveness. Still, such people were extremely rare. The overwhelming majority of free blacks were compelled to pursue the least attractive occupations. They were paid generally a lower wage than white workers and, therefore, had almost no means or hope of rising above the subsistence level.

White indentured servants occupied a fundamentally different position even though they were, for a limited period of time, bound laborers in much the same manner as slaves. The servant group, so significant in the seventeenth century, played a relatively small role by the 1770s. Comprising little more than 5 percent of the total population, indentured whites from England, Scotland, and Ireland were nevertheless found in every part of the colony. Their individual condition varied widely. Young William McLeod, a highland Scotsman, was indentured to a merchant in Queenstown, Maryland in 1770. Transferred to another merchant in Oxford, he was taught the business of a tobacco factor and general trader. By 1775 he had completed his servitude, entered a prosperous trading company, and had begun to invest in West Indies commerce where, he wrote, "I would be receiving good profits while I paid at most but a trifling commission."

Less fortunate and, alas, more typical were the servants who spent their days as struggling small farmers, many of them never even obtaining ownership of the small plots they worked. Little is known about these people, except for letters discovered in the British Public Records Office by Dr. Edward Papenfuse. James Horn published them in the 1979 *Maryland Historical Magazine*. The letters are from William Roberts who came to Maryland in 1756 and served his apprenticeship in the tobacco fields of Anne Arundel County. Sadly, he later lamented, his failure to learn "a trade or two" forced him into the life of a small tenant farmer where one "suffered the heat of sun from day break until dark." He hoped, nevertheless, "by God's blessing to live an honest life if it is a hard one." Twenty years later he appears in the records as an aging, poor, landless farmer with a wife and nine children to support.

As indicated by Table 2.2 free (non-indentured) whites made up almost two-thirds of Maryland's population and can be divided into roughly three economic groups: (1) the large planters, sometimes doubling as merchants and financiers, who lived sumptuously and provided the colony's leadership; (2) the middling planters or farmers, most of whom owned their own land, lived comfortably, and were a vital force in almost all areas of Maryland society; and (3) the small farmers, mainly tenants, and the landless agricultural workers who lived either modestly or poorly. The growth of a small urban population added a tradesman-artisan segment to the structure that stood largely, though not exclusively, in the middling rank.

The great merchant-planter class, those owning at least 1,000 pounds worth of land, slaves, livestock, other capital, and personal property, comprised not only the economic elite of the colony, but its social and political leadership as well. A man who possessed 2,000 acres, ten slaves, and lived in a large, fine house was a major local aristocrat and trade leader. He probably marketed tobacco, wheat, or other products for many of his small neighbors, rented land to a dozen or more tenant families, and provided credit to many more for purchases of goods. This last function was quite important since Maryland had no banks or other local financial institutions in the eighteenth century. While the English, Scottish, and native tobacco or wheat traders were sources of credit, wealthy local planters were most often solicited for loans. Carville Earle found that between 1750 and 1766, the top 10 percent of all Hallows Parish creditors extended 80

to 90 percent of all borrowable funds.

Among Maryland's prominent local gentry, there stood out a few dozen whose names were known by informed people throughout the colony, the Atlantic Coast, and the commercial centers of Europe. Charles Carroll of Carrollton was probably at the top of the list. In 1764 he held 40,000 acres of land in the tidewater region and Western Maryland, valuable urban properties in Baltimore and Annapolis, one-fifth share in the Baltimore Iron Works, 285 slaves, over 1,000 pounds worth of livestock, and 24,000 pounds in loans out at interest (almost ten times more than the largest creditor in Hallows Parish had ever extended). Carroll calculated his total wealth in 1764 to be 88,380 pounds. By the time of the Revolution, he was possibly worth over 100,000, perhaps the richest man in America. Over on the Eastern Shore in 1770, Edward Lloyd III held a total of 36,292 acres. These parcels stretched for almost 40 miles from Cecil to Queen Anne's County. While Carroll held more land, Lloyd's was probably of greater value. The latter's total wealth by 1770 came to almost 100,000 pounds, which made him a clear rival with Carroll for the position at the top of the "Great Planter" list.

While the elite provided most of the economic and political leadership for Mary-

TABLE 2.2

ESTIMATE OF SOCIAL-ECONOMIC GROUPS IN MARYLAND IN THE 1770s

CLASS	PERCENTAGE
Planter/Merchant Elite	5
Middling Farmers and Townspeople	25
Small Farmers	33
White Indentured Servants	5
Free Blacks	4
Black Slaves	28

BASED ON: David Skaggs, *The Roots of Maryland Democracy;* Ronald Hoffman, *A Spirit of Dissension;* and U.S. Census Bureau, *Historical Statistics of the United States.*

The members of the Lloyd family were the wealthiest and most successful agriculturists on the Eastern Shore from the late seventeenth century forward. They owned hundreds of acres of land, and diversified farming was one of the keys to their wealth. The Lloyd family home in Easton, Maryland, is pictured in 1968. Courtesy, Maryland Historical Trust (MHT)

land, its most pervasive impact may have been cultural. If they were, as some contend, the creators of Maryland's profuse and generous lifestyle, their influence is indeed far-reaching. It is equally possible that they simply reflected, more lavishly and tastefully, the deep and open enjoyment of life that can be found throughout the entire spectrum of eighteenth-century Maryland society. During the summertime the complex and demanding management of farming and the general pressure of business kept social occasions to a minimum, but in the fall, spring, and especially winter, most Marylanders availed themselves, said William Eddis, of "varied amusements and numerous parties." None proved more enjoyable to Eddis than the winter entertainments put on by the great planters at their vast country estates. In January, 1770 he wrote of a magnificent evening spent at a manor house

south of Annapolis where the dining tables were decorated with "all the good things of a plentiful country . . . the wines excellent and various; and cheerful blazing fires, with enlivening conversation which exhilarated the spirits and rendered us totally regardless of the rigors of an American winter." In Annapolis, the social center of the tidewater district, Marylanders attended the theater, danced at the innumerable balls, played cards, and enjoyed each other's company. During the spring and fall, all classes assembled at one or another of the twenty-seven tracks to watch some of the fastest horses in America (or Europe) race for large purses. These were grand social occasions and Matthew Page Andrews said that racing was "the vogue at every gathering of people, on Sundays, on Saturdays, and even at Quaker Meetings." The stables of Benjamin Tasker at "Belair" in Prince

Georges County and Edward Lloyd's famous stable were among the most valuable in the nation and formed the foundation of Maryland's horse raising tradition—a pleasant pastime and profitable business.

The great planters were not alone in the convivial social pleasures of Maryland society. The celebration of many saints days, the horse races, even the general meetings of the Quakers were attended, as several friends complained, by a "great Concorse of ... white people and great Crowds of Negroes that assemble together ... drinking to excess, and behaving in a riotous and turbulent manner." These boisterous public occasions were outnumbered, of course, by somewhat quieter and more private domestic entertainments. Weddings of the country farmers, said Eddis, were "universally performed in the dwelling houses of the parties," and provided numerous occasion for enjoyment:

The company who are invited assemble early in the evening, and after partaking of tea and other refreshments, the indissoluble contract is completed. The bride and bridegroom then receive the accustomed congratulations; cards and dancing immediately succeed; an elegant supper, a cheerful glass, and the convivial song close the entertainment.

The Marylanders zest for life's pleasures led people like John Adams to believe that they held work itself in contempt and were bringing up their children "in Idleness or what is worse in Horse Racing, Cock Fighting and Card Playing." The usually observant Adams missed the mark in this view, for his Puritan background may have led him to conclude that a people who played so hard could not work as vigorously. Such was clearly not the case. Nine out of ten Marylanders were dirt farmers who tilled the soil directly, even if they held a servant or a slave. The towns were all absolute beehives of activity. Even the wealthy planters such as Charles Carroll spent many long days administering his estates and conducting far-flung agricultural, industrial, and financial pursuits. Carroll's comprehensive

and detailed account books and his voluminous correspondence attest to his prodigious managerial labors. The direction of business enterprises on the scale of Charles Carroll of Carrollton, Edward Lloyd, or Daniel Dulaney probably comes closer to the business and financial activities of the modern bank or corporation than any other aspect of economic life in eighteenth-century America. Yet, very few of Maryland's gentry forgot the fact that their grand lifestyle would rapidly disappear without careful attention to complex, commercial agriculture.

The colony's middling farmers also managed their agricultural enterprises with considerable sophistication and skill, though obviously on a much smaller scale. This is of real importance, for it was the middle ranks of Maryland's farmers that account for the majority of real wealth, income, and consumer spending. The broad group of families, owning between 500 and 1,000 pounds worth of land and other property, represented one-quarter of the state's entire population and over 40 percent of its free whites. David Skaggs in his *Roots of Maryland Democracy* concludes that in 1771 only 37 percent of the free white adults (in the four counties he studied) were landowners, so it is likely that some of these farmers were successful tenants. Also, another small portion (approximately 3 percent) were the middle class townspeople—shopkeepers, smaller merchants, artisans, transport workers, or tavern keepers who did not necessarily own land, but did possess a fair amount of taxable wealth. The commercial and artisan trades of Maryland's townspeople were pursued by a number of farmers in the countryside, too. This non-agricultural income often boosted them into the middle rank of property holders. The number of such multiple-occupation farm families is not known, but probably ranged from 10 to 20 percent.

The middling farmers were a sizable group. Together with their wives and children, they amounted to almost 60,000 people by the Revolution. As Audrey Land states in *Colonial Maryland,* the "massive growth" of this broad spectrum of prosper-

ous farmers and moderately wealthy townspeople made them the weighty class of the Golden Age. The field crops which they produced account for the majority of Maryland's total agricultural output. Thus, they were responsible for the quadrupling of the colony's exports between 1700 and 1770. The prosperity, in turn, "created an immense market for consumer goods" that supported the growing towns with their local merchants and artisans. While the elite maintained their hold on the political leadership during the turbulent 1770s, it was the votes and, after 1775, the military forces, drawn from this middle range of Marylanders that in Land's opinion, "decided the outcome."

Below this middle strata stood the small-scale growers. These were freeholders, tenant farmers and landless agricultural workers, with less—sometimes far less—than 100 acres of land. Together, they made up close to half of all adult white males. They, too,

Above
The Baltimore Fish Market, shown in 1935, was located at Baltimore Street and the Fallsway. Built by lottery money in 1763, the fish market remained in this spot until it relocated to Jessup, Maryland, in the winter of 1984. From F.P. Stieff's Baltimore and Annapolis Sketch Book, Maryland Room, EPFL

Right
The barn seen in the background of these children, built by Jack Rohrer of Washington County in 1786, shows the German architectural influence present in Western Maryland. Courtesy, Washington County Historical Society

were arranged in a spectrum of wealth, but the range was narrow. Virtually none of these households could afford even a single slave. Those nearer to the top of the class lived modestly while those in the lower reaches usually hovered precariously between poverty and destitution. In 1770, Reverend Robert Mosley, a Jesuit priest stationed on the Eastern Shore, described a number of these Marylanders as "miserable, abandoned families, in poverty, want and misery." The Golden Age clearly had its dark underside in the lives of these sad people. Unfortunately, harbingers of difficult times loomed ahead. By the end of the 1770s, there was no longer a Maryland frontier where people could find inexpensive unoccupied land, and the state's rising towns were not yet growing rapidly enough to absorb the excess rural population. Increasing numbers of Marylanders from the older, fully settled counties, including a number who carried the name Calvert with them, headed over the mountains into Tennessee, Kentucky, and Ohio; but others stayed behind to become part of a semi-permanent class of poor, rural farmers and agricultural laborers who remained on the land until the twentieth century.

The Golden Age of the Tidewater Chesapeake was still largely supported by the tobacco leaf. On the eve of the American Revolution, the crop still accounted for almost 75 percent of Maryland's exports. The major tobacco counties (St. Marys, Charles, Anne Arundel, Prince Georges on the Western Shore and Queen Annes, Talbot, and Kent on the Eastern Shore) contained slightly over half the total population and almost the entire gentry. Tobacco trade was now over one hundred years old, but bore little resemblance to the simple, modest, and somewhat haphazard pattern of the seventeenth century. First, the scale of the Chesapeake trade increased beyond all expectations from 30 million pounds in 1700 to over 100 million by the early 1770s. It was not only the volume of trade that changed in these decades. Almost every aspect of the tobacco business was restructured in the seventeeth century except the hot, tedious work involved in growing,

processing, and packing the crop. Even the tobacco, itself, was different. After the passage of the Maryland Tobacco Inspection Act of 1747 prohibiting the export of inferior grades, the quality of the product became much more uniform. At the same time the two major types of tobacco in the seventeenth century, oronoco and sweet-scented, were augmented by new strains bearing names such as long green, thick-joint Brazil, lazy shoestring, and little Frederick. The 400-to 800-pound hogsheads of the seventeenth century were gradually enlarged until the 1770s, when the biggest weighed 1,400 pounds. The making of hogsheads, itself, became a thriving business and just prior to the Revolution, reached 100,000 a year for tobacco alone, not to mention the thousands of smaller barrels and casks used to store wheat and other products.

The most dramatic change in the tobacco

A tobacco drying barn in Calvert County is depicted in 1976, looking the same as it has for many generations. MHT

business was the rise of the continental and, to a lesser extent, Irish market for the product. By the 1770s English and Scottish merchants were re-exporting to the continent over 80 percent of all Chesapeake tobacco. Most of it went to France and Holland. Even though total exports of tobacco to Britain tripled between 1700 and 1770, the price also rose fairly steadily. There were occasional sudden "busts" in the market with a flurry of credit contractions and business failures, but they usually lasted for a season or two before the price escalated again. A second major innovation, connected with the growth of this continental commerce, was the rapid increase in Scottish tobacco traders in the Chesapeake. Almost all of these merchants represented large Glasgow firms which maintained close ties with the French and Dutch. Armed with large amounts of credit extended by these two rich continental powers, the Scots inundated the Chesapeake's tobacco ports with agents who captured about 40 percent of the whole business by 1770.

This entire commercial sector was lubricated by credit, and in the eighteenth century it reached enormous proportions. The great Glasgow tobacco houses joined older London firms in advancing credit to almost the entire middling group of planters. Virtually anyone with over 100 acres could obtain goods on credit from "factors," American agents of English or Scottish merchants. The Scots were the most bullish with their credit, providing it to some farmers who had not yet even become property holders. A prominent Glasgow merchant in 1766 wrote that the Scottish tobacco agents in the Chesapeake, acting also as importers of European goods, advanced credit simply on the future prospect and good character of young farmers:

The Agents, in disposing of the goods that are consigned them, do not always depend for payment on the real ability of the people to whom they sell them, but often trust to the labor and industry of many, who are in the Possession of little or no real property ... In a young country where land may be got at a low rent, and where a valuable staple is raised, young men soon leave their Parents, and marrying, settle Plantations for themselves. But, in order to make this settlement, they must have some household furniture and working tools. With these, they are supplied upon credit, by some Factor or Store keeper as he is called. And, thus it appears, that it is in dependence on the labor, industry and honesty of many, not if their real property, that they get goods upon credit from different store keepers.

By 1776 British factors and store keepers had advanced over 570,000 pounds in sterling credits to Maryland planters and farmers who invested it in land, slaves, buildings, and other capital goods, along with a wide variety of imported consumer items. The significance of these credits can be gauged by comparing it to the 387,000-pound sum of loans made to all New England colonies combined. Wealthy planters like Charles Carroll, Sr. feared that Marylanders were going too far into debt to pay for their "imaginary wants," which he thought included an overabundance of luxury items. Yet, this was probably not the case. The broad expansion of credit, particularly to the middle level farmers and those starting out in agriculture, played a leading role in the economic expansion of the eighteenth-century Chesapeake.

The one serious drawback to this system, however, was the occasional sharp drop in the price of tobacco which caused periodic credit "crunches." Unfortunately for the British, one of the credit contractions came in 1772, when a glut of tobacco sent the price spinning downward. Maryland and Virginia planters, taken unawares by the sudden drop in the market, found themselves unable to keep up their debt payments. Many native American merchants in Baltimore, Annapolis, Georgetown, and other Chesapeake towns, involved even more deeply in the international credit system than the planters, were threatened with legal action to pay off their large debts. Some historians have said that Chesapeake indebtedness to British merchants was a chief cause of the Revolution in 1776. Jacob Price, a leading authority on American trade in the eighteenth century, has stated that it is too simplistic to attribute the revolutionary fervor of Marylanders and their tobacco-planting neighbors in Virginia to their indebtedness to the Englishman. However, the encroaching financial crunch of 1772-1774, coinciding with already strained Anglo-American relations, "must have heightened the sense of unease fed from so many other sources." When the Revolution finally came in 1775-1776, the tidewater tobacco region "was much more enthusiastically and consistently revolu-

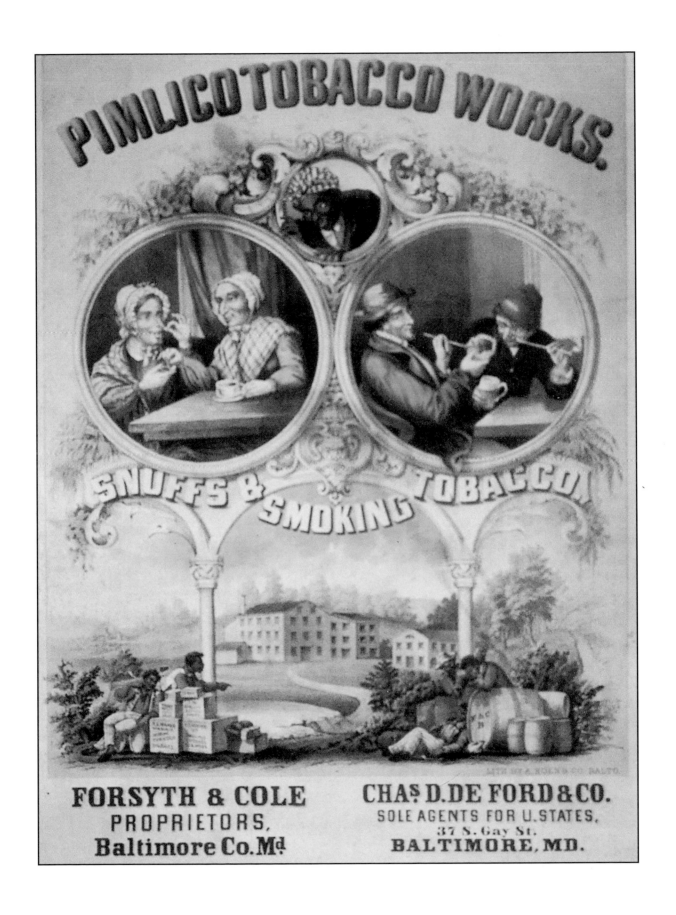

Right
Father Andrew White's mass, held upon the colonists' safe arrival at St. Clement's Island, was immortalized in this painting by artist Emanuel Lentze. Courtesy, Maryland Historical Society (MHS)

Below
This circa 1858 view of Hagerstown, as captured from the spire of St. John's Lutheran Church, looked north into the mountain landscape of the Cumberland Valley. Across the top and bottom appear several noteworthy Hagerstown structures. From the Hambleton Collection. Courtesy, The Peale Museum, Baltimore, Maryland

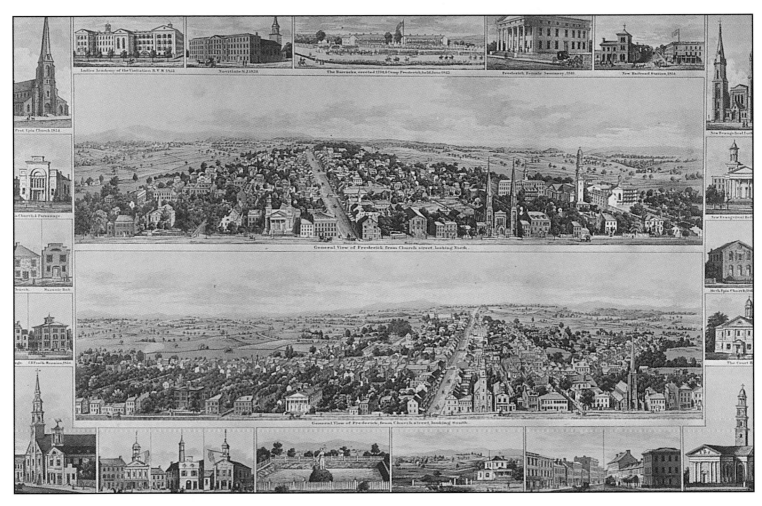

Above
These views of Frederick, Maryland, are from a lithograph printed by E. Sachse Company in 1854. The upper panorama looks north and the lower one south along Market Street. Various churches and other notable buildings in Frederick are also shown. MHS

Left
This illustration of the Baltimore Shipyard was used in an advertisement by the Chesepeake {sic} Marine Railway and Dry Dock Company of Baltimore in 1868. The shipyard, located in Fells Point from 1866 to 1884, was the only black-operated shipyard in the Baltimore area at that time. Courtesy, The Peale Museum, Baltimore, Maryland

Above
George Lovie's 1873 sketch depicted the canning process employed by a Baltimore oyster house. Courtesy, Calvert Marine Museum, Solomons, Maryland

Right
A colorful drawing from an 1872 issue of Harper's Magazine showed watermen in boats on the Chesapeake tonging the oyster beds. Courtesy, Calvert Marine Museum, Solomons, Maryland

Above
The Bare Hill Copper Mine, located near Pimlico and Falls roads in Baltimore County, incorporated this illustration into an 1870 advertisement. The insert in the lower left shows the mine's tunnel layout. The mining of copper in Bare Hill began in 1839 and lasted until the mid-1870s, when another mining company took over. MHS

Left
The works of the Peoples Gas Company of Baltimore is illustrated in this 1870 advertisement. Coal was brought to the southwest Baltimore utility by trains and used to manufacture gas, which was then stored in tanks on the company's premises. Courtesy, Commercial Credit Company, Baltimore

Above
The Fairview Inn was located on the National Road just a few miles west of Baltimore. It was the first important stop for stagecoaches headed west into the Ohio Valley and, conversely, a popular watering place for wagoners and teamsters bringing passengers from the West into Baltimore. From the Cator Collection, EPFL

Right
Exchange Place, designed by Maximillian Godefroy and Benjamin Latrobe, was completed in 1820 and became the heart of Baltimore's far-flung commercial empire. The building stood on Gay, Lombard, and Water streets in downtown Baltimore, just a few blocks from the harbor. From the Cator Collection, EPFL

Above
Construction of the C & O Canal was completed by 1850, connecting 184.5 miles between Georgetown and Cumberland. Courtesy, C & O Canal Museum

Left
This panoramic view of Ellicott's Mills shows the town and factories along the Patapsco River. A major industrial center in the first half of the nineteenth century, the valley never fully recovered from a devastating flood in 1968 that took many lives and destroyed dozens of factories and mills. From the Hambleton Collection. Courtesy, The Peale Museum, Baltimore, Maryland

Above
People journeyed by coach for five hours between Baltimore and Washington from 1825 to 1835. Phoenix Line "safety coaches" such as this one were owned by a Baltimorean. In 1838 the Washington line of the Baltimore and Ohio Railroad replaced the stagecoach as the popular way to travel between the two cities. MHS

Right
A lithograph from a drawing completed by Conrad Ludloff around 1875 shows the beginnings of a race at Pimlico Race Course in Baltimore. The clubhouse on the left burned down in 1966. From the Cator Collection, EPFL

tionary" than other parts of Maryland. Thus, the temporary failure of the British mercantilists' tobacco sector, with its regulations, subsidies, credits, and prohibitions, may have led many Marylanders to think that if a political rift occurred between Britain and the American colonies, it could not cause economic consequences worse than those invoked by the financial panic of 1772. Independence, on the other hand, could possibly open the door to superior opportunities outside of the confining economic structure. Whatever its exact role in the lives and thoughts of Marylanders, the tobacco trade and its financial system clearly played an important part in the momentous events of the 1770s.

While the tidewater tobacco trade was the centerpiece of Maryland's economy in the 1770s, it should not obscure several secondary activities which provided some commercial balance and foreshadowed the diversified economy of the following century. The most important of these activities were the raising of wheat and other cereal crops; the timber industry and its allied trades (cooperage, carpentry, and shipbuilding); iron manufacturing; and the numerous commercial, craft, and service sectors emerging in the towns.

The wheat and flour trade of Maryland began in a small way at the end of the 1600s, but it did not reach large proportions until the middle of the next century. Wheat was viewed as a cash crop in areas where soil was not as suitable for the more valuable tobacco plants. However, the increasing demand for wheat and flour in New England, the West Indies, and Southern Europe edged the price upwards, and an increasing number of both small farmers and large planters turned their attention to grain. On the Eastern Shore many farmers switched the majority of their land over to wheat in the 1760s, when bad harvests in Southern Europe sharply raised its price. The character of the Eastern Shore wheat trade can be seen in the port records of Oxford and Chestertown, showing fifty-one wheat cargoes clearing these harbors in 1769; sixteen of these headed for Southern Europe, fourteen for the West Indies, and

twenty-one for the Northeastern ports of Philadelphia, New York, Newport, and Boston. In all almost 150,000 bushels were exported. The Central Maryland counties of Baltimore, Harford, Cecil, and Frederick sent thousands of bushels of wheat and barrels of flour to these same places. Beginning in the 1740s roads opened to the rich valley area of Central Maryland, and Baltimore, the new town on the Patapsco, soon became the colony's major grain and flour exporter. In 1775 the fledgling commercial center alone shipped 250,000 bushels of wheat and 120,000 barrels of flour to northeastern American ports, Britain, Southern Europe, and the West Indies.

The lumber trade and its allied industries also became an important aspect of the Maryland economy, especially in those counties with large stands of virgin forest and poor tobacco soil. On the Eastern Shore, Worcester, Somerset, and Dorchester counties produced sizable amounts of timbers, staves, shingles, and planks. In Talbot and Kent counties, there were large stands of oak, mulberry, and pine that were regarded as some of the world's best ship timber. Located on the Western Shore, Harford County was the leading lumber producer in the 1770s. The vast forests of Frederick and Washington counties were just beginning to be commercially exploited, due to the lack of adequate roads for transporting the bulky lumber products.

Wherever good ship timber stood close to navigable water, shipbuilding proved a natural pursuit for the local population. Shipyards were established on the Eastern Shore in the seventeenth century, primarily in the small ports of Talbot and Kent counties. However, by the mid-eighteenth century, the maritime industry was also to be found in Annapolis, Georgetown, Baltimore, and other ports on the Western Shore. These enterprises, in turn, spawned ropewalks, sail makers, iron forges, and other nautical trades. There are no accurate statistics on the number of vessels constructed in Maryland's shipyards, but figures from the 1756-1775 Annapolis port books record the presence of 386 Maryland-built boats. While this constitutes a sizable business, it in no way compares with New England shipbuilding, which in the same period launched several thousand craft. Marylanders certainly could have entered the industry on a far larger scale, but failed to do so probably because they preferred to put their capital into land, slaves, and other traditionally well-paying agricultural enterprises.

Even though they could not match the New Englanders in numbers, Maryland shipbuilders proved more innovative in their design techniques, producing the famed "Baltimore Clipper," the most signifi-

This 1776 map claims to be "a new and accurate chart of the Bay of Chesapeake, with all the shoals, channels, islands, entrances, soundings, and sailing-marks." It is "drawn from several draughts [drafts] made by the most experienced navigators." LC

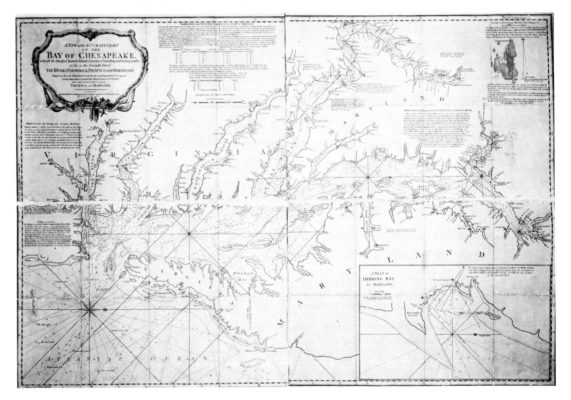

were producing their own versions, sporting even sharper molded hulls and more sophisticated rigging which were used to great effect in both the legal and illicit West Indian trade. The vessels also carried goods within the immediate area. With the coming of the American Revolution and the British blockade, this sleek, fast design was adopted by shipbuilders from New England to the Carolinas, laying the basis for the famous nineteenth-century clippers.

The smaller clipper-style vessels continued to evolve for all types of commercial

cant innovation of the eighteenth century. There is some disagreement regarding the origin of the clipper vessels, but the most often advanced theory focuses on the so-called Bermuda sloops which traded between the Chesapeake and the West Indies. These commercial ventures were unprotected by the British convoy system and, some said, involved a considerable amount of smuggling. For these reasons, the mariners engaged in this trade required smaller, sharper hulled vessels with lots of canvas and a more responsive rigging system to insure speed and maneuverability. The Bermuda sloops thus became a familiar sight in the bay. By the 1760s shipyards throughout Maryland

purposes within the Chesapeake Bay area, and before the end of the eighteenth century, were being used increasingly as pleasure yachts. George Washington was among the spectators at a 1774 yacht race on the Potomac. Relatively few of the thousands of sportspeople who now sail the Chesapeake probably know that the peculiarities of the West Indian trade and the vicissitudes of revolution during the Golden Age laid the foundation for America's tradition as the leading designer and builder of sailing craft.

Among Maryland's economic activities in the 1770s, only one stood outside the agricultural-maritime realm, but it was an important exception: the iron industry. The outcroppings of ore along the Western Shore of the bay and in Central Maryland had been noticed since the early days of the colony, but ironmaking was not undertaken in a commercially significant way until the beginning of the eighteenth century. From that point on it grew rapidly. In 1771 Maryland shipped 3,658 tons of pig and bar iron, leading all other colonies in the export of this valuable product. Most of Maryland's iron was sold in Britain, but some went to New England and the West Indies. Iron production remained largely dependent on charcoal until the 1780s, and the lack of adequate supplies of wood crippled English production. Maryland had high quality ore and its huge forests could easily provide the 300 bushels of charcoal required each day to keep an iron furnace in blast. By 1770 there were at least eighteen furnaces and an equal number of forges in operation at a wide variety of locations in Maryland. The majority, however, were situated near the Chesapeake Bay and its navigable tributaries because roads were too unpredictable for hauling the heavy loads required in the metal business. The ore of the Patapsco Valley near Baltimore was regarded as the best. There were five furnaces located right in that region, and ore was also shipped to other locations in Maryland and Virginia.

The iron furnaces themselves were among the largest structures in the colony—usually twenty-five feet on a side and thirty or forty feet tall. Forges used to refine the crude pig iron were almost as large. The latter were tended by anywhere from twenty to forty workers, many of whom were slaves and indentured servants. While the British Iron Act of 1750 prohibited Americans from manufacturing finished metal products, the regulation was ignored. Maryland's furnaces and forges made a very wide variety of items: nails, hardware, pots, pans, blacksmithing tools, axes, agricultural implements, ship fittings, barrel hoops, Dutch ovens, and dozens of other items for the home, farm, and shop.

Ironmaking was a profitable enterprise. The Principio Iron Company, established by a group of British investors on Principio Creek at the head of the Chesapeake Bay,

In 1788 settlers near the Pocomoke River attempted to extract iron ore from the Nassawango Creek because of its rusty color. Pictured is the Nassawango Iron Furnace, built in Snow Hill in 1832. Fifteen years later the furnace was abandoned due to the lack of ore. Photo by M.E. Warren

Iron was mined in the Catoctin Mountains during the 1750s and the Catoctin furnace iron works produced everything from iron bars to machinery parts during the early industrial period. The Catoctin Iron Furnace is pictured as it stood in 1935, fifty years after its closing. Courtesy, Hughes Company. From the Maryland Room, EPFL

became the colony's largest producer. By 1769 the firm had invested more than 10,000 pounds in two large furnaces; over 130 slaves; additional numbers of indentured servants and hired laborers; a sloop and a schooner for carrying raw materials and the finished "pigs" and bars. It also possessed 30,000 acres of woodland. These investments paid off: 182 tons of iron were sold in England and large amounts of Patapsco ore went to Virginia. Company managers thus returned a quarterly profit of nearly 1,000 pounds to the shareholders. By this time, however, the firm was in competition with almost a dozen other Maryland iron compa-

This 1828 lithograph depicts an early view of an iron foundry along Jones Falls, above North Avenue in Baltimore. The Baltimore region has been an important iron-making center since the 1760s, and by the 1820s contained dozens of furnaces, forges, and metal shops. MHS

nies which also turned handsome profits. The Baltimore Iron Works was begun in 1731, and thirty years later the value of its shares had risen from 700 to 10,000 pounds, returning an annual dividend of 400 pounds. During the American Revolution, canon and shot were produced at the Elk Ridge Furnace by Samuel Dorsey, who at this point had begun using coal for fuel. The Baltimore Iron Works and the Mt. Etna Furnace in Washington County also contributed to the American arsenal. Yet, the leading manufacturers of heavy weapons for the Continental Army were Samuel and Daniel Hughes, owners of the Antietam Furnace on the Potomac River. Their company supplied General Washington with dozens of large canons. Maryland's iron industry continued its growth in the post-Revolutionary era, but was soon overshadowed by Pennsylvania. Nevertheless, it provided the historic basis for the state's larger-scale metals industry in the nineteenth and twentieth centuries.

It is striking how rural the Maryland economy remained throughout the Golden Age. Plantations and farms set the scene for the major economic activity; flour and grist mills were almost all located in rustic areas; many artisans and craftsmen worked in their own farmhouses; and even the large iron furnaces and forges were a distance away from the towns, many surrounded by fields where food crops were grown and livestock raised for their large labor forces. In part, the dispersed nature of the Maryland economy made its little towns more important than their size would suggest. They were the centers of trade; the official sites of local, provincial, and imperial government; and the focus of much social life. To be sure, they remained quite small. In 1776 Baltimore, with a population of approximately 5,700, was the largest community in Maryland. Annapolis and Frederick, the respective centers of the tidewater tobacco counties and the western wheat region, each claimed somewhere between 1,500 and 1,700 people, although Frederick probably held a slight edge on the capital. Beside these three major settlements, nine other towns gained significance in the 1770s: Oxford, Chestertown, and Pocomoke on the Eastern Shore; Elkton and Havre de Grace at the head of the bay, Upper Marlboro, Bladensburg, and Georgetown in the Potomac region; and finally, on the Maryland frontier, Hagerstown.

While Baltimore, with its huge grain trade, was already recognized as Maryland's city of destiny, it was still a fairly raw commercial boom town where local merchants appeared more intent on business affairs than cultural or even religious life. Visiting the Patapsco metropolis in this era, one Jedediah Morse noted the variety of church buildings in the town. Yet, he observed that the object of the majority "appears to be to make their fortune in this world—while preparation for another is either unthought of or deferred to a more convenient season." It is, of course, not known how much the piety of Baltimore's merchants was sacrificed to Mammon, but there is no doubt that they proved to be skilled and venturesome businessmen in an astounding variety of enterprises. William Lux, for example, was one of the town's chief shipowners and traders, having partial or total possession of ten vessels during the years 1764-1775. He exported Baltimore's major items: wheat, flour, bread, iron, lumber, and hides, and his ships traded in Virginia, Boston, Barbados, Newfoundland, North Carolina, Italy, Spain, and Ireland. In addition, Lux was involved in ropemaking, ship chandlery, and flour milling. He sold wholesale dry goods in Baltimore, while maintaining a retail store at Elkridge Landing on the Patapsco. Lux was as active in politics as he was in business, organizing protests against the Stamp Act in the 1760s, pushing for independence in the crises of 1774-1776, and rendering valuable service during the Revolutionary War as a purchasing agent for the Continental Army. In almost every respect Lux was typical of the leading merchants of Baltimore in the 1770s—involved in a wide variety of local and international business transactions, continually critical of the shortcoming of the British economic policy, and, in the end, decisively supportive of the Revolution.

Annapolis in the Golden Age was a rather different sort of place. Its radicalism in economic and political affairs was tempered by the fact that it was the capital of the colony and residence of the chief civil and maritime officials of the British Crown. Governor Robert Eden was a man who relished his position at the center of social life. His large expenditures for entertainment set a grand style in the little capitol, while rankling a number of leading Marylanders who in one way and another paid for a significant part of these costly pleasures. Nevertheless, the gaiety, as well as commercial and administrative enterprises, drew some of the colony's most respected families to Annapolis. These newcomers built houses in the town, and by 1772 its streets were lined with a number of striking residences costing as much as 6,000 to 8,000 pounds. The Chase-Lloyd House on King George Street, the Hammond-Harwood House on Maryland Avenue, and the magnificent home and formal garden of William Paca on Prince George Street, can still be seen by visitors who wish to gain a first-hand look at the sumptuous but tasteful splendor of these urban estates. Affluent Annapolis residents also spent money freely on a whole range of imported luxuries which, along with the expenditures of government officials and those staying in town during the sessions of the colonial legislature, ran into the thousands of pounds.

The suppliers of the Annapolis elite added to the already long established shipbuilding, tanning, and artisan trades. Together they brought a 28 percent increase in population between 1764 and 1775. Joshua Johnson, writing in 1771 to a friend who had been away for several years said, "Annapolis cuts quite a different figure to what it did when you left it, it increases fast, both in inhabitants and society." The shear variety of crafts and trades in the town is noteworthy. Edward Papenfuse in his book *In Pursuit of Profit: The Annapolis Merchants in the Era of the American Revolution,* found over forty different occupations among its residents. A 1783 tax list for Annapolis reflects the administrative and mari-

Mulberry Fields, *erected around 1767, is an excellent example of the Georgian architecture to be found in Southern Maryland.* MHT

time activities of the town, showing eight lawyers, twelve clerks, eighteen merchants, sixteen ship captains, and twenty-three tavern/boarding housekeepers. Its artisans included sailmakers, clockmakers, watchmakers, silversmiths, goldsmiths, printers, cabinet makers, carpenters, blacksmiths, harnessmakers, hatters, musicians, teachers, and painters.

The focal point of Annapolis life was the colonial legislature, but by 1770 the old state house, erected sixty-three years earlier, was described as "an emblem of poverty." Thomas Jefferson, visiting the Maryland legislature in 1766, observed that it met "in an old courthouse, which, judging from its form and appearance, was built in the year one." Governor Eden, along with many Maryland leaders, resolved to build a structure more befitting the recently-acquired wealth and cultural sophistication of the colony. The magnificent new Georgian state house was begun in 1772 and finally completed eight years later, after a delay caused by the Revolutionary War.

Governor Eden, who presided over the laying of the cornerstone, did not see the finished project. The crises with the British Crown, simmering ever since the Stamp Act in 1765, deepened significantly in 1774 with the Boston Tea Party and the closing of that port. Marylanders formed a political convention, which gradually became the core of a revolutionary government. Poor William Eddis, who enjoyed so much the social life of the planter society in Maryland, was bewildered by their sudden turn toward rebellion. "All America is in a flame," he wrote in May 1774: "I hear strange language every day. The colonists are ripe for any measures that will tend to the preservation of what they call their natural liberty ... where will these matters end?" Within twenty-four months both Eddis and Eden fled back to England. The Maryland leaders with whom they had been so cordial now sat in control of the state house, raising a formidable military force to defend their "natural liberty."

Maryland's farmers and artisans, who formed the famed Maryland Line in the Continental Army, proved to be among the best regiments that served in the war. At the Battle of Long Island, the Quaker Colonel William Richardson held off the British and allowed Washington with the main body of the army to escape capture. They fought at White Plains, Brandywine, Germantown, and Monmouth, always holding their position. Switched to the Southern theater of war in 1780, they saved the rout of the American troops at the Battle of Camden and almost turned it into a triumph. Furthermore, they played the decisive role in the Cowpens victory, and at Guildford Court House, shattered one of General Cornwallis' best brigades. As the English general retreated toward Yorktown, the Maryland Line continued hammering away at the other major British force in South Carolina. By the time Yorktown surrendered, the Maryland Line had been so reduced by casualties that it was taken out of active service.

The skill and tenacity of Marylanders during the Golden Age—whether it be at raising tobacco, expanding the frontier, exploiting new markets for wheat and flour, forging iron, building elegant homes, or mounting murderous attacks on Britain's best regiments—was remarkable. The political independence directed by the planter-merchant aristocracy and so ably defended on the battlefield by the Maryland Line, had profound ramifications for the state's economy. Far less dramatic, but perhaps even more profound in its consequences, were the technological and engineering innovations already evident in England by the end of the Revolutionary war: the steam engine, the canal, and the factory. It took about four decades for these developments to prominently manifest themselves in Maryland, but many of those who supported the Revolution of 1776 lived to see the beginning of the Industrial Revolution. Charles Carroll of Carrollton signed the Declaration of Independence in 1776. Forty-six years later, he laid the cornerstone for the first railroad in America, just a few miles outside Baltimore. With the development of the Baltimore and Ohio line, Maryland and America would never be the same again.

Opposite, top
Tulip Hill *was built about 1756 on an Anne Arundel County tobacco estate. Its design incorporates facades that are equally impressive regardless of whether they are approached by the driveway or the river. MHT*

Opposite, bottom left
The Hammond-Harwood House in Annapolis, *constructed in the early 1770s by William Buckland, exemplifies the trend of copying English styles as an expression of Maryland's increasing wealth. MHT*

Opposite, bottom right
Ocean Hall, *a fine example of a seventeenth-century Southern Maryland tobacco plantation, is believed to have been built by Robert Slye. Its medieval roof construction enhances its beauty. MHT*

Chapter III:

RAILROAD, CANAL BOAT, AND STEAMER:

MARYLAND IN THE 1850s

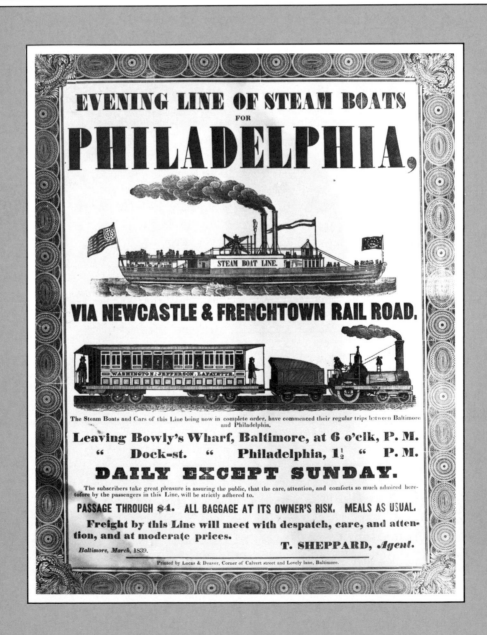

The 1850s represent a watershed decade in the development of Maryland's economy. The vast network of transportation facilities that were begun in the early years of the nineteenth century were almost all in place by the 1850s. Nothing so comprehensive or costly was undertaken again in Maryland until the highway program of the 1950-1980 era. Maryland's "transportation revolution" of the 1810-1860 era exerted a profound effect on the state economy. It assured Marylanders of new economic opportunities in commercial, industrial, and service occupations at a time when the state's agricultural sector had begun its long decline as a source of livelihood. The focus of the transportation system on Baltimore assured its overwhelming role in the emerging commercial-industrial economy and allowed its businessmen to organize and control the agricultural, mineral, and industrial wealth of the entire state to a degree unmatched in either the eighteenth or the twentieth centuries.

The census of 1860 provides a convenient overview of the profound changes that had occurred in the demographic and economic structure of the Old Line State during the four or five decades in which the new turnpikes, canals, railroads, and marine transport system were put in place. The twelve counties composing Southern Maryland and the Eastern Shore (Anne Arundel, Calvert, Prince Georges, Charles, St. Marys, Kent, Queen Annes, Talbot, Caroline, Dorchester, Worcester, and Somerset), held only 30.7 percent of the state's 687,000 res-

This lithograph depicts the Oakland Steam Saw and Planing Mills located on Leeds Creek in Talbot County in the 1870s. They later became known as the Tunis Mills. MHS

idents in 1860. Over half the population (53.8 percent) now lived in the six counties (Montgomery, Howard, Baltimore, Carroll, Harford, and Cecil) plus the city of Baltimore that comprise the Central Maryland region. Even the three counties of Western Maryland (Frederick, Washington, and Allegany) included 15.5 percent of the state's residents—almost half the number that lived in all twelve of the tidewater counties. The demographic profile of present day Maryland had clearly emerged by the end of the 1850s. As can be seen in Table 3.1, the tidewater region simply stopped growing after the opening of the nineteenth century. Between 1820 and 1860 the state added 280,000 people to its population, but the tidewater counties contributed only 9 percent to this increase. Baltimore city, with an increase of almost 150,000, accounts for 53 percent of this era's population growth and was obviously the dynamic core of the entire society. However, the population increase in the central and western regions was also impressive.

The demographic shift was the result of the commercial and industrial boom that largely bypassed the tidewater region and centered on Baltimore and the surrounding countryside. The 1860 census of employment showed that for the first time in the history of the state, jobs in agriculture had slipped to less than half of the total.

The manufacturing sector most clearly exhibited the tendency to concentrate in the Central Maryland region. Table 3.2 reveals

that Baltimore was the great center of industrial employment, with almost six out of every ten manufacturing workers employed there. However, a good deal of this activity existed in the countryside around Baltimore. Baltimore and Frederick counties contained 6,216 manufacturing jobs in 1860, amounting to 22 percent of the entire sector. The tidewater counties were left almost totally out of the race for factories and shops. They held, by 1860, only 4.3 percent of the manufacturing labor force and accounted for 4 percent of the manufacturing capital. Even the four predominantly rural counties of central Maryland (Howard, Carroll, Harford, Cecil) had more industrial-related jobs than all twelve tidewater counties put together. The turnpikes, canals, and railroads largely bypassed or ignored the tidewater region, and its more enterprising businessmen and craftsmen left in increasing numbers for Baltimore. By 1800 Southern Maryland and the Eastern Shore had entered that long economic and social sleep from which they did not begin to reawaken until the very end of the century.

While many factors are involved in the growth of Maryland's trade and industry, there is little disagreement among historians that the spectacular innovations in transportation lay at the center of this economic transformation. Maryland's location and geography made it a natural focus for transportation improvements. It occupied a strategic position midway between the northern and southern states and had, for this reason, been selected in the 1790s as the site of the national capital. The few square miles of land then given up by Montgomery and Prince Georges counties were seen as a small price to pay for having the seat of national government at Maryland's doorstep. The economic benefits which the state hoped to reap from this windfall never lived up to their expectations in the nineteenth century, but in the twentieth century they had more than fulfilled the fondest dreams of the "Capitol-on-the-Potomac" promoters.

While Marylanders were proud of their proximity to the national center, their economic efforts focused largely on Baltimore. The key to the city's success in the late eighteenth century had been its easy access

from the rich farmlands of Baltimore, Carroll, and Frederick counties and the adjacent areas of southern Pennsylvania. However, as the agricultural frontier pushed further west into the Ohio Valley and as farming in the settled regions increased, the old system of dirt roads proved woefully inadequate for the shipment of goods and supplies. The key to economic growth was the extension and betterment of the transport routes linking the hinterlands with the tidewater.

The first major effort to modernize transportation in Maryland was an immense road building and improvement program which began in the late eighteenth century and continued into the 1820s. After a num-

TABLE 3.1

MARYLAND POPULATION INCREASES BETWEEN 1820 AND 1860

COUNTY	1820	1860	INCREASE
Allegany	8,654	28,348	+ 19,694
Anne Arundel	27,165	23,900	− 3,265
Baltimore	33,463	54,135	+ 20,672
Baltimore (City)	62,788	212,418	+ 149,630
Calvert	8,037	10,447	+ 2,410
Caroline	10,108	11,129	+ 1,021
Carroll	—	24,533	—
Cecil	16,048	23,862	+ 7,491
Charles	16,500	16,517	+ 17
Dorchester	17,739	20,461	+ 2,722
Frederick	40,459	46,591	+ 6,132
Harford	15,924	23,415	+ 7,491
Howard	—	13,388	—
Kent	11,453	13,267	+ 1,814
Montgomery	16,400	18,322	+ 1,922
Prince Georges	20,216	23,327	+ 3,111
Queen Annes	14,592	15,961	+ 1,009
Saint Marys	12,974	15,213	+ 2,239
Somerset	19,579	24,992	+ 5,413
Talbot	14,389	14,795	+ 406
Washington	23,075	31,417	+ 8,342
Worcester	17,421	20,661	+ 3,240
	407,350	687,049	+ 279,699

SOURCE: U.S. Department of the Interior, Census Office, *Compendium of the Eleventh Census: 1890, Part I - Population* (Table 2, "Aggregate Population by Counties, 1790-1890: Maryland").

TABLE 3.2
MANUFACTURING IN MARYLAND IN 1860

COUNTIES	NUMBER OF ESTABLISH- MENTS	CAPITAL INVESTED	PERSONS EMPLOYED	ANNUAL VALUE OF PRODUCTS
Allegany	135	$4,235,850	1,346	$ 1,849,087
Anne Arundel	77	85,225	182	181,709
Baltimore City	1,100	9,009,107	17,054	21,083,517
Baltimore County	210	4,780,650	4,788	8,508,241
Calvert	8	38,900	37	38,293
Caroline	33	72,950	52	151,022
Carroll	144	400,250	370	743,214
Cecil	190	895,200	958	1,656,595
Charles	5	6,100	8	21,660
Dorchester	3	5,500	18	9,850
Frederick	501	1,470,446	1,428	2,894,169
Harford	255	508,030	525	797,285
Howard	49	558,900	469	1,190,822
Kent	50	126,765	105	194,300
Montgomery	44	307,980	129	380,267
Prince Georges	12	242,770	325	423,700
Queen Annes	16	36,850	36	89,260
St. Marys	54	80,750	317	153,910
Somerset	32	145,900	47	90,023
Talbot	41	90,650	102	192,805
Washington	124	263,000	407	1,085,398
Worcester	NA	NA	NA	NA
	3,083	$23,230,608	28,703	$41,735,157

SOURCE: U.S. Department of the Interior, Census Office, *Eighth Census of the United States: 1860, Part III - Manufacturers of the United States,* (Table 2, "Manufacturers by Counties").

ber of false starts, the Maryland Legislature incorporated three turnpike companies in 1805 to construct better toll roads from Baltimore toward Frederick, Reisterstown, and York. It also authorized the raising of $480,000 for the three roadways. The final cost was considerably higher. By 1815 other turnpike companies were busily constructing toll roads from Baltimore to Havre de Grace and Washington, Westminster to Taneytown, Frederick to Harpers Ferry and, most important, westward from Frederick toward Hagerstown and Cumberland. Ultimately, nine major roadways fanned out from Baltimore and remained the city's major thoroughfares until the 1950s and 1960s. The Baltimore-Frederick-Cumberland turnpike project received the greatest attention because in 1805 Congress had authorized a federally funded road from Cumberland westward to Wheeling, (West) Virginia on the Ohio River. This "National Road" was begun in 1811 and completed in 1818 at a cost of seven million dollars. It soon extended across Ohio and Indiana into Illinois. Until the coming of the railroad in the 1850s, the National Road (or Cumberland Pike as it was then called) was the major link between the east and the west. Even today, under the names Route 40 and I-70, it is one of the nation's most important highways. In the 1820s and 1830s, travel on the road was heavy. Westbound traffic consisted of settlers heading toward the Ohio Valley frontier, along with traders, suppliers, and the mail. Eastbound, there came "large droves of livestock ... from the banks of the Ohio" and hundreds of huge conastoga wagons loaded with flour, corn, oats, whiskey, hay, wool, butter, flax-seed, and other products from Western Maryland, Pennsylvania, and Ohio. *Nile's Weekly Register* reported in 1827 that "a gentleman traveling thirty-five miles on the road between Baltimore and Frederick met or passed 235 wagons in his journey, nearly seven for every mile." This transport link was Baltimore's and Maryland's economic lifeline.

In addition to Baltimore's location at the terminus of the major east-west highway, it was the primary line between the North and South. Everyone moving between the two regions, whether by boat on the Chesapeake Bay or along the Old Post Road

The approach to Cumberland from the East, down Baltimore Avenue, is shown in 1868. From the Herman and Stacia Miller Collection. Courtesy, the Mayor and City Council of Cumberland, Maryland

In the Allegheny Mountains, near Cumberland, there is a scenic gap called the Narrows. The Narrows formed a natural route for the National Road, the nation's first federally funded highway linking Maryland (and the nation's capital) with the Western frontier. The road, now known as Route 40, was built in 1811. Later the B & O Railroad was built through this same gap. MHS

(today's Route 1 and I-95), stopped in Baltimore. Its world famous inns and hotels were jammed at every season of the year. As early as 1810 an English traveler was surprised to come down to an early breakfast at the Indian Queen Hotel in Baltimore and "see the number of well-dressed men who sat down to the table, amounting to about eighty ... and I was told this is partly accounted for by Baltimore being the great thoroughfare between the northern and southern states; and the number of people passing to and fro, on business and pleasure, is immense." The fact that the major north-south route and the chief east-west link intersected at Baltimore accounts in large measure

for its phenomenal growth in this era.

The primary difficulty with the roads was their cost of repair. Wagons hauling up to two tons of cargo on narrow wooden wheels rutted the crushed stone highways and heavy storms often washed portions of them away. Before the age of high power machinery and concrete or asphalt surfaces, repairs were constantly required and gravel was made by day laborers who broke up stone with small hammers. In spite of the energetic and efficient work of the U. S. Army Corps of Engineers in supervising repairs along the National Road, it cost well over a million dollars to keep the Maryland and West Virginia portions in reasonable condition during the first twenty-five years of its existence. The private turnpike companies, lacking the revenues of the national government and having already expended $9,000 to $10,000 per mile to construct their roads, passed the tremendously expensive repairs to users in the form of higher tolls. Between the tolls and freighting costs, the shipment of goods was expensive. In 1827 a barrel of flour sold for one dollar in Wheeling but by the time it reached Baltimore, its price rose to five dollars.

The high cost of turnpike travel naturally impelled Marylanders to look to the possibility of using the Potomac as an inland transportation route. The river was not navigable above Georgetown, but as early as the 1780s, George Washington and a group of Virginia promoters had succeeded in getting the Virginia Legislature to charter the Potomac Canal Company. Ultimately both Maryland and Virginia contributed to this venture. By 1802 the company had built four short canals around the chief "falls" in the river and started deepening the channel so it could open for traffic. Unfortunately, the canals and locks were too small; traffic never sufficiently covered construction and maintenance costs nor left anything to the stockholders. By 1822 the Potomac Canal Company had spent $279,000 but had paid only one small dividend in the previous twenty-two years. In fact, without substantial loans from the states of Maryland and Virginia, it would have failed. The major stimulus to further improvements came in the period 1817-1825 as New York State constructed its Erie Canal. The linking of New York City with the great lakes via the Erie Canal was immediately perceived by businessmen in both Maryland and Northern Virginia as a serious threat to the Chesapeake. Virginia attempted to establish a new canal company that would construct a large waterway the entire distance from Georgetown to Cumberland and, by a series of inclined planes, roads, or canal tunnels, connect with the Youghiogheny and Monongahela rivers to Pittsburgh and the Ohio River. The state of Maryland quickly divided over the issue. Baltimore's businessmen, fearing the effect of the canal on their turn-

pike trade, opposed the plan, while the counties bordering on the river warmly endorsed it. Finally, in 1825 the Baltimoreans backed the Chesapeake and Ohio Canal project, in return for a promise from the Maryland Assembly that it would sponsor the construction of a feeder canal from Baltimore to the Potomac. With the states of Maryland and Virginia, the District of Columbia, and the federal government all pledging direct financial aid, plans moved ahead. The Army Corps of Engineers, which surveyed the best routes for the canal, threw a pall over the undertaking in 1826 when they estimated that the total cost of a Georgetown to Pittsburgh canal would be twenty-two million dollars rather than the four or five million quoted by the civilian promoters. Ignoring the estimate of the Corps, the Chesapeake and Ohio (C & O) Canal Company was formally organized in 1827 and on July 4, 1828 President John Quincy Adams turned the first spadefull of dirt for the new project. Twenty-two years later the canal reached Cumberland at a cost of over eleven million dollars. Needless to say, it was never completed to Pittsburgh, but it did become an important trade route for the Potomac Valley and for the growing coal fields of Western Maryland. Nevertheless, when it finally reached Cumberland in 1850, the 184-mile canal had been eclipsed by its overland rival—the Baltimore and Ohio (B & O) Railroad. Had the railroad come to Maryland even two or three years earlier, it is possible that the C & O Canal might never have been built. The whole affair underlines the difficulties that every generation has experienced allocating economic resources on the technological frontier.

The building of the B & O Railroad was pioneered by a group of twenty-five Baltimore businessmen who met together on February 12, 1827 to discuss the handful of experiments in transporting goods along rails. They were particularly interested to hear a first-hand report on the Stockton and Darlington Railroad in England which had been seen by Evan Thomas, a prominent Baltimorean. Evan, and his brother, Philip E. Thomas, the president of the Mer-

chants Bank of Baltimore, were convinced that the new technology could be successfully applied for long distance transportation—could, in fact, provide Baltimore with a trade route to the Ohio Valley superior to both canal and turnpike. The group, which included George Brown, the son of Alexander Brown, and the great merchant-shipper, William Patterson, boldly recommended that city leaders put aside all further canal plans and concentrate its resources on the construction of a railroad between Baltimore and the Ohio River. This decision, revealed in their committee report, was clearly based upon the English experiments:

Railroads had upon a limited scale been

used in several places in England and Wales for a number of years and had in every instance been found fully to answer the purposes required. ... The idea of applying them upon a more extended scale appears, however, only recently to have been suggested in that country; but notwithstanding so little time has elapsed since the attempt was first made, yet we find that so decided have been their advantages over turn-pike roads, or even canals, that already 2000 miles of them are actually completed or in a train of rapid progress in Great Britain, and that the experiment of their construction has not in one case failed ... Indeed, so completely has this improvement succeeded in England that it is the opinion of many

Horses are shown pulling a boat over the stone arch canal bridge on the Williamsport section of the C & O Canal in Washington County in 1903. From the Robert G. Merrick Archive. Courtesy, Maryland State Archives (MSA)

The Thomas Viadict, which crosses the Patapsco River, is one of the oldest stone-arch railroad viaducts in the United States. It took two years to build and was completed in 1835 and is still in regular service. From the Cator Collection. Courtesy, Maryland Room, EPFL

judicious and practical men there that these roads will, for heavy transportation, supercede canals as effectually as canals have superceded turnpike-roads.

The Baltimore and Ohio Railroad Company was chartered by the Maryland Assembly on February 28, 1827 and its stock was opened for sale in March. The State of Maryland agreed to purchase one-third of the three-million-dollar issue, Baltimore City bought $500,000 worth, and the remaining 1.5 million dollars was quickly sold to the public (36,788 individuals and corporations). The Army Corps of Engineers surveyed the best route and actually supervised the construction of the first thirteen miles from Baltimore's Mt. Clare station to Ellicott's Mills on the Patapsco River. The huge, gala groundbreaking ceremony for the railroad was presided over by the venerable Charles Carroll who turned the first spade of earth on the same July 4th holiday where, some thirty-five miles south, President Adams was digging the first dirt for the C & O Canal. In May 1830 the road opened to Ellicott's Mills—the first passenger and freight railroad in the United States. The line extended to Frederick in December 1831 and reached the Potomac at Point of Rocks in April 1832—a distance of sixty-nine miles. Legal, financial, and engineering problems slowed the progress of the railroad from this point. It did not reach Cumberland until 1842. Finally, after constructing eleven tunnels and more than one hundred bridges (the Monongahela Bridge

was 650 feet long, the largest iron bridge in America), it completed the final link over the mountains to Wheeling on the Ohio River in 1852. At that time the B & O was the longest railroad in the United States, measuring 379 miles. It forged the first direct rail link between the Chesapeake and the Ohio Valley, and had accomplished this great engineering feat at a cost of $15,628,000, almost seven million less than what had been spent on building the C & O Canal to Cumberland.

By this time the B & O Main Stem, as the western line was called, was part of Maryland's emerging rail network. In 1835 the B & O also had completed a route from Baltimore into Washington and five years later, opened a branch line to Annapolis. The Baltimore and Port Deposit Railroad linked the city with the Susquehanna River at Harve de Grace in 1837 and, by ferry, to a line running up to Wilmington and Philadelphia—the forerunner of the present Amtrack line. A year later the Baltimore and

The first train line to Annapolis began in 1840. The Annapolis and Elkridge Railroad Station on West Street is shown circa 1890. Courtesy, M.E. Warren

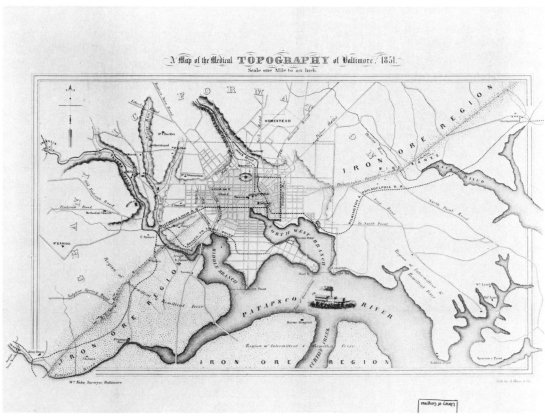

This 1851 map of Baltimore City and its surrounding counties shows the expansion of railroad routes. In addition, as a map of Baltimore's medical topography, areas of intermittent and remittent fever are speckled. LC

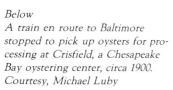

Susquehanna Railroad opened for traffic between Baltimore and York, Pennsylvania, with several branch lines to neighboring towns. By the close of the 1850s the B & O had built a second line to the Ohio River at Parkersburg, (West) Virginia. The Eastern Shore Railroad Company also commenced construction of its first line on the Delmarva peninsula, and the Northern Central Railroad (which consolidated the Baltimore and Susquehanna with several other short lines) was extending its routes from Baltimore to several new areas in Maryland and Pennsylvania. In addition, the Western Maryland Railroad, chartered to link Baltimore with Hagerstown, had opened its line as far as Reisterstown. Thus, by 1859 Baltimore could boast of its five rail lines fanning out in every direction just as the turnpike roads had done a generation before. In all, Maryland had 572 miles of railroad lines which, together with their rolling stock and other equipment, represented an investment of thirty-five million dollars. The B & O, accounting for 70 percent of this investment, owned 235 loco-

The Embrey & Cushwa warehouse in Williamsport is depicted in this 1877 lithograph. Embrey & Cushwa sold and shipped George's Creek coal, grain, and fertilizers. The Western Maryland Railroad carried coal and other goods from Cumberland to Baltimore. MHS

motives and 3,548 rail cars valued at $3.6 million. In 1859 it earned $3,618,000 and paid stock dividends amounting to $303,348. If the B & O had been the pioneer of American rail transportation in 1828, by the 1850s it was also a pioneer in the age of big business. It attracted men of large vision. Among these none stood out more than Robert W. Garrett who served as the B & O's president from 1858 to 1884. Not only did Garrett see the railroad through the difficult years of the Civil War, he improved its efficiency, increased its profitability, and expanded its operations. He was a driving force behind the development of the port facilities of Baltimore and, even before the Civil War, gave attention to the tourist and vacation business. In short, Garrett was both the chief executive of a private company and a major promoter of the entire Maryland economy. Garrett County, established in 1872 and named after the B & O president, is the only county in the state named for a business leader, and Robert W. Garrett is perhaps the best choice since he was clearly Maryland's

greatest industrial statesman of that century.

The focus of the transportation system on the port of Baltimore assured its pre-eminent position as the state's manufacturing and commercial center, but local business leaders could not expect this monopoly of transport facilities to guarantee prosperity. The port of Baltimore had to compete in a rapidly changing and increasingly competitive international maritime economy. While the Patapsco metropolis was 150-200 miles closer to the Ohio Valley than her rival ports of Philadelphia and New York, ships calling at its wharves had a considerably longer voyage if they were bound for any Northern port or European nation. They had to sail 185 miles south to pass out of bay and then back up the coast to Northeastern cities or Europe. It was for this reason that during the late eighteenth and early nineteenth centuries, Baltimore began to specialize in the West Indian trade. Yet, this enterprise was interrupted by the War of 1812 and never fully recovered afterwards. During the 1820-1860 era, the great expansion in international commerce focused on England and her industrial port of Liverpool—commerce that became dominated by New York. New York merchants organized the cotton trade of the South, and after the repeal of the import restriction grain, they took the lead in shipping wheat via the Erie Canal and New York railroads. Baltimore's tobacco trade was still lucrative, but competition from the Southern states and other nations, combined with the decline in the productivity of Maryland's tobacco fields, precluded its continuation as a growth sector of the export trade.

By the 1840s Baltimore shippers had established a new trading area—South America. The grain, corn, beef, and port that flowed into Baltimore on the new turnpikes and railroads, along with locally manufactured goods, often found their way to the southern hemisphere, particularly Brazil. The West Indies, while falling to second place, did continue to be an important secondary market. Enterprising millers in and

loaded with flour from Ellicott's, Gambrill's, or the several dozen other mills surrounding the city. Other ships, newly arrived from Brazilian ports, could have been seen off loading bags of rich dark coffee. As Norman Rukert says in his book *The Port: Pride of Baltimore,* one can walk through Brown's Wharf warehouse today "and still smell the aromatic odor of coffee impregnated in the timbers."

Baltimore shipbuilding, which had been a significant industry in the early years of the port, gradually declined, but in the 1840s and 1850s the Fells Point shipbuilders launched some of the greatest of the Bal-

These young boys are pictured in front of a busy shipyard in the Baltimore Harbor circa 1890. LC

around Baltimore developed a special type of flour for these areas called "family flour." Ground from winter wheat and of a higher grade than superfine, it kept better in the hot, humid climates of the Caribbean and South American coastal areas. The flour also proved popular in the Mediterranean. In return, Baltimore shippers imported South American coffee, copper, guano (for fertilizer), bananas, and other marketable commodities. By the 1840s Brown's Wharf at the foot of Broadway (owned by the same George Brown at whose home the B & O Railroad was born), was the center of several fleets of fast sailing ships—outbound vessels

timore clippers. The *Mary Whitridge,* constructed by Hunt and Wagner in 1855, occupies a unique place in the history of sailing. This 978-ton trading ship was among the finest examples of the speedy clipper-style craft, but she also had the cargo capacity of the slower packet ships. On her maiden voyage she crossed the Atlantic to London, a distance of 2,962 miles, in thirteen days and seven hours—a feat that appears never again to have been equaled by a sailing vessel.

By the time the *Mary Whitridge* was breaking trans-Atlantic records, the age of the sail was rapidly giving way to steam. In

BALTIMORE BAKERY.

THOMAS RITCHIE & C?.
FROM RICHMOND
BAKERS AND CONFECTIONERS TO HIS DEMOCRATIC
MAJESTY.

*All manner of ... Messes cooked to order, hot or cold
with or without ... sauce and trimmings, Public Dinn...
gotten up at the ... shortest notice, Political Hashe...
every evening ... Flummery DOUGH FA...
done brown, ... Sugar plums .*

...ESIDENTIAL OVEN.

*In 1848 the Democratic party held
its national convention in Baltimore. This suggestive cartoon reflects the political views of the time.
From the Merrick Collection, MHS*

1813, only six years after Robert Fulton's *Clermont* ushered in the era of steam navigation, Captain Edward Trippe of Dorchester County built the first Chesapeake Bay steamboat at William Flannigan's shipyard at the end of McElderry's Wharf in Baltimore. The *Chesapeake,* as it was appropriately named, was already used in the well-established service of carrying New Yorkers and Philadelphians from Frenchtown, at the head of the Chesapeake Bay, to Baltimore. By the 1830s there was a substantial fleet of steamboats plying the bay and its major rivers. To save time boats would sometimes transfer passengers and baggage in the open waters of the Chesapeake. In 1837 Tyrone Power (the great grandfather of the movie actor) described such an event as he was steaming down from Frenchtown toward Baltimore on the *Washington*:

Whilst steering through the waters of the Chesapeake, (I) perceived a large steamer standing right for us, with signal flying. Learned that this was the Columbus, *bound for Norfolk for which place we had several passengers, who were now to be trans-shipped to the approaching vessel.*

We were out in the open bay, with half a gale of wind blowing, and some sea on; it therefore became a matter of interest to observe how two large ships of this class would approach each other.

The way they managed this ticklish affair was really admirable: before we neared, I observed the Norfolk ship was laid head to wind, and just enough way kept on to steer her; our ship held her course, gradually lessening her speed, until, as she approached the Columbus, *it barely sufficed to lay and keep her alongside, when they fell together, gangway to gangway; warps were immediately passed, and made secure at both head and stern: and in a minute the huge vessels became as one.*

Here was no want of help; the luggage and the passengers were ready at the proper station, so that in a handful of minutes the transfer was completed without bustle or alarm. Meantime the interest of this novel scene was greatly increased by the coming up of the inwardbound Norfolk-man, which flitted close by us amidst the roar occasioned by the escaping steam of the vessels lying-to, a noise that might have drowned the voice of Niagara.

As we thus lay together, I noticed that the upper or promenade deck of the Columbus *was completely taken up by a double row of flashy-looking covered carts, or tilt-waggons, as they are called here. Upon inquiry, I found that these contained the goods, and were, indeed the Yankee pedlars, just setting forth for their annual win-*

Horses and carts stood ready to transport baggage as the S.S. St. Mary's steamed into Plum Point Wharf in Calvert County in 1903. Courtesy, Calvert Marine Museum, Solomons, Maryland

Horses and carts stood ready to transport baggage as the S.S. St. Mary's steamed into Plum Point Wharf in Calvert County in 1903. Courtesy, Calvert Marine Museum, Solomons, Maryland

ter cruise amongst the plantations of the South . . .

Arranged in a half circle about the bow on the main-deck, I observed the horses of these royal pedlars: they stretched their necks out to examine us with a keenness of look worthy their knowing masters' reputation and their own education.

Our business being completed, the hissing sound of the waste-steam pipe ceased, this force being once more applied to its right use; the paddles began to move, the lashings were cast off, and away the boats darted from each other with startling rapidity: the Columbus, *with the gale aft, rushing down the great bay of the Chesapeake, and the* Washington *breasting its force right for Baltimore.*

The two chief steamboat companies to gradually take over this business on the Chesapeake were the Baltimore Steam Packet Company, popularly known as "the Old Bay Line," and the Weems Steamship Line. By the 1850s they operated more than a dozen vessels—a number of them twice the size of Trippe's *Chesapeake*. The Bay Line's

Louisiana measured 266 feet and had cost $234,000. Even this mighty vessel was dwarfed, however, when in 1860 the British-built *Great Eastern*, measuring 679 feet, dropped anchor off Annapolis. A dozen bay steamboats did a rush business, carrying thousands of sightseers, including President James Buchanan, out to see what the Baltimore *Sun* described as "the Nautical Monster of the Age." Baltimoreans were naturally eager to have the awesome ship visit their port, and Robert W. Garrett of the B & O even offered its captain 2,500 tons of coal free of charge if he would call at the Chesapeake's major port. Probably fearing navigation of so large a vessel in the shallow waters of the harbor's entrance, the captain refused this lucrative offer.

The episode pointed to a problem of which Baltimore's business leaders were already keenly aware, namely, the need to deepen the channel approaches to their harbor. Ever since 1798 the city had spent small sums dredging its inner harbor, but deepening the approach channels was expensive and the city turned to the federal government for aid. In 1830 the Army

Above
The circular layout of Annapolis becomes very apparent in this aerial view of the city. The building in the lower center is St. Anne's Episcopal Church. Courtesy, M.E. Warren

Left
This lithograph of Baltimore City's harbor was drawn by E. Sachse and Company in 1858. Federal Hill can be seen in the foreground. From the Cator Collection. Courtesy, Maryland Room, EPFL

Corps of Engineers surveyed the harbor and between 1836 and 1838 Congress appropriated $55,000 for channel dredging. Political controversies in Washington over federal financing of "internal improvements" held up further expenditures until 1852. By this time Captain Henry Brewerton had arrived in the city as the Corps' Baltimore District Engineer. A West Point graduate and first-class designer, Brewerton created the nine-mile channel extending out from Fort Carroll which even today remains the main entrance to the harbor. The Brewerton channel was planned to have an average depth of twenty-two feet and a width of 150 feet. At the time, the removal of such a huge amount of spoil from the harbor was a prodigious engineering feat. By 1857 the city had two dredges and the federal government had three more at work clearing the channel. It was a great turning point in the history of the port and indeed, the economy of the whole state, when in 1858 the *Empress of the Seas,* drawing nineteen and one-half feet, entered the port through Brewerton's new channel. From the 1850s to the present day, the economic leaders of Baltimore and Maryland have maintained a close relationship with the Corps of Engineers, since their work in enlarging the harbor channels has been absolutely vital to

the state's continuing growth and prosperity. As historian Harold Kanarek observes in the official history of Baltimore District Corps of Engineers, the century-long program of harbor improvement "stands as its foremost achievement" and allowed Baltimore to retain, in an age of ever larger ships, its role as one of the great ports of the world.

While the turnpikes, canals, railroads, and harbor improvements focused the Maryland economy on Baltimore, these same innovations in other parts of the nation put the city into more direct competition with its seacoast rivals—Philadelphia and New York. In addition, the national market created by the transportation revolution combined with the sharp variations in international trade to produce a series of boom and bust cycles which deeply effected all businessmen. The result of all this was, as explained by Gary Browne in his study, *Baltimore in the Nation, 1789-1861,* was a period of spectacular growth, frightening economic turbulence, and an almost total change in the structure and methods of conducting business.

By the 1850s Baltimore's oldest merchants, who began to trade before the Panic of 1819, found it difficult to believe how much their world had changed. In the heady days of

This view of Baltimore Harbor circa 1908 looks southeast toward Light Street, where a row of steamboats are docked. Courtesy, Calvert Marine Museum, Solomons, Maryland

the early nineteenth century, Baltimore was an urban economy dominated by a small number of great merchant-shipping families who did business in much the same way that it had been conducted when the port was founded in the 1730s. These men directed their enterprises in a grand manner as private individuals or small partnerships, looking upon their shipping, Browne says, "as an 'adventure'—risky, daring, and highly profitable." Shunning specialization, they would plunge into any trading venture that looked promising. They seldom bothered with insurance and they gave or received long-term credit on a handshake and their personal reputation. They were a small, elite fraternity. The Pattersons, the Samuel Smith family, the O'Donnells, Gilmors, Hollins, Olivers, and a couple of dozen more comprised the core of this trader aristocracy, upon whom Baltimore's several hundred smaller merchants depended for leadership and economic resources. As business conditions changed, the old elite failed to adjust.

Many of them, including the city's leading partnership, Buchannan and Smith, went into bankruptcy when the Panic of 1819 hit the city.

Slowly, over the next three decades a new business community emerged that was quite different from the old swashbuckling adventurers. The new merchant-traders tended to specialize in a particular venture or commodity. Alexander Brown, founder of the nation's oldest existing banking house, told his son in 1819: "One business properly conducted is the surest and safest way to make money." Alexander Brown and Sons led the way for a generation of financiers who favored safe, steady investments over the more risky adventures of their forebearers. It was this new group that put up much of the private funding for Maryland's transportation system and her new industrial and mining operations.

Financial investment fell increasingly into the hands of banks, and the corporate form of organization began to replace the more

The William Wilkens Steam Curled Hair Manufactory published this lithograph in an advertisement circa 1856, shortly after a plant was built on Frederick Road in Baltimore. MHS

traditional partnership. The business institution came to prevail over individual or family-operated establishments, but the transition did not come overnight. The Savings Bank of Baltimore, founded in 1818, took ten years to attract even 1,000 depositors. By 1838 it had over 3,000. A decade later the institution claimed 4,700 and in 1858 its depositors numbered 18,834. Banking apparently had become a regular practice for thousands of Marylanders who did business with the Savings Bank of Baltimore, Alexander Brown and Sons, or one of the city's many other financial and savings institutions. The banks, in turn, made loans to many of the younger merchants who were taking advantage of the new transportation facilities to build up new, more specialized wholesale and retail businesses. Johns Hopkins, during the early years of his career as a wholesale merchant in the 1830s and 1840s, was a continual borrower from the Savings Bank of Baltimore. A study of the records of this hallowed institution by Lester Payne and Lance Davis also documents its important role in loaning money to the pioneering generation of Baltimore and Maryland industrialists. In 1855, when its total assets had reached $4.1 million, the Savings Bank of Baltimore advanced $95,000 to industrial firms, and its total investment

in Maryland industry stood at almost a quarter of a million dollars. Its loans to merchants were even more substantial.

In spite of the impressive growth of Baltimore's financial institutions and the increasing efficiency of their operations (Baltimore established a banking clearinghouse and incorporated a Board of Trade in 1852), its rate of financial development was considerably slower than that of Philadelphia, New York, or Boston. Not only was Baltimore losing out in the race for the most lucrative trade (with Liverpool and London), its merchants, states Gary Browne, "commonly diverted portions of their capital accumulated from trade into land, for speculation and for agricultural production as well as for status." Since investment in Maryland land during this century was seldom as profitable as commercial or industrial ventures, it served as an impediment to the state's economic development.

Putting aside these problems, Baltimore in the 1850s was by far the largest industrial center south of the Mason-Dixon Line. Over 17,000 people were employed in its factories and shops in 1860. Two trades dominated the industrial sector: Clothing producers employed over 6,000 men and women and the iron industry boasted approximately 4,000 workers. Over 1,300 were

Piles of oyster shells accumulated in front of C.H. Pearson and Company, an oyster fishery and cannery located in Baltimore, circa 1882. These shells could be crushed for road paving, or ground and used as fertilizer or chicken feed. Courtesy, U.S. Fish and Wildlife Service. From the National Archives, Washington, D.C.

The cycle of the oyster season—
from tonging the oysters at sea to
shucking in the factories—is
brought to life in this 1882 illustration taken from Harper's Magazine. *Courtesy, Calvert Marine
Museum, Solomons, Maryland*

Above
This lithograph by A. Hoen & Company depicts the Alberton Cotton Factory in Ellicott City circa 1855. The factory was a leading manufacturer of cotton duck and drill. Courtesy, Commercial Credit Company

Right
Baltimore boasted several important textile mills near the turn of the century. The Mount Vernon-Woodberry mills (shown circa 1900) were located along Jones Falls in Baltimore. The Hamden-Woodberry Mills claimed distinction as the world's largest producers of cotton duck for sails during the nineteenth century. Among the first textile mills in the United States, the Jones Falls Mills continued to produce textiles into the twentieth century. From the Maryland Room, EPFL

TABLE 3.3

LEADING OCCUPATIONS IN MARYLAND IN 1860

OCCUPATIONS	NUMBER EMPLOYED
Day Laborers	29,244
Farmers	27,696
Servants	16,683
Farm Laborers	12,920
Carpenters	5,572
Clerks	5,503
Shoemakers	4,536
Tailors/Tailoresses	4,049
Laundresses	3,349
Seamstresses	2,903
Blacksmiths	2,495
Carters & Drivers	2,141
Teachers	1,462
Coopers (barrel-makers)	1,424
Ship-Builders & Rigging Makers	1,394
Painters	1,198
Miners	1,144
Butchers	1,096
Physicians	1,093
Storekeepers	1,083
Dressmakers	1,079
Machinists	1,046
Brick-Makers	995
Cigar-Makers	915
Overseers	903
Wheelwrights	849
Cabinet Makers	808
Oystermen	739
Innkeepers	739
Bakers	737
Clergymen	731

SOURCE: U.S. Department of the Interior, Census Office, *Eighth Census of the United States: 1860, Part I - Population,* (Table 6, "Occupation: Maryland").

engaged in making boots and shoes, while 1,200 packed oysters. Many others were employed in agricultural implements, brickmaking, cigar rolling, barrel making, furniture construction, machinery and railroad equipment manufacturing, piano making, textiles (particularly cotton duck for sails), and the production of tin, copper, and chemicals. Altogether, there were 107 different industrial trades in Baltimore in 1860, conducted by 1,100 separate firms. The majority were still small shops employing two to ten people and turning out just a few thousand dollars worth of products. Still, thirty industries produced more than $100,000 worth of goods annually.

The dominance of a relatively few industries like clothing, iron, and machinery indicates that Baltimore's economic base came into existence as a rather highly specialized structure aimed at particular markets. It also displays the large-scale character often associated with the final years of the century. A study by Edward Muller and Paul Groves indicates that there was a rapid concentration of ownership in the clothing industry of 1860. While 152 firms operated, a cluster of fifteen had 4,200 of the 6,000 clothing workers on their payrolls. The majority employed less than ten. Thus, the dual structure of the clothing industry, and even its location in the area just north and west of the Inner Harbor, was well established by the 1850s and did not change for almost a century.

The city's other industrial giant was iron and machinery. The six large iron furnaces, thirteen major foundries, and numerous metal and machine shops gave Baltimore its tough, gritty reputation and also made it famous as a manufacturing center. Horace Abbott opened his iron works at Canton in 1836. Among its most memorable products were the heavy iron plates for the Civil War iron-clad *Monitor.* Poole and Hunt opened their foundry and machine shop in the 1840s—the same decade in which Hayward and Bartlett expanded their business from the production of stoves to the fabrication of structural iron. The splendid cast iron work of both firms remains visible today in the corridors and the great dome

Above
A rear view of the Patapsco flouring mills is depicted in 1906. It was built on the same site as the Ellicott and Company's milling operations, opened in 1774 by John, Joseph, and Andrew Ellicott. Ellicott City derives its name from this enterprise. The much enlarged descendent of the original mill is still in operation today, under the name of the Wilkens-Rogers Flour Mill. Courtesy, Jack D. Brown

Right
Among the stone blocks in the foreground, men are hard at work building the 220-foot long arch support for the Cabin John Bridge in Montgomery County in 1859. A major engineering feat, the bridge was built by the U.S. Army Corps of Engineers to carry both traffic and the main water supply conduit for the District of Columbia. The bridge can still be seen today in suburban Washington. From the Robert G. Merrick Archive, MSA

Bottom
A horse-drawn streetcar passed by a Patapsco Baking Powder carriage on Reisterstown Road circa 1890. Courtesy, Baltimore Streetcar Museum (BSM)

of the capitol building in Washington and in famous nineteenth-century landmarks from New York City to Portland, Oregon. These large, internationally known firms provided between 200 and 300 jobs each. Yet, the biggest employer of foundrymen, machinists, and ironworkers was the B & O Railroad. By 1860, the more than 1,000 men working at the Mt. Clare Shops on Pratt Street turned out equipment for its expanding rail empire. Roughly 190 locomotives and sixty railroad bridges, the latter designed by the brilliant engineer Wendel Bollman, were produced between 1848 and 1851 alone.

Baltimore City was not, of course, the only center of manufacturing in this era. Baltimore County had 210 manufacturing establishments in 1860, employing approximately 4,800 people. The county's river valleys—the Patapsco, Jones Falls, Gwynns Falls, and the Little Gunpowder Falls—were the sites of thriving strings of textile mills, flour mills, saw mills, and iron works which formed the base of the predominantly rural area's industrial sector. The Patapsco Valley and Jones Falls served as the major centers of the county's industrial life in the 1850s. The Union textile mill on the Patapsco was opened in 1809 and by the mid-century the valley was a beehive of activity. Numerous flour mills, begun by the Ellicott brothers in the 1770s and soon joined by other investors, reportedly produced over 200,000 barrels of flour annually by the 1850s. The site of the Ellicott brothers' first mill (across from present day Ellicott City) after two centuries is still the site of Wilkins-Rogers Flour Mill. Farther down the valley was the Avalon Iron Works which rolled rails for the B & O during the 1840s. In 1850, it employed 110 men to make nails—turning out 44,000 kegs.

Much of the capital and leadership for these "rural" industries came from Baltimore, and their products were inevitably marketed through the city. Farmers throughout the state also purchased their agricultural equipment from Baltimore firms or smaller companies in the secondary towns (who in turn bought their machinery and tools in Baltimore). Retail merchandise in the city's large dry-goods shops could

A train pulled in as passengers got ready to board on the platform of the Baltimore, Chesapeake, and Atlantic station at Mardela Springs in Wicomico County, circa 1900. Courtesy, Talbot County Free Library

now be examined and purchased by those living in distant Washington County or St. Marys County simply by taking a day trip on the railroad or steamer. Even in the region farthest from Baltimore, the area that eventually became Garrett County—the recently opened coal mines were almost entirely owned by Baltimore interests who shipped virtually all raw materials to the furnaces and mills of the city and its surrounding industrial region.

The old grain port on the Patapsco—handling the produce of farmers in the immediate hinterland in 1800—had been transformed by a new generation of businessmen into an industrial and commercial giant whose influence extended hundreds of miles inland to the Ohio Valley, north into Pennsylvania, and down into Virginia. In the early decades of the nineteenth century there were fleeting hopes expressed by some of its more optimistic citizens that Baltimore might surpass Philadelphia and rival New York. These wild dreams were gone by 1850. After the death of Alexander Brown, his sons continued to operate one of their most important offices in Baltimore, but they moved the headquarters to New York following the Panic of 1837. Nevertheless, the city's businessmen had combined some daring innovations in transportation with a more regular and institutionalized way of doing business which carved for them—and for many others throughout the state—a prosperous agricultural and industrial economy that survived the terrible upheavals of the Civil War and allowed Maryland to remain, for the balance of the nineteenth century, the most prosperous southern state in the Union.

Chapter IV

RICHES FROM THE LAND AND SEA:

MARYLAND AT THE TURN OF THE CENTURY

A t the opening of the twentieth century Maryland's economy and human resources were still concentrated in the Baltimore metropolitan region and in a dozen small, provincial towns. Urban areas at the turn of the century accounted for 50.8 percent of the total population, obviously a great milestone in the state's demographic history. Even so, rural Maryland was not an economic backwater. This was, in fact, the era of the most extensive use of Maryland's farms, forests, mines, and fisheries. In 1900, 81 percent of state territory was held in farms, the largest percentage of agricultural land use ever recorded before or since. Its full-time agrarian population, which numbered 92,000 out of a total labor force of 458,000, probably swelled to 125,000-150,000 during the picking season when the wives and children of non-agricultural workers went out to the fields and the rural packing houses.

Maryland's fishermen and oystermen reached their largest numbers in this era and the harvests from the Chesapeake Bay waters from 1870-1900 were far greater than at any time before or after. During the same period timber and coal production peaked in mountainous Western Maryland. It was a golden age of resource exploitation. Like almost every other state, Maryland gave little consideration to the long-range management of its fishing, lumber, and mining wealth, and the "golden age" was followed by a long decline in both production and employment in these industries. Agriculture, on the other hand, has become more effi-

Above
Poorer Maryland farmers in the nineteenth and early twentieth centuries used ox carts for transportation. Courtesy, Maryland Hall of Records

Top
The employees of the Consolidated Coal Company, located at George's Creek, Allegany County, are pictured preparing to enter the mine circa 1910. Courtesy, Allegany County Historical Society

cient and productive each decade. The so-called "decline" of farming in twentieth century Maryland is a steady retrenchment in farm acreage and a reduction in agricultural employment to one-quarter of the 1900 figure. Nevertheless, crop production has increased substantially.

In 1900 the Eastern Shore and Southern Maryland remained the most intensely rural and agricultural regions of the state. Visitors to these tidewater counties were captivated by the seemingly timeless quality of their bayside marshes, the flat, rich farmlands, the pine forests, and the lonely majesty of their ocean beaches. Such scenes, which were indeed beautiful in the eyes of sightseers, spelled economic hardship for the majority of permanent residents. For most of the nineteenth century the Eastern Shore was an economic backwater. However, between 1865

and 1910 a variety of men and women had begun to change this picture. By the first decade of the twentieth century tidewater farming was a dynamic sector of the Maryland economy. On a much smaller scale, but of tremendous importance, the vacation industry added vitality to the Eastern Shore.

The stimulus for the economic reawakening of the tidewater region was the railroads. In 1860 there were only seven miles of track in the whole Maryland portion of the Eastern Shore and none in Southern Maryland. Their "railroad age" finally came in the 1865-1890 era when over 300 miles of track were laid on the Eastern Shore. Even Southern Marylanders began to hear the whistle of trains.

By 1890 two trans-peninsular lines serviced the Eastern Shore. As John Hayman notes in his book *Rails Along the Chesapeake,* the "backbone" of this network was the New York, Philadelphia and Norfolk Railroad which ran from New York and New Jersey through Delaware and down

onto the Delmarva peninsula, crossing into Maryland just above Salisbury. From Salisbury it continued down to Princess Anne, Pocomoke City, and on through the Virginia portion of the peninsula to Cape Charles City at the mouth of the Chesapeake Bay across from Norfolk. An east-west line, completed in 1890, ran from the steamboat landing at Clairborne (near St. Michaels) through Easton, Vienna, Salisbury, and Berlin and across Sinepuxent Bay to the little resort village of Ocean City. Important branch lines sprung from the main routes into the principal Eastern Shore towns: Crisfield, Cambridge, Oxford, Queenstown, and Centerville.

The railroads made access to the Baltimore agricultural region much easier, but the major gain came with the opening of the huge Philadelphia and New York produce markets. Farm goods could now reach these two cities in a matter of hours. The production of corn, grain, and the other traditional crops of the Eastern Shore shot upwards, but the primary increases were in fruits and vegetables. By 1909 the Eastern Shore and Southern Maryland (primarily Anne Arundel and Prince Georges counties) yielded 53 percent of the state's vegetables, 58 percent of its fruits, and 37 percent of its poultry and eggs. Tidewater farmers took a renewed interest in agricultural management. With the income earned from new markets, they invested in agricultural machinery, fertilizer and, in the marshy areas of the Eastern Shore, drainage tiles and digging equipment. The results were often spectacular. Maryland's Bureau of Industrial Statistics noted in 1903 that areas "where 25 or 30 years ago the chief crops were scrubby bull pines, broom sage and briers" now sprouted with "everything in the shape of fruit from delicious strawberries to . . . the best peach grown in the world." By 1900 Eastern Shore fruit trees were world renowned. The huge Harrisons' Nurseries outside Berlin, Maryland in Worcester County shipped millions of young saplings to all parts of the United States and Europe.

The best measure of the quickening pace of tidewater agriculture is the increase in farm values. Between 1900 and 1910, when the average value of all Maryland farms increased by 40 percent, every Eastern Shore county, plus Anne Arundel and Prince Georges on the Western Shore, exceeded

crops demanded auxiliary laborers, thousands of Baltimore women and children were brought out by wagon, train, or steamboat during the picking season. However, Anne Arundel farms, like those scattered throughout the state, were not huge factories in the fields. Their mean size was 102 acres, which was very close to the Maryland average of 103. Only seven percent of Anne Arundel farms held over 500 acres, so the typical establishment was a relatively small, single-family operation which was augmented at harvesting season by temporary laborers. But even small farms with a rela-

Maryland's black farmers were considerably better off than their counterparts in the states to the south where the average income and rate of farm ownership were both substantially lower. Sixty-three percent of Maryland's black farmers possessed their own land in 1910. Along with Virginia, this represented the highest rate of black farm ownership in the entire South. As far as the average value of black farms, Maryland led the region.

In the lower counties of Southern Maryland tobacco still provided the single most important source of agricultural income. By

Young boys had loads of fun playing on tobacco hogsheads at the Shoe Point County Wharf in Galesville, a community on the West River in Anne Arundel County, in 1907. From the Barker Collection. Courtesy, Maryland Room, EPFL

tively low investment could produce handsome profits in an area like Anne Arundel County. In *Anne Arundel County: A Bicentennial History,* a writer noted that Charles Thomas, a black farmer, owned 130 acres of land valued at $1,500 which reportedly produced a $500 income at the turn of the century. This comfortable income was achieved by producing ten acres of corn, a variety of market vegetables, and fifteen acres of peach trees yielding 800 bushels of fruit. Thomas also owned four horses, ten cows, a dozen pigs, and a large flock of chickens.

1900, however, it failed to equal the total for all other crops. Thus even in the historic cradle of the American tobacco agriculture, the golden leaf had ceased to reign supreme. According to Regina Hammett in her *History of St. Marys County,* tobacco might have practically disappeared from Southern Maryland farms had not the cigarette industry begun to prosper in the 1870s. The excellent burning qualities of Maryland tobacco were required for cigarettes, so growers in the state could now sell their crop locally rather than compete in the chronically depressed European market.

Even so, tobacco farming had become expensive, requiring about 300 pounds of fertilizer per acre which at the turn of the century cost about eleven dollars compared to the roughly one dollar spent to nourish most other crops. Between 1880 and 1910, when the Eastern Shore and the Anne Arundel-Prince Georges areas were starting to grow, the lower portion of Southern Maryland was still losing population.

In spite of the significant agricultural gains by the tidewater region, Central Maryland continued to dominate farm production. Five counties here were responsible for 48.5 percent of the state's total output in 1909. Maryland yielded $55.9 million in crops, of which Baltimore County produced $6.1 million; Frederick, $5.7 million; Carroll, $4.6 million; Washington, $3.9 million; and Montgomery, $5.7 million. Corn, wheat, and other cereals constituted the largest single item grown in this five-county area, accounting for 37 percent of the state's total output, but Central Maryland's wealth came

from almost the full range of agricultural commodities. Vegetables and fruits, especially apples and peaches, flourished across the entire length of the state. In 1900 Maryland ranked first in the nation in the production of canned fruits and vegetables, with California and New York close behind. Ten years later, California took over first place, but Maryland remained second. Considering its size, this was a remarkable achievement which owed largely to Baltimore's and Maryland's pioneering efforts in the development of the American canning industry.

Baltimore's influence on agriculture was also apparent in the dairy industry. Baltimore, Frederick, and Carroll counties sent over 30,000 gallons of milk, along with thousands of pounds of butter and cheese, to the city each working day. Much of it went directly to dairies in and around the urban area. However, many Frederick County farmers shipped their milk to Baltimore and Washington via the White Cross

Lewis Hine photographed these migrant berry pickers' shack at Bottomley's Farm, Rock Creek, in 1909. Usually three or four families lived in two-room shacks such as this one. Courtesy, Special Collections, University of Maryland Baltimore County

An oyster fleet is pictured returning home after a long day of dredging on the Potomac, near Breton Bay, in Southern Maryland circa 1920. From the Maryland Room, EPFL

Dairy Company in Frederick. This large plant, built in 1909, could process and store 10,000 gallons—delivering it in concentrated form to local distributors in the two major cities.

Half of Maryland's total dairy income went to farmers in these three counties, and a number of the huge barns are still operating there. It was ironic and almost unfair that Baltimore County, the most industrialized of Maryland's counties, should also be its leading agricultural producer. Yet, its rich soil and proximity to the state's metropolis were overwhelming advantages.

In contrast to the improving management and increasing fertility of the land, Maryland's fishing industry provided a classic example of thoughtless over-harvesting—and drastic decline. The Chesapeake Bay and Atlantic coast had abounded in astonishing numbers of fish, crabs, and oysters. Commercial packing at the turn of the century was huge—employing 35,000 to 40,000 people and yielding an annual product worth millions. Topping the seafood list was the Chesapeake oyster which was harvested at the rate of about six to seven million bushels per season by approximately 25,000 watermen.

Baltimore served as the major center of oyster processing. The Baltimore *Sunday*

Herald in 1899 described the Pratt Street and Canton wharves as a "forest of masts" during the oyster season, when an estimated 2,500 boats unloaded their catch at forty nearby shucking houses. The vessels probably held 21,500 watermen, while the oyster houses worked about 5,000 to 6,000 shuckers. Thousands of other fishermen took their boats into packing plants at other points along the bay. Crisfield, Maryland was literally built on a foundation of oyster shells.

It should be mentioned that crabs had not yet achieved the popularity they were to attain later in the twentieth century. So abundant were these tasty crustaceans that most fishermen regarded them as a nuisance and dumped them on the shore when they were part of a catch. In some areas, watermen received fifty cents a dozen for large sized crabs, but an 1893 publication on the Maryland fishing industry stated that "in many places they are so numerous that there is no market for them . . ."

In the eighteenth and early nineteenth

Top, center
This jovial fishing party gathered at Chesapeake Beach circa 1915. The amusement park, complete with a somewhat formidable looking roller coaster, can be seen in the background. Courtesy, Calvert Marine Museum, Solomons, Maryland

Left
It was important to keep a close eye on the gauges of the seafood-processing kettles, as demonstrated by this Baltimore man circa 1900. From the Robert G. Merrick Archive, MSA

Right
The boats and a simple hut of oyster fishermen near Sherwood, Maryland, can be seen behind these three neighbors. From the Robert G. Merrick Archive, MSA

Bottom left
Crabbing on Chesapeake Bay at the turn of the century was a simple pastime—all one needed was a crab net in hand and a cart to haul the catch home. Photo by William L. Amoss. Courtesy, McKeldin Library, University of Maryland College Park

Left
One job for young girls in the early 1900s was picking the meat from a pile of steamed crabs to sell at the marketplace. Crabs are blue when alive, but turn bright red when steamed. From the Robert G. Merrick Archive, MSA

Bottom, right
In 1905, shortly before an oyster-bed leasing bill was finally passed, oystermen continued to harvest a generous supply of the tiny mollusks out of Chesapeake Bay. LC

Bottom, center
It took several hands to unload oysters from the boats to the docks at the Baltimore Harbor in 1905. Notice in the lower left two women and a small boy at work. This was typical of the labor force supplied cheaply by the immigrant community. From the Robert G. Merrick Archive, MSA

In 1903 Johns Hopkins University was located in Mount Vernon Place in downtown Baltimore. This photograph of Johns Hopkins University was taken from the Washington Monument, looking east. LC

centuries, New England provided most of the commercial oysters, but as these beds became depleted by over-harvesting, watermen turned to the Chesapeake. The first Baltimore oyster packing plants opened in the 1830s and by 1868, there were eighty. At the same time the bay's oyster yield rose from approximately 700,000 bushels to nine million. Chesapeake fishermen resisted almost all efforts to regulate the industry, including laws which called for leasing of certain oyster beds and a summertime moratorium on harvesting. The catch peaked at fourteen million bushels in 1874 and then declined to 10.5 million by 1879, prompting the first of several major investigations. A commission in 1882 recommended ending the free-for-all system of the oyster harvesting. As Victor Kennedy and Linda Breisch explain in their recent study, *Maryland's Oysters: Research and Management,* conservation was ignored because of short-term gains. When the commission's ideas came up

for consideration by the Maryland Assembly, a record yield of fifteen million bushels seemed to prove ridiculous the dire predictions of oyster decline.

Even as the harvests again slumped, watermen foretold another great rebound. It failed to come. By 1905 the catch tumbled to six million bushels, but the only regulation which the fisherman allowed was the 1890 Cull Law, requiring young oysters to be thrown back on the beds. Dr. W. K. Brooks of the Johns Hopkins University, a member of the 1882 commission, attested to the impossibility of convincing Marylanders that they were committing economic suicide by over-harvesting. Writing in 1905, Brooks said that his international reputation as a biologist, as well as an expert in Chesapeake oyster physiology and ecology, were no match for the waterman, shucker, or Maryland politician:

I speak on this subject with the difference

Left
Oystermen used scissor-like rakes while hand-tonging for oysters near Rock Point, Maryland, in 1936. F.S.A. Photo by Arthur Rothstein, LC

of one who has been frequently snubbed and repressed; for while I am sure of the errors of the man who tonged oysters long before I was born, and who loudly asserts his right to know all about it, it is easier to acquiesce than to struggle against such overwhelming ignorance, so I have learned to be submissive in the presence of an elderly gentleman who studied the embryology of the oyster when years ago as a boy he visited his grandfather on the Eastern Shore, and to listen with deference to the shucker as he demonstrates to me at his raw-box, by the aid of his hammer and shucking knife, *the fallacy of my notions of the structure of the animal.*

In 1906 an oyster bed leasing bill was passed, but it was too limited to have any impact on production. The decline continued. By 1910 harvests had dropped below five million bushels, oyster packing houses were moving out of Baltimore, and the number of watermen had been cut in half—with further declines yet to come. A rich state resource was simply being destroyed and has never recovered to more than a shadow of its former productivity.

Above
Members of a sport-fishing fleet docked at Solomons Island in Southern Maryland circa 1930 and began to shoot the breeze. Courtesy, Calvert Marine Museum, Solomons, Maryland

Above
One of the most popular attractions at Chesapeake Beach was delightful salt-water bathing, complete with white sand and no undertow. These people enjoyed the swimming pier located behind the boardwalk circa 1916. Courtesy, Chesapeake Beach Railway Museum (CBRM)

The oyster and crab house at Chesapeake Beach did a booming business selling delectable shellfish to summer resort visitors. The house also sold crab and fish bait and hired out sail, motor, and row boats in this building on the boardwalk, depicted around 1910. CBRM

The one entirely new economic sector to emerge in tidewater Maryland by the opening of the twentieth century was the excursion and vacation business. It was a trade based on an important natural resource, the state's 4,000 miles of shoreline. Marylanders had been taking steamboats out of Baltimore and Annapolis to picnic areas on both sides of the bay since the 1840s and 1850s, but the establishment of major resorts did not begin until the 1870s. The Anne Arundel and Calvert county shorelines were dotted with hostelries and picnic groves to which thousands went each summer. The most well-known of the Western Shore resorts, Chesapeake Beach in Calvert County, celebrated its gala opening in the year 1900. Reached by train from Washington and Baltimore, it attracted many with its boardwalk,

beaches, amusement park, beer gardens, band concerts, and animal acts. On opening day an estimated 5,000 people came to enjoy these pleasures.

Maryland's most famous excursion spot, however, lay just across the bay from Baltimore at Tolchester Beach. Established in

1877, it became so popular that the Tolchester Beach Improvement Company, which owned the resort area, developed a whole fleet of steamships to transport vacationers. The *Emma Giles,* built in Baltimore in 1877 by the William E. Woodall Company, could carry up to 1,500 passengers. Further down the Eastern Shore, the coastline was sprinkled with hotels, cottages, and boarding houses which by the 1890s did a thriving business, serving vacationers who crossed the bay or rode the trains from New York and Philadelphia. Oxford and St. Michaels became major summer resorts. Even tiny bayside villages like Royal Oak boomed with the vacation trade: its Pasadena Hotel (1901) advertised in the Baltimore and Washington papers for "summer boarders—$5 a week—children, half rates."

Ultimately, the most valuable piece of the state's shoreline was the thirty-mile stretch of beautiful ocean beaches which are actually two long barrier islands, Fenwick and Assateague. Separated from the mainland by the shallow Sinepuxent Bay, the islands were uninhabited until an enterprising hostler, probably trading on the fame of Newport, Rhode Island, opened the small Rhode Island Inn in 1869. During the next decade the Sinepuxent Beach Corporation began a more systematic development of the area. The 400-room Atlantic Hotel, the first of the really elegant seaside accommodations, opened in 1875. Major growth of the resort

Above
This 1911 photograph shows paint being manufactured at the Hanline Paint Company in Baltimore. Courtesy, Baltimore Museum of Industry (BMI)

Right
A crowd gathered in the rain outside the Parrish Baking Powder Company in Cumberland circa 1890. From the Herman and Stacia Miller Collection. Courtesy, the Mayor and City Council of Cumberland, Maryland

Baltimore Harbor, viewed from Federal Hill in 1903, has changed drastically, due in some part to the huge 1904 fire that destroyed the downtown area. By 1984 the former working harbor had become a tourist attraction, with Harborplace now centered where the piers were, the Maryland Science Center in place of the smokestacks on the far left, and the Aquarium located near the Patapsco Flouring Mill piers. LC

Joseph S.M. Basil's Steam Saw, Grist, and Planing Mill was one of several thriving businesses located on the Baltimore Harbor. This shot of lower Main Street and City Dock, as viewed from the State House dome, was taken in 1889. From the Maryland Room, EPFL

Right
This young boy had the opportunity of trying his hand at the wheel of an automobile in Baltimore around 1905. Courtesy, Baltimore Camera Club, Maryland Room, EPFL

Below
An early automobile cruised along Park Avenue in Baltimore on a quiet day circa 1900. LC

"destined to become one of the largest inland towns of America." No doubt the locals in Hagerstown and Frederick also shared glimmering thoughts of such a metamorphosis. There was a steady expansion, but nothing approaching Greeley's prophecy. Nevertheless, the Western Maryland cities did emerge as important local economic centers. By the 1880s and 1890s a second wave of industrial growth hit the towns, and hopes rose once again.

Frederick, with a 1910 population of 10,411, was the oldest and smallest of the three western towns. By the 1880s it had several factories, but began a more concerted effort to attract larger-scale manufacturers. According to Thomas Williams, Frederick County's historian at the turn of the century, part of the original problem rested with local residents who deemed the employment of females in factories, mills, or even stores demeaning. However, says Williams, during the 1880s there surfaced:

Frequently expressed desires of some level headed girls to engage in some clean, light occupation, whereby they might secure for themselves an honorable and independent livelihood (which) was communicated to certain businessmen in Frederick who after careful and intelligent consideration took up the idea of establishing a Hosiery Mill.

The Union Knitting Mill opened in 1887 and employed over 300 women by the dawn of the twentieth century. It was one of Frederick's most successful businesses. Nevertheless, one suspects that the local prejudice against female employment, plus the pull of Baltimore's nearby labor market, made it difficult to turn Frederick into a large-scale industrial center. The fact that by 1910 only 21.9 percent of the city's manufacturing labor force was female (compared to 37.6 percent in Baltimore) indicated that the example of the Union Hosiery Mill was not followed by many other Frederick entrepreneurs.

Hagerstown, with a population of 16,507 in 1910, maintained excellent railroad connections and an almost incredible array of manufacturing enterprises for a town of

its size. Located in the so-called "Great Appalachian Valley" (referred to as the Cumberland Valley in Pennsylvania and the Shenandoah Valley in Virginia), it was the cross-roads of four railroads. In 1907 Hagerstown claimed 203 manufacturers producing $4.6 million worth of goods. They made furniture, doors, sashes, paper, pipe organs (the famous Moller Organ Company), textiles, leather goods, beer, whiskey, brushes, foundry iron, machinery, glass, wire, bricks, books, carriages, and even automobiles (the Pope Manufacturing Company). There was little apparent difficulty attracting women into factory employment here. Updergraff's famous glove factory had over 300 on its payroll, and at least four large silk and hosiery mills engaged several hundred others. The 1910 census showed 40.1 percent of Hagerstown's labor force to be female—the highest proportion of any city in the state.

Western Maryland's economic life, particularly in Allegany and Garrett counties, rest-

This horse-drawn sled with wooden runners was used for collecting maple syrup in Garrett County during the winter of 1926. Courtesy, Maryland Department of Forestry. From the Maryland Room, EPFL

ed firmly in the mountainsides and deep valleys. Coal from George's Creek in Allegany County, and the Casselman and Youghiogheny basins in Garrett County, provided the area's lifeblood. It also spawned industrial growth at Cumberland, economic capital of the region.

The "Pittsburgh of Maryland" had begun as a strategic trading center at the eastern

Allegany Company miners at George's Creek took a lunch break after a long, hard morning in 1895. From the Herman and Stacia Miller Collection. Courtesy, the Mayor and City Council of Cumberland, Maryland

entrance to the Cumberland Gap through which the National Road, and later, the railway threaded. In the 1830s and 1840s, Cumberland became the gateway to 475 square miles of Allegany and Garrett county property which was blessed with some of the most valuable coal in the world. At the turn of the century, nearly 6,000 men worked in its mines. The city maintained five railroad connections and served as the western terminus of the C & O Canal.

While over forty separate mining companies together owned 88,129 acres of Allegany and Garrett county lands, two firms produced almost 70 percent of the region's coal. George's Creek Basin was at the center of this activity as the twentieth century began. A four mile wide and twenty-five mile long valley just west of Cumberland, it held

the so-called "Big Vein" of coveted semi-bituminous coal. High carbon content made George's Creek coal unsurpassed for blacksmithing and metallurgical purposes, but its greatest market was for use in steam boilers. The British Navy stockpiled it at their Caribbean stations, and it powered the U. S. fleet which defeated Spain in 1898.

Katherine Harvey's *The Best Dressed Miners: Life and Labor in the Maryland Coal Region, 1835-1910,* documents the fact that the George's Creek miners were a relatively fortunate, small aristocracy in a generally low-paying and dangerous nationwide industry. They were "pick and shovel men" even in 1910 when mining almost everywhere else relied on machines. The George's Creek coal veins were nearly horizontal, easily reached through tunnels rather than the

Left
An enterprising Cumberland photographer decided to develop a new concept in business environments with a studio on the C & O Canal in 1890. From the Herman and Stacia Miller Collection. Courtesy, the Mayor and City Council of Cumberland, Maryland.

Below
These two women, dressed rather conservatively for a swim, deliberated jumping into the icy C & O Canal, near Lock House 26, circa 1920. From the Herman Miller Collection. Courtesy, C & O Canal Museum

more typical deep shafts found in other areas; they also contained little flammable gas. Consequently, the Maryland accidental death rate from mining was substantially lower than in Pennsylvania and far better than in West Virginia. Even so, coal mining was a dangerous trade, and the Maryland Bureau of Industrial Statistics reported that it was difficult to find a miner over the age of thirty who had not met with a serious accident.

The George's Creek Basin was a world unto itself, described in 1881 as "one continuous street and town, twenty-four miles in length inhabited by miners and their families." The residents were for the most part native-born Americans, in addition to English, Scottish, Irish, German, and Welsh immigrants who got along well with each other and built a remarkably sober, comfortable, and cultured community. Although they never successfully established a permanent miner's union in this era, strikes and strike-threats saved them from the severe labor exploitation common in neighboring

Right
Cumberland also had its share of breweries. The work crew at the German Brewing Company took a break from their duties to pose for this photograph circa 1910. From the Herman and Stacia Miller Collection. Courtesy, the Mayor and City Council of Cumberland, Maryland

Below
The R.E. Roberts Company in Baltimore packed oysters, and was one of the many canning plants still going strong in 1930. Oyster canning in particular was a staple of this industry. From the Edward L. Bafford Photography Collection, Albin O. Kuhn Library and Gallery. Courtesy, University of Maryland Baltimore County

however, their role was important to the city. Baltimore's black population, 15.6 percent of the total, comprised 20.6 percent of its urban labor force. This rate exceeded that of both native whites and immigrants, marking blacks as the hardest working group in the city.

An extensive analysis of Baltimore's economic development by Eleanor Bruchey indicates that the city's industrial growth during the last decades of the nineteenth century could be characterized as a steady forward march rather than a spectacular series of expansions or contractions. Baltimore was not, according to national standards, an industrial giant. Maryland had ranked twelfth in manufacturing production in 1860 and fourteenth by 1900. The per capita value of its industrial output increased roughly four times between 1860 and 1909, while the national rate expanded five times. The Old Line State was, however, still leading the South.

Baltimore's labor force, 156,449 men and 60,901 women, are listed in the 1900 census as working in more than 100 different

trades and professions. The local economy also boasted a good deal of continuity over the six decades from the 1850s to World War I. In 1860 the leading areas of employment were in the trade, commerce, and service categories, and this remained true in 1900 or 1914. Furthermore, the manufacturing area showed considerable stability. Its major employment sectors right before the Civil War were, in rank order: men's clothing, oyster and fruit packing, boots and shoes, bricks, cigars, ships and shipbuilding, and iron forging. Men's clothing, copper, tin and sheet-iron, railroad cars, foundry and machine shops, tobacco manufacturing, and canning/preserving engaged the greatest numbers of employees in 1909. The port and the commercial activities associated with it still dominated the urban economy, but the proportion of those employed in industrial and mechanical pursuits had increased from an estimated 20 percent of the city's total labor force in 1860 to 36 percent in 1900.

The core of Baltimore's manufacturing sector was the clothing business, of which

Bottom, center
Baltimore's harbors contributed to the growth of the iron industry, as rail and water shipments were conveniently available. These employees of the prosperous Patapsco Iron Works posed for a picture in 1917. From the Edward L. Bafford Photography Collection, Albin O. Kuhn Library and Gallery. Courtesy, University of Maryland Baltimore County

Below
As Bethlehem-Fairfield shipyard workers commuted each day on a former pleasure boat, the refreshment stand became a popular spot during the long trip to and from work. During World War II Baltimore increased its employment with over 160,000 new jobs, most of them in the city's war industries. Photo by Marjory Collins, LC

The Polan Katz Company of Baltimore employed over 200 women in its umbrella-tipping department during the early 1900s. BMI

90 percent specialized in men's wear. By most measures—employment, worth of product, and value added by manufacture—this trade was by far the most important to the local economy. In addition, Baltimore stood as the fourth largest clothing manufacturer in the United States. By 1910, 349 firms, employing 20,670 people, produced men's clothing and shirts, while another 2,953 people made women's apparel. For this huge industry the city was indebted to a relatively small group of German Jewish immigrants, who operated almost every one of the city's large clothing factories at the turn of the century. Topping the list was Henry Sonneborn. He had come to Baltimore from Germany in 1849 and by 1911, employed 2,500 people in his seven-story factory loft at Pratt and Paca streets. When operating at a peak capacity, Sonneborn's shop turned out 3,000 suits per day—it was thought to be the largest men's clothing company in the United States. In addition to Sonneborn, Schloss Brothers and Co., Strouse Brothers, Isaac Hamburger and Sons, L. and A. Frank, J. Schoeneman, and Philip Kahn ("the overcoat king") were all among giants of the trade. Most of these firms were located in the loft factory district just west

of the city's financial and retail center. This area also housed many of the other light industries—straw hats, umbrellas ("born in Baltimore, raised everywhere" was the motto of Ganz Brothers, the largest firm), tobacco products, pianos, and additional items. Indeed, the twelve square blocks enveloping the West Baltimore loft district provided more manufacturing employment than the total number of factories, shops, and mills in all the other cities, towns, and villages of Maryland.

In the heart of downtown was the commercial and retail center, with the major dry goods and department stores in the Howard Street vicinity across to Charles, Light, Calvert, and Guilford streets. There, one found the city's major banks, insurance companies, commission merchants, import-export firms, the headquarters of the Baltimore & Ohio Railroad, and the various steamship lines. Based on an analysis of the 1900 census returns, this central retail and commercial district employed well over 30,000 people—bankers, agents, bookkeepers, secretaries, clerks, merchants, sales people, and wholesalers. Premier department stores—Hutzler Brothers, Posner's, O'Neils, and several others—each retained 500 or more people.

Left
Horse-drawn carriages and auto-mobiles shared the trolley's tracks on Baltimore's Charles Street in 1907. Looking north up the street from Preston Street, the University of Baltimore can be seen in the middle left. From the Edward M. Smith Collection, BSM

Below
This 1919 view of Howard Street at Fayette Street in Baltimore illustrated the reason the area was considered the heart of downtown. It was packed with candy stores, lunch rooms, barber shops, jewelry stores, hat shops, and department stores—causing streetcars, horses, and automobiles to fight for equal space. BSM

The Baltimore Bargain House, the city's largest dry goods dealer, had over 1,000 people
in its employ by 1910, and sent out 10,000
cases of merchandise per day. A 1903 survey
of twenty-nine department and dry goods
stores in downtown Baltimore showed 5,108
workers. This represented only a small portion of the area's retail outlets.

When one adds to this commercial, financial, and retail labor force the transportation
and service employees—Baltimore's 1,204 sa-
loon keepers, 400 restaurant workers, 7,000
teamsters and hackmen, employees in 60-70
downtown livery stables, the 2,198 messen-
ger boys and telegraph/telephone operators,
and another dozen or so major downtown
occupations—it would appear that approximately 70,000 men and women labored in

the central business district. So vital and dynamic was this area that when almost half of it burned down in the disastrous fire of 1904, it was rebuilt and operating within a few months. The rapid revival of the central business district at the same location stemmed from the fact that it was both the geographic and economic center of the whole city, state, and region. From downtown Baltimore fanned the streets, roadways, trolley routes, railroads, steamship lines, telegraph and telephone wires, along which moved the raw materials, finished products, and financial resources of the city and its economic hinterland. The years 1890-1910 represented the high water mark for Baltimore's centrality in the Maryland economy. Never before and probably never again will such a large percentage of the state's total goods, services, and financial resources pass through so few square miles of land fronting on the Patapsco Basin.

In 1900 it was still easy for Baltimore's hundreds of "drummers," who marketed the city's wares through Maryland and the South, to walk quickly from the loft district or the wholesale merchant houses over to the B & O's Camden Station or down to the Light Street wharves where the steamboats waited to take them to Easton, Cam-

bridge, Norfolk, Charleston, or Savannah. The B & O's gigantic Camden Street warehouse, completed in 1905, was at the time the largest commercial structure in the United States. Its construction coincided with the climax of inner harbor development which began in the years following the Civil War. Since the 1880s and 1890s, an increasing amount of port shipping had started to move out to new locations farther down the Patapsco River. The keys to the development of what came to be known as the "outer harbor" were dredging and rail

Above
This illustration accompanied a circa 1875 advertisement for Thomas W. Anderson and Company's Business House in Cambridge, Dorchester County, Maryland. The store dealt in "dry goods, carpets, oil cloth, and general merchandise." "Cloths, cassimeres, and ladies goods" were their "specialty." MHS

Five members of the C & P telephone crew took a break and posed for a picture next to their truck in Cumberland circa 1920. From the Robert G. Merrick Archive, MSA

Conduit lines were laid for the wires of the Wilmington-Washington telephone service along the trolley tracks in suburban Washington, D.C. around 1910. From the Robert G. Merrick Archive, MSA

terminal building. The United States Army Corps of Engineers conducted prodigious dredging programs under the direction of William P. Craighill, the greatest of all Baltimore District engineers. When Colonel Craighill arrived in Baltimore in 1866, its harbor possessed a channel 150 feet wide and twenty-two feet deep. When he finally left in 1895 to become Chief of Engineers, the waterway attained world prominence

with a main channel 600 feet wide and 30 feet deep and plans for extension to Curtis Bay. By 1916 the primary passage had been deepened to thirty-five feet.

The entire forty-year program of channel expansion had cost the federal government over nine million dollars, but the resulting commercial increase far exceeded that sum. Foreign trade skyrocketed from $33.8 million in 1870 to $131.1 million in 1906. Most of this centered on bulk commodities. The major exports in 1910 were, in order of value: refined copper, tobacco, corn, flour and wheat, raw cotton, lard, and steel rails. The chief imports consisted of iron ore and pig iron, copper, soda, potash, coffee, cement, manganese, and cork. These commodities were shipped in and out of Baltimore by the thousands of tons on newer, bigger, deep draft freighters that could no longer crowd into the old inner harbor. Until the channel's enlargement in 1916, many of the large freighters could not enter at all.

Equally important, there were almost no substantial stretches of land left along the old harbor for the development of manufacturing plants. Therefore, beginning in the 1880s and 1890s, the industrial expansion of the city spread down both the south and north banks of the Patapsco River. With its new ship channel, the once remote and uninhabited Curtis Bay district sprang to life, and train lines were brought into the water's edge. At Port Covington, another little-used waterside area, the Western Maryland Railroad began construction of its huge coal loading facility. Locust Point, where B & O docks had been expanding since the late 1860s, continued to grow. On the north side of the river—out beyond the eighteenth century Fells Point piers—new wharves, docks, and railheads were built at Canton, Dundalk, and Sparrows Point. Harborside factories and mills, fed by coal cars from Western Maryland and the other Eastern fields, processed raw materials unloaded at their doorstep by the huge, new, steam-powered freighters. In 1876, when the harbor channel dredging program was started, ninety-nine steamships and 1,260 sailing vessels left the port for foreign countries. Thirty years later, 764 steamboats but only ninety sailing craft cleared. By 1910 the number of sailing vessels had dropped to twenty-four. The new "outer harbor" grew up to meet the needs of the age of steam navigation.

In the 1850s Baltimore's industries had surrounded the old inner harbor from Federal Hill to Fells Point—slightly over two and one-half miles of waterfront. At the turn of the century one had to travel over twenty miles of shoreline to view Baltimore's industrial centers. Curtis Bay became the site of the Baltimore Car Works, the largest manufacturer of railway cars in the southern United States. South Baltimore, surrounded on three sides by water, had been completely built up by 1910 with brickyards, glass factories, foundries, the city's main gas plant, and the repair shops of its street car company. Almost half the area was devoted to the seemingly endless B & O and Western Maryland Railroad yards which fed into the marine terminals at Locust Point and Port Covington. On the western edge of the city beyond the loft district was the cluster of heavy manufacturers. Surrounding the great Mt. Clare Shops of the B & O Railroad, this vast array of stores, mills, and foundries often employed more than 3,000 men during the peak work seasons.

In the Jones Falls Valley north of downtown and, prior to the annexation of 1918, beyond the city line, lay a string of industrial villages: Hampden, Woodbury, Mt. Vernon, and Druidville, where a cluster of textile mills comprised the world's leading center for the production of heavy canvas. The workers in this industrial valley, numbering over 2,500 in 1910, exhibited a degree of residential stability and community solidarity rare in most American cities of the era. This phenomenon has also appeared in other parts of the city. Baltimore's rate of home ownership was higher than that of all other Eastern cities, a further indication of the deep rootedness of its working class neighborhoods. By this time it also had achieved a reputation as a place where the necessities of food, clothing, and housing were considerably less expensive than in cities like Boston, New York, or Philadelphia—a fact that is still true today.

In East Baltimore and Fells Point, many of the new Southern and Eastern European immigrant groups displaced older native American, Irish, and German neighborhoods. However, once the new immigrants settled, they continued to remain in a given locale from the turn of the century until the 1960s and 1970s and, indeed, many of the ethnic enclaves survive today.

Above
Employees of the National Ink Company in Baltimore spent their days filling and packing ink bottles for shipment during the 1920s. From the Edward L. Bafford Photography Collection, Albin O. Kuhn Library and Gallery. Courtesy, University of Maryland Baltimore County

In 1900 or 1910 East Baltimore was a tangled welter of small stores, fledgling factories, and sweatshops in which thousands of struggling men, women, and children worked ten to fourteen hours per day making clothing, loading ships at Fells Point docks, and laboring in the local lumber yards, printing plants, and canning factories. East of Fells Point lay the industrial and shipping center of Canton. The area was owned by the Canton Company, a land holding and industrial development firm established in 1828 on the 2,500-acre waterfront estate of Baltimore's great eighteenth-century merchant-shipper, John

O'Donnell. The company had induced a variety of manufacturing and shipping enterprises to locate on its land beginning in the 1840s. By 1900 its extensive holdings housed hundreds of acres of foundries, chemical and fertilizer plants, copper works, grain elevators, and coal yards, half of which lay in the city and the other half, in Baltimore County. The Canton Company's smelting facilities were merged at the end of the century into the Baltimore Copper Smelting and Rolling Company, soon to become the world's largest plant of this type. The numerous breweries and beer gardens of Canton and neighboring Highlandtown were open on Sundays, and thirsty Baltimoreans flocked across the city line to dance and sip lager on their day off.

Out beyond Canton lay Dundalk, with its scattered shops and mills still operating in a semi-rural atmosphere. Further east, where the Patapsco enters the Chesapeake Bay, stood Sparrows Point, site of the city's greatest industrial complex—the Sparrows Point Steel Mill and Shipbuilding Plant. Opened in 1891 by the Pennsylvania-based Maryland Steel Company, the sprawling plant was purchased in 1916 by Bethlehem Steel Company, which subsequently turned it into the largest integrated steel mill in the United States. Its scale was gigantic and its character, international. Using coal from

Pennsylvania and West Virginia, limestone from Maryland, iron ores from Cuba, Spain, and Algeria, its 4,000 men turned out 1,200 tons of iron and 1,500 tons of steel per day. The products were sold in Europe, Latin America, Asia, and Australia. In 1891 the company opened one of the largest shipyards on the East Coast and quickly came to dominate the entire harbor's naval architecture and repairing industry. By 1904 its yards accounted for 70 percent of the port's $3.2 million shipbuilding business. Sparrows Point was the most dramatic example of an increasing trend for sizeable numbers of national corporations to locate new plants in Baltimore or buy out and merge with local firms. The infusion of outside capital be-

for decades to site ships as they entered the harbor, was closed because the industrial smoke had made it impossible to view much beyond Ft. McHenry. As the author Walter Lord remarked several years ago after completing his book, *The Dawn's Early Light,* it was fortunate that the British attack on Ft. McHenry occurred prior to the industrialization of the outer harbor, since the air pollution would have prevented Francis Scott Key from seeing either flag or fort in those early morning hours.

Not only did the breakneck pace of Baltimore's economy overtax the local environment and eat up natural resources, it called forth an enormous effort from the work force. Labor-saving machinery was growing

Opposite, top
The Baltimore Gold Dust Soap Factory used an assembly line to complete the various steps involved in soap production circa 1920. Hughes Company photo. Courtesy, McKeldin Library, University of Maryland College Park

Left
The J.S. Farrand Packing Company of Baltimore employed child workers to help string beans. Those too small to work were held on their mothers' laps. Photo by Lewis Hine. Courtesy, National Archives

came a paramount factor in Baltimore's growth from the late 1890s onwards.

Clearly, it was Baltimore, not Cumberland, that became the "Pittsburgh of Maryland"—its foundries, car works, copper smelters, and steel mills provided well over 20,000 jobs by 1910. Unfortunately, when these profitable activities were combined with the sugar refineries, slaughter houses, oil refineries, and fertilizer plants (twenty-seven of which dotted the harbor), Baltimore's water and air reached what was probably its lowest level of quality at any time in history. The water of the inner harbor was so polluted that nothing could be seen below an inch or so of its surface, and in 1899 the Federal Hill Observatory, used

steadily in importance, especially in old hand-labor trades such as can making. Still much of the work was either arduous, tedious craft or heavy pick-and-shovel labor. One cannot help being impressed and a bit dismayed at the prodigious efforts of over 200,000 people aged 12 to 90 who toiled from ten to twelve hours a day for wages that were, even in 1900, rather meager. Why did they work so long and so hard? First, those who did not get fifty to sixty hours most weeks of the year fell into poverty, a far more physically grinding poverty than we have in the late twentieth century. On the other hand, those who could work sixty or seventy hours a week and send their children out at age twelve or fourteen to

The Bethlehem Steel Company employed thousands of workers in its mills and shipyards. Employees of the S. S. Steelose Engine Room are depicted in 1922. From the Edward L. Bafford Photography Collection, Albin O. Kuhn Library and Gallery. Courtesy, University of Maryland Baltimore County

earn extra dimes and quarters, could finally achieve the dream of a lifetime—ownership of one of Baltimore's comfortable little row houses, decent clothing for the family, a variety of good foods, and some modest entertainment—all the things that urban life had never included these luxuries.

What the late twentieth-century American has come to expect as a matter of birthright, the generation of 1900 regarded as the reward for tremendous physical and mental effort. Coming from backgrounds of stark rural poverty in Southern Maryland, Central Poland, or the northern coast of Sicily, having no hope for any real advancement within the agricultural economy, Baltimore's working classes were, for the most part, literally willing to kill themselves working. Even shameless exploitation was overlooked by many workers in their efforts to acquire carpeted row houses and horsehair sofas rather than dirt floor, rural shacks furnished with benches.

The per capita hours of labor expended

by Baltimore's population probably reached its peak in the late nineteenth- and early twentieth-century era. People went to work at younger ages and continued laboring until they died or became physically unable to carry on. They toiled ten hour days, often six days a week, and many worked longer than that. In 1896 the *Baltimore Sunday Herald* remarked on the oyster shuckers in East Baltimore whose days lasted from 6:00 a.m. to 6:00 p.m. Even though allowed a lunch break, they usually did not take it. "They eat between blows, some of them not at all. Their chief concern is to make as much money as possible." At the B & O Mt. Clare Shops, workers were cut back to a nine-hour day as orders slowed down. When business increased and the men could resume a ten-hour shift (thus advancing their per diem wages from eighty-eight cents to $1.10), one employee told a reporter that the news of a longer day "was too good to be true."

The women and children hired by downtown department stores, dry goods houses, and retail shops generally worked ten hours during the week and fourteen to fifteen hours on Saturdays. These employees consisted of youths from the ages of eleven and twelve to older adults in their seventies and eighties. Maryland's first Child Labor Law in 1886 prohibited those under twelve from working in factories (except canneries). In 1902 the minimum age was raised to fourteen.

While the majority of Baltimore's young people left school when they were ten or eleven, figures from the year 1900 recorded that only 4,311 children of the ages fifteen and under were working in factories. Without a doubt, these numbers are low. Thousands of other youth also toiled in the non-industrial occupations which were not required to report their employment statistics. A survey of child labor in 1889 nevertheless showed 2,280 girls working in oyster/vegetable/fruit packing houses. Their average age was twelve years. Such children coalesced into a productive, defenseless, and easily exploitable labor force. An item from the 1903 report of the Bureau of Industrial Statistics stated:

STRIKE AT THE CROWN CORK AND SEAL WORKS

About seventy-five boys, ranging in age from twelve to sixteen years, employed in the stamping rooms of the Crown Cork and Seal Company's works went on strike July 6. The cause of the strike was the demanding of a nine-hour work-day instead of ten hours and for a half holiday on Saturday. There was no organization of the boys and they attempted to get the girls in the establishment to go on strike with them, but they failed in this. The firm reports that several mothers of the boys interfered in a forcible manner, and in a day or so many of them returned to work. No losses were reported.

From Curtis Bay to the loft district to Sparrows Point, Baltimoreans in 1900 were reaping the new profits and coping with the new problems evolving from the great industrial and commercial expansions of the previous two decades. Much of the boom had been along traditional lines; thus, area residents were not thrown off balance by the increasing size and scale of economic activity. Even in this era of enormous growth,

Baltimore always appeared to be a well settled community and a civilized, urbane city. The metal industries, clothing trade, canning and preserving operations, great retail and wholesale outlets, and the shipping of Maryland's agricultural bounty were all familiar sites in the city since the 1850s. Like the tobacco planters of the eighteenth century, however, many business leaders in the city and throughout the state expected commerce to continue along these lines for many more decades to come. This was not to be the case. Technology changed and both domestic and global patterns shifted. By 1950 the economy of Baltimore and Maryland had once again undergone a major series of transformations. Its industrial captains, working classes, and public officials were all forced to come to terms with a new business environment. Yet Marylanders responded as they had during the dangerous and eventful period from 1800-1860: they contemplated altered circumstances and remodeled their economy to fit dynamic demands and opportunities. Residents of the Old Line State were fortunate in one large respect: by the dawn of the twentieth century, their security rested on a truly firm economic base.

Employees of the Armstrong Stove Foundry put down their buckets and tools and posed for the camera in Perryville, Cecil County, circa 1910. From the Robert G. Merrick Archive, MSA.

109

Chapter V

WORLD WAR AND THE MODERN ECONOMY:

MARYLAND FROM 1920 TO 1950

When Ocean City began opening tourist hotels in the 1870s, people were willing to travel by boat, train, or stagecoach just to have some fun in the sand and surf. By 1935 the resort's popularity had increased to an even more remarkable degree, mainly due to the automobile and modernized roads and bridges. This amazing popularity is clearly evident in a shot of the crowded boardwalk in 1937. Photo by Photolyte Studio, Salisbury, Maryland. From the Maryland Room, EPFL

Two world wars, from 1914-1918 and 1939-1945, thrust the United States onto the center stage of world history. Possessing one of the great Atlantic ports and containing the nation's capital within its original boundaries, Maryland was profoundly affected by this transition. World War II and resulting global involvement by the U.S. brought an influx of new people and new economic forces into the Old Line State. The growing size and scope of international trade increased the importance of the port of Baltimore, attracting maritime industries and businesses that remain today at the core of the metropolitan economy. In response to the nation's defense requirements and domestic responsibilities, the federal government also expanded. The District of Columbia grew accordingly, transforming neighboring Montgomery and Prince Georges counties into one of the nation's major suburban districts.

Like many turning points, the changes of the 1940s had their precursors. America's rise to world economic power began in the 1880s and 1890s. From the opening of the twentieth century, the Sparrows Point steel plant greatly affected Baltimore's economy in war and peacetime. World War I brought changes not only to Baltimore, but to other parts of Maryland, too. Its most significant impact was the increasing size and number of federal installations in the state. Since 1845 Maryland had housed the U.S. Naval Academy in Annapolis, but during World War I, Edgewood Arsenal, the Aberdeen

A streetcar chugged slowly up Sara-
toga Street circa 1920, amid both
horsedrawn buggies and horseless
carriages. This particular view looks
east from Liberty Street. From the
Edward M. Smith Collection, BSM

Proving Ground, and Ft. George Meade
were all established here. Enlarged during
World War II, these facilities have been joined by over a dozen more large civilian and
military installations.

The expansion of Washington began at
the turn of the century, but its greatest leap
came in the 1940-1960 era. While much of
this growth was due to federal employment
increases, the capital city attracted burgeoning numbers of non-government workers—
thousands of foreign embassy officials and
support personnel, employees of national
associations and business groups, and hundreds of private contractors supporting federal projects. Although the U.S. government
lies at the heart of this white-collar economy, the private sector has always been
dominant. The tremendous growth of federal agencies and civil service employment in
the Washington area since 1940 continues
to be exceeded by the growth of local busi-

nesses and larger corporations. Thus, the
federal presence in Maryland stimulated,
rather than replaced (or retarded), the development of the state's private enterprises.

The most striking change resulting from
the Second World War was that Maryland's
population rate soared. From 1860 to 1940 it
grew on the average of 12.9 percent per decade, amounting to an increase of 1,134,000
persons. In the three decades from 1940 to
1970 mean population growth jumped to
29.1 percent, a figure never equaled during
any previous ten-year period. Maryland
added over two million people to its census
figures, rendering it one of the fastest growing states in the union. The majority of this
increase came from new people entering the
state, and their destinations within Maryland were quite specific—the Baltimore and
Washington urban regions. The Baltimore
area's population expanded by 512,000 between 1940 and 1970, while at the same time

Montgomery and Prince Georges counties welcomed 1,011,000 new residents. Taken together, the two areas accounted for 72 percent of the growth during this great population boom. Baltimore City and County, claiming 56 percent of Maryland's residents in 1940, held 38 percent by 1970, as Montgomery and Prince Georges figures rose from 9.5 to 30 percent. The port city remained the state's leading population center, but it was clearly merging into an even larger urbanized region which some began calling the Baltimore-Washington metropolitan corridor.

In 1940 few people could have predicted the momentous changes about to descend on Baltimore, however, it was already apparent that new, long-term influences were being felt in the city's economic circles. In spite of losses suffered during the Great Depression of the 1930s, Baltimore's leaders could look back on the previous twenty-five years with some genuine satisfaction. An industrial study of the city had revealed its manufacturing growth for the 1900-1914 era to be far behind the national average. Yet, a second survey, taken in 1939, showed a dramatic reversal of this trend with growth substantially exceeding that experienced by the rest of the country. Part of the change clearly stemmed from the recommendations

of the 1914 study commission. These proposals resulted in the establishment of a series of organizations aimed at expanding small, local firms and attracting new industries which had proven successful in other major cities. In 1924 the economic development groups merged to form the Baltimore Association of Commerce which, as the 1939 industrial survey noted, "has waged many a successful battle to publicize, protect

Above
Two young fishermen began a long and painstaking day as they started repairing their nets on the Chop-tank River in Cambridge in 1933. LC

Left
The bandstand and pier in River-view Park, Baltimore, can be seen behind the construction of the boardwalk in 1916. From the Edward M. Smith Collection, BSM

and advance the city's industrial and commercial interests." The other factor in the economic upturn was the coincidence of business and promotional efforts with the coming of World War I. National defense needs provided Baltimore the opportunity to show its value as a port city and industrial complex which could expand rapidly under pressure. Together, diverse local manufacturers and shipyards with the great productive capacity the Sparrow's Point made Baltimore a natural choice for foreign and domestic shipbuilding. The Cunard Line ordered a number of large freighters, the U.S. Navy purchased fifty vessels, and employment in this sector rose from 2,000 to 20,000. Sensing its great future, the Bethlehem Steel Company purchased the Sparrows Point plant in 1916 and began to enlarge it rapidly, buying hundreds of additional acres of waterfront land for shipbuilding. At Dundalk the U.S. Emergency Fleet Corporation built an entire community for its employees. Furthermore, the B & O, Pennsylvania, and Western Maryland railroads spent millions expanding their facilities around the outer harbor. Long-established Baltimore firms, as well as newcomers, reached out into Curtis Bay,

Above
Two steelworkers at the Bethlehem Steel Mill in Sparrows Point appear to be having a jovial disagreement during their labor in this shot from 1940. F.S.A. Photo by John Vachon, LC

Right
Iron ore is pictured being unloaded at the Bethlehem Steel Mill at Sparrows Point in another 1940 photo. F.S.A. Photo by John Vachon, LC

Fairfield, Sollers Point, and other locations made accessible by the trains. U.S. Industrial Alcohol erected a $5-million plant at Curtis Bay, while the venerable Bartlett-Hayward Company enlarged its work force from 4,000 to over 22,000 and turned out over 20,000 artillery shells per day. During the five years between 1914 and 1919, Baltimore's labor pool increased by one-third. More important in the long-run, however, investment in plants and machinery doubled. Finally, the city annexed most of its major industrial suburbs (excepting Sparrows Point), thereby increasing its territory from thirty to eighty square miles. Sherry Olson's *Baltimore: The Building of An American City*, tells of an observer who summarized this explosive growth by boasting that "the city has put on seven-league boots."

The spectacular upsurge of the 1914-1919 era simply could not be sustained during the 1920s, but the Baltimore region continued to attract a number of important businesses that were to become cornerstones of the state's economy. Overall growth substantially exceeded that of the 1900-1914 period. One after the other, national and international manufacturing firms began locating in Baltimore: Lever Brothers, Proctor and Gamble, Crosse and Blackwell, Revere Copper, and Rustless Iron and Steel (Armco Steel) all entered in the mid-1920s. The year 1928 alone welcomed forty-four new businesses and 4,000 jobs to the urban area. Among these arrivals, the two most significant were the Glenn L. Martin Airplane Company and Western Electric, the equipment manufacturer for American Telephone & Telegraph. Martin had been producing planes for the navy in Cleveland, Ohio, but chose to move the entire operation to Baltimore because it was close to Washington and the government facilities at Norfolk. The huge Western Electric Company's decision to locate its primary Eastern cable production facility in Baltimore was

Towson's streetcar #8 is pictured on a typical July day in 1922 as it stopped to pick up waiting passengers on York Road at Regester Avenue. From the Edward L. Bafford Photography Collection, Albin O. Kuhn Library and Gallery. Courtesy, University of Maryland Baltimore County

A crab fisherman proudly displayed one of his prize catches at Rock Point, Maryland, in 1936. F.S.A. Photo by Arthur Rothstein, LC

An oyster bed at Rock Point appeared ripe for tonging in September 1936, as evidenced by the hearty catches of these eager fishermen. F.S.A. Photo by Arthur Rothstein, LC

Left
Once harvesting was over, piles of oysters were unloaded from the oyster boat to the dock, where they would be sold. This man and his abundant catch were photographed at Rock Point in 1936. F.S.A. Photo by Arthur Rothstein, LC

Bottom, left
These workers shucked oysters for twenty-five cents a gallon at Rock Point in 1936. The average oyster shucker could do about five gallons a day. F.S.A. Photo by Arthur Rothstein, LC

Below
Once at the wharf in Rock Point oystermen received forty cents a bushel for their oysters in 1936. F.S.A. Photo by Arthur Rothstein, LC

The main entrance to the Poole and Hunt Union Works is pictured in 1930. At one time Poole and Hunt was Maryland's leading iron foundry. It manufactured steam engines, trains, and iron pipes and tools, along with some of the iron used in the columns of the United States Capitol. Courtesy, The Peale Museum, Baltimore, Maryland

Employees of the American Fruit Growers are shown circa 1930 grading and sorting apples that will later be loaded into barrels at a packing shed in Tonoloway, Maryland. Courtesy, University of Maryland Agricultural Experiment Station. From the Maryland Room, EPFL

expansion of the Chesapeake and Delaware barge canal into a full-size facility large enough to accommodate freighters. The old canal, connecting Delaware Bay with the upper Chesapeake, was purchased by the federal government in 1919 and by 1938, the Army Corps of Engineers had enlarged it to a depth of twenty-seven feet and width of 250 feet. The modernized canal cut off hundreds of miles for vessels moving down the coast to Baltimore and brought a surge of new shipping.

Like the rest of the nation, the port city had been hurt by the Great Depression of the 1930s, but its unusually diverse economy made it less vulnerable than many other cities. During the worst period, from 1931-1934, several hundred Baltimore businesses failed, but this was reversed after 1935 when a number of new firms opened in the urban area. The largest of these arrivals was the General Motors Company which located a Chevrolet assembly plant there in 1935. By 1939 Baltimore's industrial employment exceeded the 1929 level and while joblessness remained at 9.9 percent, the figure was about four points lower than the national average. Finally, although there were a number of failures among the state's small, rural banks during the financial crises of 1931-1933, none of Baltimore's major financial institutions were permanently closed—again, revealing a significantly better record than that of most other American cities.

Maryland experienced high levels of unemployment during the years 1930-1937, but a variety of federal employment programs relieved some of the problem and made real contributions to the state's infra-structure. Among these public works projects, none advanced future economic development more than highway construction. History taught Marylanders that transportation had always been a crucial factor in its economic growth. With the coming of the motor vehicle in the early decades of the twentieth century, the state had launched one of the first and most comprehensive road building programs in the nation—turning approximately 2,000 miles of dirt and gravel roads into modern, hard-surface highways. This activity actually amounted to a series of im-

described by the Association of Commerce as "the major event in the city's industrial life since the conclusion of the World War."

Many of the industries were attracted to Baltimore because of the excellent port facilities, and major improvements in their efficiency continued to be made through private investment and state bond issues. Large new terminals and a holding yard for 3,000 rail cars were built at Port Covington and leased to the Western Maryland Railroad. In 1923 the Pennsylvania Railroad constructed a pier and a four million-bushel grain elevator that was the largest and most modern on the East Coast. It replaced its old wooden piers at Canton with a $14-million facility capable of unloading four large vessels at the same time. As in many other areas of Baltimore's economy, smaller firms were also important in port development—companies such as the Rukert Terminals Corporation expanded during the 1920s from a small facility at Jackson's Wharf to a 400-foot pier (with six acres of adjacent land) at South Clinton Street.

Another great boon to the port was the

U.S. #1 at the junction of Rhode Island and New York avenues in Hyattsville, Maryland, at the entrance to Washington, D.C. is pictured in 1935. F.S.A. Photo by Jack DeLano, LC

provements to roads which had, for the most part, been built between 1650 and 1800. In 1922 the Crain Highway, connecting Baltimore with Southern Maryland, was begun—the first new highway in the state for over a century. Other roadways of similar quality were planned, but the depression cut short these efforts until New Deal programs came to the aid of the state.

Between 1934 and 1939 federal funds for unemployment relief were used to build 167 miles of highways and eighteen bridges. Thus, by 1940 transportation planners had sketched the beginnings of an entirely new system which would largely bypass the old horse-and-wagon roads. The Ritchie Highway was completed in 1938, linking Baltimore and Annapolis via a modern landscaped roadway, and the Pulaski Highway (U.S. 40) replaced the historic and narrow Philadelphia Road. The Baltimore National Pike—the first stretch of the old National Road—was being circumvented by an entirely new dual highway just to its north. Most importantly, however, the decade of the 1940s opened with the publication of the Maryland State Commission's monumental survey and report, "Maryland Highway Needs, 1941-1960." The report recommended what seemed at the time to be an enormous $216-million transportation program, focusing on the construction of an entire trunk-line system of limited access, dual highways with 200-foot rights-of-way. Submitted on the eve of U.S. entry into the

World War II, these proposals could not be enacted. Nevertheless, the farsighted program envisioned in the report governed the state's transportation policy after 1945 and laid the groundwork for Maryland's magnificent superhighway system of the post-war decades.

The road construction programs of the 1920s and 1930s also had a major effect on Maryland's rural life and the agricultural

The Catonsville branch of the Baltimore Post Office (left) at the corner
of Frederick Road (across photo)
and Sanford Avenue (on which automobiles are parked) is pictured in
1938. From the Maryland Room,
EPFL

Farms still clearly dominated the
landscape in 1940 along U.S. #1 between Washington, D.C. and Baltimore. F.S.A. Photo by Jack
Delano, LC

economy. In 1920 seven out of ten farmers
in Maryland lived on dirt roads. By 1950
the number had been cut to only three out
of ten. Adoption of the motor vehicle was
more dramatic yet. Even in 1920, 38 percent
of all farmers had an auto or truck; within
two decades the figure reached 92 percent.
Tractors were more expensive and only 16
percent of the farms possessed one in 1930.
The depression slowed sales so that ownership increased to only 22 percent by 1940.
However, the next decade was the turning
point, with tractor purchase increasing 300
percent. Almost every Maryland farm in excess of fifty acres had at least one such vehicle by 1950, while over 5,000 farms owned
two or more. The war, itself, played some
role in this development. Severe farm labor
shortages (only the employment of German
war prisoners saved the 1943 tomato crop)

A farm in Cambridge, Maryland, employed this young boy as a bean picker in 1937. The bushel basket of string beans he carried when through was almost as big as he was! F.S.A. Photo by Arthur Rothstein, LC

Above
George Pernell (left) and Lucas Barnes (right) picked peas for a canning factory in St. Marys County as an occasional source of extra income. The men are pictured at their toil in 1940. F.S.A. Photo by John Vachon, LC

Left
A representative of the Resettlement Administration is pictured talking to a family of mountain people on a farm in Garrett County in 1936. F.S.A. Photo by Arthur Rothstein, LC

Shelling corn certainly became a simpler task when one used the "Invincible" electric corn sheller, shown here at Whitehall Farm in Harford County in 1930. Courtesy, Consolidated Gas and Electric Light Power Company. From the Maryland Room, EPFL

A large kettle sits nearby, boiling and ready for a freshly butchered hog on a snow-covered farm in Frederick in 1940. F.S.A. Photo by Marion Post Wolcott, LC

resulted in far more extensive rental or lease of tractors and other farm machines. The University of Maryland trained approximately 37,000 farmers in equipment repair so that by the war's end, almost everyone was familiar with farm machine maintenance. Finally, the 40 percent increase in agricultural sales during the war gave many farmers the extra income required to purchase expensive equipment.

The electrification of Maryland's agricultural region also occurred during these years. In 1930 only one quarter of the state's farms, primarily those in the Baltimore and Washington suburban areas, had power. Largely through the efforts of the federal Rural Electrification Administration, the figure jumped to 61 percent by 1945 and 84 percent by 1950. By the end of the 1940s,

Maryland farmers had entered fully into the new age of gasoline and electricity.

The tractors, trucks, and power lines allowed many important changes, but they did not alter any fundamental trends in the agricultural economy. The number of farms continued to decline along with total acreage, while remaining lands became increasingly concentrated in the hands of fewer operators. Maryland claimed 47,908 farms in 1920, but only 36,107 three decades later. Over half of this decline occurred in the 1940s. Indeed, 1945 marked the beginning of the great contraction in the number of Maryland farms—a phenomenon still evident today. From 1920 to 1950 over 700,000 acres had passed out of agricultural use. Much of this was marginal land in Western Maryland and the Eastern Shore, but a size-

These workers were at last ready to load the final basket of string beans they had picked into a truck parked next to fields near Cambridge in June 1937. F.S.A. Photo by Arthur Rothstein, LC

Right
These employees of the Phillips
Packing Company are placing tomato juice in sealed cans into baskets,
which they will then carry to a
chilled water pool for cooling. F.S.A.
Photo by John Collier, LC

Right
These employees of the Phillips
Packing Company are placing toma-
to juice in sealed cans into baskets,
which they will then carry to a
chilled water pool for cooling. F.S.A.
Photo by John Collier, LC

Below
The captain of this Chesapeake Bay
freight boat took off his shoes for
better footing on the melon-
smeared hold of his ship. Someone
had not been careful! F.S.A. Photo
by John Collier, LC

able and ever increasing proportion came
from the highly fertile Baltimore and Washington suburbs. Baltimore County, for
example, lost 61,000 acres to suburban development between 1920 and 1950 and another 122,000 by 1982. Only 25 percent of
its land was then designated for farming,
and the area dropped from second to
twelfth place in state agriculture production.
The five most rapidly urbanizing counties
of Central Maryland witnessed the conversion of 84,000 acres to non-agricultural uses
during the 1920-1982 period, with the major
shift coming after 1945.

Fewer operators claimed what remained of
Maryland's once abundant farmlands. By
the end of the 1940s, 39 percent of these
holdings were under fifty acres, amounting
to approximately ten percent of the state's
agricultural territory. In addition, most small
"farmers" were actually employed in unrela-
ted jobs which yielded a higher income.
The middle range growers, owning 100-219

acres, comprised 52 percent of all farmers and worked approximately 45 percent of the arable soil. In 1982 holdings of 50 or less acres accounted for 42 percent of the state's farms, but only about 7 percent of its land. Middle-range farmers, those possessing 50-179 acres, cultivated roughly 27 percent of Maryland's fields. Growers with 180 or more acres claimed the remaining two-thirds of the state's farmland. Since the amount of land does not translate directly into more income (one-fourth of farms with less than fifty acres did manage to sell more than $10,000 worth of agricultural products in 1982), the degree of economic concentration is somewhat exaggerated by acreage figures. Nevertheless, the typical, genuine commercial farm in Maryland, (that is, one selling more than $10,000 worth of agriculture products in 1982) averaged 257 acres; represented a mean investment of $568,000 in land, buildings, and equipment; and sold about $123,000 of its crops. Roughly 8,107 "typical" operations existed, accounting for 97 percent of the sales generated by all 16,184

Maryland farms. Obviously, the major agricultural changes occurring since the 1940s have turned farming into a large-scale enterprise.

In terms of the state's agricultural products, the most spectacular event has been the rise of the Eastern Shore poultry business. Chickens had always been raised there, but Central Maryland out-produced all other areas until the war. With the coming of electric service and improved roads to Eastern Shore farms, hatcheries were built and the business began to expand rapidly. The area accounted for only a quarter of the poultry business in 1940, but by 1949 it had captured over 80 percent. World War II was the turning point, with the production of broiler chicken increasing from twenty-one to 127.6 million pounds between 1939 and 1945. In 1982 the eight Eastern Shore counties accounted for 91 percent of the $366 million dollar poultry sales.

The building of modern highways on the Eastern Shore during the inter-war years was a boon not only to poultry and truck

Mrs. Eugene Smith, whose husband is a Farm Security Administration borrower, met in her chicken yard in St. Marys County with F.S.A. Supervisor Margarite Chappelle for some sound advice in September 1940. F.S.A. Photo by John Vachon, LC

The growth of the resort industry, along with the increasing use of automobiles, ended the rural isolation of the Eastern Shore. Pictured is the state road in Bethlehem, Caroline County, in 1938. Courtesy, The Baltimore Sun

farmers, but to the tourist trade, also. Louis Drexler, Chairman of the Del-Mar-Va Resorts Commission, told an Eastern Shore business convention in 1927 that the local resort industry had experienced "a remarkable awakening" due to highway construction. The assessed valuation of Ocean City, he said, had increased from $200,000 to over six million dollars since 1921, and the growing availability of auto travel was making the area "a mecca for tourists." He added that the "summer resorts should grow by leaps." Drexler's forecast was ultimately correct, but the depression slowed the pace of development until 1940. Although wartime gas rationing severely curtailed vacations from 1942-1945, growth indeed began to leap ahead in subsequent years.

While Ocean City's expansion may be linked to better highways and general prosperity, some boardwalk observers have noticed an uncanny relationship between increasing wealth and decreasing modesty in swimwear. The reduction of the male bathing suit to shorts and a sleeveless shirt coincided with the prosperity of the early twentieth century. Those affluent Roaring Twenties similarly saw women shedding cumbersome "swimming dresses" for form-fitting one piece suits. During the depressed 1930s neither bathing attire nor the resort business improved, but the 1940 season, heralded as the best since the 1920s, was the first one in which men went "topless."

Once again, the enormous boom of the 1950-1980 era seemed to reduce both male and female suits to an almost absolute minimum. One hesitates to suggest the effect of any future economic surge on beach attire.

The auto and the truck also influenced retailing on the Eastern Shore. Area merchants found themselves in competition with the new chain stores which began to appear in the larger towns during the 1920s. Small business people complained that consumers shopped with cash at the franchises and used credit to complete their purchases at local stores. Although some grumbled about better roads inducing more people to shop in Baltimore and Philadelphia, Frank

Left
*Mrs. Harper's Tourist Home was lo-
cated at 5530 Wisconsin Avenue in
Chevy Chase, Maryland, right
above the district line. Her door was
always open, and Mrs. Harper
charged $2.50 a night in 1942. F.S.A.
Photo by Marjory Collins, LC*

Short, a farsighted retailer from Salisbury, said that this phenomenon could be advantageous to area merchants. In a speech in 1927 he said:

There will always be a percentage of our people who will go to the city for certain commodities. As our highways are improved the accessibility of the large city is increased, but as our roads are improved we also make the Peninsula centers more accessible for our local trade. The fact ... may be recognized as an advantage to the local merchant for his patrons become familiar with a higher standard of quality {which} develops a demand for similar commodities on the Peninsula and which if displayed in a 'large store' way will be bought by the Peninsula consumer.

In the long-run, Eastern Shore businessmen were deeply interested in modernizing the transportation link between the Delmarva peninsula and the Baltimore-Washington area. Having discussed the possibility of a bridge across the Kent Island narrows since the turn of the century, they argued their case to the legislature during the years between the two wars. The Maryland Assembly authorized a bridge, but could not find the $14 million to build it. Finally, in 1947 Governor Lane made it a top priority and construction began. Upon its completion in 1952, the Chesapeake Bay Bridge carried a $45-million price tag, yet the four mile long structure remains one of the nation's finest. When it opened it was also the longest continuous steel bridge in the world, and its 186 foot height assured easy passage of the largest ships. Most important-

Bottom, center
*Gasoline sold for twenty-three cents
a gallon at this Dome gas station in
Takoma Park, Maryland, in 1921—a
low price by today's standards! LC*

A good source of income for Deal Island fishermen during the 1940s was taking summer tourists on fishing parties. W.D. Webster was one such entrepreneur. F.S.A. Photo by Jack Delano, LC

ly, its creation marked the beginning of the Eastern Shore's full integration into the economic and social life of the Baltimore-Washington region.

In contrast to the economic strengths realized by the Eastern Shore, Western Maryland during the inter-war years suffered a series of difficulties from which it is still attempting to recover. In the view of Harry Stegmaier, Jr., the leading authority on this region in the modern era, Western Maryland's fundamental economic problem was the gradual concentration of industrial employment in three large firms. The largest by far was the Celanese Corporation which began in 1924 to manufacture a cellulose acetate yarn at a huge plant near the Potomac River just south of Cumberland. By 1940 Celanese employed approximately 11,000 people and had become the chief contributor to Western Maryland's manufacturing employment. The Kelly-Springfield Tire Company opened its factory in Cumberland in 1918. Quickly establishing itself as a permanent feature of the city's industrial base, it provided jobs to several hundred coal miners who had been thrown out of work when many of the George's Creek mines closed after the war. Finally, the Virginia Pulp and Paper Company, located on the Potomac at Luke, Maryland, expanded during the 1920s. This company employed both ex-miners and ex-farmers from surrounding Allegany and Garrett counties. During the same era, however, many of the older and smaller firms which offered the city of Cumberland and the neighboring region a diverse economic base went out of business. The local glass industry almost totally disappeared, the George's Creek coal mines declined to a shadow of their former prosperity, and even the famous Footer's Dye works finally closed in 1937. By 1940, 83 percent of Allegany County's factory employees were engaged by one of the three large firms that had grown up in the area during the 1920s. In addition, the railroads supported several thousand additional workers. Hence, the region's labor force was dependent upon a small number of major employers and, as Stegmaier points out, "if anything serious happened to any of the big four employers economic disaster would result."

Above
The William Wilkens Steam Curled Hair Manufactory began operating during the 1840s, when processing animal hair to be used for stuffing mattresses, sofas, and carriage seats was a major business. After World War I, however, the business rapidly declined. In this photograph from 1939 the change is illustrated by the many empty factory buildings. From the Maryland Room, EPFL

Left
An abandoned, yet interesting, Garrett County coal mine—complete with icelike stalactites—is pictured in 1937. F.S.A. Photo by Arthur Rothstein, LC

Right
Many of Maryland's textile and canning industries can be picked out of
the background of this panorama of
Cambridge, Dorchester County, in
1940. From the Maryland Room,
EPFL

Below
The Phillips Packing Company's
camp for migratory workers in Vienna, Maryland, is pictured in 1940.
Living quarters are on the left, and
the cooking areas are on the right
near the single water pump. F.S.A.
Photo by Jack DeLano, LC

The Second World War brought prosperity back with a rush to Western Maryland. The Celanese plant began producing a synthetic yarn, Foristan, used in making parachutes and a variety of other items from anti-mildew underwear for soldiers in the tropics to gas mask parts and pistol grips. Celanese's production rose 35 percent and employment peaked at 13,000; almost half of these workers were women. The Kelly-Springfield Tire Company turned to the manufacture of .50 caliber armor-piercing cartridges and mortar shells, and when synthetic rubber became available in 1943, it also began making tires again. Two years later the firm returned to civilian production and became the mainstay of the county's economic life for the next thirty-five years. Its payroll increased from 1,000 to 6,500. In conjunction with George Washington University, Kelly-Springfield also built the Allegany Ordnance Plant on the West Virginia side of the Potomac seven miles west of Cumberland. Here approximately 500-600 Marylanders helped develop

the bazooka, aircraft rockets, and the Jet-Assisted Take-Off devices called JATO's. The ordnance plant continued to play an important role in the local economy far into the post-war era. Similarly, the giant Luke papermill expanded during the war and has remained an employer of around 2,000 workers ever since.

Although many industries fared well in the years following World War II, Allegany County's economy was seriously wounded by massive layoffs at the Celanese plant. A nation-wide depression in the textile industry and the removal of most Celanese operations to other parts of the country were responsible for this event. Rail service also declined. Local highways traversing Maryland's mountainous terrain could not completely replace the trains, and transportation problems added to the other difficulties. All of these developments cut deeply into the local economic base; by 1949 Allegany County had an unemployment rate of 23 percent.

Hagerstown did a good deal better during the 1920-1950 era. Its extremely diversified economy survived the depression remarkably well, and then was transformed by the war. The Fairchild Engine and Airplane Company, which began in Hagerstown in 1925 and employed 200 people by 1939, contributed much to local prosperity. As the 1930s drew to a close, the Army Air Corps ordered 270 training planes, necessitating an expansion of the company. By 1945 Fairchild had built 5,000 training planes, 1,000 C-82 cargo carriers, plus thousands of parts for the Glenn L. Martin Company. The government financed a massive series of production facilities on the outskirts of Hagerstown, but Fairchild was still so desperate for space that it leased the Odd Fellows Hall and even private homes. By 1943 the company employed 8,000 people and appeared to have subcontracts with almost every firm in the city—down to the venerable M. P. Moller church organ factory which grew from 185 to 1,200 employees and turned out airplane wings for Fairchild and training gun turrets for the Navy. While Fairchild emerged as the region's industrial giant, there were no grave setbacks among

In October of 1937 this train of the Western Maryland Railroad was photographed as it chugged through the center of Hagerstown, arriving from Baltimore. F.S.A. Photo by Arthur Rothstein, LC

the diverse collection of manufacturers which had for so long characterized the economy of this valley town. The later decline of Fairchild Industries in the 1970s had a serious impact, but never dealt such serious blows as were felt in the Cumberland area when Celanese and the railroads suffered their financial difficulties.

Although of great local importance, the economic changes in Western Maryland and the Eastern Shore were but a side show to the enormous upheaval in the Baltimore region. The Second World War brought to the port city an unprecedented volume of military contracts, shipping, plant expansions, and employment increases. Maryland ranked twenty-eighth in population, but stood twelfth on the list of government contractors during the war, receiving $5.5 billion between 1940 and 1945. In per capita

contract dollars, it ranked fourth in the entire nation. The Baltimore region captured 78 percent of the state's war work—almost 60 percent of which went to six firms: Bethlehem Steel, Martin Aircraft, the Eastern Aircraft Division of General Motors, Westinghouse, Western Electric, and the Bendix Corporation. Ships, airplanes, and communication equipment were the backbone of the city's war production economy. However, the concentration of Maryland's prime military contracts in the hands of a few corporations tends to obscure the wide range of businesses that shared these profits. The city's Association of Commerce reported in 1945 that over 600 area firms had participated in war work. Baltimore's great diversity of trades facilitated the rapid conversion to military production, and the secondary contractors, many of them small businesses, were quite significant. General Motors, for example, hired forty-six subcontractors to transform its Chevrolet plant into a fighter plane factory in 1942. Remarkably, only twenty-four weeks passed between the time when the last auto rolled off its assembly line and the first "Avenger" and "Wildcat" fuselages began to be shipped out. Almost one-third of the Glenn L. Martin Company's $1.6-billion job was performed by smaller subcontractors, and the Bethlehem Steel shipyards relied on hundreds of firms to outfit their vessels.

Practically the full spectrum of Baltimore's business community shared some of the work originally assumed by the major corporations. This included firms that were old and new, large and small. Many war contractors were in the 500-1,000 employee range, but the average size was fifty to 200, and a surprising number had payrolls under that amount. The three workers at the Diez & Hynson Brass Foundry made propellers and a variety of fittings which found their way into the hundreds of ships being built or repaired down at the harbor. In terms of age, the military contract firms listed in the official history of the Maryland war effort were divided as follows: 46 percent were businesses founded (or established in Baltimore) before 1917, 44 percent had come on the local scene between 1917 and 1939, and 10 percent were established between 1940 and 1945. Revered old shops such as Samuel Kirk & Sons Silversmiths, founded in 1815, made silver-soldered components for radar units and dozens of other electrical devices embodying the latest scientific and technological knowledge; on the other hand, brand new firms like the Londontown Manufacturing Company, established in 1943, produced raincoats for the Army—a trade in which Baltimore clothing factories had been involved since the Civil War.

There is no question that the greatest single enterprise in Baltimore's war effort was Bethlehem Steel's herculean shipbuilding program. Its Sparrows Point shipyards built ninety-eight vessels, including a number of oil tankers weighing over 200,000 deadweight tons—at the time these were among the largest ships afloat. Bethlehem's most spectacular effort, however, was the construction of 508 vessels, mostly Liberty ships for the merchant marine, across the harbor at Fairfield. In the fall of 1943 the Fairfield yards were completing four ships per week, constructing them in thirty days from keel laying to launching. At peak employment, Bethlehem had over 60,000 workers on its Baltimore payrolls—46,700 at Fairfield alone. To feed the shipyards with enough steel, the Sparrows Point production complex was enlarged and modernized. Combined with expansions in the late 1940s, it remained efficient and competitive in the post-war era. A $200-million addition in 1957-1959 made Sparrow Point the largest steel mill in the free world, with a labor force of 29,000.

Glenn L. Martin Aircraft expanded rapidly in 1939 as it received orders from England and France, and began production on its B-26 Marauder for the United States. By 1945 it had manufactured over 10,000 aircraft and countless components. Between 1938 and 1940 employment rose from 3,500 to 13,000 and at its peak in 1943, the number reached 53,000. Net sales increases were equally impressive from $24.1 million in 1939 to $598 million in 1943. To provide trained workers for the company, the University of Maryland and Johns Hopkins each instructed approximately 10,000 men and women in the fields of engineering, math, chemistry, metallurgy, and management. In 1945 Glenn L. Martin made a large gift to the University of Maryland for the establishment of a School of Engineering which played an important role in developing the institution's entire science and technology program.

The third largest wartime employer in Baltimore was a relative newcomer to the city. The Bendix Corporation had opened a modest facility on Fort Avenue near Ft. McHenry in 1937 to expand its production of aircraft radio equipment. By 1940 the company had grown to about 700 workers, and three years later it employed over 8,000 in plants scattered throughout the urban region. Its Friez Instrument Division engaged 2,000 additional persons. From that time onwards Bendix has been a major part of the

Maryland economy. The University of Maryland and Johns Hopkins again helped to train its technicians.

Johns Hopkins' role in the Maryland war effort was not limited to the instruction of industry employees. As one of the world's major scientific and medical research centers, its scientists were involved in over a hundred important military projects—the two most significant of which were the atomic bomb and the proximity fuze. The latter invention electronically detonated anti-aircraft shells as they reached the point closest to their target. It was a devastatingly effective weapon and one of the most significant pioneering efforts in the field of electronic miniaturization. Following the war, the university's Applied Physics Laboratory, which had developed the proximity fuze, began a long-term program to perfect guided missiles and other military hardware for the Defense Department. Eventually, Johns Hopkins led the nation's universities in government research contracts, primarily in the military, medical, and health fields.

The staffing requirements of the Baltimore area war industries were far in excess of the local labor market. In 1940 approximately 400,000 people were employed in the Baltimore region, and about 130,000 of them worked in manufacturing. Even with the demand for labor, there were close to 28,000 jobless persons. In the fall of 1943 total employment in the Baltimore area reached 560,000 and manufacturing consumed over half of the labor pool. The shipyards alone employed 77,000. At the same time 55,000 young men and women were taken *out* of the area's work force for the armed services. The U.S. Employment Service reported that it had filled the labor deficit through the absorption of all the unemployed, the migration of approximately 110,000 workers into the Baltimore area, the entrance of 35,000 young people into the job market, the hiring of 10,000 elderly or handicapped workers, and the entrance of 20,000 women "not customarily in the labor force." The engagement of female and black workers in manufacturing increased substantially. Women constituted 9 percent of this work force in 1941 and 29 percent in 1944, while

black employment rose from 7 to 18 percent. A few Baltimore manufacturers hired blacks voluntarily, but most did not do so until persuaded, pressured, or forced under Executive Order 8802 which forbade discrimination in employment. The opening up of better paying manufacturing jobs to women and black workers marks a major turning point in the economic and social history of Maryland. While the proportion of minority group members in manufacturing (and other more important positions) declined sharply at the end of the war, it never returned to the former level. Karen Anderson in her book *Wartime Women* states that thousands of Baltimore's black and white female defense workers found new factory occupations better paying and more interesting than most traditional women's jobs. Near the end of the war, a woman at the Bendix Corporation told a federal interviewer: "I love my job and hate the idea of giving it up. I can hardly wait to get there. I never thought I could do such exciting work ... and I am really proud." Black employees were taught skills they had never been given an opportunity to learn and gained work experience that launched many of them on permanent careers in industry. While Maryland's color line remained strong for another twenty-five years, its solidity was broken and gradually overcome by the war experience.

The radical shifts in the structure of the Maryland and Baltimore economies engendered fears that peacetime readjustment would bring even higher unemployment than had been the case in the 1930s. A larger population would burgeon with vast numbers of relocated war workers intending to remain in the state, females wishing to stay on the job (a majority of those interviewed by the government in 1945 expressed the desire to do so), and the returning veterans. The Maryland Commission on Post-War Reconstruction and Development predicted high unemployment for several years, but fortunately the reconversion to a peacetime economy moved quickly and joblessness never reached the figures estimated by the group. While the state's population increased 18.6 percent during the 1940s, total employment rose 31.3 percent. Manufacturing jobs expanded by 23 percent in spite of an absolute decline in Baltimore's garment industry—the first such downturn in its history. A decrease of 11,000 household servants (over 90 percent of which were black) was a sign of real progress, since many of these workers left the low-paying field for higher wages in manufacturing and growing new service areas. Employment figures for 1950 showed that Maryland's economy had started to move with the rest of the nation towards more professional, communications, transportation, wholesale, retail, and other non-manufacturing occupations.

The war marked the emergence of Baltimore County as the state's largest industrial and business center after the port city, itself. The county had always possessed a sizeable portion of manufacturing firms, and Sparrow's Point, too, was within its boundaries. During the war, however, the expansion of the Martin Aircraft Company in Middle River, Bendix Corporation in Towson, and a variety of other plants meant that almost half of the state's total military work was performed in Baltimore County. After 1945 an increasing number of companies began to move there from older, cramped, city quarters, while many establishments just coming into the area also chose the suburban location. In 1947 alone sixty-five million dollars worth of new manufacturing investment entered the Baltimore region—with a larger percentage than ever before going into the county. As residential development boomed, retail and service businesses grew by the hundreds to provide for the new suburban population.

Rapid growth in the county prompted officials to develop a more efficient highway system. By 1949 the first plans for the Baltimore Beltway and the Harbor Tunnel Throughway had been announced, and both projects were completed in the 1950s. This was only part of the gigantic statewide highway program first unveiled in 1940; yet, it expanded far beyond that ambitious original plan.

In addition to these highway construction efforts, Maryland and Baltimore moved into the forefront of air service. The city's old municipal terminal was outdated by 1945, and blueprints were immediately made for a much larger, modern facility. The sprawling new complex was erected eight miles south of the city on the new Baltimore-Washington Parkway. When it was opened in 1950, Friendship International Airport (now called Baltimore-Washington International Airport), was the most modern terminal in the U.S. Five times larger than Washington National Airport, BWI became a major regional center for air travel and cargo. As has happened elsewhere, the terminal stimulated the growth of many new businesses in surrounding Anne Arundel County, turning its ancient farms and tobacco fields into industrial parks and residential developments.

In spite of the growing importance of its suburban areas, Baltimore City and its harbor remained at the core of the state's economy. Port shipping continued to increase after the war, and in terms of tonnage, it even temporarily surpassed New York in 1947 to become America's leading export center. A 1948 *Business Week* article entitled "Baltimore: New Export Leader," explained that the port's closer proximity to the coal and wheat supplies, shorter rail connections to many Midwestern cities, and lower loading costs gave it the advantage over its East Coast rivals. The city did not hold the premier position for long, as New York resumed leadership. Nevertheless, Baltimore's brief jump into first place indicated the tremendous increases of the war and post-war years. In 1950 Sparrows Point and the other metals industries employed over 31,000 in a dozen locations around the harbor, while 148 chemical plants and their more than 10,000 workers also depended on the port for their supplies of raw materials. A 1952 study by the state's planning commission showed the total extent of maritime activities. Fully 956 establishments with almost 142,000 workers (about two-thirds of the entire area's manufacturing sector), owed their existence to the port, and another 1,004 firms employing 49,000 were partially dependent on the facilities. It was not an understatement when the Baltimore Association of Commerce said in 1947: "As the Port Goes, So Goes the City."

During the late 1940s, in the midst of great prosperity, a number of leaders recognized that major changes were required to maintain maritime supremacy. Baltimore area business groups had been successful in getting Congress to deepen the harbor from thirty-five to thirty-nine feet, ensuring that the facilities would keep pace with the increasingly deep drafts of the bulk cargo ships so vital to the area's economy. Yet, other equally serious problems remained. In 1950 Baltimore was still moving approximately 80 percent of its cargo through the port by rail, while many other maritime cities were carrying as much as half their cargo by truck. This gave competitors a real advantage in the general transport business, because motorized vehicles were far more efficient than trains. Since all of Baltimore's waterfront loading areas and terminals were owned by the railroads, trucks had relatively poor access to the ships and were charged higher dock fees than what they paid in other parts. At the same time, the railroads were failing to expand their general cargo facilities and in some cases were not even maintaining them sufficiently. These factors made it very difficult for Baltimore to vie for the more lucrative general cargo business, rendering the port increasingly dependent on its traditional bulk trade.

Truck access to the port improved with the state's highway building programs of the 1940s and 1950s, particularly the opening of the tunnel under the harbor in 1957. However, total solutions to the trucking problem did not arrive until the construction of the federal interstate system in the 1960s.

The real breakthrough for the harbor as a whole, nevertheless, came in 1956 with the creation of the Maryland Port Authority. Its vigorous program to improve terminal facilities, particularly for general cargo; its equalization of dock fees for both trucks and railroads; and its aggressive promotional efforts opened one of the most successful chapters in Baltimore maritime history.

Of all of Maryland's many economic changes during the 1940s, one of the most striking was the growth of the federal government as the largest single "industry" in the state. By 1972 over 126,000 federal employees lived within the state's borders. Nothing indicated the growing importance of the federal government and the city of Washington more than the spectacular rise of Montgomery and Prince Georges counties. In 1930 Montgomery ranked seventh and Prince Georges fourth in population; both were still regarded as largely agricultural areas. Prince Georges County provided the easiest access to Washington, since it stretched over two-thirds of the Maryland-District of Columbia boundary. Even in 1930 nearly half of the Prince Georges population lived in suburban areas adjacent to the District. The rest of the county appeared to be occupied chiefly by centuries-old tobacco farms. In Montgomery County the towns of Bethesda, Chevy Chase, Kensington, Silver Spring, and Wheaton were small suburban enclaves set amidst rolling farmlands and pastures. Their total population did not exceed 25,000. Rockville and Gaithersville were country towns.

Fortunately, the Montgomery County political "boss" of the 1920-1950 era was a powerful, farsighted businessman and politician named E. Brook Lee. Lee was instrumental in modernizing the government, establishing the Maryland National-Capital Park and Planning Commission, and pushing through local legislation which by 1940 gave Montgomery County the best school and recreational systems in the state. He also worked with public officials to build a modern network of roads and highways that lured both buyers and home builders into the county. Lee, himself, was a real estate developer who profited from these improvements, but his direction brought wealth to the county and the state far in excess of his very large personal gain. In this regard, he may be considered as the leading member of a whole generation of civic-minded Maryland businessmen who worked in the other counties to modernize local government, improve conditions for economic development, and make their local areas more attractive and efficient places in which to live, work, and invest. Lee's own efforts paid dividends in every way. Affluent Washington-

ians moved into the county in increasing numbers throughout the 1920s and 1930s. Beginning in 1945 the flow of residential development became a floodtide as the nation's capital expanded in all directions. From 1945 to 1950 the county grew from 85,000 to 164,000. In 1970 it contained 523,000 people, a figure far exceeding the combined populations of both the Eastern Shore and Western Maryland. A variety of federal installations also began to relocate along the county's new highways. By 1943 the Naval Research Ship Center, the National Institute of Health, the Bethesda Naval Hospital, and the Army Mapping Service had moved there. The National Institute of Health alone counted over 11,000 employees in 1973.

To the east, Prince Georges County absorbed an even larger share of Washington's expansion. Through it ran the main rail lines from Washington to Baltimore and the Northeast, as well as the nation's oldest inter-regional highway, Route 1. After World War II this road was paralleled first by the

Baltimore-Washington Parkway and then by Interstate 95. In addition, almost three-quarters of the Maryland portion of the Capital Beltway crossed through the Prince Georges County, as did Route 50—the main highway from Washington to Annapolis and the Eastern Shore. Within its D.C. suburban region, the county came to house Andrews Air Force Base, the National Agricultural Research Center, Goddard Space Flight Center, the Census Bureau, the Federal Records Center, and the Naval Surface Weapons Center. It is also the location of the main campus of the University of Maryland.

Few wonder why the county grew from 89,000 in 1940 to 357,000 in 1960 and 660,000 by 1970. Montgomery and Prince Georges counties then made up 30 percent of the state's population—and 25 percent of the labor force in these jurisdictions were federal employees. Another 25 percent, often holding upper-level, high income jobs, worked in government-related private businesses. Moreover, 47 percent of Montgom-

Montgomery County used to be mainly farmland, as illustrated in this photograph of one of its rustic grocery stores in 1940. F.S.A. Photo by Arthur Rothstein, LC

ery County's labor force were professional and managerial, which primarily accounts for its emergence in 1970 as the nation's second wealthiest county. This same jurisdiction also boasted one of the largest concentrations of highly educated scientists, engineers, technicians, and administrative managers in the United States, thus becoming a natural location for businesses requiring a pool of talented employees.

It was in this rather swift manner that Old Line State was shaken out of its slow, comfortable existence as a quiet agricultural society surrounding the compact and bustling port city of Baltimore. By 1950 the entire central portion of the state stretching from Harford down to Montgomery and Prince Georges counties was showing clear signs of melding into a rich, economically diverse, and semi-urbanized region. Relying on the advanced technologies developed during the war and using skilled workers from the large defense contractors, many new businesses flourished in the late 1940s and beyond. The accelerated pace of economic life was felt throughout the state. Maryland was too small and communication had improved too much for changes in the central core not to reverberate from Garrett County to the Eastern Shore.

Partially facilitated by educated newcomers, one of the most significant statewide effects of the thriving economic and social climate was a dramatic upgrading and expansion of the antiquated, racially segregated school system. Maryland's five teachers' colleges were transformed into four-year institutions, offering affordable higher education to local residents in almost every section of the state. The state government poured millions of dollars into the University of Maryland, and it soon became one of the nation's major institutions of advanced learning. In 1964 the school opened a second campus in Baltimore County near the intersection of the beltway and Interstate 95, finally giving the urban area a publicly-supported, research-oriented university. All of this academic activity has caused a revolution in the education level of the state's adult labor force. In 1940, 20 percent of Maryland's adults were high school graduates, but forty years later, 67 percent had received their diplomas and 36 percent could boast at least some college training. Obviously, more than just the landscape of Maryland had been transformed since the early 1940s. The new generation of citizens, more educated, skilled, and affluent than any of their ancestors, gradually began to assume a major role in the state's business and economic arena. By the 1970s and 1980s, that arena has grown more diverse and interesting than ever before in Maryland's long history.

Chapter VI

GROWTH, CHANGE, AND REINDUSTRIALIZ-ATION:

MARYLAND FROM 1970s TO EARLY 1980s

During the 1960s Maryland's economy appeared to be in some difficulty, but today the state is wealthier, more productive and innovative than at any time in its history. Analysts in earlier decades could see certain signs of economic hardship. For example, Maryland's population increase had drastically slowed. In the 1970s the state grew by only 7.5 percent compared to an average rate of 29.1 percent for each decade from 1940-1970. Even more ominous was the erosion of the large manufacturing base.

Baltimore's heavy industries suffered the same decline seen in many other aging Northeastern cities, and its once great garment trade had almost vanished from the old loft district. The metropolitan area lost a devastating 56,100 manufacturing jobs between 1970 and 1983. As the *Wall Street Journal* commented, Baltimore appeared in the 1960s to be "a dull blue collar town with a fancy hospital (Johns Hopkins), an occasionally successful baseball team (the Orioles) and little else." Its downtown district, aside from the brave (some thought foolhardy) urban renewal project called Charles Center, seemed outmoded and unprofitable—particularly the semi-abandoned and forlorn-looking inner harbor area. In the Washington suburbs the rate of federal employment had started to slow down, and it was expected to eventually decline (as indeed happened after 1980).

Rather than fading, however, Maryland's economic growth rate proved better than the national average during the 1970-1983 period. This was due to the tremendous surge in non-

manufacturing jobs—particularly the wholesale/retail trades and service industries. The change caused a historic restructuring of the state's economy as can be seen in Table 6.1. Even the industrially depressed Baltimore region responded with a net gain of 189,000 jobs from 1970 to 1983. The state's employment climbed by 499,000, representing a 32 percent increase while the population grew by only 10.1 percent. Unfortunately, the last great surge of baby boomers and an unprecedented number of women became permanent members of the labor force during this time. Combined with factory workers whose jobs were permanently lost, these two groups kept the state's unemployment rate between 5.5 and 7.5 percent for most of the 1970-1983 era, except during the great recession of 1981-1983 when it hit 9.6 percent.

While lower than the national average for almost the entire postwar era, joblessness was a continual problem in certain regions of Maryland, primarily the industrial quarters of Baltimore and Western Maryland. Migrants from rural areas and their children added to Baltimore's pool of unskilled, poorly educated workers (both black and white) who experienced difficulty in entering an increasingly technical job market. The city's blue-collar to white-collar transition further impaired its

The Avalon Nail and Iron Works, located just outside of Baltimore, rolled rails for the Baltimore and Ohio Railroad during the 1840s. In the next decade, it employed 140 men—turning out 40,000 kegs of nails in 1850! The foundry housed a rolling mill and seven steam-powered puddling furnaces, depicted in the center of this illustration from a circa 1857 advertisement. In the background, the famous Thomas Viaduct spans the Patapsco River, carrying the B & O's trains between Baltimore and Washington. Heavy industry and transportation has formed the economic core of Maryland's economy for much of the nineteenth and twentieth centuries. From the Hambleton Collection. Courtesy, The Peale Museum, Baltimore, Maryland

Above
Tourists enjoyed dressing up for a stroll in the sun along the boardwalk in Ocean City, Maryland, around the turn of the century. Bathers were a bit more casually attired. Courtesy, M.E. Warren

Right
People are pictured enjoying the afternoon sun at Betterton Beach around 1915. The Chesapeake, a popular hotel at the time, can be seen on the left. Courtesy, M.E. Warren

Above
Depicted is a typical mid-eighteenth-century tobacco plantation on Chesapeake Bay. The family's large brick house is surrounded by formal gardens and several out-buildings for their servants. Farming activities can also be seen. MHS

Left
The lithograph firm of A. Hoen & Company used this illustration of the Baltimore Harbor in an eye-catching advertisement in 1890. The most famous of Baltimore's many printing firms, A. Hoen & Company was one of the world's leading printers of atlas and highway maps and an unsurpassed master in litho-graphy. From the Cator Collection, EPFL

*During the 1850s Baltimore's main
thoroughfare was Baltimore Street.
This view of Baltimore Street, printed by E. Sachse Company, shows
the Baltimore Museum on the right,
along with various other shops and
businesses. From the Cator Collection, EPFL*

Above
A Bird's-Eye View of the City of Annapolis *was lithographed by E. Sachse Company around 1860. Annapolis is surrounded by the Severn River (right), Chesapeake Bay (front), and Spa Creek (left). The naval academy is on the right, and the statehouse can be seen in the center. From the Cator Collection, EPFL*

Left
Isaac Friedenwald published this last panorama of Baltimore City and Harbor in 1889. The long building on the left is the Camden Railroad station. Baltimore's industrial growth is clearly evidenced by the numerous smokestacks. From the Cator Collection, EPFL

The United States Naval Academy calls Annapolis home. Pictured above is the Chapel and to the left are cadets on parade. Courtesy, Annapolis and Anne Arundel County Conference and Visitors Bureau

The Maryland State House is the oldest state house in the nation still in legislative use. Courtesy, Annapolis and Anne Arundel County Conference and Visitors Bureau

St. John's College is home to the Great Books Program, where the curriculum is based on a chronological study of the seminal works of Western civilization. Courtesy, Baltimore Visitors and Convention Association

Above: Power Plant Live is one of downtown Baltimore's latest entertainment attractions. Young people from throughout the region meet to eat at the development's restaurants, comedy clubs and cafes. Photo by William Priddy

Baltimore City Hall was begun in 1867. It is built in the Second Empire style, a Baroque revival made popular by Napolean III. Courtesy, The Greyhound, Loyola College in Maryland

The Kunte Kinte Heritage Festival has celebrated African history since 1989. Courtesy, Annapolis and Anne Arundel County Conference and Visitors Bureau

C & O Canal at Violets Lock, Maryland. Photo by David Kelsey

Above
Ego Alley is famous for boat shows, organized or otherwise. Courtesy, Baltimore Visitors and Convention Association

Opposite page top
The Drum Point Lighthouse has been lovingly restored and can be found today at Calvert Marine Museum in southern Maryland. Photo by William Priddy

Opposite page bottom
Because of its proximity to the State Capitol Building, the water, and its architecture, Main Street Annapolis has become one of Maryland's favorite daytrip destinations. Courtesy, Baltimore Visitors and Convention Association

The annual Eastport May Basket Contest is hosted by the Annapolis Maritime Museum to welcome the spring season. Courtesy, Annapolis and Anne Arundel County Conference and Visitors Bureau

The Anchorage Marina is filled with the boats of those who treasure the Chesapeake. Photo by William Priddy

The City Dock was once a colonial port and is now home to a waterfront park. Maryland State House is the in the background. Courtesy, Annapolis and Anne Arundel County Conference and Visitors Bureau

Above
The Power Plant has had many incarnations. Today, it is one of Baltimore's most popular tourist destinations, and includes a Barnes & Noble bookstore, a Hard Rock Cafe and ESPNZone. Photo by William Priddy

Below
The Naval Academy's Blue Angels are a highlight of the annual air show. Courtesy, Annapolis and Anne Arundel County Conference and Visitors Bureau

Top
Baltimore celebrates the Preakness every year with an extensive parade. Courtesy, The Greyhound, Loyola College in Maryland

Above
Montgomery County community of Hyattstown in the winter. Photo by David Kelsey

Dining by the water is a favorite Maryland pursuit. Courtesy, Baltimore Visitors and Convention Association

The annual Renaissance Festival has been a Maryland tradition for nearly three decades, and celebrates medieval culture and history. Courtesy, Annapolis and Anne Arundel County Conference and Visitors Bureau

Farmland near the Potomac, Maryland, alive with the colors of autumn. Photo by David Kelsey

Annapolis bills itself as the nation's sailing capital. Courtesy, Baltimore Visitors and Convention Association

ability to engage those whose sole market-able skill was a willingness to perform physical labor. However, there were reasons to think that these problems would be somewhat less troublesome during the balance of the decade. Primarily, the state's total economic growth became stronger throughout the 1970s; Maryland even rebounded quite rapidly from the great recession of 1981–1983. While by no means ended, the massive decline in the old manufacturing areas bottomed out. Furthermore, fewer young people entered the labor force, yet increased numbers of older workers left. During the balance of the 1980s, 50,000 persons per year were needed simply to replace retirees. In addition, an estimated 26,000 new jobs were created annually. Migration in and out of the state slowed down, but it was always a wild card in predicting the size of the future labor force.

The state's new economic structure differed considerably from that of the 1950s. At that time manufacturing ranked first; wholesale/retail trade, second; government employment exceeded manufacturing; the services pushed past government, as well. Important changes also occurred within several of these sectors. The service industry, for example, included a much higher proportion of skilled and professional positions. Similarly, the surviving manufacturing jobs often required more technological know-how and increased productivity than had been the case in 1950. Industrialists who depended on cheap, unskilled or low-skilled labor tended to leave Maryland. Most of their displaced workers eventually entered into the state's booming trade and service areas, but some experienced long periods of unemployment and others only found steady work if they agreed to accept a permanently lower standard of living. These were the state's "new poor," casualties of economic transition. On the positive side, the same changes also enhanced (or forced) a large class of people to obtain the new, higher paying jobs which boosted them and the entire state into

TABLE 6.1

MARYLAND EMPLOYED LABOR FORCE IN 1950 AND 1980

OCCUPATION	1950 (numbers/percentage)	1980 (numbers/percentage)
Agriculture, Forestry, Fisheries & Mining	62,071 (6.9)	33,266 (1.7)
Construction	68,270 (7.6)	127,840 (6.6)
Manufacturing	223,201 (24.9)	279,740 (14.4)
Transportation	56,818 (6.3)	84,957 (4.4)
Communications & Public Utilities	25,513 (2.9)	56,009 (2.9)
Wholesale Trade	29,271 (3.3)	66,590 (3.4)
Retail Trade	139,397 (15.6)	299,592 (15.4)
Finance, Insurance & Real Estate	32,174 (3.6)	115,619 (5.9)
Business & Repair Services	20,397 (2.3)	95,333 (4.9)
Personal, Entertainment and Recreational Services	69,983 (7.8)	72,699 (3.7)
Professional & Related Services	78,593 (8.8)	435,047 (22.3)
Public Administration	76,383 (8.5)	279,920 (14.4)
Not Reported	12,704 (1.5)	N.A.
Total	894,775	1,946,612

BASED ON: U.S Department of Commerce, Bureau of the Census, *Report of the Seventeenth Decennial Census of the United States, Census of Population: 1950,* (Table 28, "Class of Worker of Employed Persons") and *1980 Census: Congressional Districts of the Ninety-Eighth Congress, Part XXII,* (Table 5, "Labor Force Characteristics").

Mrs. Orem Lowery was very careful when cleaning soft clams for Orem Lowery Seafood in Broomes Island, Maryland. Mrs. Lowery is pictured at work in 1957. Courtesy, Calvert Marine Museum, Solomons, Maryland

One of Kelly-Springfield's tire-manufacturing factories is pictured at its location in Cumberland in 1975. Courtesy, Department of Economic and Community Development

the nation's upper income brackets. Maryland's per capita income reached $12,994 in 1983, making it the seventh wealthiest state in the union.

There appear to have been five key elements contributing to the economic success of the previous decades. First, the Baltimore region benefited by reindustrialization and the rapid growth of the trade and service sectors. The introduction of more productive (high-tech) elements was also a boon to virtually all businesses—from traditional steel mills to fledgling bioengineering firms. Second, the almost rebuilt port continued to prosper, paying great dividends in terms of income and jobs. Third, success breeds success. After the beautifully renovated Baltimore Inner Harbor drew praise from *Time Magazine,* the *Wall Street Journal,* and the network news shows, an even larger influx of private investment flowed into almost every section of the city. Fourth, the near completion of Maryland's excellent interstate highway system, along with a major upgrading of key state roads, allowed the entire Baltimore-Washington-Frederick region to develop into a single, gigantic common market. Its 5.4 million residents

boasted a higher median income than was found in any other of the nation's metropolitan areas. Finally, Prince Georges, Montgomery, and Frederick counties housed vast research, development, and professional service complexes, attracting what was probably the largest concentration of skilled engineers, technicians, analysts, and research specialists in the United States.

Just under half of Maryland's total labor force in the 1980s was concentrated in the Baltimore urbanized region, while the Washington suburbs held over one-third. As a result, the Baltimore-Washington common market employed eight out of ten Marylanders.

Greater Baltimore, itself, consists of the city and county by that name, as well as Harford, Carroll, Anne Arundel, and Howard counties. However, over two-thirds of its employment remained in the city and built-up portions of lower Baltimore County. With the new interstate highways fanning out from Baltimore in much the same fashion as nineteenth-century turnpikes, the metropolitan region is traversed by auto and truck in less than 60 minutes. Both people and goods therefore move quickly

The lighthouse at the Maritime Museum in St. Michael's, Talbot County, is viewed in 1979. The Maritime Museum is a popular tourist attraction for all on the Eastern Shore. Courtesy, Maryland Tourism

TABLE 6.2

AVERAGE ANNUAL EMPLOYMENT BY INDUSTRIAL GROUP, BALTIMORE METROPOLITAN AREA 1983

INDUSTRY	NUMBER EMPLOYED	PERCENTAGE
Manufacturing	139,800	14.9%
Construction	45,100	4.8
Transportation, Communications, and Utilities	57,700	6.1
Mining	100	—
Wholesale Trade	54,900	5.8
Retail Trade	165,600	17.6
Finance, Insurance, and Real Estate	59,500	6.3
Services	212,800	22.8
Government (Federal)	54,000	5.8
Government (State)	57,400	6.1
Government (Local)	91,600	9.8
Total	938,500	100.0%

SOURCE: Maryland Department of Employment and Training, Research and Analysis Division.

and easily between the six counties whose activities are coordinated by the Baltimore Regional Planning Commission. Regionwide businesses, too, have created an effective voice through the Greater Baltimore Committee. These two economic development organizations are headquartered in the city, but maintain a metropolitan perspective.

The distribution of employment in the Baltimore region can be seen in Table 6.2. The major change was the decline of the manufacturing sector, yielding losses of jobs in the metals, garments, glass, transportation equipment, textiles, and food processing industries. Still, manufacturing was important to the region's economy, and traditional firms continued to upgrade facilities as new high-tech enterprises established themselves. Baltimore County included fifteen industrial parks, which attracted fledgling companies, in addition to corporate giants —Bendix, Westinghouse, Martin-Marietta, Aircraft Armament, Inc. and Black and Decker. Some of these firms also operated major production and development centers in adjacent suburban jurisdictions.

Baltimore County business investments have been particularly strong since the end of the last recession. Between July 1982 and July 1984 they totaled $260 million and may be able to create nearly 14,000 new jobs. The area's labor force includes some of the best educated and most affluent people in the state and nation. While leading public schools give impetus to this tradition, Baltimore County also houses the second and third largest state-funded institutions of

higher learning. The University of Maryland-Baltimore County offers undergraduate and graduate curricula in the social sciences, humanities, and natural sciences, and is particularly proud of its biochemistry, math, computer science, information systems management, and health care programs, the latter sponsored jointly with the University of Maryland Medical School downtown. Towson State also provides the full range of academic instruction; here, communications and business administration are most prominent. Finally, as Maryland's leading employer, Baltimore County possesses vast physical, economic, and educational resources which continue to fuel its long-term growth.

Located on either side of Baltimore County, Carroll and Harford counties have also begun to attract major businesses. Overwhelmingly rural districts until the late 1970s, these two jurisdictions recently launched programs to build industrial parks, provide utilities, and smooth the way for new investment through the efforts of economic development commissions. Carroll County had one of Black and Decker's largest production plants within its boundaries, and nearby was the 9.5 acre main distribution center for Random House Publishers. About 72 million books flowed in and out of the giant facility each year, monitored by the latest computerized ordering and inventory systems. Formerly rural Carroll County had also drawn several clothing and shoe manufacturers away from Baltimore, most notably London Fog and Joseph A. Bank. In the electrical field, both Westinghouse and McGraw-Edison maintained large plants.

The most distant of the Baltimore area counties, Harford houses the U.S. government's Aberdeen Proving Ground which employs approximately 15,000 people. Yet, along the mainline tracks of Conrail and the Chessie System, an increasing variety of manufacturing firms are growing and expanding—old companies like the famous Beta Shoe Factory and new enterprises like Maryland Computer Services, a homegrown corporation producing re-engineered equipment and software packages for the vi-

sually impaired/blind. The latter was once listed as one of America's 500 fastest growing firms.

Perhaps the major "high-tech" innovation in the Baltimore region, however, involved one of its oldest and largest companies: Bethlehem Steel. In the 1970s the Sparrows Point plant built its famous "L" furnace, considered to be the factory's greatest leap forward since the Second World War. In 1983 Bethlehem also announced plans to install a state-of-the-art continuous castor which, when linked to the "L" furnace, would make Sparrows Point one of the world's most technologically advanced steel plants and a strong competitor in the international market. The $250-million project provided reasonably good assurance that the city and the eastern section of Baltimore County would continue to have 10,000-15,000 jobs "at the point," at least through the rest of the century.

Across the line in East Baltimore

General Motors Company was doing the same thing to its huge Chevrolet plant. At a cost of over $270 million, the most modern robotic machinery rendered this assembly line equal to any in the world. Similar changes were going on in hundreds of smaller production facilities throughout the Baltimore region. Firms which could be made more efficient through automation and computerization had little choice but to go high-tech or go out of business. Outdated plants would not be able to match standards for efficiency nor compete with lower labor costs in some areas of the U.S. and foreign countries.

The high-tech revolution may have very well transformed the Maryland economy as profoundly as the steam-powered engine did during the last century. In the 1840s and 1850s the state's artisans—blacksmiths, coppersmiths, handloom weavers, and other craftspeople were steadily replaced by factory/machine producers. Most were forced

These space-age looking computer control panels observe and operate Bethlehem Steel's "L" furnace. The control center has a backup computer system as well as manual controls linked to the huge blast furnace by 20,000 wire terminals. Courtesy, Bethlehem Steel Corporation

Opposite,
The busiest spot in Baltimore's sprawling Outer Harbor is the huge Dundalk Marine Terminal, operated by the Maryland Port Administration. As one of the largest container terminals in the United States, Dundalk is the destination of hundreds of ships from all over the world. Every day over a thousand trucks enter and leave the facility, moving goods between Baltimore and the nation's industrial heartland. Courtesy, Maryland Department of Transportation, Maryland Port Administration.

Below
Fishing boats docked at Crisfield in Somerset County were photographed in 1975. After all these years Crisfield's main industry is still crabbing! Courtesy, Maryland Tourism

to bury their handcraft tools and methods in the face of the nineteenth-century version of high-tech: steam-powered equipment. Those artisans who successfully adjusted often made fortunes, but even the majority of factory workers ultimately enjoyed an increased standard of living. Similar to the events taking place during the last century, high-tech revolution appeared to reduce the labor force to a degree unimagined by the previous generation. Foreign competition weighed more heavily in the 1980s than it did 100 or so years ago, but the same processes were still at work.

The real tragedy of economic change was with those workers who suddenly found their jobs and, indeed, their often substantial skills no longer marketable. At the national, state, and local levels, both private and public sector leaders recognized this problem and began to deal with it. Nevertheless, in Maryland—and particularly the Baltimore area—structural unemployment was exacerbated by the 1981-1983 recession.

Despite a fine, stable work force, Baltimore County found itself with a 10 percent joblessness rate. Furthermore, its eastern section, the home of Sparrows Point and other heavy industries, despaired in a 20 percent unemployment figure. The county government, Economic Development Commission, and business leaders funded a study and held discussions aimed at finding ways to cope with these conditions. Soon afterward the U.S. Congress passed the Job Training Partnership Act, giving Maryland (and other states) a structure in which to begin private sector job retraining activities. As a result, Baltimore County developed some very successful programs. It transferred its Occupational Training Administration (OTA) into the office of the Economic Development Commission (EDC) for the purpose of gearing vocational education to the most rapidly developing local employment sectors. Working in conjunction with

these county agencies, local business-government councils regularly reviewed the state of the job market. Two training centers, located at the eastern and western ends of the county, provided self-paced, intensive study in entry-level vocational skills. As local employment needs changed, trainees were guided to those areas in greatest current demand. The Eastern Skills Center, which bore the brunt of the major factory layoffs in this heavily industrial zone, concentrated on computer-related training. Those whose English and math skills needed improvement received help in these subjects. In addition, the county's three community colleges—Dundalk, Essex, and Catonsville—developed a variety of special programs for both dislocated workers and new entrants into the labor force.

Clearly, job seekers of all sorts looked toward non-manufacturing sectors for employment. Such positions had in fact grown in Baltimore County and the "suburban" jurisdictions. In the city, however, economic expansion depended on the revitalization of the port and the downtown renaissance.

Both antedating and supporting its general renewal, the first real breakthrough for Baltimore was the port's refurbishment. This project began in the 1960s when the Maryland Port Administration (MPA), set out to reorganize, rebuild, and expand maritime facilities—particularly those general cargo services which had been in decline since the war. Second, as Joseph L. Stanton, the MPA's first administrator, recalled, "we had to sell the port of Baltimore to the shippers of the world." Aided by chief engineer Dr. Walter Boyer and Greg Halpin, later head of the MPA, Stanton reversed the port's decline and turned it into one of the world's major competitors for containerized cargo. At the same time he increased its traditional bulk trade. Two crucial MPA actions marked the real turning point of development. First, officials convinced the B & O and Pennsylvania railroads to turn their terminal facilities over to the MPA. Second, the port administration purchased the old Baltimore Municipal Airport and transformed it into the Dundalk Marine Termi-

nal—a general cargo facility.

When the railroads owned all of the terminals, they charged trucking firms substantial fees, forcing these companies to focus on ports which were more hospitable to highway transportation. The MPA equalized all fees, worked hard to facilitate good highway access, and provided efficient loading facilities for motor vehicles. An immediate increase in truck-hauled general cargo was seen, but the shift received its greatest stimulus from the growth of containerized shipping. When the S.S. Mobile landed a containerized cargo at the MPA's Canton Marine Terminal in April 1963, Stanton and other foresighted port officials envisioned a revolution in marine transportation and set out to prepare Baltimore for the event.

Baltimore's Inner Harbor is a dynamic example of the city's economic renaissance. Along the waterfront spreads James Rouse's magnificent Harborplace, a complex of shops, food stores, and restaurants. Behind it stands the thirty-story World Trade Center and to the left are the sleek glass walls of the Baltimore Hyatt Regency Hotel. Photo by Bob Willis. Courtesy, Baltimore Office of Promotion and Tourism

Their predictions proved to be correct. A 1970 MPA report stated: "Probably at no time in modern maritime history have such sweeping and radical changes taken place in ocean shipping, port requirements and transportation facilities in such a short time as have occurred in the 1965-70 period." Containerized shipping reached a million tons by 1970 and exceeded four million thirteen years later, making Baltimore the second largest East Coast facility oriented to this type of transport. The Dundalk terminal proved to be admirably suited to containerized cargo handling. A 550-acre area improved by the MPA's investment of over $200 million, it generated many times that figure in revenues. In 1965 the MPA also supported the effort of

Sea-Land Services, Inc. to build a pioneering container terminal at Canton. Speaking at a meeting to mark the twentieth anniversary of this trade in Baltimore, Sea-Land's president remembered that the city "was willing to take a chance with us. Their boldness gave birth to a new generation in transportation history—the intermodal container "generation." By the mid '80s Sea-Land shipped somewhere around 30,000 containers through the port, and yielded revenues and benefits in the millions.

Comfortable in its possession of the old Canton and Locust Point railroad facilities and the Dundalk Terminal site, the MPA set out in 1959 to "sell" the world's shippers on Baltimore. Before that time the port had kept permanent representatives only in New York, Pittsburgh, and Chicago. No overseas branches existed. In 1959, however, the first foreign office opened in Brussels, the headquarters of the new European Common Market. Shortly after a second branch was established in London, chartering center for the world maritime industry. MPA representatives came to Tokyo in the 1960s and Hong Kong in the 1970s. One port authority official said that in the early days, many shippers who had traditionally traded through New York or Philadelphia were uncertain as to where Baltimore was located. Happily, MPA agents conveyed an important message: not only was their port 200 miles closer to the Middle Western industrial and consumer market than any of the other East Coast cities, but Baltimore was creating facilities which would make cargo handling more efficient and less costly than those of its rivals. Today every major international shipper knows where Baltimore is located; they are also familiar with the full range of services offered along these 45 miles of waterfront. Furthermore, foreign vessels sometimes literally have to stand in line to load or unload cargos. The MPA, therefore, worked to expand its facilities in order to meet the annual growth in trade.

The most visible evidence of the port's coming of age was the MPA's 30-story World Trade Center (WTC) on the inner harbor where in the 1740s and 1750s, Baltimore maritime history began. Opened in 1977, the WTC offered a permanent home, four floors, to the Maryland Port Authority. The rest of the building was rented to over 100 firms doing business in the harbor district. These companies, in fact, represented only a fraction of those using or depending upon the maritime facilities.

The Port of Baltimore today is a giant enterprise serving over 300 foreign cities wishing access to the U.S. market stretching from Harrisburg and Pittsburgh out to Chicago and Minneapolis, and down to St. Louis. Its scale of operations is simply staggering to those unfamiliar with the life of a major world trading center. In 1983, 22.6 million tons of bulk and general cargo moved through the port, a decrease of just

over eight million from the previous year (due to one of the periodic slumps in the coal and grain export market). General cargo, of which 71 percent was containerized, increased to 5.1 million tons. Since each ton generates anywhere from five to twenty times more jobs and economic benefits than most bulk commodities, the port had a very fine year.

Baltimore's cargo consists of coal, grain, petroleum, chemicals, ores, and a wide variety of other goods. One of the more and unusual bulk items is scotch whiskey. This celebrated beverage arrives at the Port Covington Marine Terminal where it is pumped by the thousands of gallons into special tank cars for shipment to bottling plants and consumers—at a substantially lower cost than already-packaged scotch.

Coal leads all other bulk exports, and in spite of periodic fluctuations, it is destined to remain on top for many years to come. America's high-quality coal finds great demand in Europe. The Dutch, for example, import about half of their coal from the U.S., most of it through the Port of Baltimore which in 1982 sent 310,000 tons to Rotterdam. The railroads carry all of this trade to the harbor, and several of the world's largest coal companies have established gigantic new loading facilities in Baltimore. At Curtis Bay the Island Creek Coal Company, a subsidiary of Occidental Petroleum, opened a $100-million terminal which could handle up to 3,500 tons of coal per hour and had an annual capacity of 10 million tons. The entire transfer from train to storage to ocean-going vessel is managed electronically from a single control tower. Over on the Patapsco part of the harbor, the Consolidation Coal Company, a Conoco subsidiary, has followed Island Creek's lead. The newer facility, however, can be quickly expanded to accommodate 20 million tons. Here, the coal is dumped directly from rail cars onto 75-foot high piles. Hence, the cars never have to remain idle. When it is ready for shipment, the coal is scooped up by two mammoth "stacker/reclaimer" machines which appear to be taken out of a science fiction book. The equipment reaches out 180 feet to loft 7,000 tons

A tobacco auction in Upper Marlboro brought these experts together from miles around in 1979. Courtesy, Department of Economic and Community Development

of coal per hour. Like oil tankers, coal-handling vessels had grown from big to gigantic. After World War II, 10,000-ton, ex-liberty ships achieved popularity in the trade, but they were gradually replaced by 20,000-ton bulkers and later, by the 65,000 *Panamax,* the largest boat able to navigate the Panama Canal at that time. Baltimore was a very competitive port for these huge crafts, but 150,000-ton coal ships would not be able to use the port until the U.S. Congress finally deepened its channels from forty-two to fifty feet. Authorization for the project was obtained and a large artificial island created for the purpose of depositing dredged materials. But as was the case with previous channel deepenings, the government moved like a glacier. Fortunately, the delay was the only cloud hanging over the port's future.

Unimpeded by the 42-foot channel depth, the general cargo trade, nevertheless, continued to grow through boom and bust cycles. Its centerpiece was the Dundalk Marine Terminal, where ships unloaded at

thirteen berths. Containers, automobiles, or loose goods were removed by cranes which hovered about ninety feet above the wharf. The latest generation of these computer-aided machines was built by Hitachi, Ltd., of Japan. They weighed over 600 tons, had an outreach of 118 feet, were capable of moving forty-eight containers per hour, and cost just over three million dollars each in 1982. Over 80 percent of the cargo moved through the Dundalk Terminal is containerized, but the largest category of non-containerized cargo is even more valuable: automobiles. In 1983, 174,341 vehicles, transported by 251 ships, came to the United States via Dundalk. The autos, containers, and other cargo were hauled to and from the terminal by 2,560 rail cars and 405,379 trucks. Dundalk was open seven days a week. This meant that every day of the year (except Christmas), approximately 1,100 trucks checked into the facility through its eleven-lane Gateway Plaza. In addition to the Dundalk Terminal, the MPA offered services at Locust Point and Canton. Private firms, like Sea-Land and Ruckert Terminals, also handled container trade—accounting for 21 percent of the 1983 total. In spite of the heavy traffic at the port, access was quite good and would become even better in 1985 with the opening of the eight-lane Ft. McHenry Tunnel, extending I-95 under Baltimore harbor to near the historic site. This $80-million endeavor, the largest single interstate highway construction project executed to that date, provided the central and final link in the Maryland and Mid-Atlantic system. Motor access to the port would be improved, and the city as a whole, which had very poor through-traffic facilities in 1956, would possess one of the nation's best metropolitan road systems. The only problem for the existing terminals was that they were now nearly filled to capacity with shippers, allowing little room for expansion. Fortunately, a new 2.2-million ton facility, called Seagirt Marine Terminal, was under construction. It would sit on land filled with spoil from the 115-foot deep trench dug on the bottom of the harbor to accommodate the Ft. McHenry Tunnel. Seagirt opened for use in 1990. Beyond this terminal, the MPA started to fill a 350-acre marsh area near the Fairfield shipyards (of World War II fame) for another facility that opened in the 1990s. Together with existing services, these two additions easily met shipping demands well into the twenty-first century.

The economic revival of the central city of Baltimore—the Baltimore Renaissance—was the one aspect of modern Maryland that became genuinely legendary. The city's inner harbor in the 1950s and 1960s was a crumbling, half-abandoned, waterfront area through which most Baltimoreans would not walk. By 1984 it had been transformed into a dazzling complex of shops, restaurants, and hotels surrounding the National Aquarium, Maryland Science Center, Baltimore Convention Center, and a variety of other facilities which attracted over twenty million visitors—more people than went to Disney World. Shabby-looking, old commercial buildings in the adjacent central business district which sold for $100,000 in the early 1960s were snapped up at one or two million. Private investment in the

Charles Center-Inner Harbor area totaled approximately two billion dollars and continued to escalate. New construction was estimated at $400 million during 1984, but nearly $600 million was on the drawing boards. Eight hotels would grace the area.

The Baltimore Renaissance also represented a vast rebirth of inner city housing. Private developers converted entire neighborhoods from slums into elegant middle and upper income residences. Investors who never dreamed of putting a dime into the city twenty years ago scrambled to buy up land and buildings in ever-widening circles around the original redevelopment areas. In the opinion of many of these people, Baltimore became the leading example of nationwide urban renewal. Visually, Baltimore's inner harbor today probably has no rival on the North American continent. The American Institute of Architects recently described it as "one of the supreme achievements of large-scale urban design and development in U.S. history . . . a masterpiece of planning and execution."

How did this happen? First, a stronger fundamental urban economy than appeared to be the case in the 1950-1980 era actually existed. Second, Baltimore provided an almost unparalleled natural setting and physical environment for the type of center city revitalization that has become popular throughout urban America. Third, renewal efforts were forged by a longstanding, close spirit of cooperation between local government and business leaders. Finally, a small group of individuals possessing the relatively rare combination of ability, vision, and power worked on the city's behalf.

As indicated previously, the long-term economic health of the Baltimore region was probably never in as much jeopardy as some believed. Actually, the groundwork for the area's resurgence was laid during the 1960s when newspapers, urban "experts," and the radio/TV commentators spoke of the inevitable collapse of old, Northeastern cities. The port clearly reached its low ebb in the late 1940s and early 1950s, but by 1959 positive developments started to occur.

Manufacturing plant closures, nevertheless, were a real blow to the city's wage earn-

Horse racing has traditionally been a popular sport, and it still is today in Baltimore County. Courtesy, Maryland Tourism

These cows belong to the United States Department of Agricultural Research Center, located in Beltsville, Maryland. Courtesy, Maryland Tourism

Maryland's first statehouse stood in St. Marys City, the original capital of the state from 1634 to 1694. After the capital was moved to Annapolis, the statehouse was used as a church. A reconstruction of the original building is pictured in 1975. Courtesy, Maryland Tourism

ers, tax base, and the adjacent Baltimore County area. The local recession hit hardest in the 1960s and 1970s. Soon, though, the worst seemed to be over. Maryland's Department of Employment and Training projected a relatively small loss in the number of industrial jobs, 15,800, for the 1982–1990 era, compared to a decline of over 50,000 positions during the decade of the 1970s. Early signs of downtown Baltimore's office boom and the strong growth in the trade and service areas had not been apparent when the dismal forecasts had been issued. This type of economic development activity was quite obvious in the suburban areas, but after

the manufacturing decline and upswing in central city trade/service jobs. During this grim period it seemed as if Baltimore was about to suffer the economic equivalent of cardiac arrest. While serious problems of joblessness, underemployment, and industrial hardship remained, the city's prospects looked better than at any time in the previous several years.

It should be recognized that some of this economic turnabout would have occurred even without the inspired leadership of the 1960-1984 renaissance. Based upon the relatively successful experiences of cities much less able and bold than Baltimore, with no

Fishing Village in Choptank, Maryland, is yet another place where boats frequently appear tied up at the dock. Courtesy, Maryland Tourism

1970 or 1975 they became increasingly apparent in the central business district, too. Furthermore, the metropolitan region's strong, long-term employment gains accelerated Baltimore's service industry and created a new market for the urban labor force. Between 1960 and 1980 the number of employed residents commuting from the city to their suburban jobs rose from 13 to 25 percent. This trend, however, placed a heavy burden on many low income workers who could not afford automobiles and found it very difficult to get to the new employment centers. In addition, the city endured a ten-to-fifteen-year lag time between

asset as great as the inner harbor, it is difficult to imagine that Maryland's chief metropolitan area, with its two million residents, would have functioned without a large administrative-service area in its central business district. What the leaders of Baltimore's renaissance did was to take an almost inevitable, modest central city recovery and turn it into a colossal achievement—bringing many office and services outlets into downtown Baltimore not because they had to be there, but because they *wanted* to be there. Beyond this success, area leaders created two entirely new spheres of economic growth: tourism and housing. This aspect of the

Baltimore Renaissance is a real triumph of vision and courage, but spokespeople for urban renewal a mere 20 years ago were regarded as dreamers.

Baltimore's greatest asset in developing reconverted housing, central city tourism, and even a burgeoning entertainment trade is its basic physical plant—one of the most spectacular inner harbors in America and a huge stock of "charming" former low income dwellings which thousands of middle and upper income people love to restore. The waterside area was so naturally picturesque that it was bound to attract some of the facilities that have sprung up in many historic and/or visually interesting districts throughout the U.S., yet the Baltimore harbor is not just another "colorful spot." Its resplendent sweep of shoreline and wharves has been carefully enhanced by a stunning combination of buildings, open spaces, promenades, and ships. The inner harbor currently must rank near the top of the national list for sheer visual drama. Counting almost two billion dollars of investment, the prospects for expansion are high and the greater portion of its shore still awaits reconversion. To date, approximately one and one-half miles have been transformed, but the potential redevelopment area, stretching from Ft. McHenry around to Canton, measures almost four miles. Conceivably, the region could be extended to six or eight miles as shipping and waterfront industry move further along to the "outer" harbor. It is a waterside developer's dream—easy to build, boasting spectacular vistas on every side, and void of the elevated highways which impede one's view in so many other port cities.

Baltimore's housing renaissance extends much farther than the 800- to 900-acre inner harbor area. It stretches for dozens of blocks in almost every direction from a redeveloped core and appears to be rapidly engulfing the entire nineteenth-century physical plant: an area of fourteen to eighteen square miles. Again, one big reason why Baltimore has done so well in housing redevelopment is that the city probably has retained a larger percentage of its older dwellings than any other major urban cen-

ter. Because most of Baltimore's twentieth-century physical plant developed on new land, few of the earlier structures were destroyed. The central business district never grew large enough to threaten surrounding residential areas, and the Baltimore fire of 1904 was contained in a relatively small district. Thus, in the 1960s when the first real wave of back-to-the-city people began to turn old row houses (as Baltimoreans unassumingly called them) into "townhouses," they had literally thousands of splendid buildings from which to choose. The inner city seemed like a vast storehouse of used furniture which had suddenly gained recognition as a valuable antiques repository. Prices were right, too. People familiar with the cost of townhouses in the Georgetown or Capital Hill sections of Washington, D.C. or similar "old town" areas in other cities, could not believe that Baltimore's large, elegant, revered residences could be purchased for far less than an undersized suburban tract home. Consequently, a flood of middle and upper income residents continue to pour into all the neighborhoods surrounding the central business/inner harbor area. In doing so, they have replenished the tax base, drawn other residents and tourists to town, and spawned hundreds of businesses which serve their now vibrant neighborhoods. A rush of new home construction (in styles compatible with the older dwellings) completes the list of benefits.

Due to its leaders and close cooperation between the public and private sectors, Baltimore has capitalized on its economic and physical assets to a degree which is probably unmatched among the nation's large cities. This entire renewal effort originated through the efforts of a business group, the Greater Baltimore Committee (GBC), and a civic association, the Citizens Planning and Housing Association (CPHA). The GBC began as an informal organization of retail shop owners concerned about the decline of the central city district. Their rallying cry had been the 1954 closing of O'Niel's department store, the first of the major downtown businesses to call it quits. The GBC then decided that a dramatic, new urban renewal project would demon-

strate the center city's continuing economic viability. In 1958 the group presented Baltimore with a striking thirty-three acre office complex called Charles Center—the first development of its type to be built there in over thirty years. This $130-million jewel was a great economic success and sparked the whole series of projects which now cover almost 600 acres. With Charles Center's financial success to its credit, the GBC also advocated the establishment of the Maryland Port Administration, the Jones Falls Expressway construction, and the building of the Baltimore Civic Center.

The CPHA had a different mission. Created in 1941 primarily to deal with low income housing problems, it gradually embraced the entire range of redevelopment activities. For example, it played an important role in the 1968 consolidation of all city housing and community service agencies into a single municipal department of Housing and Community Development (HCD). CPHA also aided in the growth of Baltimore's exceptionally strong group of neighborhood associations, and from this core of local activists came several of the key leaders in the entire redevelopment effort.

Through organizations like the GBC and CPHA, businesspeople and public officials have been able to work closely together in guiding urban renewal. The largest projects are overseen by a series of quasi-public corporations such as the Charles Center-Inner Harbor Management Corporation, led by representatives of both sectors. In the early phase of the waterside area's redevelopment, public investment outshadowed private funding because site preparation was a prerequisite to building. By 1984 the situation changed, with business investment greatly surpassing government money. Both private profits and public revenues, however, have exceeded the most optimistic estimates.

It also is generally agreed that a relatively small group of key people played a critically important role in the redevelopment process. Typical of the larger movement, this group contains almost equal numbers of public officials and business leaders. First on the list is James Rouse, a Marylander from the Eastern Shore who came to Baltimore in the 1930s. An internationally famous developer, he served as a prime mover in the creation of the GBC, Charles Center, and especially the waterside area, where his firm built Harborplace, the centerpiece of the entire renewal endeavor. Of course, Rouse is best known for his development of the new city of Columbia in Howard County. Its 14,000 acres of residential properties, offices, industrial parks, wooded open spaces, and lakes offer a model of attractive suburban life; but Rouse's interest in Baltimore never flagged. Today thousands of his suburban Columbia residents enjoy themselves regularly at the restaurants and shops of the inner harbor. Next to Rouse, Walter Sondheim is the most significant "founding father" of the Baltimore Renaissance. Leaving his position as one of the chief executives of Hochschild Kohn department store, Sondheim played a central role in the Charles Center project, the inner harbor's development, and almost every other major undertaking in town during the past thirty years. On the public side, there is no question that Baltimore's Mayor William Donald Schaefer was the central figure not only in the downtown renewal, but in generating a positive attitude towards the entire city. He did more than any other individual to make the public aware of Baltimore's heritage, diversity, and rich, colorful communities. The city had a very strong sense of neighborhood at the opening of the twentieth century, but that spirit faltered after World War II. Schaefer along with the CPHA, promoted community identity as one of the city's greatest social and political assets. In the 1950s when the mayor first entered politics, Walter Sondheim said that Baltimore "had a pretty low opinion of itself." To residents and visitors alike, this dismal attitude obviously disappeared. As president of the city council and mayor, Schaefer's visibility allowed him to speak for the city and pledge its aid to investors with an authority that no other local American official could match. He has been recognized as one of Baltimore's greatest mayors and probably one of the most significant of the twentieth-century.

America. Perhaps the best indication of Schaefer's stature was his ability to attract and retain for long periods of time some of the nation's most talented public administrators. Robert Embry and Jay Brodie, for example, directed the city's housing and community development agency and gained reputations as two of the nation's leading experts in this area. Indeed, Baltimore received more than its fair share of truly remarkable and loyal leaders whose personal stamp will remain for decades. It had been suggested that the city should build a statue of these urban pioneers, but anyone standing in front of Harborplace could look all around and see a massive tribute to their talents, energy, and intelligence.

In the midst of heaping well deserved praise on Baltimore's shining achievements it must be borne in mind that the city still suffered from some large economic and social problems. Its industrial base declined, many of its black and white middle class families continued to leave for better school

districts, and its low income households showed no sign of disappearing. In spite of the fact that Baltimore had spent the bulk of its financial resources on educational, social, and medical services for moderate and poorer residents, high unemployment (especially among black youths), poverty, crime and substandard housing conditions still plagued many sections of the city.

The gleaming structures of the inner harbor could be disheartening when very little appeared to be improving for the Baltimore's admittedly large underclass—approximately two out of every five residents earned less than $10,000 per year. Some of these citizens sharply criticized the city's leaders for ignoring their needs while pandering to the big developers and posh in-town residents. The problem, of course, was that Baltimore's public and private sectors simply could not retain much of the traditional manufacturing upon which many unskilled workers had depended. No American city was able to swim against this vast tide of economic change. Although Baltimore could not

An object of inspiration to photographers and artists traveling through the rural portions of Frederick County, the B & O station at Point of Rocks remains a shrine to the golden age of railroading, long past. This Victorian Gothic classic, built between 1871 and 1875, initially stood at the junction of the Metropolitan branch to Washington, D.C. and the Old Main Line destined for Baltimore. Continually declining services and the construction of a new facility eventually reduced the majestic terminal to its present use: as a railroad maintenance office and commuter train station. Photo by Richard A. Flom

179

forced investors to locate within its boundaries, government officials quite successfully created several small industrial parks under the direction of BEDCO, the Baltimore Economic Development Corporation. Yet, BEDCO was in competition with the rest of the state and nation; it could at best hope to minimize manufacturing losses.

At the root of Baltimore's economic and social problem was its distinction as being the only place in the entire state where poorly educated, low skilled people could find affordable homes and at least some access to positions for which they were qualified. Housing remained cheaper and the environment more wholesome in Western Maryland or on the Eastern Shore, but there were hardly enough jobs to support the already sparse populations. Baltimore City provided the only alternative for the poor. Lack of good transportation and generally high costs of living meant that low skilled jobs in the prosperous suburbs went by default to local youth who were happy to have extra spending money. On the other hand, Baltimore's minimum wage positions were snapped up by people desperately seeking to support themselves and/or their dependents. The central city redevelopment continued to offer increasing numbers of these low paying service jobs, but they would not replace the old manufacturing positions which offered higher salary rates and greater opportunities for advancement. Baltimore's underclass remained unskilled, undereducated and unhopeful of finding a way out of the minimum wage trap. In addition, massive cutbacks in federal funding, beginning in 1981 exacerbated the situation. Sad to say, some of Baltimore's underclass citizens felt that they were lucky to have any job which made up for lost entitlement programs.

In terms of upward mobility, the City of Baltimore has almost heroically tried to improve the education level and vocational skills of its poorer residents. Still, the task extended beyond current financial resources. The school system was overwhelmed by large Numbers of students with serious learning disabilities, difficulties at home, personal problems, and the weighty burden of being "ignorant" and poor in a well-educated and affluent society. The eighteenth- and nineteenth-century economy could, and did, exploit the unskilled; but it also rendered small niches of opportunity for these people. Few doors remained open to those without schooling or technical expertise—especially in cities like Baltimore which converted from blue-collar to white-collar employment. This problem represented the greatest single economic and educational challenge to the state of Maryland in the remaining years of the twentieth century.

Yet, the situation was far from hopeless. Those who could not find traditional blue-collar jobs would not necessarily have to settle for a career of fast food service or broom pushing. Nor would they need college degrees to become members of Baltimore's white-collar labor force. Many reasonably well-paying service jobs existed for people having only a high school-level education. Other positions could be obtained by learning job-specific skills at local training centers or at one of the city's two community college campuses. Individuals earning associate's degrees in a technical or paraprofessional field had a better chance of moving into middle income jobs. As a past study indicated, even high-tech companies drew about half of their labor force from high schools and community colleges.

Baltimore's chief problem was that its educational system was waging a brave, but losing, classroom battle. During the (1983-1984) year, the city faced a drop-out rate three and a half times greater than any other school district in Maryland. Furthermore, the academic performance of its graduates at every level was sadly below the state average. Baltimore also granted fewer diplomas (48.8 percent) to its youth than any urbanized county in the Old Line State; in places like Montgomery and Howard counties, 87 and 83 percent, respectively, finished high school.

Money (or specifically, the lack of it) presented the greatest obstacle. The city's expenditure per pupil in 1981-1982 ranked

Opposite
The Lavale Tollhouse in Allegany County can still be visited today, with original toll rates posted on the side of the building for the tourist to read. Courtesy, Maryland Tourism

Part of the Goddard Space Flight Center in Greenbelt, Maryland, is pictured in 1979. Courtesy, Maryland Tourism

C & O Canal Lock #31, on the Maryland side, is depicted in 1979. Courtesy, Maryland Tourism

sixteenth out of Maryland's twenty-four school systems, yet Baltimore received the largest percentage of state and federal education funds. Somehow, Maryland needed to increase its investment in the city school system to give Baltimore's underclass an equal chance to enter the employment market and become an asset to the state.

When discussing economic problems germane to the Baltimore area, it is important to keep a broader perspective in mind. Despite the many hardships found in the old port city, Maryland as a whole had done well over the previous decades, maintaining an unemployment rate well below the national average and showing very healthy expansion in many of the country's major growth sectors. The single most important reason for overall prosperity is the continuing spectacular development of the Washington region, unquestionably the star performer in Maryland's economy. One can quickly gain some feeling for the

size and character of the area by driving east on Interstate 270 from Frederick around the Washington Beltway and out Route 50 towards Annapolis, with perhaps a short side trip up Route 29 to Columbia in Howard County. Along this fifty-mile itinerary the observer notes huge federal installations; the private laboratories of many of the nation's leading high-tech companies; clusters of large, new office buildings; corporate headquarters; and major research and development centers for dozens of telecommunications, electronics, and biotechnic firms. Finally, the driver marvels over a vast network of beautiful residential neighborhoods and one of the nation's greatest concentrations of elegant shopping malls, restaurants, and retail outlets—services which satisfy an extremely affluent labor force of approximately 615,000 people. Certainly large sections of the Baltimore or Annapolis regions can match Washington suburban opulence, but the latter boasts a massive size and uniform prosperity which sets it apart from the rest of the state and nation.

This rare distinctiveness comes from an unusual economic base. While a clear and growing Baltimore-Washington common market exists, divisions occur between the two halves of this supermetropolis. Baltimore, for example, engages 15.9 percent of its residents in manufacturing, a figure which would be much higher if Howard and Anne Arundel counties were not considered to be a part of the metropolitan area. On the other hand, only 6.3 percent of the Washington suburbanites work in industry. Futhermore, the national capital district's economy thrives on a significantly higher level and more professionalized service sector. Using figures from the U.S. Bureau of Labor Statistics and the National Science Foundation, a study by the Maryland Department of Economic and Community Development indicated that by 1981 this area possessed the greatest concentration of professional and technical workers of any of the nation's fifteen major high-technology centers. In Montgomery County alone there were approximately 250 research and development firms. Here, too, Interstate 270 provides a 30-mile display of many facilities employed numerous scientists, engineers, technicians, and computer specialists. These companies are involved in telecommunications, electronics, biomedical and genetic research, and the development of automated systems. The Greater Washington Research Center calculated 105,000 people worked in the region's high-tech firms in the early '80s. Companies were initially drawn to the area because the Defense Department, the National Institutes of Health, and many other federal agencies contract out hundreds of billions of dollars worth of research and development projects. But private corporations benefit from the government's presence in other, sometimes more important ways. Since information spawns new technology, firms also gain knowledge from an unmatchable pool of federal experts in the Defense Department, NASA, Environmental Protection Agency, Federal Communications Commission, National Institutes of Health, National

Bureau of Standards, and the Department of Energy. In addition, the area's libraries and information centers contain by far the world's largest collection of general and technical data. With such a tremendous concentration of resources, many local companies also gravitate toward the private research and development sector, thereby achieving greater independence from government work.

An extremely high level of professional employment in the technology-related companies is further enhanced by a large group of immensely skilled federal workers. (Approximately 56,000 government employees reside in the Montgomery-Prince Georges area compared to the 560,000 people engaged by the private sector). All of these technical, administrative, and managerial experts have made the Washington area among the most affluent in the nation. Montgomery and Prince Georges counties accounted for 36.2 percent of Maryland's entire personal income in 1981, while the city and county of Baltimore, with 200,000 more residents, contributed only 32.2 percent. In terms of family and per capita income, Montgomery County outdistances every other county by a significant margin. Its average family income in 1983 was $50,600 which placed it among the ten richest counties in America. As one might imagine, these same suburban residents were a very well-educated group, with a full 42 percent of the total adult population having completed four or more years of college. Maryland, too, shined in this category as 20 percent of its residents attained college degrees, and only two other states could claim a more educated population.

With the spread of the research, development, and service industries into the entire Baltimore-Washington region, it is imperative that the percentage of college and graduate/professional people in the work force increase. This should occur since Maryland has a history of attracting those who are young and highly educated. To its credit, the state also possesses a very large, already affluent and well-schooled population whose children have the advantages of achievement-oriented families, superior and

Left
These young boys seemed intent on catching some crabs, as they waded in Chesapeake Bay with their crab nets in 1978. Courtesy, Maryland Tourism

Below
Men crabbing with traps near Calvert Cliffs in Southern Maryland are pictured in 1970. Courtesy, R.E. Miller, Chesapeake Biological Laboratory and the Calvert Marine Museum, Solomons, Maryland

competitive institutes of learning, and the funds to pursue both undergraduate and graduate degree programs. Young Marylanders thus become a great asset to the economy when they return from the universities—as so many of them do. Moreover, they seek to remain in the Old Line State because its future looks bright. Indeed, Maryland does not suffer from the unhappy phenomenon endured by so many other states whose best college graduates, unable to find either the employment or the exciting lifestyles they desire, leave for more attractive areas. Blessed with a strong and growing "modern" economy, a moderate climate, and almost the full variety of environments available to the nation, it has rightfully been called "America in miniature." The international flavor of Washington; Baltimore's inner harbor; the mountains replete with hiking, fishing, and skiing adventures; the Chesapeake Bay; and the ocean shore are all within a short drive. From the earliest settlement of the nation, Marylanders have revelled in these abundant natural gifts—plus a strategic economic location—a rare combination of assets among the nation's fifty states. And while a business atmosphere attracts the private sector, environmentally conscious developers ensure that physical features are not sacrificed to the crane. Suburban Columbia, for example, has captured 25 percent of all foreign firms which have opened in Maryland. Sophisticated executives choose the city for its new, highly efficient, beautiful surroundings —the type of settings in which skilled and affluent employees cannot only conduct their business profitably, but may also lead a rich, full life. The same thing may be said of many other areas throughout the entire central portion of the state.

The future of Maryland's economic and demographic heartland is clearly bound up with the destiny of the Baltimore-Washington common market, a metropolis exceeded in size only by the New York, Los Angeles, and Chicago regions. It runs from Fairfax County, Virginia through Washington up to the harbor city and its adjacent suburbs. Claiming about 35,000 square miles, Greater Baltimore-Washington is about the same size as the Philadelphia and Chicago metro-

politan regions, but somewhat smaller than Los Angeles. The 1980 population of 5.4 million placed it fourth in the nation behind New York/New Jersey, Los Angeles/ Long Beach, and Chicago. In a number of respects, however, it is the most fortunate of all the nation's large metropolitan agglomerations. Among the top ten urban regions, the Baltimore-Washington area has the highest median household income and the largest percentage of professional and administrative workers in its labor force. Its 1980 retail sales, $26 billion, ranked fourth after Los Angeles, New York, and Chicago, and the office market here was one notch higher. In the period from 1970 to 1980, this region's total retail construction was exceeded only by Dallas/Ft. Worth and Los Angeles; residential construction in Greater Baltimore-Washington led the nation.

For most of the twentieth century, America's metropolitan areas have been the leading centers of economic growth. The Baltimore-Washington region is in many respects the southern anchor of the Boston to Washington urbanized corridor, sometimes referred to as this country's megalopolis. Yet, for several reasons it has escaped the more severe economic problems which have effected the other large Northeastern cities. The majority of the Baltimore-Washington region's population and employment, approximately 60 percent, centers around the District of Columbia, but the Baltimore subsector also includes the second most important port on the East Coast, and the entire region's most important airport. In addition, Maryland is a Southern border, sitting astride a long established line of demarcation. Therefore, it has inherited the Northeast's firm tradition of economic growth, while reaping far greater benefits from the recent Southern (or Sunbelt) boom than its sister cities of Philadelphia, New York, and Boston. With almost eight out of ten residents living and working in the affluent and growing twin cities region, Maryland looks forward to a bright economic future. Progressive, resilient, dynamic, the Old Line has indeed led to new prosperity.

Chesapeake's famous steamed blue crabs. *Courtesy, Annapolis and Anne Arundel County Conference and Visitors Bureau*

Above
Tobacco at one time was Maryland's primary crop. It was used as currency to pay taxes, purchase land, and buy goods. Today it is a declining industry centered in Southern Maryland. Here on a sunny day in 1985 it was trucked to market for sale later at a Marlboro auction house. Photo by Dave Kelsey

Right
In 1943 the Washington Surburban Sanitary Commission built Brighton Dam to form the Tridelphia Reservoir. Named for the town its waters now cover, Tridelphia provides both water and recreation to suburban Maryland residents. The dam was photographed in 1985. Photo by Dave Kelsey

Above
Rock concerts, Bullets basketball, Capitals hockey, Ringling Brothers Barnum & Bailey Circus, boxing matches, and ice shows all appear in the Capital Centre, a 19,000+ capacity all-purpose arena serving the Baltimore-Washington metropolitan areas. Photo by Dave Kelsey

Left
The National Library of Medicine in Bethesda was dedicated in 1962 and serves as a national reference library for medical research. A number of biological research companies are located in suburban Maryland, supported by access to the library and the National Institute of Health. Photo by Dave Kelsey

189

Above
Because of its proximity to Washington, D.C. the I-270 corridor in Montgomery County has attracted numerous high-tech industries and businesses dependent on government contract work. From consulting on social problems to weapons design, a myriad of small businesses and large cluster here. Photo by Dave Kelsey

The Poolesville National Bank building, constructed in 1907, is now the Poolesville Town Hall. When George Peter sold land that was not on the road, he successfully petitioned to have the old road abandoned and a new right-of-way granted. The bank building sits between the old and the new roadways. Photo by Dave Kelsey

One of the first United States government facilities to locate outside the District of Columbia was the Naval Hospital in Bethesda. The medical complex provides treatment and hospitalization for Navy, Marine, and Coast Guard personnel. Photo by Dave Kelsey

Chapter VII

THE MARYLAND MIRACLE:

MARYLAND FROM MID 1980s TO 2003

M aryland, as one of the nation's oldest economies, has found it necessary to reinvent itself year after year, generation after generation. Over the past 25 years, Maryland has redefined itself numerous times, including during the 1980s when Ronald Reagan introduced an agenda dramatically different from his predecessor's. Marylanders responded as they always have, with timely adjustments to changed circumstances. While many Americans remember the Massachusetts Miracle of the 1980s, a phrase used frequently during the failed 1988 presidential run by then-Massachusetts Governor Michael Dukakis, less well-known is the Maryland economic miracle.

Indeed, Maryland, supported by a boom in financial services, defense contracting and commercial construction, experienced breathtaking economic expansion during the 1980s. Downtown Baltimore added several new office towers, as did cities and towns across the state. Bethesda, Rockville, Greenbelt, Columbia, Frederick, Towson, Hunt Valley, and Owings Mills emerged as business centers in their own right as construction activity swept through markets large, small, and medium.

As evidence of the boom of the 1980s, by 1990 the proportion of Marylanders working in the construction industry was 50 percent higher than the corresponding proportion for the nation. Rapid growth in the population of Marylanders aged 25 to 34 also kept retailers and residential builders flush with opportunity.

The driving force in Maryland during the 1980s was federal spending. On the same side of the Potomac and joined to the nation's capital, Maryland

Baltimore's skyline is one of the nation's most dramatic, and represents a mixture of architectural styles. Courtesy, Baltimore Area Convention & Visitors Association

The American Can Company represents one of Baltimore's finest examples of creative reuse. This former abandoned factory is now home to cafes, shops and other popular venues. Photo by William Priddy

is a natural home to defense contractors, beltway bandit consulting businesses, lobbying firms, and others who seek to serve federal needs. As a result, when the federal government spends, Maryland tends to out-perform. Such was the situation during the 1980s. Federal spending in Maryland for wages and salaries by the Department of Defense rose 37.7 percent between 1983 and 1990. Total federal spending in Maryland was up almost 50 percent during the same period. Jurisdictions closest to D.C. like Montgomery County fared particularly well during this period.

By 1986 Maryland ranked twelfth in the U.S. in employment growth, an impressive ranking for an old-line East Coast state. The state's labor force expanded by over 4 percent that year as the mobile portion of the American labor force flocked to Maryland to take part in its resurgence. Despite the rapid increase in people looking for work, the state's unemployment rate fell to 3.6 percent by 1990, one of the lowest rates in the nation. Several prominent Maryland economists went on to proclaim the state recession-proof, pointing to the fact that Maryland's dependence on the federal government helped to insulate the state's economy from the vagaries of global business cycles.

The rising fortunes of defense contractors, commercial developers, and their financiers hid the fact that older parts of Maryland's

economy remained in steep decline. While defense manufacturers continued to expand, Maryland's traditional manufacturers found themselves giving way to competitors from states to the south and from abroad. Between 1980 and 1988, the state's manufacturing industries actually declined by 28,000 jobs, leaving older, more industrial communities like Dundalk, Essex, Middle River, Cumberland, Oakland, Hagerstown, and Cambridge with large gaps in their employment bases.

Predictably, the losses were concentrated in those industries expanding most rapidly in other parts of the world. Steel and other primary metals manufacturing employers shed almost 17,000 jobs between 1980 and 1987. Maryland's apparel and textile manufacturing industries eliminated 5,500 jobs between 1980 and 1987. Losses in shipbuilding, a favorite and traditional Maryland pastime, help explain the 3,100 jobs lost among transportation equipment manufacturers.

In short, Maryland's economy shifted dramatically during the 1980s, creating big winners and big losers. Older industrial communities found themselves scrambling to participate in the boom of the 1980s even as shiny suburbs sprouted through much of metropolitan Maryland.

By the late 1980s, Marylanders were generally looking at a bright horizon. The fall of the Soviet Union and dismantling of the Berlin Wall signaled an end to the Cold War, and Marylanders, like other Americans, could look forward to a time of relative international peace and harmony. In the meantime, money flowed freely as savings and loans and banks rushed to lend money to growing businesses. Marylanders had little idea of what was to follow.

"What goes up must come down" is to economists as important an insight as are supply and demand, but economists (among others) largely ignored this fundamental economic/gravitational insight. The recession of the early 1990s saw Maryland's economy unravel. It also served to further discredit the economic profession. Rather than protecting Maryland from the recession of 1990–1991, the dependence of the state's economy on the federal government served to intensify the economic downturn that proved much milder in the balance of the nation.

The data are consistent with this assertion. As an example, federal outlays rose 11.1 percent in fiscal year 1985, but just 2.0 percent in 1993, a decline in real terms. Defense contractors experienced a sharp falloff in revenues as Department of Defense procurement fell, and they began laying off engineers and physicists by the hundreds. This pattern lasted through much of the 1990s. For instance, Defense procurement in Maryland, declined from $4.46 billion in fiscal year 1995 to $4.09 billion in fiscal year 1996, leading to large losses in the state's defense electronics and instruments sector. Thousands of production workers, often with annual salaries in excess of $50,000, were let go. Many left for Texas, North Carolina, Georgia, and other states that held up better than Maryland. Personal income growth in both the Washington and Baltimore metropolitan areas stalled, eventually stunting growth among retailers and homebuilders statewide.

Federal employment also began to fall rapidly. While "reinventing government" and the "peace dividend" were looked upon favorably by a broad cross-section of Americans, the loss of high-wage federal and federal contracting jobs wrought havoc on Maryland, particularly in the large metropolitan counties that had expanded so magnificently during the 1980s. Montgomery, Prince George's, Baltimore, and Anne Arundel counties all found themselves with high office vacancy rates, a rise in joblessness, and widespread disgruntlement among highly educated workers. Unlike previous recessions, which had largely battered Maryland's blue-collar workers, this one also deeply affected white-collar professionals. During the first half of the 1990s, what had been one of the nation's most vibrant economies turned into a national laggard. Even the state's Chamber of Commerce had difficulty finding positive things to say, and Maryland became tagged as a high-tax, low-growth, anti-business state.

The savings and loans (S&L) crisis of that period didn't help matters. With thousands of white-collar workers being laid off and many leaving the state altogether, the demand for office space collapsed. Banks and S&Ls began to fold as the value of their real estate portfolios began to crumble, leading to a so-called credit crunch as financiers burned by eco-

nomic events chose to grip their money more tightly. Maryland was among the 20 states hit hardest by the S&L debacle, and the crisis eventually cost state taxpayers and the state deposit insurance fund $185 million. Maryland's weakened banks became prime acquisition targets for banks in North Carolina, New Jersey, and elsewhere, leading to consolidation in the financial services industry

The Concorde Point Lighthouse in Havre de Grace is one of the oldest lighthouses in continual use on the East Coast. Photo by William Priddy

The Drum Point Lighthouse has been lovingly restored and can be found today at a Southern Maryland museum. Photo by William Priddy

Camden Yards, home of the
Baltimore Orioles. Courtesy,
Baltimore Area Convention &
Visitors Association

Camden Yards, home of the
Baltimore Orioles. Courtesy,
Baltimore Area Convention &
Visitors Association

and a loss of headquarters jobs. Maryland National Bank, USF&G, and the Bank of Baltimore were among those financial service providers acquired by out-of-state concerns. The loss of headquarters jobs and decision-makers gradually affected advertising firms, architectural firms, engineering firms, and others providing services to locally based corporations.

Amidst the gloom came occasional good news. The arrival of Southwest Airlines at Baltimore/Washington International Airport in 1993 positioned the airport to become the region's discount leader, a status that would benefit it greatly in subsequent years.

Professional sports also came to play a greater role in the lives of Marylanders. In 1992 Oriole Park at Camden Yards was completed. The park was an instant sensation, selling out routinely and serving as the model for subsequent stadium development in Cleveland, Denver, and other cities. Several years later, the Cleveland Browns decided to leave that city for Baltimore, which offered to build the Browns a new stadium.

Decline persisted in many traditional Maryland pursuits as well. The town of Solomons, on the western shore of the Chesapeake Bay in Calvert County, was once a center of a flourishing community of commercial fishermen and boat-builders. During the last few decades, an influx of suburbanites have contributed to a decline in the productivity of the Chesapeake as pollution of the Bay and its tributaries have forced many watermen and other economic users out of business.

On Maryland's Eastern Shore, small-scale commercial fishing remains viable and water-towns are reasonably intact. Much of Maryland's Eastern Shore is isolated from the metropolitan communities of the western shore, and, therefore, does not face the suburban encroachment experienced by other water-dependent communities. Still, the arrival of second-home construction and recreational tourism comes at a time when many traditional uses of the Bay and its waterfront have become less viable economically, and steadily, the waterman disappears from Maryland's economic profile.

During the 1990s, another institution nourished by the water continued to struggle. The Port of Baltimore has traditionally enjoyed competitive advantages as the most inland port on the eastern seaboard of the United States. That has served it well as Baltimore has been positioned to link global markets to the industrial markets of the Midwest, including Chicago, Detroit, Cleveland, and others. But despite aggressive promotion and public investment, the 1990s saw an acceleration of the global forces that had been turning the tide against the Port for a quarter-century.

Baltimore's inland location emerged as a liability, as shippers sought to avoid the time-consuming trip up the Chesapeake Bay. Hampton Roads, Virginia, at the mouth of the Bay, began taking away market share. In 1982 Baltimore had been the number two port in the U.S. for container ships, named for the modular, metal cargo packages that dominate today's industry. By the late 1990s, its ranking had fallen to 15th, and many came to view it as a second-tier port.

The state's government found itself unable to do much to stem the economic decline. Maryland was in the midst of a fiscal crisis. During the 1991–1993 period, then-Governor William Donald Schaefer was forced to initiate eight rounds of executive cost containment and legislation. All told, these moves led to budget cuts in excess of $1.6 billion, and included the layoff of hundreds of state employees and furloughs for others. Education aid for teachers' benefits and student transportation were slashed, as was other aid to counties and municipalities. The state's Rainy Day Fund was completely drained.

The Port's sagging fortunes symbolized the decline of Maryland's largest city. By the early 1990s, Baltimore's decline was virtually unparalleled among American urban centers, a stark contrast from its 1980s renaissance. Between 1990 and 1998, Baltimore ranked second among the nation's major cities in terms of population loss, behind only Washington, D.C. By 1998 the city's population had fallen below 700,000 residents, down from a historic census year peak of roughly 950,000 in 1950. Thousands of vacant homes sprouted up as a result, igniting scourges of crime, fires, rats, and the occasional structural collapse.

The loss in residents was accompanied by a loss in jobs. During the first quarter of 1989, the city recorded nearly 456,000 jobs. Nine years later, this figure had plunged to 378,000 jobs, equivalent to a loss of one-sixth of its employment base in less than a decade. During this period, the surrounding counties of the metropolitan area added roughly 104,000 jobs, and suburban Baltimore County, not Baltimore City, is now the region's leader in both population and jobs.

Contributing factors to Baltimore's difficulties are almost too numerous to dwell on in detail, but include city-specific issues such as deteriorating public education, violent crime, property crime, grime, taxes, parking, high auto insurance, an aging population, unparalleled drug addiction rates, disease, grinding and concentrated poverty, economically unviable commercial and industrial structures, and contaminated sites.

A myriad of non-city specific factors also fueled Baltimore's diminution, including a combination of federal policies and changing

Despite fierce competition from other East Coast ports, the Port of Baltimore remains a leader in several key niches, including automobile cargo. Photo by William Priddy

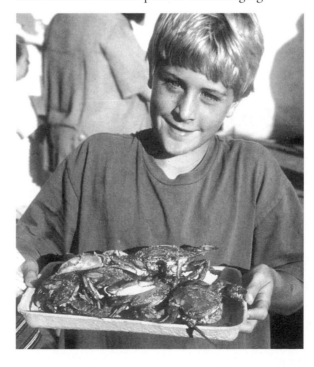

Maryland is famous for its crabs. Young people continue the tradition. Courtesy, Annapolis and Anne Arundel County Conference and Visitors Bureau

Johns Hopkins is today Maryland's leading non-government employer, and is a world leader in medical research and education. Courtesy, Baltimore Area Convention & Visitors Association

technologies that have weakened the comparative advantage of urban areas and helped drive decline. In this way, Baltimore is not unique among American cities.

Statistics characterizing the condition of Baltimore's civil society paint a similarly grim picture. During the late 1990s, Baltimore was rated number one in the nation for hospital emergency room admissions involving legal/illegal drugs. The city also emerged as the fourth or fifth deadliest in the nation depending on data source, and the city's murder rate had climbed to a level seven times higher than in the average American city.

Analysts from other parts of the country noticed Baltimore's decline, dedicating treatises to what had become one of America's most disheartening urban stories. In his 1996 work *Baltimore Unbound*, scholar David Rusk writes that, "Quite simply, Baltimore City is programmed for inexorable decline." Subsequently, he writes that, "There are 34 American

cities, including, by 1980, Baltimore City, that have passed the point of no return . . . . No combination of urban renewal, downtown development, model cities programs, community development corporations . . . has ever reversed the downward slide of such cities. There is no factual basis for believing that more of the same . . . will reverse Baltimore City's decline . . . . "

Baltimore was not the only city in Maryland to find itself in high waters. Cambridge, Maryland, was another historic city that found itself in decline during the 1990s. Founded in 1684 as the seat of Dorchester County on Maryland's Eastern Shore, the community emerged as a thriving center for agriculture. As one of the state's only two deep-water ports, Cambridge also became a prime location for shipping and seafood industries. But the city's economy began declining in the 1950s when major food packing operations moved elsewhere. The city's population declined by approximately 500 people between 1990 and 2000, falling to just under 11,000 residents.

Cumberland in western Maryland also has experienced a decline in recent years. The difficult times began during the 1970s as manufacturers Celanese Corporation, PPG Industries, and Kelly-Springfield Tire Company closed their Allegany County plants. A series of other job losses helped to cut Cumberland's population from 38,000 in 1950 to about 21,500 by 2000.

In Silver Spring, Maryland, a different form of decline occurred. Proximate to Washington, D.C., Silver Spring emerged as a model of suburbia, a town that emerged around its rail line and location as a bedroom community for workers in the nation's capital. It also became a retail destination, with shops and department stores lining its major thoroughfares. Eventually, Silver Spring became home to one of the nation's first shopping centers where customers parked in a lot in front of the building, a precursor to the modern mall.

Ironically, it was the emergence of the mall that led to Silver Spring's decline in the late 1970s and 1980s. As newer suburbs pushed away from Washington, so too did residents, who no longer shopped in Silver Spring, but opted for their newer local shopping venues. Montgomery County has pursued several plans to revitalize downtown, but until recently, most have fallen through. The most well-known project was the American Dream mall, an enormous retail center that would have been accompanied by an indoor wave pool and amusement park. But like several previous attempts to breathe life into a decaying downtown, it flopped in 1997 when Montgomery County balked at the high price tag.

Thus, after the terrific run of the 1980s, Maryland suddenly found itself without momentum and without identifiable engines of growth. The state would have to redefine itself once again. The need was pressing. For much of its history, Maryland has enjoyed one of the nation's lower unemployment rates, but by 1997, Maryland's unemployment rate had come to exceed that of the nation's. Moreover, the state found itself in vigorous economic competition with neighbors such as Virginia and Delaware. The trials and tribulations of Maryland's largest city were also more than a

The Power Plant has had many incarnations. Today, it is one of Baltimore's most popular tourist destinations, and includes a Barnes & Noble bookstore, a Hard Rock Cafe and ESPNZone. Photo by William Priddy

bit worrisome. Somehow, within the span of 10 years, Maryland had transitioned from a position of seeming blissful invulnerability to one of profound uncertainty.

Even the greatest societies experience periods of loss, doubt, and disappointment. By the mid-to-late 1990s, Maryland found itself in this situation. But all great societies find a way to reinvent themselves, and to identify new avenues to prosperity. Just as quickly as Maryland's fortunes had faded, they would re-emerge. Marylanders, among the most educated states in the nation, would find a way to rally.

Despite the tough years of the early- and mid-1990s, Maryland still possessed numerous highly valuable assets. Federal research is a hallmark of the state, with institutions such as the National Institutes of Health in Bethesda, the Patuxent River Naval Air Station in St. Mary's County, the National Security Agency in Anne Arundel County, Aberdeen Proving Grounds in Harford County, Fort Detrick in Frederick County, NASA Goddard Space Flight Center in Prince George's County and numerous other centers of scientific endeavor. The state is also known for its university research, and is home to the Johns Hopkins University, the University of Maryland, College Park, and the University of Maryland, Baltimore.

This great mass of intellectual capital found a way to make its presence felt during the technology boom of the late-1990s. This was particularly true in biotechnology, a natural for Maryland given its concentration of leading researchers and scholars. But now, rather than confining themselves to the university laboratory, a greater proportion of this scientific talent sought out opportunities in the private sector, leading to a boom in employment growth and innovation in Maryland's rapidly developing biotech industry.

Among the biotech segments in which Maryland excelled was gene therapy. Rockville-based Human Genome Sciences Incorporated has emerged as a pioneer in the sequencing of the genomes of pathogenic bacteria. Gaithersburg-based Genetic Therapy Incorporated became the first company in the nation to enter into Phase III gene therapy trials.

Maryland's biotech sector made national headlines on May 4, 1998, when Rockville-based EntreMed saw its shares leap 330 percent in one day as investors rushed to the stock on speculation that the company was close to developing two new treatments for cancer. More than 23 million shares of the company traded hands that day, compared to the company's average daily trading volume of 64,000 shares.

But no firm has exemplified the continued maturation of Maryland's biotech industry as well as Gaithersburg-based MedImmune

Incorporated. The company has emerged as the nation's fourth largest biotech company, and is responsible for the development of Synagis, a treatment designed to strengthen a tiny baby's immune system against respiratory virus. In a majority of cases, the treatment is enough to prevent infection from progressing to serious illness.

Maryland's biotechnology industry went on to make global headlines and human history thanks to Celera Genomics. The company was founded to sequence and assemble the human genome. By identifying the chemical makeup of more than 80,000 human genes, Celera successfully mapped the genetic makeup of one human being, a scientific first. The breakthrough opens up avenues for new research including the development of medicines customized to a person's specific composition that prevent dangerous diseases long before symptoms appear. In short, Celera's accomplishment was one of the century's greatest, and left no doubt as to the potency of Maryland's emerging biotech cluster.

There were other technology segments to emerge in Maryland during the late 1990s, including fiber optics. Companies like Ciena and Corvis added jobs by the hundreds as they developed and manufactured leading-edge telecommunications equipment. Young knowledge workers also arrived in Baltimore, to be a part of the city's emerging Digital Harbor. All

The B&O Railroad Museum is a prominent landmark in a working class neighborhood in southwest Baltimore, and ranks as one of the preeminent locations in U.S. Railroad history. Courtesy, Baltimore Area Convention & Visitors Association

of a sudden, Maryland, which had become accustomed to being one of the slowest growing states in the nation during the early- and mid-1990s, was returning to its former glory. By the end of the decade, job growth in Maryland was approaching 60,000 per year, a massive total for a state Maryland's size.

Experts recognized that Maryland had made enormous strides in just a few years. In its Science and Technology Index, the Milken Institute, a highly respected center of research in California, ranked Maryland fourth in the nation for its technology preparedness, behind only Massachusetts, Colorado, and California. Maryland, mired in doldrums just years earlier, suddenly found its economy to be more dynamic than those of Virginia, Washington, Texas, Georgia, North Carolina, New Jersey, Connecticut, and other perennial high-flyers.

Data from the U.S. Bureau of the Census confirmed Maryland's reemergence. By 1998–1999, Maryland reported the highest median income in the nation. Technical talent flocked to Maryland to participate in the state's miraculous return to economic health. By 2000 Maryland ranked first in the nation in terms of the percentage of its population holding advanced degrees. As the new millennium approached, Maryland was more than participating in the nation's economic boom, and prosperity was reestablished just as quickly as it had vanished several years prior.

Even sports fans had something to celebrate. In 2001, the Baltimore Ravens defeated the New York Giants 34-7 to win the Super Bowl. The next year, the Maryland Terrapins won the National Collegiate Athletic Association championship in men's basketball, trouncing the Indiana Hoosiers 64-52. Suddenly, being a Marylander was a very fine thing.

This expansion of prosperity made its impact felt in Baltimore City as well. After years of steep decline, the citizens of Baltimore concluded that enough was enough. That Baltimore would reverse its decline should come as no surprise despite the view of some that the city was beyond the point of no return. Baltimore's economic history may be viewed as a series of booms and busts. The better part of the 1990s had come to represent more bust than boom, but with grinding

determination, momentum was reestablished.

Without fail, Baltimore's periods of economic growth and prosperity have followed periods of substantial investment in commercial infrastructure that induced private investment. During the very early periods of Baltimore's history, this investment often took the form of improvements to transportation infrastructure, including investments in seaports and railroads. After watching New York gain access to the markets of today's Midwest with the construction of the Erie Canal during the early 19th century, Baltimore, determined not to be left behind, invested its resources in the Baltimore and Ohio B & O Railroad, giving it access to markets to its west.

Renamed in 2003, M & T Bank Stadium is the home to the Baltimore Ravens, winners of Super Bowl XXXV. Courtesy, Baltimore Area Convention & Visitors Association

Maryland celebrates African and African American heritage in many ways, including with the Anne Arundel County sculpture. Courtesy, Annapolis and Anne Arundel County Conference and Visitors Bureau

Federal Hill is one of a number of waterfront neighborhoods now packed with young professionals embracing the lifestyle offered by Baltimore's renaissance. Courtesy, Baltimore Area Convention & Visitors Association

After World War II, this spirit of public investment continued as the city modernized its central business district and created the Inner Harbor. Once home to rats, failing businesses, rotting piers, and abandoned buildings, the Inner Harbor area is today one of the nation's leading urban tourist destinations.

But Baltimore had during much of the 1990s forgotten the lessons of the past. The mayoral regime that prevailed from 1987–1999 worked diligently to maintain the city's reasonably high bond rating, spending and investing little in key infrastructure such as parks and parking. Decline invariably followed.

With a new mayoral administration in 1999, a new spirit emerged. The administration of Martin O'Malley began with a pledge to shut down 10 of Baltimore's most active open-air drug markets, a feat that was accomplished within the administration's first six months. Improved policing led quickly to a dramatic reduction in the city's crime rate. The FBI's uniform crime statistics revealed that over a three-year period, Baltimore led the nation in reducing violent crime. By 2003 crime was down 25 percent compared to 1999, bucking the flat national trend.

The reduction in crime and renewed job creation conspired with favorable demographics to generate a housing boom in the city. The children of the baby boomers, a massive group

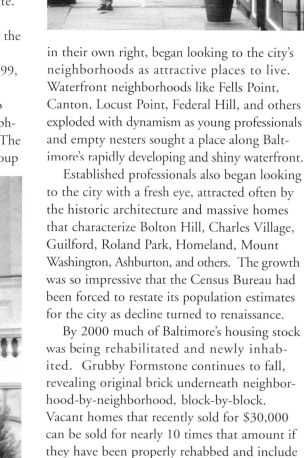

Mayor Martin O'Malley urges Baltimoreans to "Believe" in front of City Hall. Courtesy, The Greyhound, *Loyola College in Maryland*

in their own right, began looking to the city's neighborhoods as attractive places to live. Waterfront neighborhoods like Fells Point, Canton, Locust Point, Federal Hill, and others exploded with dynamism as young professionals and empty nesters sought a place along Baltimore's rapidly developing and shiny waterfront.

Established professionals also began looking to the city with a fresh eye, attracted often by the historic architecture and massive homes that characterize Bolton Hill, Charles Village, Guilford, Roland Park, Homeland, Mount Washington, Ashburton, and others. The growth was so impressive that the Census Bureau had been forced to restate its population estimates for the city as decline turned to renaissance.

By 2000 much of Baltimore's housing stock was being rehabilitated and newly inhabited. Grubby Formstone continues to fall, revealing original brick underneath neighborhood-by-neighborhood, block-by-block. Vacant homes that recently sold for $30,000 can be sold for nearly 10 times that amount if they have been properly rehabbed and include the accoutrements that Baltimoreans demand: rooftop decks, sweeping views, exposed brick, wood floors, cathedral ceilings, and an abundance of old-world charm.

Part of Baltimore's momentum can be traced to shifts in public policy. Beginning in the summer of 1995, Baltimore began to tear down its largest housing projects, one by one. The demolitions of Lafayette Courts, Lexington Terrace, Murphy Homes, and other public housing was pursued because these projects, once so filled with promise, had become dirty and dangerous. In their place are emerging new communities like Pleasant View Gardens in East Baltimore where residents have access to healthcare, modern streetscapes, and attractive housing.

Commercial development also accelerated. For many years, Baltimore did not experience the construction of one new office building downtown. After the construction of an office tower at 1 South Street was completed in 1992, downtown's skyline remained unaltered for nearly a decade. That has changed. By 2000 office development began anew, and by 2003, Baltimore's skyline was much altered from prior years.

The momentum continues. The entire West Side of Baltimore's downtown is currently being redeveloped. The West Side redevelopment project ultimately involves nearly $1 billion of new investment in the city's former cultural and retail core. By the end of the current decade, more than 2,400 apartments will become available through new construction and restoration of historic buildings. More than 400,000 square feet of office space will also be available, as will an additional 250,000 square feet of retail and entertainment space.

While all of this translates into new jobs, tax revenues, and vitality, nothing excites Baltimoreans like the redevelopment of the historic Hippodrome Theater, the linchpin of the West Side's renaissance. Decades ago, the Hippodrome anchored Baltimore's cultural life. It was one of the first theaters in the city to show motion pictures and is one of the last remaining theaters built by Thomas Lamb, a leading theater architect of the early 1990s. Its $63 million restoration revives the theater to its former glory, and provides Baltimore with a modern center with 2,250 seats, a five-story stage house, and a capacity to host headline Broadway shows.

The renewed vigor of urban life in Maryland has not been confined to Baltimore. In

Cambridge, Maryland, second home purchasers have flocked to the city that sits along the banks of the Choptank River. A new Hyatt has opened, which, by employing 500 people, is now the city's largest employer.

In Silver Spring Discovery Communications new headquarters and the American Film Institute's refurbished Silver Theater have opened along with a new town center replete with shopping and restaurants. The development is part of a seven-year, $1 billion urban renewal project that will redefine a 360-acre section of downtown from a largely abandoned wasteland of boarded-up shops to a cultural and commercial center.

Built between 1758 and 1764, this colonial home incorporates dramatic views of the South River. Courtesy, Annapolis and Anne Arundel County Conference and Visitors Bureau

Maryland Avenue is one of Annapolis' most beautiful thoroughfares. Courtesy, Annapolis and Anne Arundel County Conference and Visitors Bureau

In 2002, Republican Robert Ehrlich and Democrat Kathleen Kennedy Townsend represented their respective parties in the gubernatorial race. Robert Ehrlich won, becoming the first Republican to win the governor's election since 1966. Courtesy, The Greyhound, Loyola College in Maryland

In Cumberland shops are opening at Canal Place, attracting residents and tourists alike. The city has become a haven for cyclists, who come via the Allegheny Highland Trail, part of a planned biking and hiking route that will eventually stretch from Pittsburgh to downtown Cumberland. The trail will end at the Western Maryland Railway Station, a restored depot adjacent to Canal Place.

Today, Maryland's cities can be characterized as healthy, growing, and viable. From the mountains of Western Maryland to the beaches of Ocean City, cities and towns across the state continue to participate in the expansion of one of the nation's fastest-growing economies. While markets have played a major role in helping Maryland's cities to prosper, public policies have also contributed.

As a state of small land area, the efficient utilization of property has always been of concern to Marylanders since at least the 1930s, when state planning began in earnest. Still, with growth, there is sprawl and congestion.

In response, Maryland's then-Governor Parris N. Glendening announced in 1995 his priority commitment to develop and secure passage of legislation to empower the state government to direct growth and promote the redevelopment of older developed areas. Among the legislation passed subsequently were the Smart Growth Areas Act, which limits most state infrastructure funding related to development to existing communities or to those places designated for growth, and the Rural Legacy program, which provides grants to create greenbelts to protect geographically large rural areas. Few states in the country were as active in growth management as Maryland, and the determination to redirect growth to the cities explains part of the resurgence that has been experienced in Maryland's older urban communities.

Maryland had managed to reestablish its economy as one of the nation's most dynamic during the late-1990s and into the current

Each year, this Memorial Day Parade held in Annapolis grows in attendance and popularity. Courtesy, Annapolis and Anne Arundel County Conference and Visitors Bureau

decade without the benefit of rapidly increasing federal expenditures. After September 11, 2001, however, the American people and the federal government concluded that defense and homeland security would need to be stepped up.

As a result, even as the nation's economy remained mired in a recession and subsequent jobless recovery, Maryland continued to expand, as defense spending found its way to Maryland corporations, national security agencies, and to centers of research. Maryland remains one of the five or six most active defense procurement states in the nation, and the state's economy often excels during times of conflict. Such was the case in World War II when Maryland's factories were humming in the production of airplanes, ships, and other implements of defense. Such is the case today.

By 2003 Maryland's unemployment rate was nearly two percentage points lower than the nation's. Job growth continued statewide even as the country found itself mired in the deepest labor market slump in over a decade.

Maryland continues to position itself for the economy of the future. In early 2003 the first business incubator in the nation dedicated to serving the nation's homeland security needs was established in Anne Arundel County. As home to the National Security Agency and the U.S. Naval Academy, the county has always been at the forefront of the nation's defense establishment, and will continue to be.

Tourism also has emerged as one of Maryland's leading growth engines. In part, this is reflected at Baltimore/Washington International Airport (BWI). By the late 1990s, BWI was one of the nation's fastest growing airports. Even after 9/11, the airport has continued to expand, and is presently in the midst of a five-year, $1.8 billion expansion program that began in April 2001.

But tourism's role in Maryland has manifested itself in other ways as well, and has been particularly important to the economies of several of Maryland's most rural areas. One example is Garrett County, the westernmost of Maryland's 24 jurisdictions. Characterized by the same rugged beauty as neighboring West Virginia, Garrett County has become established as a year-round resort community, which has at its epicenter magnificent Deep Creek Lake.

Named for Benjamin Banneker, the Maryland-born mathematician and surveyor who assisted in laying out the nation's capital, and Frederick Douglass, the brilliant orator and abolitionist leader, the Banneker-Douglas Museum was built in 1874 by free blacks. Courtesy, Annapolis and Anne Arundel County Conference and Visitors Bureau

Deep Creek Lake has emerged as a prime vacation destination for residents in the Washington, Baltimore, and Pittsburgh metropolitan areas. Visitors boat, fish, ski, white-water raft, and golf depending on the time of the year. The influx of tourists has generated a wave of

BWI Airport has emerged as one of the nation's fastest growing airports in recent years, and is considered the East Coast's discount fare leader. Courtesy, Baltimore Area Convention & Visitors Association

new development and job opportunities in Garrett County, which once had one of Maryland's highest unemployment rates.

The momentum for Maryland's economy can also be found at the Port of Baltimore, which has managed to capitalize on several promising niches. Founded in 1706 on the banks of the Patapsco River, the Port has continued to redefine itself. Though still an important player in the containerized cargo market, Baltimore's greatest success in recent years can be traced to its establishment as one of the leading ports of entry in the U.S. for foreign-made automobiles and for the export of roll-on/roll-off cargoes overseas. The fact that Baltimore is one of only two Eastern U.S. ports where the main shipping channel reaches a depth of 50 feet remains an important competitive advantage, and the state of Maryland remains committed to its long-term success.

In 2001 the Port signed its biggest deal ever, a 20-year agreement with Scandinavian shipping line Wallenius Wilhelmsen that has transformed the Dundalk Marine Terminal into a hub for roll-on/roll-off cargo. Baltimore's share of the East Coast's roll-on/roll-off market topped the 50 percent mark for the first time in 2002.

But the state of Maryland's greatest in-dustrial priority remains biotechnology. No wonder. Baltimore is the nation's leading city in attracting National Institutes of Health grants, and Montgomery County possesses one of the nation's greatest biotech firm clusters. As home to the National Institutes of Health, the Food and Drug Administration, the Center for Medicare and Medicaid Services, and other health-related institutions, biotech and healthcare are natural elements of Maryland's long-term future.

Increasingly, local universities have sought to leverage their academic talent by creating new private sector opportunities. Two universi-ties in Baltimore have served as the vanguard. The University of Maryland, Baltimore, now a top-flight research center in its own right, announced that it would develop a biotech park with a total price tag of $200 to $300 million. The announcement took Balt-imoreans by storm, since its location will be on five acres of uninhabited land in West Baltimore, property that in prior years has been used as a dumping ground for snow. Ultimately, the bio park will include six buildings totaling 700,000 square feet of lab and office space.

Then, another major announcement followed, one that has the potential to forever change the economic history of Baltimore's East Side. The Johns Hopkins medical campus announced that it too would develop a biotech park. The East Baltimore Biotech Park, planned for an expanse of property adjacent to Johns Hopkins, is expected to generate 8,000 jobs,

Once home to rotting piers, Baltimore's Inner Harbor is now one of the nation's leading urban tourist destinations. Courtesy, Baltimore Area Convention & Visitors Association

37 percent of which will be available for those with lower education and training, a plus for a city as diverse as Baltimore.

The East Baltimore Biotech Park will be located in one of Baltimore's poorest, most violent sections. Over the course of a decade, this section of East Baltimore will be transformed into a center of cutting-edge research, development, and commercialization. It is part of Maryland's continuous rebirth and redefinition. And, it is a project typical of Mary-land's economic history and ambitions.

Conclusion

As one of the oldest economies in the nation, Maryland has enjoyed many forms. Early in its history, Maryland was like most of America: a state of watermen and agrarians living off the land. But by the 19th century, Maryland had emerged as an industrial powerhouse, fueled by its railroads, seaports, and strategic location on the eastern seaboard.

This industrial character persisted well into the 20th century. But with the deindustrialization of much of the northern United States, Maryland had to change, as did its cities and towns. Slowly, a service sector economy emerged: an economy of engineers, bankers, investment brokers, entertainers, medical researchers, federal workers, consultants, and academics. Maryland, blue-collar for much of its history, came to be one of the most white-collar-intensive states in the nation. For older communities like Baltimore, Cumberland, and Cambridge, this meant difficult adjustments. Newer communities thrived, with suburban cities eventually dotting metropolitan Maryland.

The boom of the 1980s was driven by service sector growth coupled with an expansion among defense manufacturers. Financing was readily available, and Maryland experienced rapid expansion among both large and small employers. But the 1990–1991 recession brought difficult times to Maryland, as losses in manufacturing conspired with deep job cuts among service sector providers to leave Maryland as one of the slowest growing economies in the nation. By the mid-1990s, Maryland's future looked uncertain.

But just as quickly as Maryland's fortunes faded, they returned. Biotechnology, information technology and other cutting-edge segments of the economy expanded rapidly in an environment characterized by the nation's most educated workforce. Cities reestablished their viability by renewing their central business districts and promoting large-scale redevelopment. By the early years of the millennium, Maryland's economy had re-emerged as one of the most rapidly growing and dynamic in the nation. Aggressive economic development efforts continue, including in the renaissance city of Baltimore. Other cities are also renewed daily, and a spirit of newfound optimism has come to characterize the Old Line State.

Aerial view of the University of Maryland. Courtesy, University of Maryland

CHRONICLES OF
LEADERSHIP

There is a richness and diversity in Maryland's business history that can be matched by few other states. Blessed with a wide range of natural resources in its four major sections—the Eastern Shore, western Maryland, the southern counties, and the Baltimore urban area—Maryland's economy has never rested on just one product or group of products.

A review of the business biographies in the following section will provide solid evidence of the diversified nature of Maryland's economy over the past century. Virtually all of the companies included herein were founded after 1880, by which time the basic infrastructure and development patterns of Maryland's economy had been established. The founders of these firms recognized the opportunities presented by a state with an excellent port, a growing and prosperous population, and a reliable labor base, and their companies have remained valued members of the Maryland business community.

Many of these firms were founded in the last decade of the nineteenth century or in the first two decades of the twentieth century, after the initial wave of industrialization following the Civil War had passed. This was the progressive era in America, which historians often have described as a time of economic tensions, when big business had begun to close the doors of opportunity to aspiring entrepreneurs. Judging from the experience of these companies, especially those in the Baltimore area, there clearly remained a number of open avenues to commercial success. There also were a surprising number of firms founded during the Great Depression, when some Maryland businessmen obviously saw opportunity rather than despair.

In the years since World War II Maryland has undergone an extensive economic revitalization that shows no signs of slowing. The most well-known symbol of this renaissance is Baltimore's Inner Harbor, the famous project that was begun in 1975. Ocean City, long the favorite summer resort of Marylanders, has witnessed a tremendous boom in growth, especially since 1960. In Columbia and St. Charles, Maryland has two of the nation's most successful "new communities," and the state enjoys one of the nation's highest concentrations of scientists and engineers to serve high-technology industries.

When Maryland's first settlers arrived in 1634 at the Indian town of Yoacomico, which they renamed St. Mary's, the land welcomed them with an environment that would support a variety of crops, and with excellent water transportation to bring in supplies and ship out the colony's products. Over the next 350 years Maryland gradually built upon its natural advantages to develop businesses and businessmen of whom the state could be proud.

The organizations whose stories are detailed on the following pages have chosen to support this important literary and civic project. They illustrate the variety of ways in which individuals and their businesses have contributed to the state's growth and development. The civic involvement of Maryland's businesses, institutions of learning, and local government, in cooperation with its citizens, has made the state an excellent place to live and work.

ACTION PRODUCTS

The remarkable story of Action Products, Inc., and its founder reads like a modern-day fairy tale. Founded in 1970, this Hagerstown-based company has established itself as a leading manufacturer and distributor of cushioning products used in the medical and medical-related industries throughout the world.

Most of the company's products are derived from an ultra-soft synthetic rubber-like material, called Akton® polymer. This unique, shock-absorbing material was invented by the company's founder in the basement of his home more than 30 years ago. What began as a scientific pursuit to develop padding that would help prevent pressure sores in immobilized patients has today spawned a corporation that sells over 2,000 products for hundreds of applications. Its diversified markets include hospitals, home healthcare dealers and therapists, military and law enforcement agencies, equine and shooting sports and a wide variety of Original Equipment Manufacturers.

Wheelchair cushions and bed pads were the first products sold by the company. In the mid-1980s, Action Products expanded its market to include hospital operating rooms. Research indicated anesthetized patients were developing

Home to the McElroy family and birthplace of AKTON polymer, Olean, New York.

Founders, Dr. and Helen McElroy, with son and current vice-chairman, Ben McElroy.

pressure sores during surgery, similar to those seen on bedridden or wheelchair-bound individuals. A product that could prevent such tissue trauma was found to be in high demand. By 1990 the company had designed approximately 50 products for its operating room line. These products include table pads, head pads, chest rolls, patient positioners, pediatric positioners and specialty surgical frame pads.

The company's second major line of medical products serves the home health care industry. Besides the standard wheelchair seating and positioning cushions and surface support pads, Action also manufactures shoe insoles, elbow and heel protectors, ankle braces, knee pads and hand exercisers for rehabilitation.

The shock-absorbing attributes of Akton® polymer present limitless applications for its use that extend far beyond the reaches of the medical field. The material is used in gun recoil pads for hunters and law enforcement personnel, in gloves for jackhammer users, in padding for race car driver helmets and seats and in various pads for horses to prevent tissue trauma.

Remember Danny DeVito's penguin suit in the movie *Batman Returns*? That, too, was made of a thick coat of—you guessed it—Akton® polymer.

The wonder polymer has also been used in a nasal mask to treat sleep apnea, as an absorbent in high-energy electron and photon radiation therapy for cancer, and was even attempted in breast prosthesis.

Research and innovation remain the hallmark of the company, which boasts a burgeoning international market and sales exceeding $10 million a year. Sometimes success must be invented before it can be achieved, however. And that's what makes Action's story so compelling.

To understand the essence of Action Products, Inc., one must first become acquainted with its founder, chairman and guiding spirit—Dr. Wilbur R. McElroy. The ingenuity and resilience of this sprightly 89-year-old are the foundations for the company's present-day success.

McElroy was born outside of Chambersburg, Pennsylvania, in the small farming community of Fayetteville. His grandfather raised apples, peaches, cherries and tomatoes and operated a canning factory. As a young boy, McElroy was fascinated by the steam engine and mechanisms in the factory, and particularly the large vats outside where lime sulfur was heated for use as an orchard insecticide.

His interest in horticulture grew and McElroy thought that would be his future career—until he became captivated by chemistry in high school. He enrolled in Gettysburg College and was greatly influenced by one of his professors, Dr. Zinn, who had attended Johns Hopkins University. Following in the footsteps of his mentor, McElroy entered Johns Hopkins to study chemistry. The department at Johns Hopkins was oriented toward physical chemistry, however, and McElroy wanted to study organic chemistry. After one year, McElroy left Johns Hopkins University and enrolled in Pennsylvania State University, where he received his master's degree in organic chemistry.

He landed his first job with The Texas Company, or Texaco as it is known today, in Beacon, New York, working in the analytical and testing department. The company gave him a leave of absence so he could go to Purdue University and earn a doctorate degree. While at Purdue, he worked on National Defense Research Council projects from 1941 to 1943. A rapid method to analyze gun powder was developed, and a machine was made for each of the seven arsenals to do this. He synthesized several new explosives with exceptional brisance, resulting in patents. He also cooperated with other universities to synthesize antimalarials.

When McElroy returned to The Texas Company, he knew he wanted to specialize in organic chemistry. The opportunity arose in 1945, after The Texas Company opened the Jefferson Chemical Company in Port Arthur, Texas. McElroy was given the chance to oversee process development in their pilot plant. So he relocated there with his wife, Helen, and six-month-old son, Ben. Unfortunately, the climate proved unfavorable for his wife's health, and after four years, the McElroys moved back to New York.

For some time McElroy had entertained thoughts of running his own business. An opportunity arose in his wife's hometown of Waynesboro, Pennsylvania, to purchase a private consulting and laboratory business that performed chemical analysis and testing. Although he loved working for The Texas Company, McElroy felt it was time to test his own wings, and in

First site of Action Products, Inc., Scutt's Dairy in Portville, New York, 1969.

1949 he bought Wayne Laboratories. He also took the test required to become a registered Professional Engineer in Pennsylvania and has been a P.E. for over 50 years.

While enjoying the freedom of his own business, McElroy once again found himself doing unfulfilling analytical chemistry work. So he and his family moved again, this time to Alexandria, Virginia, where he accepted a job with Melpar, a subsidiary of Westinghouse Airbrake Company. Much of the work involved government research and development, particularly relating to the space industry. McElroy headed up the chemistry department there, and the company decided to move its top scientists to a central research lab in Alexandria. He was one of the scientists

Second site of Action Products, Inc., Hinsdale, New York, 1972–1978.

Flag-raising ceremony to commemorate "E" Award at Action products, Inc., 1987.

assigned to the new location. After one year, however, Westinghouse closed the research lab, giving its employees only one month's notice.

McElroy found a position with Mobay Chemical Corporation and was responsible for bringing some of the technology of polyurethane coatings that had been developed in Germany over to the United States. He was sent to Alabama in 1955 and spent an observation period in Germany, so he could help to design a full-scale plant in the United States with that knowledge. He helped jumpstart a plant in New Martinsville, West Virginia, where he spent ten years working in research and process development. He later moved to Olean, New York to get a job with Conap, making polyurethane systems for paint and adhesives. While at Conap, he also developed a coating for printed circuit boards that were used in the first U.S. computers in space.

But his dream to operate his own business would not die. So in 1969, at the somewhat ripe age of 55, McElroy left his job with the chemical company and set up shop in the basement of his Olean, New York, home. Acting upon the suggestion of a friend who worked in the medical products business, McElroy began to design a quality material for wheelchair pads. At the time existing products, such as foam and gel pads, were only partially effective

in preventing decubitis ulcers, or pressure sores. While experimenting in his makeshift lab, McElroy supported his family by doing consulting work on the side. He still owned Wayne Laboratories in Waynesboro, Pennsylvania, and started his research operations as a division of that business. A year later, he had developed a product that he believed would be marketable. He named the material *Akton®*, a derivation of the Guatemalan word for "natural rubber".

Timing is everything. In 1970 the Veterans Administration was planning to initiate a medical/engineering study to test all the wheelchair pads available on the market and identify the one of highest quality. McElroy learned of the project, contacted the Veterans Administration, and at the last minute was placed on the testing schedule.

"I had to catch a plane and flew the pad to Chicago myself for testing," recalls McElroy. "We came out number one in every category, medical and physical. As a result, we got the Veterans Administration contract to supply pads to their hospitals in the United States. That's what got us started."

Dr. McElroy and his wife officially established Action Products, Inc., that year. The company contracted with the Veterans Administration to supply Action® Flotation Pads to its hospitals for five years between 1973 and 1979. During this period, the company's commercial medical business grew and it began to export products on a small scale.

Soon McElroy's basement could no longer accommodate his blossoming operation. He rented a former farm dairy building in Portville, New York, for $50 a month and set up shop there. His operations were rudimentary, to say the least. The chemicals arrived in 55-gallon drums weighing 500 pounds each. McElroy was short on funds for expensive, cumbersome machinery, but he did purchase an electric lift truck to lift the drums onto concrete blocks. All the mixing was done by hand and the chemicals were weighed out into plastic buckets. Once the proper mixture was

Dr. McElroy (3rd from left) and Chris McElroy (center) with European distributors at the 1998 awards ceremony in Oslo, Norway.

created, the liquid material was poured into polyurethane bags suspended in boxes and laid flat to cure for 18 hours. The following day the pads were sealed with an adhesive McElroy developed himself, then fitted with covers.

After one year, McElroy moved his operations to an abandoned feed supply company in Hinsdale, New York. He stayed there until 1979, when high taxes in New York prompted him to look elsewhere. He relocated the company to Hagerstown, Maryland, not far from his boyhood home in Pennsylvania. The former Southern Shoe Manufacturing Company on Mulberry Street became his new headquarters.

At the time Action Products had one employee in Hagerstown, his son Ben, who moved from Raleigh, North Carolina, to join his father and take over production operations. Ben handled every aspect of operations, from sales to manufacturing to answering the telephone—a daunting task. Help would soon arrive, however. In 1980 Troy McKnight, an engineering student from Johns Hopkins University, obtained a summer job with the company. His duties ranged from assisting in the manufacture of the products to janitorial work. It wasn't long before

Three generations of Action: founder Dr. McElroy (seated), granddaughter and director of corporate development, Mistie McElroy, and son and vice chairman, Ben McElroy.

he became involved in sales and started attending trade shows.

"I liked what I saw and decided to stay here," says McKnight. "The company started growing and I grew with it. I saw the tremendous opportunities that existed here."

Twenty-three years later, McKnight is now president of Action Products, taking over for Ben who retired last year after serving in that role for a decade.

The company has continued to prosper, presenting unique challenges for a historically family-run operation. "We're trying to maintain a small family-oriented culture, while at the same time trying to get bigger and make the organization more flexible, faster and able to respond in order to be competitive," says McKnight.

In the late 1970s, Action began to recognize the tremendous export potential of its products but had few resources to devote to the project. Then in 1982, Chris McElroy made the acquaintance of Jon Bredal, a Norwegian businessman who was also involved in a family-run medical products company. A perfect fit was formed between Action Products, Inc. and Tollef Bredal, AS. Together, Chris McElroy and Jon Bredal tackled Europe, seeking to develop a solid network of European distributors. Twenty years later, Action Products has earned a reputation for export; having earned both the prestigious "President's 'E' Certificate" in 1987 and "President's 'E' Star Award" in 1997 for excellence in export. Today the company's products can be found worldwide on five continents, with sales concentrations in France, Germany, the

Owners, Chris McElroy (left) and Ben McElroy (center), with Vince Serra, vice president of research and development, at 1998 MedTrade show.

United Kingdom, Australia and Japan.

The company built a new manufacturing facility in Hagerstown Business Park in 1997—and today the business does remain much like a family operation, despite its growth and expansion. Action now has 160 employees and operates from two Hagerstown-based operating plants. Dr. McElroy is chairman of the board. Ben is vice-chairman and treasurer. Chris McElroy began her career with Action Products by sewing covers for pads. Now she is senior vice president and is in charge of international sales and marketing. Their daughter, Mistie, earned her master's degree in business administration from George Washington University and is the director of corporate development at the company.

As for the company's founder, he still goes to the office several times a week and continues to experiment and develop new polymers in the research laboratory. Dr. McElroy and his second wife, Maggie, travel frequently and live life to the fullest every day.

Like the Frank Sinatra song, McElroy says he is proud that "I did it my way." "I started the company and was able to develop it with planned strategies and complete honesty. And now we're well-respected all around the world."

ACTION and AKTON are registered trademarks of Action Products, Inc., USA.

213

AMERICAN COMMUNITY PROPERTIES TRUST

In 1968, Jim Wilson, founder of Interstate General Corporation, bought acreage 23 miles outside of Washington, D.C., along Maryland Route 5 and the U.S. Route 301, the two most-heavily-traveled highways in Charles County. The small town of St. Charles already existed nearby, and Wilson decided it was the perfect location for an adjacent planned community of the same name. St. Charles led to the creation of a public company, American Community Properties Trust (ACPT), a land development and property management company that is applying the smart growth principles of St. Charles to other planned communities.

Wilson had already experienced success with Interstate General Corporation, L.P. (IGC), which he started in Puerto Rico in the 1950s as a construction and building firm, gaining vast experience building everything from bridges to shopping malls, houses, and roads. In the 1960s Wilson set his sights on the mainland, specifically the state of Maryland.

To make this dream a reality, Wilson enlisted the services of such notables as Robert O'Donnell of the planning firm Harmon, O'Donnell and Henninger. O'Donnell had a reputation for being a master planner and was considered one of the founding fathers of the prestigious Urban Land Institute. Wilson also called on Bethesda-based architect

Construction of a bridge over railroad tracks on Smallwood Drive in St. Charles. Since its inception, St. Charles has built a collection of arterial roads that serve its residents and provide important traffic relief for the rest of Charles County.

Maryland Governor J. Millard Tawes (left) attended the grand opening of St. Charles' Carrington community in 1965.

Arnold Kronstadt, who had become known for his sophisticated and efficient apartment design concepts. Wilson's plan called for a city based on the principles of "Smart Growth," with a mixture of residential, industrial and commercial property.

In 1972 the government's Docket 90 designated St. Charles as a planned unit development that allowed the company to apply for government funding, which in turn provided the framework upon which the community was built. Wilson knew that for a "Smart Growth" community to be successful it had to offer a variety of housing options and permanent open space. Under the development agreement between ACPT and Charles County, 50 percent of the planned community would consist of single-family homes, 25 percent townhomes or duplexes, and 25 percent apartment units.

Wilson added a transportation grid of more than 12 miles of divided lane roadway, as well as an extensive water and sewer infrastructure to serve businesses and residents of St. Charles and the greater Waldorf, Maryland, commercial district.

Designed around a New England town model, the overall community contains five villages, with each village divided into several neighborhoods. Each village includes schools, shopping centers, places of worship, and a large variety of recreational amenities. The model also provides housing for people of all income brackets and from

all walks of life. In addition, St. Charles has been the largest provider of income-assisted housing in Charles County since it was first developed. It also provides apartment facilities for senior citizens. Single-family homes are built on a curvilinear, cul-de-sac system, as opposed to the more common grid system. This design maximizes land use and is also another way in which the community preserves open space. In the completed villages, single-family home prices range from $160,000 to approximately $270,000 in 2003.

Through a creative, compact design strategy and higher density levels, the community of St. Charles is a forerunner in preserving open space in Charles County, Maryland. In the two completed phases of the community are the villages of Smallwood and Westlake. Smallwood Village, the first to be completed,

ACPT board members Antonio Ginorio, T. Michael Scott, J. Michael Wilson, Thomas Shafer, and Edwin L. Kelly at the American Stock Exchange.

contains the Smallwood Village Center, Business Park North, and the Henry Ford Circle. Westlake Village contains three neighborhoods with nearly 5,000 housing units. The two villages also contain a thriving industrial park that is home to the local branch of the Maryland Department of Motor Vehicles, the United States Post Office, the largest county newspaper, and the largest collection of private sector employers in Charles County.

An aerial view of Smallwood Village, the first of five villages that will eventually comprise St. Charles. St. Charles has been called a model for smart growth policies because of its successful mix of commercial and residential land use.

Miles of trails connect the neighborhoods in each village, providing paths to its nearby lakes, playgrounds, shopping areas and community centers. The trails will also serve a greater role as part of the efforts being undertaken by the Southern Maryland county governments and the Tri-County Council in creating hike and bike paths, which will connect Charles, Calvert, and St. Mary's counties. Fairway Village, the third of five villages that will comprise St. Charles, includes an active adult community scheduled for construction in the Glen Eagles neighborhood. There are also ongoing road construction projects beneficial to all of Charles County.

One of the ways that a planned community can weigh its success is if the homes they offer maintain their value and appeal while also easing the pressure to develop remaining open space. ACPT's community of St. Charles has proven successful in this area for more than 30 years.

Today, 35,000 people call the growing community of St. Charles home. Statistically, this number includes approximately one-third of all Charles County residents.

The community's balance with commercial space has proven to be a plus for Charles County as well. It is home to the largest regional mall in the county, the 1.1 million-square-foot St. Charles Towne Center Mall—one of the largest generators of property tax, and the largest source of state sales tax, in the county. Adjacent to this property is the St. Charles Towne Plaza, a 400,000-square-foot shopping center. The Simon Property Group developed both properties.

A significant factor in St. Charles's success is the vital role its residents play in the daily and routine management of their communities. Charged with maintaining the architectural diversity and integrity of the community, volunteers sit on the St. Charles Planning and Design Review Board, assuring that all site plans are approved and meet community requirements. In addition, the community is governed by a three-tiered neighborhood management system, which includes neighborhood associations, townhome associations, and village councils, each sharing in the responsibility for storm water management, as well as maintaining pools, common areas, and neighborhood centers.

At more than 9,000 acres, ACPT's St. Charles is considered a case study in optimal mixed-use land development. By 2035 St. Charles will have a population of 65,000 in a high-density area that does not sacrifice any aspect of healthy living, and at the same time adding to the community's prosperity and to the health and stability of Charles County. In October 1998 ACPT became a publicly-traded company on the American and Pacific Stock Exchange under the symbol APO.

Today, J. Michael Wilson, son of James Wilson, is ACPT's current CEO and chairman, while Ed Kelly serves as president and COO. They will lead both the company and the community into the next dynamic stage of growth in Maryland and beyond.

Bottom left: Part of the Dorchester Mews community in St. Charles. Through arterial land use and design, St. Charles' neighborhoods average about three homes per acre, preserving open space within and outside of the planned community.

Bottom right: Village Lake apartments in the Wakefield community of St. Charles. St. Charles currently includes just over 2,000 apartments that provide a mix of housing for people from all walks of life, from young families to senior citizens.

AMERICAN MICROWAVE CORPORATION

American Microwave Corp. (AMC) began operations on September 5, 1978, in the Damascus, Maryland, residence of its founder, Raymond Sicotte. Raymond was born and raised in Waltham, Massachusetts, and graduated with electrical engineering degrees from Northeastern University in Boston and The University of Connecticut in the mid-1960s. He went to work in the Satellite Communications Division of MIT Lincoln Laboratories in Lexington, Massachusetts, upon graduating as a microwave electronics design engineer. He moved his family to Maryland in 1969 to accept a staff position at Comsat Laboratories in Clarksburg, Maryland, designing advanced microwave solid state circuits and systems for the burgeoning commercial satellite communications industry.

By the time the workload at Comsat Labs slowed down, Raymond and his wife Margaret (Peggy) realized they had fallen in love with the central Maryland area and decided to start American Microwave Corporation in order to remain in the area and raise their family of three children. They took out a second mortgage of $12,000 on their residence to serve as the initial "seed capital" money, and Raymond began designing, manufacturing and selling the initial product lines, power dividers and switches. Margaret became the office manager, and son, Bradford, began building products as a teenager after school and on Saturdays.

With its motto "In Pursuit of Excellence Through Engineering," the company struggled to ship $40,000 in the first full year of operations in 1979. Sales were mostly to customers in the Washington, D.C., area. In 1981 the company expanded its product line to include microwave solid state switches and leased a 1,000-square-foot facility in Gaithersburg, Maryland, that spring. It shipped $100,000 in 1981 and $145,000 in 1982 with five full-time employees, as it expanded its customer base to New York, California and Canada.

Ashok Gorwara and Raymond Sicotte (left to right) holding the award as the SBA Exporter of the Year presented to AMC in 1999 by the Small Business Administration.

In 1984 the company moved to a 6,000-square-foot facility in Frederick, Maryland, as customer demands for its products required a staff of 15 employees to meet its production obligations. The company reached a milestone of $1 million in sales in 1985.

The year 1986 saw the introduction of another major product line, high precision, electronically variable solid state attenuators, a product with significant demand in the defense electronics market. Variable attenuators are circuits that add variable loss to a microwave signal as it passes through the circuit.

The company had developed a sales representative network across the U.S. by then, and began advertising in major microwave trade magazines. Margaret retired from the business to pursue her first love as a medical assistant. Bradford rose through the ranks from assembly to test department to sales and marketing, while he majored in electrical engineering at the University of Maryland.

Products were being sold to the UK, France, Italy and West Germany through the company's agents in western Europe, and 1986 also saw the first award for AMC. The U.S. Small Business Administration recognized the company as Small Business of the Region for 1986.

In 1990 Raymond had a chance meeting with his former colleague at MIT Lincoln Lab, Ashok Gorwara. Ashok had started and built two companies since his departure from MIT in the early 1970s. One was Planar Microwave International in California, and the other was Vitroc Elektroniks Ltd. in his native India. He had recently returned to America and was looking to restart in the microwave electronics industry with his new company, Planar Monolithics Industries (PMI), Inc. Raymond and Ashok decided to join forces, with each holding equity

American Mirowave Corporation's employees from its four companies.

positions in both AMC and PMI, and each having his own unique product line. Ashok not only brought additional sales and engineering design expertise to the organization, but also brought modern management and organizational techniques from his training at the Sloan School of Business Management at MIT.

The combined AMC/PMI operations grew steadily through the 1990s in spite of the downturn in the Defense Electronics Market. Growth was most dramatic in international sales as that sector grew from 7 percent of total sales in 1990 to 25 percent in 1996.

In April 1997 Ashok and Raymond formed a third company, Planar Electronics Technology (PET), Inc., to address the burgeoning requirements for solid state amplifier products at AMC and PMI, as well as the Defense Electronics and the commercial electronics markets.

In October 1998 Ashok and Raymond formed Planar Filter Company (PFC) to address an urgent need for filter and switched filter products in the marketplace. It employs the solid state switch technology developed at AMC and combines it with state-of-the-art filter products to serve both the commercial and military markets.

In 1999 AMC won its second SBA Award as Exporter of the Year for the Maryland Region for having exported over $1 million in business to customers outside of the U.S.

With a common management philosophy of managing from the ground up as well as from the top down; building relationships with each and every customer; employing a Total Quality Management System with authority, responsibility and accountability for each employee's assigned job; and installing a comprehensive financial and operational Management Information Systems—all four companies continue to grow and flourish today.

The four combined companies produce a wide variety of microwave electronic products that are employed on electronic defense platforms, such as the Patriot Missile Radar System, APR-46 radar warning receivers for the Hercules C-130 and other military aircraft, as well as critical parts for radar and avionics

systems on the F-15 and F-5 fighter aircraft. The companies' products also form vital parts on electronic support systems such as radar simulators used to develop stealth aircraft and other vehicles—as well as test sets used to verify proper operation of radar warning receivers and radar jammers on military aircraft prior to critical missions over hostile territory. The products of PET and PFC support commercial communications systems requirements.

The combined operations currently lease 15,000 square feet of space in four locations and provide work for 40-plus employees in and around Frederick, Maryland.

Logarithmic amplifier produced by American Microwave Corporation.

AMERICAN REGISTRY OF PATHOLOGY

"This site provides information about the pathogenesis and imaging of inhalational anthrax. The content represents the combined efforts of the Armed Forces Institute of Pathology and the American Registry of Pathology, Washington, D.C. We invite collaboration with other institutions that have experience with anthrax. Our goal is to provide information that improves the understanding and recognition of inhalational anthrax."

This statement, taken from the Armed Forces Institute of Pathology's (AFIP) Pulmonary and Mediastinal Pathology website, provides a good example of the work undertaken by the AFIP and facilitated by the American Registry of Pathology (ARP). Formally recognized by Public Law 94-361 in 1976, ARP was originally founded as a medical society in 1921 by the American Society of Ophthalmology. Today it continues to serve as AFIP's liaison to the civilian medical community. ARP assists the AFIP by serving as a mechanism to perform diagnostic consultation, education and research to benefit the U.S. military and the civilian medical community worldwide.

Both AFIP and ARP have undergone monumental changes since their inceptions. AFIP, founded in 1862 as the Army Medical Museum to study diseases and injuries sustained during the Civil War, operates today as the pathology reference center for the Departments of Defense and Veterans Affairs. ARP, under the guidance of Executive Director William Gardner, M.D., serves as AFIP's nonprofit link to the worldwide medical community. ARP facilitates many of AFIP's activities, including offering individual diagnoses to civilians and member of the military; offering, both nationally and internationally, over 50 annual post-graduate continuing educational courses in diagnostic pathology for thousands of pathologists, medical and scientific professionals; offering a large number of fellowships and other training opportunities; annual symposia consisting of special lectures in various disciplines for members of the medical profession; and publishing

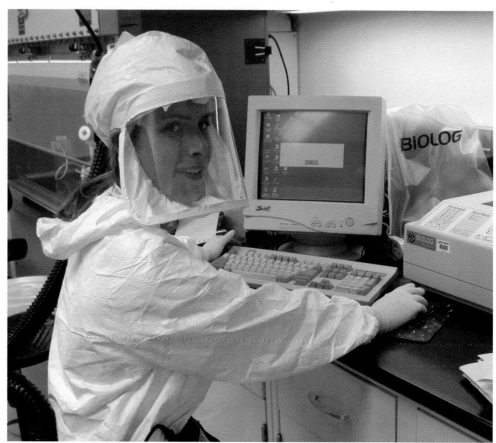

Dana Kadavy, Ph.D., prepares tests for biochemical identification of Bacillus anthracis conducting critical anthrax testing following the October 2001 attacks.

and marketing pathology textbooks. In 2001 alone, AFIP provided over 500,000 hours of professional post-graduate education.

That same year, AFIP's Center for Advanced Pathology performed diagnostic consultations on over 100,000 cases worldwide. The services offered through AFIP are "tertiary," constituting a second opinion option for cases where there is a real need for advanced diagnoses. ARP's initial establishment as a medical registry serves the institutions well in this respect: AFIP's Department of Repository and Research Services maintains the National Tissue Repository, located at the Institute's Forest Glen Annex in Silver Spring, Maryland. The Repository contains over three million case files of pathogenic tissues relating to every imaginable illness, some as unusual as leprosy. Colonel Charles Pemble, AFIP's director of Field Operations and Force Health Protection, notes that the services are available "to anybody in the world," and that AFIP's diagnoses can represent "a last line of defense" in cases of very obscure illness.

Colonel Brion Smith, AFIP's chief deputy medical examiner and program director for the Department of Defense (DoD) DNA Registry, calls ARP a "fascinating, unique organization" and "a good idea for government," which is highly valued by the civilian community. In 1988 the Department of Defense established AFIP's Office of the Armed Forces Medical Examiner (OAFME), located at AFIP's Annex in Rockville, Maryland, to provide the Department of Defense and other federal agencies with the latest advances in forensic medicine. The DoD DNA Registry became an early leader in the utilization of the polymerase chain reaction (PCR) of DNA to identify deceased service members. A system for collection, storage and testing using DNA identification methods was in place by the beginning of the Persian Gulf War in 1991, and it was used to establish the identity of two soldiers killed in that conflict. Most of the scientific and support staff assigned to the DoD DNA Registry are ARP employees.

The U.S. Army has always excelled in accounting for deceased military personnel, with recovery, identification and burial priorities since the American Revolution, when casualties were often identified by their fellow soldiers. The large number of casualties suffered during the Civil War led to soldiers wearing metal identification tags, and to the 1906 establishment of the War Department policy of issuing "dog tags" to every soldier. Fingerprints and comparisons of dental records helped identify the deceased during World Wars I and II and the Korean and Vietnam conflicts. Identification through DNA ushers in an era of unprecedented forensic diagnostic capabilities in an era of unprecedented "post-mortem challenges," including thermal injury.

December 1991 saw the formal establishment of the Armed Forces Repository of Specimen Samples for the Identification of Remains (AFRSSIR). In June

The American Registry of Pathology editiorial office, located in Silver Spring, produces publications which provide authoritative encyclopedic references for diagnostic medicine around the world.

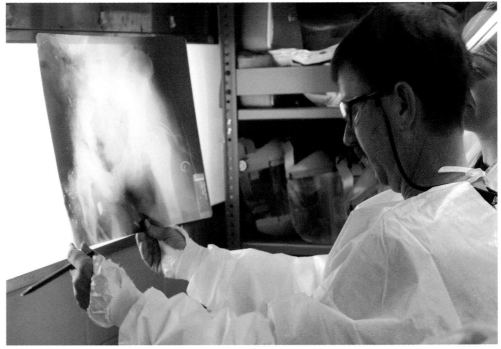

1992 the lab preserved sample DNA in the form of blood specimens and buccal swabs taken from U.S. Army trainees at Fort Knox, Kentucky. The goal of the new laboratory was "no more unknown soldiers." Between 1992 and 1999, similar collections would be made for military personnel deployed to Somalia, Rwanda, Haiti, Bosnia, Latin America and Kosovo. The new laboratory met its goal in part in May 1998 with its identifi-

Navy Commander Joe Hodge, a forensic pathologist, examines a radiograph during casualty identification operations. The Armed Forces Medical Examiner System is headquartered in Rockville, Maryland.

cation of Air Force Lieutenant Michael J. Blassie, interred in Arlington National Cemetery as Vietnam's "unknown soldier." Blassie was lost in May 1972 near An Loc, Vietnam. His remains were identified through tracking mitochondrial DNA, inherited only through maternal lines. Due in large part to AFIP's DNA expertise, historians, anthropologists, medical personnel and technicians at the U.S. Army's Central Identification Laboratory in Hawaii now had a means of identifying servicemen killed in earlier conflicts, including World War II and the Korean War, through reference specimens submitted by relatives of deceased service members.

In June 1993 OAFME assisted the FBI in identifying the remains of over 80 individuals who died during the Branch Davidian incident in Waco, Texas. Throughout the 1990s, the Office would assist in identifying passengers and crew members killed in national and international civilian air crashes, as well as Americans killed in terrorist bombings in Daharan, Saudi Arabia. In August 1998

in identifying victims killed during the terrorist bombing of the U.S. Embassy in Nairobi, Kenya.

OAFME would serve in an even more dramatic way during the fall of 2001. Following the terrorist attacks of 9/11, legal authorities confirmed the Pentagon as an area of exclusive federal jurisdiction, ensuring that the Armed Forces Medical Examiner held authority for the forensic investigation relating to victims of the attack. Over 100 AFIP personnel, led by the OAFME, participated in one of the most comprehensive federal forensic investigations in U.S. history. OAFME successfully identified 178 of the 183 Pentagon attack victims. AFDIL personnel played a critical role in the OAFME mission, providing DNA identifications on most of the Pentagon victims and on all 33 passengers and seven crew members killed in the hijacking of United Airlines Flight 93 near Shanksville, Pennsylvania.

Most core AFIP functions are conducted at the Institute's headquarters, located in Washington, D.C., on the Walter Reed Army Medical Center installation. It's there that AFIP Principal

Navy Captain Douglas Arendt, a forensic dentist, utilizes digital technology at an aircraft accident site to provide a dental radiograph identification. Digital technology often allows AFIP's forensic specialists, headquartered in Rockville, Maryland, to capture images in remote locations, helping to ensure quick and accurate victim identification.

Deputy Director Florabel G. Mullick, M.D., characterizes the Institute's Directorate for Advanced Pathology as its "virtual heart." Mullick's appointment in 1994 as associate director for the Center marked AFIP's first appointment of a woman to a senior position. She continues to serve as chair of AFIP's Department of Environmental and Toxicologic Pathology, which tracks environmental toxins and adverse drug reactions in tissues. The department also maintains registries on the effect of Kuwait oil fires on Desert Storm veterans, the effects of Agent Orange on Vietnam veterans and illnesses suffered by prisoners of war. The department also maintains databases for medical geology, radiation biology, environmental agents and arseniasis. The Department of Infectious and Parasitic Diseases Pathology features a web page dedicated to smallpox, including detailed descriptions of pathologic features, symptoms, epidemiology and complications.

ARP also facilitates numerous AFIP courses through the Institute's Directorate of Medical Education. Offerings include the Department of Hepatic and Gastrointestinal Pathology, with a "virtual" Gastrointestinal Biopsy Course, enabling any physician with Internet access to better recognize diagnostic features of "selected benign, malignant, infectious

At AFIP's Rockvelle, Maryland site. Dr. Jeffrey Taubenberger of the Armed Forces Institute of Pathology examines an x-ray film showing a fragment of the genetic sequence of the 1918 "Spanish" influenza virus.

and idiopathic diseases encountered in the human surgical pathology of the gastrointestinal system." Previous courses offered by the Department of Medical Education include the 48th annual course for the Pathology of Laboratory Animals and coursework in medical geology, health and the environment, co-sponsored by, among others, AFIP, the U.S. Geological Survey, and the United Nations Educational, Scientific and Cultural Organization (UNESCO). The Department of Medical Education online course offerings for 2003 include the online urologic pathology series, legal medicine and a biostat course for resident pathologists. The Department also offers slide study sets for a nominal fee to civilian residents, including a slide set on the pathology of AIDS. AFIP's "What's New?" category on its website includes informational web pages on anthrax, arsenic, monkeypox, SARS and smallpox. Information relating to the imaging and pathology of severe acute respiratory syndrome (SARS) represents the combined efforts of AFIP, ARP, the

Tan Tock Seng Hospital and Centre for Forensic Medicine in Singapore and the National Taiwan University Hospital in Taipei, Taiwan.

AFIP's excellence in providing educational resources is spelled out clearly in its Department of Hematopathology website, which includes cases submitted by the Department of Defense, the Department of Veterans Affairs, and civilian hospitals worldwide. This website includes a discussion of actual cases and includes tissue samples with histologic features—features discernible only by microscope. This virtual lab is further enhanced by offering links to PubMed, the medical literature search offered through the National Library of Medicine. The Department of Gynecologic and Breast Pathology offers similar features, with an online course "Breast Lesions That Mimic Carcinoma." The site's link to PubMed features medical abstracts authored by AFIP personnel.

AFIP has been distinguished since 1950 for the publication of its *Atlas of Tumor Pathology*, authored and edited at that time by a national group of academic pathologists. Since 1990 ARP has comprised the editorial, or produc-

Megan Tiemann, mitochondrial (mtDNA) technician, at AFIP's Armed Forces DNA Identification Laboratory, located in Rockville, Md, performs a DNA amplification test. AFDIL is one of the leading DNA laboratories in the world.

AFIP's National Museum of Health and Medicine hosts thousands of visitors each year.

tion, office for the *Atlas*'s publication, assuming responsibility for its layouts. Lead pathologists in the field, many from the international community, now collaborate in producing this publication, which can be found in almost any pathologist's office. The fascicles, or divisions of the *Atlas*, which are published in parts, are available in print and on CD. The purpose of the most recent Fascicle Series, the fourth, is to promote a consistent, unified and biologically sound nomenclature to guide surgical pathologists in the diagnosis of various tumor and tumor-like conditions.

U.S. Army Colonel (Dr.) Renata Greenspan, AFIP director, characterizes the National Museum of Health and Medicine as the "soul" of the institution. The museum also enjoys a lively history: after its founding in 1862, it moved in 1888 to the "Old Red Brick" building located on the Mall in Washington, D.C. In 1965 President Johnson proposed that "Old Red Brick" be donated to the Hirshhorn Museum and Sculpture Garden. The medical museum of the AFIP moved at that time to its current location on the Walter Reed installation. This site, formerly designated by President Eisenhower during the Cold War as the National Command Center, now houses the museum as a subdivision of AFIP. Museum exhibits include the bullet that killed President Lincoln and the probe used to find it, a spinalcord section with vertebrae from the spine of John

Wilkes Boothe, and a display, popular with children, of the lungs of both smokers and non-smokers. Members of the museum staff have been interviewed for the Discovery Health Channel, the Learning Channel, the History Channel and the National Geographic Channel. Museum exhibits cover a wide range of topics, from "Doctors at the Gate: The Public Health Service at Ellis Island" in 1998, to 1997's "Inside Out: Ninth National Art Exhibition of the Mentally Ill," to 2000's "Linus Pauling and the Twentieth Century: The Quest for Humanity."

The arrival of the electronic age has advanced the provision of AFIP's services exponentially, allowing physicians in the remotest corners of the globe to access slides of pathogenic tissue through a computer screen. With the electronic relaying of tissue samples among departments, in-house experts can now produce case diagnoses within four hours. Staff pathologists respond within 48 hours to 90 percent of submitted cases. Advances in forensic pathology continue as well: OAFME recently validated a system that traces the Y chromosome, potentially doubling the possibilities of identification through DNA material. AFIP—facilitated by ARP—continues to thrive, providing both military and civilian populations with an astonishing array of services.

AMERICAN SPEECH-LANGUAGE-HEARING ASSOCIATION (ASHA)

The association dates back to the spring of 1925, when a group of doctors led by psychologist Dr. Carl Seashore met in Iowa City, Iowa, to discuss the formation of an association for professionals with an interest in communication disorders. On December 29 of that same year, 11 clinicians and researchers formed the American Academy of Speech Correction, an organization separate from its original affiliation, the National Association of Teachers of Speech. The newly created association's mission was to ensure that individuals with communication disorders received the highest quality care from members, who were required to maintain certain standards of study and practical experience.

In 1930 the organization, renamed the American Society for the Study of Disorders of Speech, offered a major convention program, voted to start its first official publication, established membership requirements and approved an ethical practice statement.

In 1936 the society published its first journal, the *Journal of Speech Disorders*, later known as the *Journal of Speech and Hearing Disorders*. In 1947 the organization formally recognized the link between speech and hearing by changing its name to the American Speech and Hearing Association (ASHA).

In 1958 ASHA opened its first national office at 1001 Connecticut Avenue in Washington, D.C., under the direction of its first executive secretary, Kenneth Johnson, with one staff person to assist him. Membership had reached nearly 5,000, and the presence of a national headquarters drew increased attention to providing knowledge and setting professional standards for speech, language and hearing specialists. The association began accrediting academic programs and clinical facilities in 1962. By the end of 1965, with membership reaching 13,617, the association built a new national office at 9030 Old Georgetown Road in Bethesda, Maryland. New programs aimed at improving and expanding services to members and people with communica-

Fred Spahr, ASHA's executive director.

tion disorders continued. In 1969 ASHA included an Office of Multicultural Affairs as part of the national office structure. The purpose was to ensure that the association continually addressed the culturally and linguistically diverse issues related to its professionals and the millions of ethnic minorities with communication disorders.

By 1976 ASHA's membership had climbed to 24,466, and it became clear that a larger headquarters was required to house the organization. The association purchased 30 acres in Rockville, Maryland, the site of its existing offices. In September 1981, with membership at 36,096, ASHA had a new headquarters and a new name—the American Speech-Language-Hearing Association.

In 1980, during this period of dram-

atic change, Fred Spahr became the second executive secretary of the association, succeeding Kenneth Johnson. Spahr began his career at the association as associate secretary of professional affairs in 1970 and spent 10 years rising through the ranks. Throughout the 1980s, Spahr applied his core values and philosophies, helping transform the association into the model of management excellence that it is today.

ASHA continued to grow throughout the 1980s, as technology increased and changes were made in the provision of healthcare services. Benchmarks include the establishment of the ASHA Continuing Education Program in 1980 and the

ASHA Political Action Committee in 1985.

By the early 1990s, the association had made strides and broken ground in several important areas, including the expansion of ASHA's base member services and adding 32,000 square feet of space to its headquarters, for a total of 79,500 square feet. In an effort to deflect any increase in local traffic due to the expansion, ASHA began offering incentives to staff. Incentives included flex-time, telecommuting and subsidized public transportation. This was also the time Spahr realized his vision of creating an even more culturally diverse and inclusive organization at all levels. ASHA membership had topped 62,000.

In 1996 Spahr introduced another successful staff program team management. Recognizing that building and maintaining an effective team management process would be a time-consuming and sensitive process, Spahr made this a

priority. There is little doubt that this program has led to considerable improvements, including better research and planning, less damage control, lower staff turnover, and better products and services.

Spahr was also the driving force in developing many socially responsible initiatives, including a mentoring program at Garrett Park Elementary School, a recycling program recognized by Montgomery County leadership and hosting the NIH charities Film Festival. This commitment to staff and community has lead to ASHA being recognized as a "Great Place to Work" by *Washingtonian Magazine* and by the State of Maryland and Montgomery County Work/Life Alliance (1999–2002).

Today, as Spahr approaches retirement, the association boasts a membership of 111,000 members nationwide. During his tenure as the executive director, the

National Headquarters , 10801 Rockville Pike, Rockville, Maryland.

association has experienced tremendous growth of its membership by more than 300 percent, staff by 250 percent, budget by 800 percent, and assests by 900 percent. In addition, the organization's workforce reflects diversity in gender, race and ethnicity, age, sexual orientation and religion.

Through Spahr's leadership, ASHA has continually evolved and shifted to ensure that what began in 1925 would grow and flourish and will continue to do so as the association moves forward with a new leader at the helm. Based on a long history of positively impacting the lives of staff, the membership and people with communication disorders, we are proud and thankful for his service.

AMPORTS

With the massive volume of imports and exports passing through hundreds of United States ports, the task of efficiently processing products has become a major technical and logistical challenge. With more than 50 years of experience, AMPORTS is the largest portside processing company in the United States. The award-winning company processes more than 600,000 imported and exported automobiles on an annual basis, and has proven itself to be an innovative leader of the industry.

Founded in the late 1950s by Rudolph G. Hobelmann, who was originally a Customs Broker, the company was approached by Volkswagen of Germany, and started what was essentially one of the first port processing businesses in Baltimore, by watching over deliveries of the famous VW "Beetle."

In the early days of port processing, automobiles, such as the Beetle, were individually hoisted from cargo holds and slung onto the docks, a roughneck operation that often damaged the vehicles. On-the-spot repairs were frequently called for, and Hobelmann quickly expanded his

company to meet that need, bringing on mechanics to repair the new cars when necessary.

By the 1970s, the number of Volkswagens being shipped from Germany to Hobelmann's U.S. facilities had swelled into the hundreds of thousands. Seeing the inevitable growth of the port processing industry on the horizon, Hobelmann expanded his business to handle the increasing demand.

The former companies known as Hobelmann Port Services, Benecia Industries and Crown Auto Processing were com-

Mr. Davis on the left, talking with the shop supervisor in their Land Rover production shop.

bined under a single company name, AMPORTS. Since that day, the company has steadily met its goal of continued growth in global transportation logistics. AMPORTS, with 545 employees, processes import and export vehicles at four locations in the United States: Baltimore, Maryland; Benicia, California; Brunswick, Georgia; and Jacksonville, Florida.

"Location, location, location" has been a key to AMPORTS' success. Because of its excellent mid-east coast location, Baltimore has always been home base to Hobelmann and AMPORTS. Thirty-two percent of the U.S. population lives within overnight truck access of the city, and with 34 percent of the country's automotive manufacturing base within overnight truck access, it is both highly cost efficient and geographically advantageous to be based in Baltimore.

With overland transportation costs being a car manufacturer's biggest expense, AMPORTS allows companies to get their product as close as possible to their customer base no matter what coast they may be near, in the most efficient manner.

Success breeds success: AMPORTS' impressive processing record constantly brings the company more business. In 2002

Specialty designed shop for accessory installations.

in Baltimore alone, AMPORTS processed nearly 260,000 imported vehicles, a total of 82 percent of the import vehicle market entering through this mid-east port. For 2003 AMPORTS projects it will process approximately 97 percent of the total imported vehicles entering through the Maryland port.

Since its beginnings, Hobelmann Port Services has experienced changes to the organization and its ownership. California-based American Port Services acquired Hobelmann Port Services and its subsidiary, Crown Auto Processing, in 1996, financing the acquisition via a stock offering on the London Stock Exchange. The company's name officially became American Ports Services, Inc., and in 1997 acquired the airport management business, Johnson Control World Services, Inc., which operated, managed, and developed airports, fixed-base operations and other aviation-related facilities.

At the beginning of the 21st century, AMPORTS was purchased by British Ports, PLC, which operates more than 20 ports in the United Kingdom, including Southampton, Grimsby and Immingham. AMPORTS continues to operate under its own name in the United States. In a decision to focus AMPORTS' energies more completely on their port processing services, the company sold off their aviation division in July 2002.

All of AMPORTS' seaport locations provide state-of-the-art facilities that are necessary for the rapid and efficient handling and processing of vehicles. Today a single cargo ship can deliver several thousand cars in one load. These features include streamlined on/off pier loading, well-lit security storage areas and the latest in technological equipment for all car preparation and service tasks. All AMPORTS terminals provide complete distribution services, which include pre-shipment inspection, rail loading and unloading, marine damage surveys, and staging for shipboard loading and inland transportation.

Facilities and logistics at all of the company's ports are efficiently organized

and equipped to meet the demands of time-pressured manufacturers. Once the vehicles arrive, they are processed and shipped with minimum delay. High security facilities are available for all AMPORTS customers who have long-term or short-term storage needs. All of the company's ports provide a full range of processing services provided by highly skilled, well trained personnel using the latest technological tools.

Under the direction of AMPORTS' Chief Executive Officer, Jim Davis, the

All units are scanned to send location and other vital information to the computer via radio frequency.

Accessory installation is one of the many services offered by AMPORTS.

company has earned an industry-wide distinction for having the finest facilities and cutting-edge technologies for vehicle port processing and computerized inventory and control systems in the nation. For example, Davis looked to his team of in-house engineers to plan and build state-of-the-art body shops, resulting in seamless, streamlined and cost-efficient vehicle processing. The company uses IBM AS400 and Radio Frequency (RF) scanning equipment in the processing of the vehicles, and recently added a second AS400 to serve as an emergency backup system. In addition, the company purchased MIMIX software, which networks and updates information in real-time from all of the company's processing centers.

Davis is also credited with extensively expanding the company's international client list, which now includes: Hyundau and Kia, Mitsubishi Imports, Mitsubishi-Fuso Trucks, General Motors Exports, Ford Exports, Chrysler Exports, Mazda Exports, Suzuki Imports, Porsche Imports, Isuzu Imports, and the new PAG, which includes Volvo and Land Rover Imports. Forty percent of AMPORTS business comes from export processing with 60 percent originating from the import side.

In keeping with the policy of heightened sensitivity and responsiveness to its customers needs, AMPORTS employs state-of-the-art radio frequency barcode technology to track all vehicles entering and leaving the terminals, as well as identifying a vehicle's exact status and location in the facility on a seven day, 24 hour basis. With such precise systems in place, a complete rundown on an individual vehicle's status can be provided immediately upon a customer's request. With as many as 15,000 vehicles at the facility at one time, it is essential for the company to operate a tracking system with the most advanced ability to handle situations unique to the port processing industry. Each vehicle is tracked by its Vehicle Identification Number (VIN), so that a customer's product can be precisely located in the system within seconds.

ISO work instructions are followed by all technicians.

AMPORTS is authorized to deal with any transportation damage that may have occurred while the vehicles were *en route*. In the company's Jacksonville, Florida, location, AMPORTS works very closely with the Dupont Company, providing a highly advanced color lab. The company has specially designed and engineered car washes and has also created a special apparatus to remove the excess water from their car wash system.

Each AMPORTS facility has also earned the International Office of Standards (ISO 9000-2000) Certification, the updated version of (ISO 9000). This internationally-recognized benchmark of quality is awarded only after a company passes a strict audit of every phase of the processing operation. AMPORTS was the first port processor to attain this certification. Each AMPORTS facility is audited by the ISO every three months in order to maintain their certification, and the company continually adheres to its rigorous requirements.

In addition, most car companies also hold their own audits. Companies such as Ford, for example, send in their own team of experts to inspect the quality and performance of AMPORTS processing and staff. Setting the example by which other port processors are measured, AMPORTS has consistently been recognized by its peers and trade organizations as "outstanding port processor of the year." Automotive manufacturers such as Land Rover, Hyundai and Kia have named AMPORTS processor of the year several times, and the company also received the prestigious Chrysler Pentastar Award in previous years.

AMPORTS' continued success points to its outstanding leadership and innovative style. The company has reinvented the term "customer service" to meet the constantly changing demands of the 21st century. Davis, the company's CEO, believes a company's success cannot be measured solely by its technological edge, but by personalized service as well. His philosophy is that company executives should maintain an active relationship with their clientele, assuring them of the personalized service that they would not receive at any other port processing facility. To enforce that policy, AMPORTS executives make regular visits to their clients. Davis asserts that it is this personal touch, coupled with the company's quick response time in meeting their customers' special needs, that has made AMPORTS the high quality, award-winning port processor that it is, and enabled it to stand out above the rest.

APOGEE DESIGNS, LTD.

Apogee started life in a garage, financed growth on a Montgomery Wards card, and grew due to dogged determination, excellent clients, a Calvinist work ethic—and by shrewdly upgrading to a Sears card. Ideally situated minutes away from Johns Hopkins and less than an hour from the National Institutes of Health, Apogee has benefited from proximity to the amazing array of biotechnology companies in the Baltimore/Washington corridor.

In 1979, a small company by the name of Bethesda Research Labs (BRL) had the foresight to realize that researchers in the burgeoning field of molecular biology needed a source for chemicals, enzymes and apparatus. Until BRL, researchers not only did research but also had to make the basic molecular tools necessary for experiments that drove the biotechnology revolution over the following decades. At that time, experimental apparatus was made in university shops at great expense and with varying degrees of expertise. Which is to say, it leaked. That's not an attractive feature when you're running thousands of volts through it on a wet bench top. Lab technicians wanted to be sure that touching the wrong place wouldn't turn them into a smoking briquette. The time was right for a reliable supply of standardized, high quality, engineered apparatus. Apogee had the talent and equipment, and was in the

Model S2 DNA Sequencing Gel Electrophoresis Apparatus.

right place at the right time, to answer the need.

Apogee's close relationship with BRL resulted in numerous electrophoresis units and led to development of the S2, a then-revolutionary DNA sequencer that shortly became the world standard. It is still sold today and is routinely seen on lab benches during PBS programs describing paternity suits, crime scene evidence and the DNA macromolecule. Apogee stuck by BRL through some dark days, and prospered when it morphed into Life Technologies, a $450 million dollar company and one of the few molecular biology firms to make money.

Apogee has developed core competency in electrophoresis, fluid transfer (micropipettes, pumps), hollow fiber bioreactors and benchtop research equipment. They made the units that Cellmark used to test the blood of a glove-challenged ex-Hertz spokesperson. Recent projects include equipment designed for Exact Sciences as part of their innovative and extremely sensitive DNA-based colorectal cancer test.

Sunrise™12·16 separates preparative and analytical quantities of nucleic acids (e.g. DNA) in submerged 12 x 16 cm agarose gels.

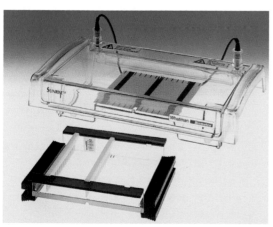

Telecommunications has established itself as another growth industry in Maryland. It's not unusual for companies to have exceptional technology but no expertise in the design and production of a housing to hold it. For lack of a case or label, a product doesn't ship. Investors become agitated, venture capitalists make nasty sounds and competitors get the sale. Apogee—easily accessible from the BWI airport and the web at www.apogeedesigns.com—provides industrial design and manufacturing expertise on a cost-effective basis. Maryland's technology-based firms have provided Apogee with ample opportunities to bring design, engineering and production value to scientists and engineers charged with taking new technology and making it old.

While the spirit of innovation remains the same, the garage is now bigger, the equipment is automated and the credit cards are used strictly for lunch.

BALTIMORE BASILICA OF THE ASSUMPTION

The Basilica of the National Shrine of the Assumption of the Blessed Virgin Mary, built from 1806 to 1821, was America's first cathedral. Beyond a beautiful Catholic cathedral, the Baltimore Basilica stands as what Pope John Paul II has called "a worldwide symbol of religious freedom." Both historically and presently, the Basilica proclaims that religious freedom is as much a part of the foundation of the United States as political freedom.

The colony of Maryland, under the English Stuart kings, enjoyed benefits of religious freedom legally from 1639 until the Glorious Revolution in 1688. This is the first instance of a codified law establishing the premise of freedom of religion in the English speaking world. After 1688 until the American Revolution however, there were strict laws governing the worship of Catholics living in the colonies. Some wealthy Catholic landowners did secretly have priests and private

Artist Rendering of the Restored Baltimore Basilica in 2006. The restored Baltimore Basilica, under architect of record John G. Waite Associates of Albany, New York, will reflect the vision of Archbishop John Carroll and the design of Benjamin Henry Latrobe. The important symbolism of natural light will be reintroduced into the interior of the Church through both the nave windows and the 24 skylights which will again illuminate the interior of the cathedral. Use of light colors in the floor, pews and walls will also contribute to the symbolic nature of the cathedral as a place of openness and freedom.

Archbishop John Carroll 1790–1815, first Bishop of the United States and member of the very important Carroll Family (the wealthiest family in the America's at the end of the 18th Century). He is the visionary for the growth of Catholicism in the United States and played an integral part in the design and form of the Baltimore cathedral, with its architect Benjamin Henry Latrobe, the father of American architecture.

chapels for themselves, and those who worked for them and neighboring Catholics could share Mass on their property. The Carroll Family were one of these families and, one of the wealthiest in the colonies.

Secretly, brothers John and Daniel, along with their cousin Charles Carroll of Carrollton, were educated by English Jesuits in Flanders. John was ordained a priest and returned to Maryland to be a missionary. John, Daniel and Charles were staunch advocates of the American Revolution and fought for political as well as religious freedom. Charles was the only Catholic to sign the Declaration of Independence, knowing full well that if the American Revolution was lost, his own family's fortune was at risk just as the others who boldly challenged George III.

In 1784 John Carroll was nominated by the clergy in Maryland to be a superior of the Catholic Church, having

similar powers to that of a bishop. He was confirmed as Superior of the Missions in the 13 United States in 1784. Then, in 1789, Pope Pius VI created the Diocese of Baltimore with Carroll as its first bishop. John Carroll did a great deal to establish the Catholic Church in the new United States and was founder of Georgetown University in Washington, DC, as well. As bishop of one-third of the continental United States, he knew there would be a tremendous need for priests in the new nation. St. Marys Seminary was soon founded and became the primary educational institution for priests in the United States.

With no cathedral in the new diocese of Baltimore, John Carroll recognized his obligation to build one in Baltimore. There was a small, simply constructed Mass House, St. Peter's, already in existence; however, Carroll wanted to make a statement with his new cathedral. It would come to symbolize the freedom for all who came to the United States in search of a new life. At the same time, the construction of the federal city (Washington, DC) had begun. Benjamin Henry Latrobe was appointed by Thomas Jefferson as Surveyor of the Public Buildings for the US government. Latrobe, the first trained architect in the US, volunteered his services to design the Baltimore Cathedral. The Capitol was being built and designed by Latrobe simultaneously, and he would commute between the two construction sites on horseback. Both buildings were constructed in the same timeless, Neoclassical architectural style. Thomas Jefferson gave a great deal of advice and counsel to Latrobe on architectural matters that benefited both the U.S. Capitol Building and the Baltimore Cathedral. The similarities in design and style of the two buildings would come to symbolize both freedom of politics and religion. The first cathedral was decidedly not Gothic, which would have harkened back to the Europe of old, but like the new nation at that time, moving forward. Built on a prominent hill in

The Pastoral Visit of Pope John Paul II, October 8, 1995. Cardinal Keeler was instrumental in having the Pope visit Baltimore in 1995. The Cardinal is a great historian and made a great effort to tell the story of Maryland's role as the place of religious tolerance in the English colonies as well as the great role subsequently played out in Baltimore and her cathedral as direct beneficiaries of freedom after the creation of the United States government. While in the Basilica, the Pope prayed intently before the Blessed Sacrament and blessed a large bronze plaque commemorating the great councils of Baltimore. (Pictured above from left to right is Monsignor James V. Hobbs, rector of the Basilica; His Eminence, William Cardinal Keeler and His Holiness, Pope John Paul II.)

Baltimore, Latrobe designed the building so that great amounts of natural light would illuminate the interior.

Unfortunately for Latrobe and the rest of the country, the British burned down the Capitol during the War of 1812. The Baltimore Cathedral, however, remained untouched, although construction was delayed for nearly 4 years. It was dedicated on May 31, 1821, by the third Archbishop of Baltimore, Ambrose Marechal. Neither John Carroll nor Benjamin Latrobe saw the first cathedral completed. Carroll died in 1815, and Latrobe died in 1820.

The Basilica plays a pivotal role in American religious history. It was the meeting place for three plenary and seven provincial councils that guided the

Roman Catholic church and its community as the country moved westward and grew in population. James Cardinal Gibbons, as spokesman for the Catholic Church, gained the respect of many Americans of all faiths when he spoke out for the common man and vehemently against the unfair working conditions of the second half of the 19th century. Visitors and dignitaries from all over the world have made the pilgrimage to the Baltimore Basilica. The website www.baltimorebasilica.org gives detailed information about its history and the events that have taken place, and are still taking place in the Basilica.

William H. Keeler was appointed Archbishop of Baltimore in 1989, and in 1994 Pope John Paul II made him a cardinal. Keeler is the driving force behind the restoration of the Baltimore Basilica. His intent is to restore the cathedral back to Carroll's original vision and Latrobe's original design. The most obvious change will be the reintroduction of the 24 skylights that once serenely lit the interior. Four have been restored, with the other 20 to be restored in time for the 200th anniversary of the Basilica in 2006.

The Baltimore Basilica reminds our nation and the world that religious freedom is as much a part of the greatness of the United States as is political freedom.

The Second Plenary Council of Baltimore, 1866. This etching portrays one of the services surrounding the Second Plenary Council of Baltimore, held just after the end of the Civil War. Besides being the first Catholic cathedral in the United States, the Baltimore Cathedral was the site of the consecration of many of the first bishops of the U.S., and it was the gathering place of the U.S. bishops for a whole series of meetings that took place throughout the 19th century. The Holy Father asked the Archbishop of Baltimore to hold periodic meetings of all the U.S. bishops in a successful effort to keep the rapidly growing Church in the United States together, despite the great pressures of westward expansion and tremendous immigration that marked 19th-century America.

BALTIMORE SYMPHONY ORCHESTRA

The internationally acclaimed Baltimore Symphony Orchestra (BSO) stands as Maryland's premier cultural institution, enjoying a preeminent position among the world's most recognized orchestras. Acclaimed for its uncompromising pursuit of artistic excellence, the BSO has attracted a devoted national and international following, while maintaining deep bonds throughout the Maryland community through innovative educational and community outreach initiatives.

In October 1997 the orchestra enhanced its tradition of excellence by hiring Yuri Temirkanov as the BSO's eleventh music director. Chief Conductor of Russia's legendary St. Petersburg Philharmonic, Principal Guest Conductor of the Danish National Radio Symphony Orchestra, and Conductor Laureate of London's Royal Philharmonic, Temirkanov was attracted by the BSO's history of artistic accomplishment.

The city of Baltimore established the BSO in 1916 as a branch of the municipal government, convinced that such a cultural institution would greatly enrich community life. The idea of bringing classical music into the lives of all of its citizens—not to just a privileged few—motivated the city administrators' efforts. Concertgoers in their 90s today recall attending the orchestra's educational concerts, a part of the orchestra's gift to the community since its inception. Nearly 50,000 school children now attend such concerts annually.

The BSO reorganized as a private institution in 1942. Philanthropist Joseph

An earlier and smaller BSO.

Meyerhoff introduced the orchestra's modern era, appointing Romanian-born conductor Sergui Comissiona in 1965 and building the orchestra's current home, Joseph Meyerhoff Symphony Hall, which opend in 1982. The new hall, built without flat walls or right angles to produce a rich, lively sound, provided a fitting setting for then Music Director Comissiona. Innovative programming and compelling performances characterized the tenure of this dynamic musician, who remains a beloved figure in Baltimore. In 1981 the BSO performed under his direction in East Germany, the first U.S. orchestra to do so.

Maestro David Zinman inherited Comissiona's orchestra in 1985, usher-

BSO Music Director, Yuri Termirkanov, leading his Baltimore orchestra in the Joseph Meyerhoff Symphony Hall. Photo by David Harp

ing in yet another era for the Baltimore orchestra—one characterized by international and critical acclaim. Critics, impressed especially with Zinman's championing of American works, hailed him as a formidable orchestral "educator." Zinman's newly revitalized orchestra traveled extensively overseas, marking his tenure in 1987 with critically acclaimed concert tours of Europe and the Soviet Union. The BSO represents the first U.S. orchestra to perform in

The interior of the 2,438-seat Meyerhoff Symphony Hall. Photo by Ron Solomon

The exterior of the Meyerhoff Symphony Hall. Architects: Pietro Belluschi, Inc. and Jung/ Brannen Associates. Photo by Richard S. Mandelkorn

Russia after the two countries resumed cultural relations following the war in Afghanistan.

During the BSO's first concert tour of East Asia in 1994, Japanese newspaper *Yomiuri Shimbun* hailed it as "the best of all the overseas orchestras" to perform that year in Japan, in a field that included the Berlin, Vienna and New York Philharmonics. The tour's stunning success prompted a return visit to Japan in 1997, with violinist Isaac Stern as guest artist. The East Asian tour provided a political as well as cultural venue for representatives from Maryland. Lieutenant Governor Kathleen Kennedy Townsend accompanied the tour as part of a trade delegation dedicated to exchanging opportunities in business and economic development. In so doing, Townsend followed a tradition of such liaisons established previously by Governor William Donald Schaefer and Baltimore City Mayor Kurt Schmoke.

In 1987 the orchestra responded to its new music director's guidance by winning its first Grammy award for Sony Classical recordings, featuring Yo-Yo Ma performing cello concertos by Samuel Barber and Benjamin Britten. Two Grammy awards followed in 1994 for *The New York Album*, again featuring cellist Ma under Zinman's direction. The BSO's *Casual Concerts* series was introduced in 1986 and heard on more than 150 radio

A BSO musician works with a local Baltimore elementary student at the BSO's annual "Musical Open House."

stations across the country. Audiences delighted in the orchestra's innovative and insightful presentations of classical works. Locally broadcast NPR programs currently include *Backstage at the BSO* and *Onstage with the BSO*.

The orchestra's focus on the importance of educational and community outreach programs sharpened considerably in 1995 with the BSO's Arts Excel program, a collaborative teaching effort for math, science, reading and language arts between the orchestra's musicians and selected area schools. Local first-graders could now differentiate between long and short vowel sounds through the strings of a violin. In 1989 the orchestra established its Community Outreach Committee, aimed at involving members of the area's African American community in all aspects of orchestral activities.

The effect of politics on culture was deeply felt during the aftermath of the World Trade Center bombings in September 2001. The BSO was the first U.S. orchestra to tour on European soil after that date. In November of 2001, Temirkanov conducted Beethoven's *Eroica*, the symphony dedicated to freedom from tyranny, at the Berlin Philharmonie. Audience members, some of whom may have witnessed World War II's devastation, listened closely to the symphony's second movement, its funeral march, as the Baltimore musicians attempted to translate the untranslatable.

Temirkanov may presage another orchestral renaissance in Baltimore: with the 1997 appointment to the BSO of this charismatic conductor, overall support in the form of gifts, capital improvements and endowments has risen consistently.

In Russia now, "the government doesn't give any money for culture," Temirkanov states. The maestro's "deeper, richer sonority" and "heightened expressivity," as described by *The Wall Street Journal*, will find a new venue in 2004, when the BSO takes up residence at its new secondary location, Strathmore Hall Performing Arts and Education Center in Bethesda, Maryland. This aspect of the BSO's continued development is an indication of the orchestra's determination to serve the entire state of Maryland, while growing artistically. He looks forward to performing within hailing distance of the National Symphony Orchestra.

In an interview with *Kultur aktuell* broadcast over Bavarian radio airwaves in November 2001, Temirkanov stated that the role of symphony orchestras within the context of recent terrorist bombings remains straightforward: "It's all about conveying spiritual values through music. Thus, as musicians, we can work our way into the fabric of society." He also states in an interview with *BBC Music Magazine* during that time that "however brilliant a recording, it can never reproduce the feeling that the music was born in that moment. That's what conductor and orchestra are always working for." The BSO, originating nearly a century ago as a branch of Baltimore's municipal government, continues to be at the heart of the community in Baltimore and through the state of Maryland.

BERETTA

Beretta is the oldest industrial dynasty in the world. Started in the early 1500s, the Beretta business has been in continuous family ownership for 16 generations. Both the family and company trace their origins back at least to the year 1500, when a lintel from a foundry bearing the Beretta family name was reportedly destroyed in a flood in Gardone Val Trompia, the small mountain town in northern Italy where the Beretta factory still operates today.

In the 1980s, a Beretta invoice submitted to the Venetian Republic by Bartolomeo Beretta was located in the Venetian archives. The invoice was dated 1526 A.D. and was for a shipment of arquebus barrels provided by Beretta to Venice, proof that the company was involved in the manufacture of firearm products from its earliest days of operation.

Beretta manufactured firearm barrels only until the late 1600s, at which time the company began making entire firearms. During subsequent centuries, the Beretta family manufactured elegant shotguns and rifles for sporting use, as well as small arms for military and law enforcement customers.

Beretta products today are noted for their graceful design and high quality. Beretta hand-engraved shotguns sell for up to $100,000 each, although well-made, affordable shotguns are also available for hunters and competitive shooters. The quality of these shotguns is confirmed not only by the number of people that own them worldwide, but also by the high level of accomplishment enjoyed by their owners. In the Atlanta Olympic games in 1994, for example, seven of the twelve Olympic medals won in shotgun-shooting

Cavaliere Ugo Gussalli Beretta, patriarch of the Beretta family.

Beretta Factory in Gardone Val Trompia, Italy.

in the early James Bond books, and Beretta pistols have been featured in numerous action and adventure movies, including *Die Hard* and the *Lethal Weapon* series.

Beretta entered Maryland history in the late 1970s when the Beretta family decided to establish its own manufacturing and service facility in the U.S. Located in Accokeek, Maryland, a group of investors bought the factory and office building that now house Beretta U.S.A. Corp. in 1977. The new company soon began importing Beretta products into the United States from Italy, as well as manufacturing small-frame, semi-automatic pistols for self-defense use and for use by police officers as backup weapons.

events were won using Beretta shotguns, including customers from China, Australia and Italy.

Beretta also manufactures high-quality, safe and reliable sidearms for use by law enforcement and military organizations and for civilian use. Ian Fleming wrote that a Beretta pistol was James Bond's favorite sidearm

The Beretta family has always insisted on the highest quality in its products. The Beretta motto is, "If it bears the Beretta name, it will be the best," and dramatic proof of the company's adherence to this motto came in 1985, when the U.S. Army chose the Beretta Model 92 9mm pistol as the standard sidearm for all branches of the U.S. Armed Forces. Originally employing

Beretta Wheelock Pistol dating to 1680–1690.

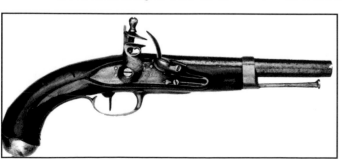

Beretta USA plant, located in Accokeek, Maryland.

about 20 people in the late 1970s, Beretta U.S.A.'s employment swelled to 500 employees by the late 1980s, as the company doubled its factory size and began the massive project of manufacturing hundreds of thousands of 9mm pistols for American soldiers, sailors and pilots. The U.S. military pistol contract was the most publicized small arms contract in the last half of the 20th century and Beretta U.S.A. soon became the second largest private employer in southern Maryland.

It is difficult to find a family in southern Maryland that has not been touched by the jobs created at the Accokeek, Maryland, Beretta facility. During the buildup to the first Iraq War in the early 1990s, the Beretta U.S.A. factory ran on three shifts, 24 hours a day, with Beretta pistols leaving the loading dock in Maryland and arriving in Saudi Arabia for immediate deployment to troops ten days later. Beretta pistols have been used in every major U.S. military engagement since the late 1980s, including prominent use in both Iraq campaigns, in Bosnia, Panama and Afghanistan. Beretta U.S.A. employees have always been proud of the role they have played in helping protect the safety of their country, the service personnel who defend the country and the causes of freedom toward which American military campaigns have been directed.

Beretta pistols are also carried by over a thousand law enforcement agencies in the United States and Canada, including the Maryland State Police, the Prince George's Police Department and such cities as Los Angeles, San Francisco and Chicago.

Begun in a small town in a narrow mountain valley in northern Italy almost 500 years ago, the Beretta company, family and tradition of excellence remain vibrant motivating forces in the Maryland economy today. Beretta Holding was established in the mid-1990s and established Benelli U.S.A. Corporation

Beretta gunsmith hard at work.

in Accokeek, Maryland in the late 1990s, dedicating that company to the importation of a sought-after line of high-quality sporting and tactical shotguns. Beretta Holding also purchased Stoeger Industries, publisher of *The Shooter's Bible*, a renowned reference book for firearms enthusiasts for almost 95 years, as well as numerous other sport-related publications. Beretta U.S.A. also expanded its activities by establishing a retail company that operates elegant retail stores on Madison Avenue in New York, and in Highland Park Village in Dallas, Texas.

By the late 1990s, with the acquisition of new companies and the growth of Beretta operations in Italy, in the U.S. and elsewhere, Beretta Holding stood as owner of the largest conglomeration of firearm manufacturing, sales and distribution companies in the world. With all of this change and growth, though, Beretta U.S.A. Corp. in Maryland and the other companies owned by Beretta Holding remain under the ownership and direction of Cavaliere Ugo Gussalli Beretta, patriarch of the Beretta family, and of his two sons, Pietro Gussalli Beretta and Franco Gussalli Beretta, with Franco's young son Carlo waiting in the wings for the day when he, too, will lead this remarkable family enterprise.

BEST AMERICAN AMBULANCE

Move over Horatio Alger and make some room in the Rag-to-Riches Hall of Fame for Willie Runyon.

What he invested in for more than 40 years of his business life has evolved into Best American Ambulance, the largest locally owned, locally operated, private ambulance service in Maryland.

Not bad for a kid from the hills, whose dirt-poor origins spurred him to a life of hard work, the accumulation of material things to enjoy, and an appreciation of the good life.

Upon his death in November 1999, Runyon had authored chapters in his life story that included service in the Army Air Corps during World War II, adventures as a vice cop for the Baltimore police department, pioneering the establishment of an ambulance service that existed on its own without a connection to a funeral home, and playing smoke-filled-room politics as a shaker-and-doer in the Maryland Democratic Party.

Runyon was born in 1923, in what is now known as Appalachia. His hometown was Delbarton, population under 1,000 in southwest West Virginia. The local folks measured distances over the hills by "hollers." Three "hollers" meant you had to climb to the crests of three hills to communicate your message.

"His father was a coal miner," said wife Pat Runyon. "His mother died a few months after Willie's birth. He was raised by whomever wanted to put up with him. He really had no home and had a very difficult childhood, which is what fueled his ambition to accumulate wealth."

As a boy, Runyon scoured the railroad tracks to pick up the coal that had fallen off the tenders. After she married Runyon, Pat visited his origins. "We swept the floor of his half-sister's home to get a layer of fresh dirt," she said. "I think that is the definition of dirt poor."

In his 16th year, Runyon took advantage of one of Franklin Roosevelt's New Deal programs to lift the nation out of the Great Depression and its economic doldrums. There was an initial stop in Charleston, West Virginia, for

"Why ride in a hearse befor your time?"

training before a trip to Baltimore, where "he talked his way into a job with Martin-Marietta," Pat said. "That was one of his talents—the ability to talk."

Another was "having a mind like a sponge." Runyon's formal schooling was practically nil, but he was "a natural learner." He was an intent listener and a keen observer.

"Willie would find somebody who knew how to do whatever he wanted to learn to do," she said, "and stick at it until he could do it better."

Whether from Appalachia or Arizona, young men were being swept up by the winds of war, and Willie Runyon was among them. Finding himself in the Army Air Corps, Runyon was trained as a pharmacist's mate and dispensed drugs at military installations, primarily at Sheppard Air Force Base north of Wichita Falls, Texas. Ironically, that's where his future wife's father was stationed.

His service record and familiarity with pharmaceuticals qualified him for Baltimore's police force, where his "street and from-the-sticks smarts" held him in good standing.

When founder Louis Orefice asked Willie to join him at the American

Ambulance and Oxygen Service Company, he hung up his badge in 1955. The firm's slogan was: "Why Ride in a Hearse Before Your Time?"

"Back in those days," Pat explained, "most ambulance services were part of funeral homes. They did the emergency runs, what we call the '911 work.' Before Lou, there was no private ambulance service. If you had to be transported horizontally to a hospital in a non-emergency situation, the funeral home's hearse would do it. Hence, Lou's slogan."

With Orefice's death, Willie assumed full control of the business. He, his first wife and their three children moved into the company's second-floor space and expanded the venture's fleet of ambulances that were maroon Cadillacs. "He took the business to the next level," Pat said. "He was something of a pioneer in the ambulance-service industry that at the time was hardly regulated."

Those days were destined to come to an end. Shortly after Pat went to work for the company in 1966, the onslaught of state and federal regulations started.

Mr. Runyon and some of his "colorful" fleet.

Willie was in the forefront of arranging for medical transportation to be included in a person's insurance coverage in the Baltimore area.

"For example, a person who needs dialysis requires transportation to get that service," she said. "Some can drive themselves, but others can't, especially those on limited incomes."

Yet, there was another side to the Medicare sword that greatly expanded coverage

The "Runyon" legacy continues with Best American.

of such medical services. The regulations piled up. What had been primarily a non-licensed brand of business became license-intense.

Fashioning his own kind of Manifest Destiny, Runyon began buying smaller ambulance companies, adding six in all to his holdings. He also absorbed a major competitor, Maple Hill Ambulance. "The story went that people only started a company," she said, "so that Willie would buy them out." He quickly became No. 1 in the Baltimore area.

"Willie's word was gold," she said. "It was his bond. If he told you there would be three ambulances in front of your house

when you needed one, you could take that to the bank. His word, his handshake, was better than any written contract."

Politics was almost a hobby. Willie was deeply involved in Democratic campaigns for mayor of Baltimore and senator from Maryland. He was a Democrat born and bred. He loved the back-room lure of politics.

His last name could not have fit him better. He mirrored a Damon Runyon character, like Nicely Nicely or Sky Masterson. He loved to gamble, to go to the race track, and to enjoy a social beverage or two.

Pat is a lifetime Baltimore resident. While attending a secretarial school, "a friend of a friend" told her Willie's company was looking for a person to handle the telephones from 4 to 11 at night. That fit well with her homework schedule and her yen to make spending money.

"I got caught up in the business," she said. "It gets into your blood. I had worked for my father, who had been an electrical contractor. I was used to being part of a family-operated business and to a high-standard work ethic."

She married Runyon, 20 years her senior in 1979, together they had a daughter, and the family business became a part of her. Upon his death 20 years later, the company, as the bureaucratic regulations and insurance providers kept up the pressure, started to flounder. Runyon, beset by illnesses, could not cope with the new stresses. "He was a Type-A personality," she said, "and still tried to run it as best he could."

When some relief was granted by regulators and lawmakers, the company began to right itself. Best American Ambulance was created by a merger on June 5, 2003. "We are sitting on the edge of greatness," Pat said.

"I worked a job that is worthwhile," she said. "I really enjoy getting up in the morning and heading for the office. I miss not being there. We are poised to move ahead.

"When you call us with an ambulance problem," she said about the local nature of the newly consolidated enterprise, "you don't get an operator in Phoenix, Arizona. You get a person right here in Baltimore."

BIORELIANCE CORPORATION

BioReliance Corporation, a Maryland fixture for more than 50 years, provides testing and manufacturing services to biotechnology and pharmaceutical companies worldwide. It works with companies from the largest to start-ups, with a range of government agencies, and has played a key role in major medical developments since the preparation of the first polio vaccine in the mid-1950s.

BioReliance, ticker symbol BREL, has been publicly traded on NASDAQ since 1997. From its headquarters in Rockville, it directs operations in the United States, United Kingdom and Germany. All told, it has more than 700 employees, serves more than 600 clients annually, and generated revenues in excess of $80 million in 2002, when sales grew almost 20 percent and earnings topped $10 million.

The company, a leading contract service organization, makes sure drugs and other products are safe and well-made. Its testing, development and manufacturing services support production of biologics (medicines and vaccines developed from living cells or tissues) and other biomedical products. Its services span the product cycle from early pre-clinical development through licensed production.

BioReliance performs all work under rigorous regulatory standards such as those employed in its Mycoplasma testing facility.

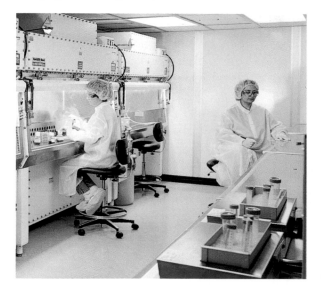

In 1985 BioReliance completed the first new laboratory in the Shady Grove Life Sciences Center, located along Montgomery County's now-famous I-270 corridor, later named "DNA Alley."

The company has two divisions. Testing and development evaluates products to make sure they don't contain disease-causing agents or have negative side effects, and that they are pure and stable. Manufacturing develops unique production processes to make microbial and viral products for clinical trials and for sale by clients.

BioReliance emphasizes customer service and support. It provides established companies streamlined product development, reducing time to market. It supports early stage companies that may lack the resources to pursue many aspects of product development. For all, it is a cost effective alternative to internal development and manufacture.

The company began as Microbiological Associates (MA). Founded in 1947 in Coral Gables, Florida, by Charles E. Bender, it produced serum ultra filtrate for the newly emerging tissue culture field. Dr. Samuel Reeder bought MA in 1951 and relocated it to Bethesda, Maryland, where it became the first commercial supplier of cell cultures and reagents.

Four years later, MA established its first contract research and development program with the U.S. government and the National Foundation for Infantile Paralysis to support development and production of the first polio vaccines.

Soon, MA began producing viral diagnostic products and entered its first contracts with the National Institutes of Health (NIH) and the National Cancer Institute (NCI). These led to MA developing new technologies for disease diagnoses of laboratory animals, including the Mouse Antibody Production (MAP) test.

Through contracts with the National Aeronautics and Space Administration, MA supported development of safety testing protocols for lunar samples brought back from the moon in 1969.

Also in 1969, MA was the first bio-science company acquired by California-based Whittaker Corporation. MA remained in Maryland, developing new diagnostic products for human infectious diseases. During the first half of the 1970s, the company was the largest contractor to the NCI and added the Food and Drug Administration (FDA), Environmental Protection Agency (EPA), Department of Agriculture and Department of Defense (DoD) to its client base. In 1978 it became the first to license and market an ELISA diagnostic test of any kind, for detection of cytomegalovirus.

In 1979 Whittaker divided MA into two parts. Testing services remained under the MA name while the tissue culture media, sera and diagnostic products businesses became a division called MA BioProducts. This division was eventually spun off as BioWhittaker and remains a leading manufacturer and marketer of research reagents and diagnostic products in Maryland.

The next year, MA began expanding its commercial development and testing services as an early Contract Services Organization. It created a biotechnology services division to pioneer new safety tests for the emerging biotechnology industry and worked with Genentech, Inc., to establish the original biosafety testing program for Activase®, the first licensed therapeutic derived from mammalian cells.

Isolation of test samples is prescribed to avoid possible contamination and maintain their integrity as much as to protect laboratory personnel.

In 1982 MA acquired EG&G Mason Research Laboratories in Rockville, establishing itself as one of the leading genetic toxicology laboratories in the world. In 1983 it began biosafety testing for the first licensed therapeutic monoclonal antibody product, Ortho Pharmaceutical's Orthomune OKT®3.

The next major corporate change came in 1984 when Daryl Laboratories bought MA from Whittaker. It retained the Microbiological Associates name for the merged company and moved product development and manufacturing operations from California to Maryland.

In 1987 MA moved most of its laboratories to a new state-of-the-art, award-winning, 40,000-square-foot facility in Rockville's Shady Grove Life Sciences Center. It also started expanding outside the United States, hiring an agent to represent its services in Japan.

The next few years contributed several business firsts: Testing for the first genetically engineered microbial pesticide approved by the EPA for field trials; MA's first major R&D collaboration with another company, which included an NIH contract to develop and validate a transgenic mouse for safety testing of chemical products; becoming the first U.S. biologics testing

Highly computerized biotechnologies, including Polymerase Chain Reaction (PCR) methods, are used routinely in the testing procedures of the company.

In 1997 BioReliance celebrated its 50th anniversary. At the podium is Capers McDonald.

contract research organization to establish its own international laboratory, incorporated as a wholly owned subsidiary in Stirling, Scotland; development of testing protocols and evaluation of the first gene therapy products allowed into human clinical trials by the FDA; being the first CDC-approved commercial laboratory approved for testing simian filoviruses, including Ebola and Marburg; first to commercialize models for validating purification processes to remove or inactivate agents such as mad cow disease and other transmissible spongiform encephalopathies from biologically derived materials; and safety testing of the first liver transplanted from a baboon to a human.

In 1992 MA produced recombinant adenovirus for the treatment of cystic fibrosis on contract for the NIH. That same year, Capers McDonald joined the company as president and CEO and put together the management team that positioned MA for its Initial Public Offering (IPO) five years later.

In 1993 McDonald co-founded a wholly

owned subsidiary—the world's first independent contract manufacturer for viral-based products, particularly gene therapies and vaccines.

In 1995 MA was selected as "High Technology Firm of the Year" from among more than 200 members of what is now the Technology Council of Maryland.

The next year, MA established an international Scientific Advisory Board to help advance new assay developments. Its first four members were experts from Germany, California and New England. It acquired BIOMEVA GmbH of Heidelberg, Germany, a successful manufacturing organization offering fermentation services using recombinant and natural microorganisms—and the company was named Employer of the Year by the Montgomery County Private Industry Council.

BioReliance Corporation was established in 1997 as parent to all of MA's subsidiaries. It completed its Initial Public Offering on August 1 and began trading on NASDAQ. It collected multiple contracts from NIH and one from the National Institute of Environmental Health Sciences to evaluate transgenic animal models for accelerated cancer risk assessment that shortened the "in-life" portion of long-term carcinogenicity studies from two years to six months. The company celebrated its 50th anniversary on September 24 by breaking ground for a new 50,000-square-foot headquarters and laboratory facility located among its other facilities in Rockville.

Expansion continued with ground breaking in 1998 for a 58,000-square-foot biologics manufacturing facility in Rockville.

In 2000 DynPort LLC selected Bio-Reliance as the principal provider for development and manufacturing services supporting the U.S. Defense Department's Smallpox Vaccine Biodefense Program.

The new millennium was marked by additional recognition of BioReliance. The company was named Emerging Business of the Year by the Montgomery

The corporate headquarters was designed to host visits from the company's worldwide clientele.

County Chamber of Commerce in 2001, and its U.K. subsidiary received the Export Award 2001 from the Scottish Council for Development and Industry. Its stock was ranked 66th nationally among 100 Hot Stocks for 2002 by *Bloomberg Personal Finance* magazine and

was added to the Russell 3000 Index. *Equities* magazine and Adelphi University honored the company's annual report with a Gemstone Award. In 2003 BioReliance ranked 11th among *Fortune Small Business* magazine's 100 fastest growing companies, and third on the *Washington Business Journal's* regional list of Largest Biotechnology Companies. The company received a national "Stevie" award for Best Investor Relations Program and was selected as the Capstone Company for the annual MBA Capstone Case Competitions of Johns Hopkins University School of Professional Studies in Business.

As CEO, Capers McDonald has successfully guided the growth of BioReliance since 1992. Here he is addressing guests celebrating the opening in 2001 of the company's 58,000-square-foot U.S. manufacturing facility in the Shady Grove Life Sciences Center.

BioReliance President and CEO Capers McDonald put together the dynamic management team that brought the company public in 1997 after five years of nearly 25 percent compound annual growth. The effort raised more than $32 million for growth and expansion.

Mr. McDonald championed information systems to improve business

effectiveness and efficiencies and led to the establishment and expansion of manufacturing services in the U.S. and the U.K.—and the acquisition of operations in Germany.

Chair of the Technology Council of Maryland, with about 700 member companies, Mr. McDonald is a founder and past chair of the Maryland Bioscience Alliance, and a member of the Maryland Governor's Commission on Development of Advanced Technology Business, the Board of Visitors for the *Washington Business Journal* and a range of other organizations.

He was named the 2002 Greater Washington Entrepreneur of the Year in the Life Sciences by Ernst and Young, one of the region's Ten Most Admired Bosses by *Techway* magazine, one of Maryland's "Power Elite" by *Warfield's Business Record*, and recipient of the Leadership in Technology Award of the Technology Council of Maryland.

Mr. McDonald holds an M.B.A. from Harvard, a master's in engineering from MIT and a bachelor's in engineering from Duke, as well as device patents in both the U.S. and Europe.

THE ASPEN GROUP

The Aspen Group of Maryland, a full-service staffing solutions provider, is firmly rooted in the belief that faith is essential to the company's success. Armentha "Mike" Cruise, founder of the business which has branched out to become the ninth largest temporary services company in the D.C. metropolitan area, credits her spiritual belief system with providing and guiding her every step.

Cruise served in the human resources department of the Mid Atlantic Region of Bell Atlantic for 23 years. In the '80s, the utility giant offered salaried buyouts in return for early retirement to many upper management staff members. Cruise, a longtime believer in having dreams and working diligently to make them reality, accepted the offer. She used her years of experience and the finances from the buyout to establish her own business.

She formulated a business plan, and with the help and support of her husband, Bob Mills, Cruise opened the doors to her staffing firm in Takoma Park, Maryland in 1988. Moving forward, she used a personal mission statement derived from a poem by Goethe as a compass: "That the moment one definitely commits oneself, then Providence moves too."

Cruise has always recognized that the tone is set at the top; therefore, she serves as an example with her spirituality to those who work for her. When a problem arises, Cruise encourages prayer with staff members. Through evoking divine order, she and her team are prepared for challenges.

And there have been many challenges over the years. At one point, The Aspen Group lost their largest client due to political difficulties. This was the contract she says "we lived on." Although the news was devastating, she realized there was a greater power to whom she could turn with her problems.

Cruise phoned her team to tell them that the contract was no longer theirs. Although the news was disappointing, the staff had something important to tell her

President and founder Armentha "Mike" Cruise.

as well. A major telecommunications com-pany called that very day and awarded them an even larger contract. Cruise considers this event not as a twist of fate, but the result of faith, a sort of divine intervention that allowed her, her employees and the company to move forward.

Over the past 15 years, The Aspen Group has grown its locations, services and sales figures dramatically. The company's growth is proof of its slogan: "Like the Aspen Tree that covers the forest, we cover the globe." The company has grown to be a $20 million revenue producer on an annual basis. Their commercial client list includes MCI, Marriott, Verizon, Lockheed Martin, Bank of America and UPS.

The Aspen Group has continued to be independently operated in an industry dominated by franchises. As Cruise likes to say, "We started from scratch and have remained completely self-sufficient. We know who we are and we know whose we are."

The high profile of a successful business-woman has given Cruise the opportunity to send a strong message. With great conviction she encourages others—whether in daily interaction, or speaking

to groups—to never give up. She proudly tells of her faith in the hope that someone who may be in the throes of adversity, as she has been, will understand that a strong belief will bring answers.

The Aspen Group has made a name for itself as the deserved recipient of many prestigious awards. The company has been named Business of the Year by the D.C. Chamber of Commerce and included in the Inc. 500 for two consecutive years. Cruise has received recognitions such as the National Supplier of the Year Award, the *Working Woman Magazine* Award for Excellence in Customer Service, recognition from *Fortune* magazine and the National Association of Women Business Owners, as well as awards from the Minority Supplier Development Council.

The Aspen Group continues to grow and flourish, providing first-rate professional staffing and human resources solutions. The future holds great promise for The Aspen Group and Cruise, as they move forward covering the globe with her unique style, passion, award-winning service, and above all the ability to believe.

CENSUS FEDERAL CREDIT UNION

From home equity loans to home banking, Census Federal Credit Union has a 55-year history of exceptional service to its members. The Suitland, Maryland, institution was created to provide financial services to employees of the Census Bureau. A branch office was opened in Jeffersonville, Indiana, in 1967.

Today membership has expanded to include 16 employers, or SEG groups. Among these groups are the Census Bureau, GSA Administration Services Maryland-East, Floyd County Government, Indiana Auditor's Office, Clark County Government, Clark Memorial Hospital, Jeffersonville Library and Visiting Nurses Association.

President and Chief Executive Officer Pamela Hout is proud of the organization's tremendous growth in the past two years alone. In 2002 CFCU received the superb rating of 1 (out of a possible 5) by the National Credit Union Administration. This year CFCU was recognized as one of the Top 100 credit unions in electronic services in the nation.

"The staff, the Board of Directors, the supervisory committee—we all worked

The Annual Meetings are held in the Auditorium at the Census Bureau Conference Center.

Dorothy Winslow, chairperson of the Board of Directors.

really hard," says Hout. "Any suggestions the NCUA recommended were implemented. We also tried to do technological improvements to make the job easier and more efficient."

Although she would humbly refuse to take credit, Hout is a major reason for the credit union's recent successes. A native of the small town of LaVale in western Maryland, Hout always had an interest in business and finance. She earned a degree in business manage-

ment from Frostburg State University and soon thereafter landed her first job in the banking industry. She worked for First Federal Savings Bank in Cumberland for eight years in a variety of roles, including teller, teller supervisor, accountant and branch manager.

In 1993 she moved to Rockville and worked for three years in the accounting department of NIH Federal Credit Union. Hout then returned to the banking industry as an accounting manager for Columbo Bank in Bethesda. Looking for an opportunity to advance her career, Hout applied for the Chief Financial Officer position at Census Federal Credit Union in 1999 and got

Eli Serrano, vice chairman of the Board of Directors.

the job. In August 2000 she was promoted to Chief Executive Officer. And the rest is history.

Hout has implemented new services and technological innovations that set CFCU apart from other credit unions. From her background in banking, Hout saw there was a demand for savings bonds. Now CFCU issues and redeems savings bonds. She also abandoned the former practice of recording check images on microfilm and converted to a CD storage system. The new imaging system takes front and rear pictures of checks. The image of the check can easily be viewed on a computer screen.

Francis Boucher, treasurer of the Board of Directors.

CFCU offers a variety of loan services, including loans for new and used automobiles, home equity and signature loans. The company offers Visa Classic and Gold credit cards, debit cards and ATM cards, as well as money orders and traveler's checks. They even sell stamps. Several savings account options are available. The main share accounts and Christmas Club accounts are among the most popular. Money market accounts and certificates such as IRAs are also offered.

Electronic banking services are in demand, and CFCU was quick to meet the challenge. Home banking is simplified thanks to the institution's user friendly website. Customers can complete a loan application or apply for a savings account in the comfort of their own homes. Through the automated teller system, called "Day and Night Audio" or "DANA" for short, customers can dial in to do balance inquiries, transfer funds, make loan payments or conduct other related business 24 hours a day, seven days a week.

To be eligible to participate in the credit union's services, a $50 savings account deposit is required. Members must be employees or family relations of employees who are active or retired from the Census Bureau or the other SEG groups. Ownership entitles members to vote for those who serve on the Board of Directors. Members also receive a copy of the credit union's quarterly newsletter, *New Horizons.*

Strong support from the staff and the Board of Directors has made Hout's sometimes-hectic job a lot easier. The employees of Census Federal Credit Union provide exemplary member service and are dedicated to making a difference within the credit union movement. The staff is committed to serving its membership and through their dedication and due diligence this goal is accomplished. Together, employees position the credit union to flourish, helping ensure the quality and level of service to its members.

The Board of Directors tirelessly volunteer their time, knowledge, and never hesitate to serve the credit union. They are committed to providing their members with the best customer service and participate in promoting the credit union's growth as an institution of strength and stability. Furthermore, the Board of Directors continues to explore

Roberta Carter, ATM/Vista coordinator, assists Christopher Volatile, supervisory committee chairman, with information on his account.

Terri Vance, senior loan officer, processes a loan application for a member.

exciting opportunities and challenges to meet the fast paced technological future.

The supervisory committee has been instrumental in the overall success of the credit union. One of these exemplary volunteers is Christopher Volatile, a telecommunications employee of the Census Bureau located in Suitland, Maryland.

Volatile was honored as the "Volunteer of the Year" by the National Association of Federal Credit Unions in 2002, representing credit unions with less than 150 million in assets. As Chairman of the Supervisory Committee, Volatile has worked hard to improve the overall efficiency of credit union operations.

He negotiated and received permission from the Census Bureau to utilize the Census E-mail network. Under Christopher's leadership, he arranged for video teleconferencing capabilities to be done through the Census Bureau, thereby reducing travel expenditures for the Board of Directors. Most importantly, Census Federal Credit Union now receives telephone service provided by the Census Bureau at greatly reduced rates. This improved service significantly reduced monthly operating expenses by thousands of dollars in local and long distance costs. Christopher was also successful in implementing uninterrupted power sources for the credit union's Audio Response and automated teller machines in Suitland.

CLARK CONSTRUCTION

A. James Clark, chairman and CEO of Clark Enterprises, Inc., and the chairman of the executive committee, one of the largest privately held general contractors in the U.S., The Clark Construction Group, Inc., is a man with a great reputation. And, to Clark, that ranks higher than any accolades he could ever receive. It is his character, entrepreneurial spirit and never-say-you-can't attitude that makes him a perfect role model for anyone trying to better himself. Taking what he already had and working from there is what catapulted Clark on his own life's path.

"I was born at exactly the right time," says Clark. With complete humbleness and gratitude, he explains that throughout his youth during the Great Depression, "I didn't realize I didn't have much." He credits his parents and teachers for inspiration.

At the age of 13, Clark began clerking and delivering groceries on weekends. He made $15 for two days of labor. "I enjoyed working," he says. "It made me independent." Clark worked for the same grocer until his third year of college at the

George Hyman Construction Company (now the Clark Construction Group, Inc.) was the first company in the area to use the steam shovel.

University of Maryland at College Park.

During his years at College Park, he began dating Alice Bratton. Her father introduced him to Benjamin T. Rome, nephew of George Hyman, founder of the George Hyman Construction Company located in Washington, D.C.

Upon graduating with a bachelor of science degree in 1950—as part of the first senior class to graduate from the Glenn L. Martin College of Engineering, which also was built by Hyman—Clark accepted an entry-level position with the company. He also married Alice that year, and they

have been together ever since. At the beginning of his career, Clark worked 14-hour days during the week and half days on Saturdays. Still, he made little money in the beginning, averaging about $60 a week.

But his hard work paid off. By 1960 Rome appointed Clark vice president and general manager of Hyman. As a team, they had already constructed many new facilities, including several buildings at the University of Maryland at College Park; the District Chapter Building for the American Red Cross in Washington, D.C.; Andrews Air Force Base Hospital; and the Dirksen Senate Office Building on Capitol Hill.

Clark was always looking for innovative technologies and creative business partnerships to foster the company. In the 1960s Hyman was one of the first contractors in the United States to use tower cranes, which are faster and more precise when lifting heavy objects from the ground. Realizing that the company needed a new angle for winning contracts, Clark contacted Oliver T. Carr, a Washington, D.C., developer, and secured Hyman's first negotiated contract, which established the company's strong business relationship with developers.

FedEx Field—Washington Redskins Stadium, Landover, Maryland.

BWI Airport Terminal C, Baltimore.

In 1965 Hyman won the largest privately bid contract ever awarded in Washington, D.C., with phase one of L'Enfant Plaza. At a cost of almost $200 million, it took eight years to complete the 3.2 million-square-foot complex in three phases.

In 1969 Clark became Hyman's president and chief executive officer. His appointment ushered in dramatic growth, as the company was awarded many contracts outside the Washington, D.C., area. They included the South Campus

University of Maryland Chapel, College Park, built in the 1930s.

at DeKalb College and the $139 million Central Passenger Terminal Complex at William B. Hartsfield International Airport, both in Atlanta, and the Richmond Museum of Fine Arts.

During the 1970s Clark established a holding company known as Clark Enterprises, Inc., which was formed to oversee the management of various business interests, including commercial and residential construction, real estate and communications. He established OMNI Construction, which secured mostly non-union contracts, and Hyman opened offices in Richmond, New York, Boston, Philadelphia and Miami. The company headquarters also moved to Bethesda, Maryland.

Growth in the 1980s continued, with projects such as Three Lincoln Center in New York, Metro stations throughout the Washington metropolitan area, and the Ronald Reagan State Office Building in Los Angeles.

In 1996 the George Hyman Construction Company and OMNI Construction merged to become The Clark Construction Group, Inc., which has only had four CEOs in 100 years. Today, Pete Forster is the CEO of Clark Construction, a company that employs more than 3,500

employees and has annual revenues in excess of $2 billion. "I see good things in the future," says Clark. "The business will do as well as our people do." Clark is extremely proud of his employees and says that businesses "shouldn't hire anyone you wouldn't want to be good friends with." He recommends Jim Collins' motivational book, *Good to Great*, which illustrates that "successful companies are based on the types of people they hire." His friendship, professionalism and expertise—along with his fairness and the company's training resources—are what make his employees stay with the company. The company formed Clark Corporate University, which promotes continual education and training, focusing on safety, general business, project management and field management.

Although Clark Construction hires many engineers right out of college, retirement is not enforced. Many employees have already celebrated 20 and 30 years with the company, something that is a bit of an anomaly in today's workplace. "We've built a company of wonderful people," he says.

Clark has many reasons to be proud, but his greatest joy comes from his family. He and his wife have three children and

Johns Hopkins University Cancer Research Building, Baltimore (also known as the Bunting-Blaustein Building).

Chevy Chase Bank headquarters, Bethesda.

University of Maryland Byrd Stadium improvements, College Park.

10 grandchildren. When one of his sons was a toddler, he almost died of spinal meningitis. "Children's Hospital saved his life," said Clark. Ever since then, he made it a priority to give to those in need. Today, along with the Children's National Medical Center in Washington, D.C., Clark's companies make donations to many organizations, such as Samaritan Inns and Jubilee Housing. Clark Construction renovated three apartment buildings for Samaritan Inns to help the homeless and those with addictions transition back into

Discovery Communications headquarters, Silver Spring.

society. "They take care of the buildings," says Clark of their new homes. "The residents help each other and run each facility themselves, with no expense to anyone."

His humanitarian efforts have garnered Clark much respect. Currently, he is on the Board of Trustees for the University of Maryland College Park Foundation, serves as Trustee Emeritus for The Johns Hopkins University and Johns Hopkins Medicine; is a member of The Moles; and is an Advisory Board Member of the PGA Tour Golf Course Properties. The University of Maryland renamed its school of engineering in his honor, and The Johns Hopkins University now calls its biomedical building "Clark Hall."

However, Clark is not comfortable with all the attention. When he is not working, he spends time with his family, playing golf, hunting or fishing. He also walks three to five miles every day. When asked what, besides his family, he is the most proud of, Clark says it is his company's reputation. "We think reputation is the thing that makes a company very, very successful." It must be true. Just by Clark's own example, he has shown that reputation, indeed, makes the man—and the company.

JOHN E. HARMS, JR., AND ASSOCIATES, INC.

John E. Harms, Jr., a native of Hagerstown, Maryland, graduated in 1943 from Johns Hopkins University with a bachelor of science degree in civil engineering. He held professional engineer licenses in Maryland, Delaware and the District of Columbia. In 1986 Maryland Governor Harry Hughes appointed him to the Board of Registration for Professional Engineers, where he was a civil engineer member until 1998.

After serving in World War II in the South Pacific, John launched his engineering career with the Baltimore firm of Whitman, Requardt and Associates. Twelve years later, in 1955, he founded the firm of John E. Harms, Jr., and Associates, Inc. (Harms & Associates).

The initial location of Harms and Associates was at Greenway and Business Route 3 in Glen Burnie. In 1962 the firm moved to its present location at 90 Governor Ritchie Highway in Pasadena, Maryland. In 1973 a second floor was added to the main building, and in 1992 the building was again enlarged to accommodate the growing staff and multiple disciplines. In June 1996 a

John E. Harms, Jr.

satellite office was established in Frederick, Maryland.

Mr. Harms' business philosophy was centered on creating an environment where dedicated, productive, family-oriented people would be comfortable. This philosophy was carried on through the years and allowed the company to attain and maintain a high-level profes-

sional staff. Managers and other members were selected based on perpetuating this philosophy.

The firm's staff members served on local committees and participated in several community events. The goal of the company was to be "service oriented." This goal was best met with a "strong project manager" system which holds them to a high standard of accountability with associated authority. Throughout the years, the firm and several members of its staff have won many awards for outstanding achievement for specific projects as well as community participation.

Some of Harms and Associates' early private sector projects were major developments, including Maryland City, Sun Valley, Chesterfield and Fox Chase. Early municipal sector projects included design, stakeout and inspection of the Cox Creek and Broadneck Wastewater Systems; College Parkway, Maryland Route 4, in Calvert County; and the geodetic survey control for the initial Anne Arundel County "Overall Mapping" Project. The firm also served as "Town Engineer" for several small municipalities in Maryland.

Other notable projects were the first order control and rights of way surveys for the Baltimore Light Rail from Glen Burnie to Towson, design of the Fallston Wastewater System for Harford County; studies and design of onsite utilities and wastewater treatment for the National Institute of Health campus; ongoing environmental assessments for the Maryland State Highway Administration; design of the Annapolis Mall Expansion; and planning, engineering and surveys for several major development projects including Shipley's Choice, The National Business Park, Annapolis Exchange, Piney Orchard and Arundel Mills.

The Pasadena office of John E. Harms, Jr. and Associates, Inc.

COLUMBIA UNION COLLEGE

Columbia Union College, located in Takoma Park, Maryland, and serving Southern Montgomery County and the state of Maryland, is a coeducational, liberal arts college operating under the auspices of the Seventh-day Adventist Church.

Founded a century ago in 1904, the college grew out of the ashes of two conflagrations in Battle Creek, Michigan. In 1903, after fires destroyed a sanitarium and a publishing house there, leaders of the General Conference of Seventh-day Adventists selected the suburban town of Takoma Park, Maryland, as the new location for the denomination's headquarters, the publishing house, a sanitarium, and a college. The place chosen for the Washington Sanitarium (now Washington Adventist Hospital) and the college was in the Montgomery County portion of Takoma Park. The attractive 50-acre wooded site overlooking Sligo Creek, was purchased for $6,000.

The college was developed on the eastern part of the land, facing the sanitarium.

H. M. S. Richards Hall has served a variety of purposes on the campus. Once the "Normal School Building" housing an elementary school and teacher training program, the building is now the home for the deparments of religion, history and political science, and the Office of the Chaplain.

The Gateway To Service has been a landmark on the Columbia Union College campus for over 50 years. It was moved to this central vantage point on campus in the 1970s.

From 1904 to 1907 three buildings were constructed: North Hall (the first men's dormitory), Central Hall (the dining hall), and South Hall (the first women's dormitory). While South Hall was under construction, women students were housed in the Carroll House, near present Grant Avenue, and the Manor House, on what is now Manor Circle; neither of these two early Takoma Park homes exists today. College Hall, the first administration building, was completed in 1908. Situated across from the present main entrance to the Washington Adventist Hospital, enlarged and faced with brick and known today as Science Hall, it is the only one of these early buildings still standing. In 1919 Columbia Hall, a new administration, classroom, and chapel building, was erected on the northwest corner of Carroll and Flower Avenues. For over 50 years it was the signature building of the college until an arsonist destroyed it in 1970. With the addition of a library in 1942, these structures formed a crescent facing the hospital; today, Science Hall and Weis Library are all that remain of that original half circle.

As the college grew, new buildings were added, and the campus expanded across Flower Avenue. Additional buildings included an elementary school/teacher-training facility (now H. M. S. Richards Hall, 1939), a central heating plant (1940), two residence halls (Halcyon Hall, 1947 and Morrison Hall, 1962), a gymnasium (1950), swimming pool (1955), and a campus center building (Wilkinson Hall, 1970). Sligo Seventh-day Adventist Church, although not an official college building, was erected on the northeast corner of Carroll and Flower Avenues in 1944.

For many years the college operated a printing press and a mill, which included among its products stepladders and lawn chairs. Enlarged and renovated, the press building is now the Health Sciences building. The mill buildings currently house the campus support services, the Information Technology Services department, and the college's radio station, WGTS-FM. Licensed by the FCC in 1957, WGTS was the first educational FM station in the Washington metropolitan area; its call letters are taken from the college's motto, "Gateway to Service." The college also owns several houses in the community which serve as residences for faculty, staff, and students. Among these is a large Georgian house on Carroll Avenue that was willed to the college by Heber H. Votaw and his wife Carolyn to be the college president's home. Mrs. Votaw was the sister of United States President Warren G. Harding.

Over the years the college has had several names. It opened as Washington Training College on November 30, 1904, with 50 students. In 1907 the original purpose of providing a liberal arts education was replaced by a more specialized objective of training men and women for missionary service, and the name was changed to Washington Foreign Mission Seminary. In 1914, as Washington Missionary College, the college resumed its original objective, and the first commencement service was held on May 22, 1915. In 1933 the lower biennium was

Built by Heber H. Votaw and his wife Carolyn Harding, sister of U.S. President Warren G. Harding, the Votaw House was given to the college in the 1960s as a residence for the college president. Votaw was the first Seventh-Day Adventist missionary in Burma (1905–1914).

organized as Columbia Junior College. The junior college ceased to exist in 1942 when Washington Missionary College received regional accreditation as a four-year, degree-granting institution, which the college still maintains. In 1961 the name was changed to Columbia Union College. In addition to regional accreditation, the institution holds the relevant approval and/or accreditation for its education, nursing, and respiratory care programs.

In 1984 the institution added an evening program for working adults. This baccalaureate program, which offers programs in business administration, organizational management, health care administration, and information systems, opened an off-campus site in Gaithersburg in 1999. In 1998 the college allied itself with the Center for Law and Public Policy in order to promote interest in law and politics. It also has a cooperative education program, which enables students to gain work experience related to their majors, and an external degree program. In 2001 the college again started offering graduate degrees, with the commencement of an MBA program.

Today, Columbia Union College offers undergraduate and graduate degrees in sciences, humanities and selected professional fields. Over 1,200 students enroll annually, primarily from Maryland, the District of Columbia, and the Mid-Atlantic states; they also come from

across North America and the world, representing a rich cultural diversity. Among distinguished alumni are U.S. House of Representatives member Roscoe G. Bartlett (6th district), and Leonard Bailey, an innovative heart surgeon at Loma Linda University in California.

The institution has a well-recognized music program, including two choral groups, Pro Musica and the Columbia Collegiate Chorale, and an internationally-known orchestra, the New England Symphonic Ensemble, which performs several times a year in Carnegie Hall. In April 2003 these groups launched the College's centennial celebration with a performance at the John F. Kennedy Center for the Performing Arts under the baton of world-renowned composer John Rutter.

The College athletic program is affiliated with the National Collegiate Athletic Association, Division II, with men's and women's teams competing in basketball, baseball, softball, soccer, and track and field. The athletic program also includes an acrobatic/gymnastic touring group called the Acro-Airs.

Each year a number of students leave this country to participate in the Adventist Volunteer Service, spending from several weeks to one year in locations around the globe as volunteers in positions ranging from teachers of English as a Second Language (ESL) to construction workers. This program originated at Columbia Union College in 1959 as the Student Missionary Program and has grown into an organization which provides opportunities for volunteer service to the youth of the worldwide Seventh-day Adventist church.

Seventeen men have served Columbia Union College as president, two of them more than once: James W. Lawhead, 1904–1907; Homer R. Salisbury, 1907–1910; John L. Shaw, 1910; Milton E. Kern, 1910–1914; John L. Shaw, 1914–1916; Benjamin F. Machlan, 1916–1921; Marion E. Cady, 1921–1922; Harvey A. Morrison, 1922–1927; Harry H. Hamilton, 1927–1935; Harvey A. Morrison, 1935–1936; Benjamin G. Wilkinson, 1936–1946; William H. Shephard, 1946–1959; Charles B. Hirsch, 1959–1965; Winton H. Beaven, 1965–1970; George H. Akers, 1970–1974; Colin Standish, 1974–1978; William Loveless, 1978–1990; Clifford Sorensen, 1990–1992; Charles Scriven, 1992–2000; and Randal Wisbey, 2000–present.

Over the span of two years, 2003–2005 Columbia Union College will celebrate its centennial anniversary under a motto of "Engage, Excel, Explore." With lectureships, performances, service opportunities, and a variety of other events, the college and its community will explore its rich heritage and the opportunities of the new century.

The current Science Hall is the oldest building on campus, known as College Hall when built in 1908. The sand, gravel and stone for the building were taken from the banks of nearby Sligo Creek. The lumber and other supplies were shipped from Baltimore.

CORVIS CORPORATION

Optical communications networks are the wave of the future—the technology that is transforming the way the world handles voice, video and the Internet. Corvis Corporation, a cutting-edge provider of intelligent all-optical solutions, saw the wave coming and is riding it to a position of international leadership.

Corvis, based in Columbia, Maryland, supplies all-optical network equipment and communications services to leading service providers, corporations and government agencies around the globe. It does so with an eye on its clients' bottom lines and their ability to expand into the wideband future.

Corvis has had a significant impact on its industry since it was founded in 1997 by telecommunications pioneer Dr. David R. Huber. Its initial public offering in July 2000 was the most successful for a start-up company in stock market history up to that time, cementing its position as a leader in the all-optical race.

Dr. Huber provides the long-term vision and strategy for the company and oversees research and development, engineering and technology.

Corporate building at 7015 Albert Einstein Drive, Columbia, Maryland.

Dr. David Huber

An electrical engineer and physicist, he has been at the forefront of his industry since he earned his Ph.D. from Brigham Young University. He holds 41 U.S. patents in optics technology and has more pending.

Dr. Huber managed the Lightwave Research and Development Program for General Instrument Corporation and held positions in optical communications development at Rockwell International Corporation, Optelecom, Inc., and ITT Industries, Inc., before founding Ciena Corporation in 1992.

He served as Ciena's chief technology officer and chief scientist as it became the first company to provide volume commercial shipments of dense wave division multiplexing equipment.

Understanding the phenomenal potential of all-optical networking in a world where demand for bandwidth grows exponentially, Dr. Huber founded Corvis with the vision of creating the world's first all-optical networking company. In the process, Corvis has helped redefine telecommunications with end-to-end optical network solutions that dramatically reduce the overall expenses associated with building and operating networks and dramatically increases the speed with which new services can be offered.

Before all-optical solutions, fiber-optic networks used by telecommunications carriers were hybrids dependent on expensive equipment to shift from optical to electrical signals and back. Optical signals had to be converted into electrical form whenever they got too weak or needed to be switched to their destinations. Once strengthened, they were converted back into light beams by small lasers. Long-distance callers didn't know it, but the limitations of traditional equipment forced their conversations to go through dozens of these conversions. Telecommunication companies did know it and had to pay the price to be competitive.

Corvis, operating to Dr. Huber's goal of creating optical innovations that drive carrier profitability faster than anyone else, is changing this reality. Its intelligent all-optical networks enable a vast array of advanced services with dramatically lower capital and operating costs. It is the only company to have built and deployed a commercial all-optical network, including the world's first and only commercial all-optical switch. Further, Corvis was the first company to have deployed commercial Raman amplifiers in terrestrial networks.

Corvis works with carriers to prepare them for the all-optical world, offering products to guide their transition from traditional equipment. Where a carrier

already has networks, Corvis' teams of experts focus on using its industry-leading field-proven optical innovations to optimize them. They work with an eye toward the client's future and eventual move to all-optical, while never losing track of the client's bottom line.

"We realize that each network occupies a unique stage in its evolution," the company's mission says, "and we are committed to accurately assessing challenging terrestrial and undersea network problems and recommending solutions to help carriers around the world move forward at a pace that reflects their business goals."

The company's flexible portfolio of optical networking solutions evolves from point-to-point links to an all-optical mesh, so carriers can expand their return on investment and lower ongoing operating costs. It enables them to grow their networks in ways that make sense of their traffic, equipment base, service requirements, and business models—and which improve the economics of their operations.

For many carriers, this means the new and the old technologies complement each other to offer a path toward an efficient, all-optical system at any time in the future. Plus, as carriers increase their capacities, the network grows easily, using legacy networks locally and regionally while transporting long-distance traffic—all optically. This compares to a road system of interstate highways connecting with neighborhood streets.

The network elements Corvis offers cover the full range of carrier needs. The Corvis optical network (ON) family of solutions provides ultra-long-haul (distances of more than 3200 kilometers) transport with all-optical switching. The Corvis optical convergence switch (OCS) combines the functions of several network elements and is structured to expand to meet each client's needs and ambitions. The Corvis XF (undersea festoon) system equips carriers with ultra-high capacity repeaterless transport for

underwater or land transmission distances of up to 350 km.

But as advanced as it is, technology is only the beginning of the reasons for intelligent all-optical networks. They generate revenue growth since faster deployment of services and compelling new wavelength services lead to increased revenues. They bolster client's bottom lines because improved manageability, lower power consumption, smaller footprint, decreased staffing needs and greater automation help reduce operating costs. They reduce capital spending because of the overall lower cost of deploying a network without regeneration and electrical switching points, an advantage that grows dramatically with network scale. And all-optical networks are easy to operate with automation to help manage capacity and planning for the future.

Corvis sells optical networking equipment to key service providers worldwide, and works with many national governments and government agencies. The U.S. government is the largest bandwidth user in the world, but hardly the only nation in this important and growing market.

On July 28, 2000, three years after starting operations, Corvis went public, trading on the NASDAQ with the symbol CORV. In subsequent years, it faced a

recession-related dip in revenues and share price. It responded by positioning itself to take advantage of future growth, and did so as 2003 advanced.

In 2002 Corvis formed Corvis Government Solutions, Inc. (CGSI), its government subsidiary and technical advisory board. CGSI's team had combined experience of more than 110 years working with government agencies.

The same year, Corvis acquired an undersea optical networking solutions provider, Dorsal. The merger made Corvis one of the few global end-to-end providers of optical networking systems.

Dorsal's President and CEO Jim Bannantine joined Corvis' executive team as president, succeeding Huber, who remains as chairman and CEO. The team also includes Lynn Anderson, senior vice president, chief financial officer and treasurer, and Kim D. Larsen, senior vice president, general counsel and secretary of Corvis and president of CGSI.

Also in 2002, Corvis introduced its Customer ONE program, combining its networking solutions with metro/access systems providers and application software companies to quickly expand revenue sources of its customers.

In 2003 CIII Communications, a 96-percent-Corvis-owned joint venture with St. Louis-based telecommunications and cable management firm Cequel III, acquired the assets of Broadwing Communications from Cincinnati Bell, Inc. This made Corvis a comprehensive optical networking company that can supply both networks and network services. Broadwing's core network, built with Corvis' market-leading all-optical equipment and the first in the world to be all-optical, began carrying live, commercial traffic in 2001. Broadwing sells data, voice and video transport to major service providers as well as complex data and network applications to companies and other enterprises.

Its technology enables Broadwing to provide the highest quality and most technologically advanced solutions—and to provision its services faster than any other service provider in the industry. Its network connects 137 cities coast-to-coast over 18,700 miles of advanced optical fiber.

Corvis, with its new subsidiary Broadwing Communications, employs more than 1,100 people at offices in North America. It seeks the most qualified professionals in the world, bringing together people from many different backgrounds, professional disciplines and cultures to make Corvis one of the greatest entrepreneurial ventures in its industry. Company values include customer service, opportunism, respect for others, producing value-added deliverables, innovation and security.

The staff provides clients with installation and turn-up services, including turnkey solutions if needed; training for their employees in all details of the system; and 24/7 pre- and post-sales support to insure that its clients deliver world-class service to their customers.

All-optical networks are becoming the telecommunications architecture of choice. While competitors play catchup, Corvis is ready to ride the next wave.

Above and below.
Corvis Buildings, Columbia, Maryland .

The Inner Harbor of Baltimore. Photo by
William Priddy

EDDIE'S OF ROLAND PARK

Impeccable customer service combined with superior quality groceries has always been the hallmark of Eddie's of Roland Park. Serving two locations in North Baltimore, this upscale neighborhood grocery store has been in operation for over 59 years. Three generations of shoppers (often in the same family) realize that Eddie's success began with its founder, Victor Cohen. His business philosophy of providing the best quality goods and services at a fair price is still maintained by his daughter, Nancy.

In 1944, customers were greeted by name at the market's doors and their children were offered Dad's Oatmeal Cookies. This tradition continues today with a personal greeting at the door and delicious cookies from their in-store bakery.

The roots of Eddie's of Roland Park began with a Jewish Russian immigrant who came to Ellis Island from Kiev, Russia. He began his grocery career at age 14, delivering groceries to neighbors of the A&P where he worked in Baltimore. At age 19 Victor became the youngest store manager in the chain's history. In 1944 he fulfilled his dream of opening a gourmet market—Victor's

A young Victor Cohen at the original Victor's Market as featured in Food World.

Market—in a shopping center in North Baltimore designed by Frederick Law Olmstead. In fact, Victor's was in the nation's first shopping center.

Nine years later, he opened a second store called Eddie's, in the same neighborhood. That store, with expansions, remains today. As in his original store, "Mr. Victor" maintained his tradition of providing the best groceries, and prime meats, along with personal shopping and delivery to his customers. The same attention to detail and service is in evidence today as Nancy Cohen, Mr. Cohen's daughter and now president and owner of Eddie's of Roland Park, continues to operate the stores with her father's dedication and care.

Going into the grocery business was never Nancy's plan. Her one foray as a teenager into the world of groceries lasted all of an hour and a half. This confirmed her father's belief that girls and the grocery business were mutually exclusive. Ms. Cohen pursued her own passions and completed a master's degree in clinical psychology. While completing that degree she worked for an agency that provided vocational counseling for the physically and mentally challenged. Pressure from relatives persuaded her to delay Ph.D. studies and give her father's business—

Nancy Cohen, president and CEO of Eddie's of Roland Park.

her family's business—a second chance.

In 1981 she joined her father at the door of Eddie's. Her father informed her that her one and only task was to stand at the door and greet people. Ms. Cohen laughs when she remembers her indignation at that assignment: she said, "I have a college degree, I have a master's degree! You want me to open a door?" Now, however, she clearly sees the wisdom in her father's methods of running the store. For the next several years, Nancy Cohen absorbed as much about the grocery business and her customers as possible, learning both from her father and his many longtime associates.

Within two years she started incorporating her own ideas into the store's operation. She updated the logo, created a unique circular, and further distinguished Eddie's by adding "of Roland Park" to its name. Facing new competition from chain stores entering the market, she refocused on Eddie's with the eyes of a customer. Typical of many women, she too worked full-time and needed to feed her family at the end of a long day. Nancy expanded an already busy kitchen by hiring a chef to create and prepare á la carte meals for busy families. Eddie's of Roland Park was the first supermarket in Baltimore to offer freshly prepared meal options. Now the Gourmet to Go counter has a menu offering over 300 items.

Many of the additions and changes Nancy made at Eddie's occurred during her father's winter vacations in Florida. She had instincts she trusted but didn't want the confrontations that would often ensue when she tried to sell her father on her newest ideas. With innovations already in place upon her father's return, he could only say, "I hope you know what you're doing."

Ultimately, Nancy's accomplishments brought her father great pride. By 1991 she was running the business—with her father still very much involved. That same year, while her father was in Florida, Nancy decided to open a second location only 2 miles from the original Eddie's. Stunned and not at all happy, her father told her to "*un*-sign" the purchase contract. Nancy responded with the drive and determination typical of her father. When confronted by his own dynamic characteristics in his daughter, what else could he do but repeat his mantra: "I hope you know what you're doing." She did. The second store is larger and busier, offering a greater depth of products and services. Both stores

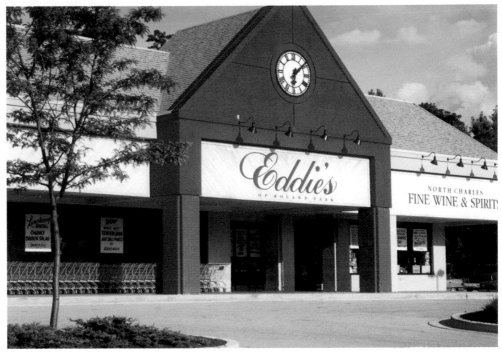

Eddie's of Roland Park 6213 North Charles Street location.

continue to offer everything from imported specialty foods to gift shops, from service meats, fish, poultry and game, to customer-oriented services that include catering, personal shopping and home delivery.

With the success of the second Eddie's, at North Charles Street, Ms. Cohen proved to those in the grocery business that in fact she was her father's daughter. As the only female CEO of a group of supermarkets in the Mid-Atlantic region, Nancy Cohen continues to keep Eddie's prominently situated within the male dominated grocery business.

Beyond its customer-driven niche as a purveyor of fine foods, Eddie's of Roland Park is also a dedicated member of the community. Of her service philosophy, Nancy says, "I am committed to the community in a larger way by making significant and meaningful contributions to local schools, churches, synagogues and civic causes in our community and the city at large.

"We get involved in neighborhood beautification projects and we carefully maintain the properties from which we do business. But our *most* important assets in cementing community relationships are our associates."

Still enthusiastically involved with the business he founded, Victor Cohen passed away in 2000 at the age of 88. Even as they mourned "Mr. Victor," customers and associates alike were comforted by their trust that his spirit would live on in his daughter.

To her delight, Nancy's sons Michael and Andrew can't wait to enter the family business. They grew up visiting the stores frequently and witnessing the excitement of the entire operation. With every new product's presentation, and the warm greeting of every customer, Eddie's remains a Baltimore institution.

Inside the original Victor's Market.

GLOBAL SCIENCE & TECHNOLOGY, INC. (GST)

Global Science & Technology, Inc. (GST) provides expert consulting services in the fields of Earth and space science to clients in government, industry and academia. One of Maryland's fastest growing technology companies, GST has been widely recognized for its top quality and innovative work and has contributed to such well-known projects as the Hubble Space Telescope and the Earth Observation System (EOS). They specialize in meteorology, software, engineering and satellite communications projects. In 2000 the Technology Council of Maryland said the following about the company: "Melding engineering and applied science in an energetic, open research environment. GST's work is on time, often below budget and designed to help their clients make decisions." Their clients include NASA, the United States Air Force, the Department of Defense, and the National Oceanographic and Atmospheric Administration (NOAA).

Headquartered in Greenbelt, Maryland, GST was founded in 1991 by current company President Chieh-san Cheng. Born in Shanghai, China, Mr. Cheng came to the United States in 1972 as a

President and CEO Chieh-san Cheng. In the past year, GST has received national recognition by being ranked in Inc. magazine's Inc 500 list, the Deloitte & Touche Technology Fast 500 list, and by winning the NASA Goddard Space Flight Center Contractor Excellence Award.

GST participated in the NASA JOULE campaign to study heating in the upper atmosphere due to sun/Earth interaction. Here, a Joule rocket is being prepared for launch. GST developed the electronic "payloads" used for the measurements.

graduate student. He obtained a master's degree in technical management from Johns Hopkins University in Baltimore and was trained as a meteorologist, earning another master's degree from the University of Maryland. In the late 1970s he worked for NASA, where he gained a working knowledge of the space technology industry. Mr. Cheng founded GST primarily to serve NASA's Goddard Space Flight Center. A core goal in starting the business was to create a good work environment for employees with openness, honesty and a commitment to ethics and integrity. In November 1999, the Washington District Small Business Administration named Cheng "The Minority Enterprise Development Small Business Person of the Year."

GST offers a variety of products and consulting services. DirectMet® is a complete direct readout and satellite analysis system for GOES and GMS satellite imagery, which is the source of information for weather reporting.

DirectMet was the first commercial product released by GST and has been sold worldwide to users such as commercial and public weather services, high schools and universities, television stations and private engineering firms. Along with DirectMet, GST has a weather product called MetLab/WAFS which is a weather workstation with the ability to integrate data sources and product types into a flexible display.

GST was one of the primary contractors responsible for the development of MODIS Ground Stations. MODIS is a key instrument in NASA's Earth Observing Satellite for monitoring interactions between the atmosphere, oceans, land surface and biosphere.

GST provides operational support, strategic planning, technical assistance and product development for the Regional Applications Center Northeast (RACNE), a NASA/Cayuga Community College-New York initiative designed to make Earth system science more relevant to resource management, agricultural and urban planning professionals in state and local government. RACNE pulls in localized satellite information and combines it with other data for informational purposes. The consulting services that this division of GST offers include developing options and solutions for geospatial and spatial technology projects.

GST also supports NASA's Geospatial Interoperability Office (GIO) to increase the scope and adoption of geospatial interoperability standards in NASA.

The company also offers support services to National Weather Service STAR4 meteorological receiving workstations worldwide.

GST's SkipWare® is an Internet-over-Satellite performance enhancement software that optimizes satellite communications.

The company's accomplishments have been recognized in many forums. In 2000, 2001 and 2002, GST was ranked on the Maryland Technology Fast 50, a list that recognizes the state's fastest growing high technology companies. In the fall of 2002 the company was listed on the Deloitte and Touche Technology Fast 500, a similar but more extensive ranking that includes companies in North America. The rankings are based on percentage revenue growth over the previous five years. GST's percentage growth from 1997 to 2001 was 627 percent. Also in fall 2002, GST was ranked on *Inc.* magazine's listing of the 500 fastest growing privately-owned companies. In May 2003 GST received the annual Contractor Excellence Award for Small

GST President and CEO Chieh-san Cheng, along with Vice Presidents Larry Roelofs and Paul Clemens, accepts the 2003 Contractor Excellence Award from Al Diaz, Center Director of NASA's Goddard Space Flight Center.

With DirectMet®, GST has created a tool that gives weather professionals a powerful weather workstation that allows capture, analysis, and display of live satellite weather images on a desktop computer.

Business/Service from NASA's Goddard Space Flight Center. The award recognizes contractors who make substantial contributions to the mission of NASA Goddard, are dedicated to continuous improvement and achieve demonstrable and measurable accomplishments.

Career opportunities at GST are varied, and include positions in mechanical engineering, electrical engineering, systems engineering, astrophysics, scientific research, peer review logistics, advanced networking and information technology. The company culture encourages creativity and strives to provide challenging and motivating work for its employees. This dynamism is reflected in the remarkably low turnover rate of 3.3 percent among the technical staff. In addition to its Greenbelt headquarters, the privately owned company has offices in Washington, D.C., the state of New York, and Beijing, China. The company also hosts a paid summer internship program

for undergraduate, graduate and accelerated high school students.

GST seeks to have a positive impact on the surrounding communities and encourages community outreach among its employees. GST provides or has provided mentoring to several small, disadvantaged, or women-owned businesses. In 2002 GST entered into a formal Memorandum of Understanding with the Sinte Gleska University, a tribal university in rural South Dakota, to help them develop and promote educational, research and training opportunities in the service of Rosebud Reservations and allied tribal communities, and to attract private sector investment in the Lakota Nation and allied Native American concerns. Toward these ends, in the first year of the agreement, GST advised on and submitted jointly with Sinte Gleska several proposals to NASA, NSF and NOAA, two of which were funded. GST often serves as their Washington D.C. area host, and helps make introductions to key personnel at NASA Headquarters and Goddard.

With its emphasis on creativity, high quality work and investment in people and resources, Global Science & Technology, Inc. is well positioned as it moves further into its second decade of existence.

HARBOR HOSPITAL, BALTIMORE

"A hospital in South Baltimore has been a long felt want. In case of any accident happening in Locust Point or along the docks, it is necessary for the injured to be taken to one of the uptown hospitals or across the ferry to Johns Hopkins. Thus it is a long time before the injured can receive medical attention."

The above quote, taken from an unmarked newspaper clipping from the early 1900s, describes the circumstances around which South Baltimore General Hospital, now Harbor Hospital, was founded. The hospital, now situated on the bank of the Patapsco River at the mouth of Baltimore's Inner Harbor, celebrates its 100th anniversary this year. Incorporated with a Board of Directors in 1903, it remains loyal to its founder's vision of community service.

Dr. Harry Peterman, Harbor Hospital's founder, taught school for three years before deciding to study medicine. The son of Jeremiah and Mary Peterman, he left Chambersville, Pennsylvania, in the late 1800s to enroll in Baltimore Medical College. The college later became part of the University of Maryland School of Medicine. Harry and his brother James both graduated in 1895 with honors

An early version of an imaging machine at South Baltimore General Hospital.

from the medical college. Dr. Harry Peterman, appointed as a resident physician to the Baltimore Eye, Ear and Throat Hospital, served patients there until 1900, when he decided to establish his own clinic. A history of the hospital compiled in 1959 notes that "his heart was urging him on to do more for the sick and needy in this special field of eye, ear and throat."

Despite South Baltimore's large population, there was not a single clinic or

hospital of any type serving its population in 1900, and "many of the people in this area did not have the street fare to take their children or themselves into Baltimore to other clinics." One of Peterman's patients, Mrs. George Frame, mother-in-law of the mayor of Baltimore at that time, "told him to let her know when he was ready to start, and she would do all she could to help him." She assisted Peterman in forming his first Board of Directors, which met at the home of a city councilman on Calvert Street, "next door to the North Avenue Presbyterian Church." The board "organized and appointed Dr. Peterman the power to select the site of his clinic, as he wanted it called. A three-story house at 1017 Light Street was selected and rented for $25 a month from Dr. Anna Koons."

On May 1, 1901, Peterman's first patient, a mother with two children, entered the South Baltimore Eye, Ear, Nose and Throat Charity Hospital. She was not charged a fee and paid only ten cents to the clinic for the cost of the bottle which held her medicine. Funds for furnishing the clinic came from Peterman's own pocket. He established his operating room on the second floor, carrying patients up the steps piggyback if they were unable to walk the stairs. Peterman's first practical nurse, Mrs. Cornelia Snyder, served without pay during her first year of dispensary work, receiving only her room and board as remuneration.

In 1903 the clinic purchased its 1211 Light Street location for $13,000. Facilities for the newly-incorporated South Baltimore Eye, Ear, Nose and Throat Hospital included "12 hospital beds, four or five nurses serving for the patients and a very large dispensary clinic." In December 1903, trustees authorized the hospital's president to form a "Board of Lady Visitors," constituting the first of the hospital's women's auxiliary groups. Duties for the first auxiliary group included superintending domestic affairs and supplying "means for current expenses," this money "to be raised by such means as the Board deemed

Operating room nurses gather instruments used for a surgical procedure.

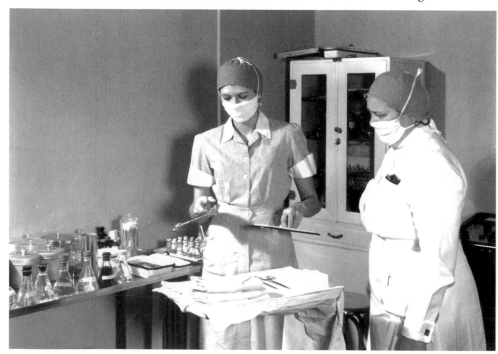

wise and proper." Agitation for a larger hospital continued, with a physician from that time noting that "the best site for a hospital would be 1416 Light Street, a large building occupied by the Charity Organization Society." The physician noted further that "the only way to make the hospital pay would be to interest every physician in the institution, or have them become stockholders."

William Grecht, a member of the clinic's board of directors, "took the building and advancement of the hospital as a very personal project," offering $10,000 in cash to start the selling of the bond drive, and then purchasing $10,000 in bonds himself. Grecht "insisted, in fact demanded, that his friends and business associates buy liberally of these bonds." A newspaper clipping from that time noted that since its inception, Peterman's clinic had "been doing the work of a good Samaritan," and added that with the construction of new facilities, its opportunities "for practical benevolence will be greatly enlarged."

Ground was broken for the new hospital on January 16, 1914. It would have "thirty-five beds, a new accident room, and a new clinic area," with "a new

An aerial view of Harbor Hospital, sitting on the banks of the Patapsco River.

building of fireproof construction, considered a model of its kind at that date." The new building "cost about $70,000 and the equipment, which was entirely new, cost about $10,000." Mrs. George Frame, the first president of the Women's Board of South Baltimore Hospital, would continue to campaign from door to door, asking for donations for building newer and larger hospital wings.

Fall of 1918 saw the opening of the hospital's School of Nursing, with nine

Preparing to lay the cornerstone at the new and present hospital location, 1968. Photo by David Parlett

students in attendance. The Woman's Auxiliary formed a sewing group in 1919 to meet the need for hospital linens, spending $258.58. Their efforts were eased in 1927 when the group purchased its first electric sewing machine. 1937 saw a $250,000 fund campaign to add 50 more hospital beds. On February 25, 1939, Peterman died suddenly of a heart attack at the age of 68. *The Baltimore Sun* eulogized the hospital founder in a lengthy tribute. Twenty-nine years later, Peterman's hospital would move to its present site, on the Patapsco River at the mouth of Baltimore's Inner Harbor.

Harbor Hospital, renamed in 1988 during the tenure of another well-loved president, Barney Johnson, continues to honor Dr. Peterman's intentions: operating as a service to its community, and treating every patient, regardless of income. More than 60,000 patients a year seek treatment at Harbor, which is now part of the MedStar Health service system. Affiliation with MedStar, which focuses on community-based hospitals offering a wide range of services, provides a solid financial backing to Harbor, easing both acquiring new equipment and updating facilities. The hospital's location one mile from northern Anne Arundel County ensures its standing as the largest provider of maternity services to that area. Its "mother-centered" maternity care ensures that area mothers-to-be enjoy a high standard of care.

Harbor Hospital's women's services include a Fetal Assessment Center, a complete prenatal diagnostic center and a Fertility Center, specializing in a wide range of fertility-related disorders. Services for new mothers include pre- and postnatal classes, grandparenting classes, specialty nursing care and support groups. To help ensure healthy pregnancies as well as births, the center offers preconception counseling and genetic counseling.

Small meditation rooms and the hospital chapel are available to all patients and families seeking a quiet place for prayer and solace, with ministers and their associates available to offer support. A language bank of employees and volunteers offers translating services for non-English-speaking patients and their families.

Harbor also serves as a teaching hospital, with a residency training program in internal medicine and a transitional program that prepares residents for other

A view of a patient unit at the current Harbor Hospital location.

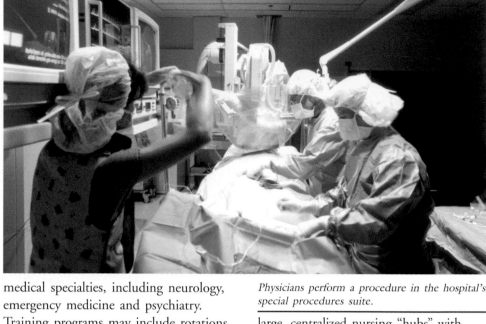

Physicians perform a procedure in the hospital's special procedures suite.

medical specialties, including neurology, emergency medicine and psychiatry. Training programs may include rotations at nearby Johns Hopkins University and the University of Maryland School of Medicine. More than 30 full-time and 80 volunteer faculty offer internal medicine subspecialties to Harbor's residents in training. Many of Harbor's over 500 physicians maintain teaching positions with area medical schools, ensuring that hospital staff is well-versed in the latest medical advances. The Harbor Hospital Nursing Scholarship Program offers funds to individuals interested in pursuing nursing as a career.

At the same time that Harbor Hospital received its new name, it replaced its

large, centralized nursing "hubs" with nursing facilities located outside patient rooms, allowing patients to enjoy a more personalized level of care. Harbor was the first hospital in the region to be updated in this fashion. The hospital opened both its Cancer Center and its LifeResource Center in 1997, further enhancing its offerings. Teams of nationally-renowned oncologists serve in the cancer diagnosis and treatment center, where a multidisciplinary team of experts—including oncologists, rehabilitation therapists, social workers and image consultants, as well as a nutritionist, a pharmacist and a chaplain—combine efforts to provide the best medical care and support to cancer patients and their families. Support groups offered at no cost to patients include an oncology support group and Bay Bridge Breathers, addressing those suffering from emphysema, chronic bronchitis and pulmonary fibrosis.

Harbor's LifeResource Center offers educational programs, lectures and self-help programs to enhance the health and well-being of the community. Program offerings include a smoking cessation seminar and a "Feel Good Friday" presentation on joint pain and treatment. LifeResource Center staff frequently present health programs in area malls, schools and churches, offering specialized programs to schools that complement existing health and science course work. The center's Health Resource Library offers books, brochures, videos and information on a variety of health topics including aging, spirituality, medication and learning disabilities. Library computers equipped with Internet access are available for use by members of the community.

In December 2001 Harbor Hospital signed a lease agreement with the National Institutes of Health's National Institute on Aging (NIA) to establish a clinical research unit at the hospital, providing support services in the form of research personnel and pharmacological, laboratory, diagnostic testing and management services to NIA's program for Advanced Studies in Translational Research on Aging (ASTRA). With Harbor's assistance, NIA would extend the clinical research efforts of the program within an acute care hospital environment. The program would facilitate collaboration between NIA and Harbor Hospital physicians, providing access for community members and patients served by the hospital to specialized medical care and consultation. Community members also benefit from Harbor's Parish Nurse program, created in 1994 to extend the hospital's healthcare mission within the community. The comprehensive outreach program, which

Harbor employees enjoying lunch and the scenery on the back lawn of the hospital.

includes volunteer parish nurses and partnerships with other health agencies, provides influenza immunization clinics to underserved, minority and high-risk populations in Baltimore City and Anne Arundel County. Free cancer screenings are offered as well.

It is a tribute to Harbor's residency training program, which attracts physicians from all over the world, that many of the residents who train through the program establish their medical practices locally, referring their patients back to the hospital and retaining medical privileges there. The nursing staff also exhibits a warm loyalty toward Harbor, with many choosing to stay on as "career" nurses. Lenora Addison, one such example, now serves as the hospital's vice president of Patient Care.

As plans move forward for celebrating

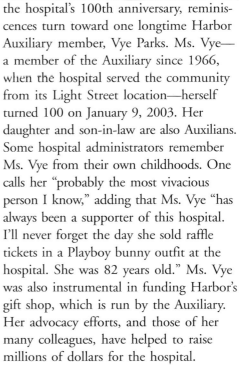

The Teleconference Room located in the Max and Rosalie Baum Medical Conference Center, Harbor Hospital.

the hospital's 100th anniversary, reminiscences turn toward one longtime Harbor Auxiliary member, Vye Parks. Ms. Vye— a member of the Auxiliary since 1966, when the hospital served the community from its Light Street location—herself turned 100 on January 9, 2003. Her daughter and son-in-law are also Auxilians. Some hospital administrators remember Ms. Vye from their own childhoods. One calls her "probably the most vivacious person I know," adding that Ms. Vye "has always been a supporter of this hospital. I'll never forget the day she sold raffle tickets in a Playboy bunny outfit at the hospital. She was 82 years old." Ms. Vye was also instrumental in funding Harbor's gift shop, which is run by the Auxiliary. Her advocacy efforts, and those of her many colleagues, have helped to raise millions of dollars for the hospital.

Harbor Hospital moves into the future under the guidance of Joseph M. Oddis, appointed in 2002 as the hospital's new president. Oddis, who brings extensive experience in hospital administration, served as president and CEO of South Carolina's Spartanburg Regional Healthcare System. He inherits Harbor Hospital's rich tradition of individuals willing to give of themselves to enhance their community's health and well-being.

HARFORD COMMUNITY COLLEGE

Named for Henry Harford, the last proprietary of Maryland and the son of the sixth Lord Baltimore, Harford County, Maryland is rich in history. It is the place where the man credited with introducing Shakespeare to American audiences lived and where the famous and the infamous once resided. Green fields and horse farms still grace this county, which today enriches the lives of its residents through its history, culture, military base and the superior higher education offered at Harford Community College.

The county has always played a role in education, whether through formal classrooms or life's harsher lessons. Junius Brutus Booth, the English classical actor, settled with his family in Harford County in 1821 and built a Gothic revival home called Tudor Hall. Booth is credited with introducing the plays of William Shakespeare to American audiences. He and his sons—Edwin, Junius, Jr., and John Wilkes—were considered some of the finest classical actors of their time. Edwin's portrayal of Hamlet was widely acclaimed, but John Wilkes became infamous as the assassin of President Lincoln.

The College played an active role with the Preservation Association for Tudor Hall (PATH) to purchase Tudor Hall and make it a museum and performance

Edwin Booth, native of Harford County as Hamlet.

space. The College hosted performances by actors Stacy Keach and Lynn Redgrave, gave interviews to the BBC, and had coverage by cable and network television. The building was sold at auction in 1999.

The Harford Community College campus lies less than a mile from Tudor Hall on over 300 acres of what was formerly known as Prospect Hill Farm. From 1828 to the 1950s, Prospect Hill was an important horse-breeding farm in a county and region renowned for thoroughbred racing. The most well-known stallion to make its home at Prospect Hill was Durbar II. Foaled in France and owned by Mr. and Mrs. H. B. Duryea, Durbar II won the highly respected Epsom Derby in England in 1914—defeating the favorite, a horse owned by King George V.

Students of all ages are enriched by international and cultural programs and services.

The owners of Prospect Hill, Robert and Anne Heighe, inherited Durbar and other quality racing stock when Mr. Heighe's aunt, Mrs. Duryea, died. Unfortunately, Durbar II died not long after coming to America and was buried on the farm in front of the original stone farmhouse, the Hays-Heighe House. Built in 1808 and listed on the National Register of Historic Places, the handsome, buff-colored stone house is maintained and used by the College to this day.

Harford Community College was created in response to a need for quality higher education on a local level. In the 1950s, a junior college development committee was organized, made up of members of the Board of Education and educators from the county's seven high schools.

The College, then known as Harford Junior College, started with a $10,000 grant from the Harford County government. It officially opened in 1957 with an enrollment of 116 students and a faculty of 16. The age of students ranged from 17 to 50. Tuition was seven dollars per credit hour.

The original curriculum of the College was created to address the needs of the Harford County business community and to offer opportunities for transfer to four-year institutions.

In 1961 pivotal legislation was introduced by Harford Countian and Maryland state senator, William S. James, which guaranteed state funding to all Maryland community colleges. Because of his leadership, Senator James is often referred to as the "Father of Maryland's community colleges."

The Harford County Board of Commissioners purchased the Hays-Heighe House and its 204 acres in 1962, which

President of the College, Claudia E. Chiesi, Ph.D.

now forms the College campus. The new campus was officially opened in 1964 and included several converted historical structures, as well as the new Aberdeen, Bel Air and Maryland Halls. The 1960s saw a rapid expansion of the physical plant of the College with the opening of

several more new structures, including Joppa Hall, Havre de Grace Hall and the Chesapeake Center. Harford opened the Susquehanna Center in 1968, housing the College's fitness center, Olympic-size pool and gymnasium.

The College changed from Harford Junior College to Harford Community College in 1971. The change was part of a national trend at the time to reflect the more comprehensive nature of the community colleges' services. Athletics were added in 1971, and over the years more than 70 Harford student athletes have received All-American recognition in intercollegiate sports.

Harford Community College broadened its educational scope even further in 1972 by opening a European Division campus in Wiesbaden, Germany, which offered courses to U.S. Air Force military personnel stationed in several European countries. Broadening its scope on the regional level, the College went on the air with its own radio station in 1975. Still broadcasting today, WHFC-FM is the only public radio station in Harford County.

A nine-member Board of Trustees appointed by the governor guides the College. Trustees collaborate in statewide and national leadership activities with the Maryland Association of Community Colleges in Annapolis and the Association of Community College Trustees in Washington, DC.

The 1990s saw an expansion of instruction, student development, international programs, facilities and community outreach services, as well as a focused commitment to environmental stewardship.

Ambitious collaborations have enhanced instruction. The opening of Edgewood Hall Apprenticeship and Training Center in 1994 was a unique collaboration between higher education and a trade association. The Harford County Electrical Contractors Association contributed to the costs of construction. The Higher Education and Applied Technology (HEAT) Center, dedicated in 1995, fulfills the College's economic development role in the region,

Thoroughbred Durbar II, winner of the 1914 Epsom Derby.

provides conference space, acts as a business incubator, and partners with other public/private institutions of higher education for upper division and graduate programs.

The College places special emphasis on its tradition of international education programs and cultural exchange. In the late '90s the College's vocal jazz ensemble performed twice internationally—at the Montreux Jazz Festival and the North Sea Jazz Festival.

Today, Harford is involved with many partnerships that span the globe. The partnership with Russia focuses on health sciences and education reform; the collaborative program with Morocco deals with telecommunications; and the partnership with Germany focuses on the environmental sciences.

The newest international program, on renewable energy, is slated to begin in summer 2004 in Denmark. These international collaborations have provided students and employees with exceptional opportunities for learning and helped those participating to recognize the essential importance of understanding global business and cultural communities.

The College's involvement in the community is demonstrated by the

Jerry Greenfield (center), co-founder of Ben and Jerry's Homemade Ice Cream, at Harford Community College Foundation, Inc. fundraiser with benefactors Roger and Elaine Ralph, April 2003.

strength of its Community Education and Training division, which annually registers over 29,000 participants in noncredit programs for professional development, personal enrichment, and workforce training.

Additionally, the College has served as a site for community dispute resolution. In 1996 the College brokered its first meeting between the local NAACP chapter and law enforcement officers. As an indication of the College's commitment to raise college attendance rates among low-income and minority populations, the College was awarded a five-year, $500,000 partnership grant from U.S. Department of Education for GEAR UP (Gaining Early Awareness and Readiness

Visiting students and faculty from Harford's sister college L'institut National des Postes et Telecommunications, Rabat, Morrocco, April 2000.

for Undergraduate Programs). Minority enrollment continues to grow.

In 1997 Harford Community College launched its impressive Sustainability Program to promote environmental stewardship. Prompted by the National Wildlife Federation publication *Ecodemia*, the College continues to take bold and positive steps in addressing environmental issues in the areas of landscape design, grounds maintenance, recycling, building design and construction, materials purchases, and renewable energy resources and conservation.

Harford Community College President, Dr. Claudia E. Chiesi, introduced four major elements to address campus environmental stewardship: student learning, program development, honoring the environment, and serving as a model for emerging sustainable practices. These elements provide the focus to develop and implement programs that will educate individuals on the meaning of sustainability and the importance of human and environmental interdependence. Through instruction, capital construction, outreach and example, Harford expects to serve as a model for emerging environmentally-friendly practices by showcasing their uses and benefits.

To involve and educate the campus community, faculty, staff and administrators made numerous site visits to green-designed buildings in Maryland, Washington, D.C., Ohio, Pennsylvania and Canada. As a result, the College has incorporated sustainability into its plan for renovation of many of the older buildings. Following the U.S. Green Building Council's LEED™ (Leadership in Energy and Environmental Design) system, the College uses environmentally responsible practices and materials such as recycled/recyclable carpeting, wood from sustainably managed forests, increased natural lighting and renewable energy.

In spring 2003, President Chiesi presented Harford's efforts in environmental stewardship at the National Wildlife Federation-sponsored forum at the University of Maryland. Senior administrators routinely present at conferences, symposia and meetings with elected officials and civic leaders. Recently, the College participated in national conferences at the University of Tennessee and Ball State University, Indiana. On Earth Day 2003, President Chiesi signed the Tailloires Declaration, an international commitment of over 200 colleges and universities to the principles of environmental stewardship and social justice.

In 2000 Harford opened four new buildings. Evidence of the College's cultural and arts commitment is shown in the state-of-the-art William H. Amoss Performing Arts Center. The 908-seat Amoss Center brings nationally-acclaimed artists in the fields of opera, theatre, music and dance to Harford County.

Shortly after the opening of the Amoss Center, the College entered into a formal partnership with the nationally-recognized Washington Ballet. The Ballet is in residence for a week prior to a performance of newly choreographed work, including the world premiere of *Peter Pan*, *The Jazz-Blues Project*, *Cinderella* and *Carmen*. Harford students are offered the opportunity to take master classes with some of the world's finest ballet dancers and choreographers when the Ballet is in residence at the College twice a year.

Complementing its arts programs, the College holds one of the largest public art collections in the county, which is displayed throughout the campus. The College uses its public gallery to promote regional and national contemporary artists.

The College's 50,000-square-foot Library was also dedicated in 2000. Containing 65,000 volumes, the library offers a fully networked digital library available for use by students, employees and interested community members.

The third building to be dedicated in 2000 reaffirmed the College's commitment to the sciences. In conjunction with the Harford County Astronomical Society, the College had operated an observatory for student and community use since 1978. The new Observatory, opened across from the main campus, contains state-of-the-art research and observation equipment, placing Harford on the cutting edge of astronomy and planetary sciences.

The fourth building was the College's adult day care center, strategically situated next to its child day care facility. The intergenerational activities are comple-

Sculpture by Harford County native and former HCC student Amy Butcher Parker in the Library Reading/Reference Room.

mentary to the College's early childhood education program.

The College received its ten-year reaccreditation in 2002 from the Middle States Commission on Higher Education with 47 commendations for excellence in instruction, publications, facilities, service and institutional effectiveness.

Among other notable honors are multiple First and Second Place awards for College publications from the National Council of Marketing and Public Relations. In 2000 Dr. Chiesi received the regional CEO of the Year award from the American Association of Community Colleges. President Chiesi and Naomi Tutu, daughter of Archbishop Desmond Tutu, presented peace and conflict resolution models at the 2001 Peace Conference at Hofstra University in honor of the 100th anniversary of the awarding of the Nobel Peace Prize.

From a junior college with an enrollment of 116 students and funded by a $10,000 grant, Harford Community College has seen its enrollment surpass 5,400, having risen 37% in the last five years. In 2003 the Harford Community College operating budget was more than $29 million with a physical plant value in excess of $44 million.

On the edge of its 50th anniversary and continuing its quest for excellence, Harford Community College has established itself convincingly as a college of character and distinction.

HEFFRON COMPANY

The Heffron Company is a classic study of one man's dream that has flourished through three generations of one family. Founded in 1922 as a small plumbing and heating concern, the company has grown into a highly specialized family-run corporation that now works on the cutting edge of its industry, leading the way into the 21st Century.

Shortly after returning from World War I, where he served as a sergeant, Joseph Heffron set about making his dream of owning his own business a reality. From a stable he purchased along with a house on 12th Street and Independence Avenue in southwest Washington, D.C., Heffron built the first mechanical firm in the city. Remodeling the stable into offices, Heffron created a company that would specialize in commercial and industrial heating and plumbing.

Heffron founded the business on a solid set of core values, which included treating all individuals with respect and dignity, maintaining the highest standards of integrity and loyalty, and providing model leadership that promoted perseverance, a positive attitude, goal achievement and the successful delivery of products and services. He also created a mission statement that included goals such as earning the respect, trust and

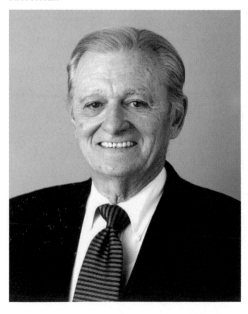

George Dunn Sr., 1955. Refined the direction and core values that have made Heffron successful.

Joseph Heffron, 1927, founder of Heffron Company.

confidence of customers, being a team player in solving their problems, and enhancing company and employee performance through focus and commitment. Heffron's original set of core vales and his mission endures in the company to this day.

Starting with a staff of a heating estimator, a plumber, and three office clerks, Heffron built a company which prospered throughout the 1920s. By 1928 he employed more than 750 people, installing plumbing and heating systems for a rapidly-expanding clientele, as well as continuing to service his original clients.

The stock market crash of 1929 had a tremendous impact not only on the company, but also Heffron himself. Known as a sensitive and generous man, Heffron had signed a great number of promissory notes for employees and others to help them obtain loans during their times of financial difficulty. After the crash, the banks came to Heffron to collect on the notes. At the same time, Heffron's own business shrank to one-tenth of the size it was before 1929. The banks urged Heffron to file for bankruptcy, but he did not want the stigma of bankruptcy upon the family, and devoted

himself to finding a way to pay off the promissory notes as well as his own debts so that the business could once again thrive.

Although he had lost dozens of accounts in the crash, Heffron still had one good customer, Potomac Electric Power. His good record with the giant utility brought Heffron just enough business to keep the company afloat during those dark days, and helped him to persevere. He eventually found enough work for the company to keep his employees on the payroll, and paid off all the debts. It was a great victory for Joseph Heffron, but the stress of the ordeal took a toll on his health. Suffering from diabetes and unable to aggressively solicit new business as he once had, Heffron restructured the company to focus more on service work.

Shortly after that restructuring, the United States government approached Heffron. They wanted to purchase the land where his home and business was located. Heffron sold the plot of land, which became the current site of the Department of Agriculture, moved his business to the northeast section of the city and continued to operate the business from the new location.

Throughout the years of World War II,

George Dunn, Jr. pictured in 1995, ten years after he assumed the presidency of the company.

George Dunn, Sr., Eileen Dunn, George Dunn, Jr. and former Executive Project Manager Safeway Distribution Center, Dino Mostardi.

Heffron's health continued to deteriorate, and though he was unable to participate on a day-to-day basis, he somehow managed to keep the business alive with the help of his wife and employees. In March of 1945 Joseph Heffron died, and the future of the Heffron Company was thrown into limbo. The banks urged Mrs. Heffron to bring in someone to manage the business, but by now Joseph Heffron's dream had been instilled in his wife and she searched for a way to keep it a family-run company. Mrs. Heffron decided to ask her daughter Eileen and son-in-law George Dunn Sr. if they would consider taking over the business.

Eileen and George Dunn Sr. were living in Dallas, Texas, where he had a promising career as a chemist with Sherwin Williams. Dunn, a graduate of the Drexel Institute and only 26 years old, had been co-credited with creating the formula for the camouflage paint used on the hulls of warships, allowing the ships to move through water virtually unnoticed. Even though he was on a fast track to success as a chemist, the couple decided to make a go at the fledgling

family business and keep the Heffron Company alive.

The move was a challenging one. Though Eileen Dunn was raised while her father ran the company business, she had not been a part of its operations. George, whose expertise was in chemistry, had little if any knowledge of the mechanics of plumbing and heating systems. Nonetheless, the couple took

on the challenge. Eileen learned all she could about company finances and bookkeeping and George spent his days learning about piping and systems. His innate analytic skills proved to be extremely useful in understanding how plumbing and heating systems were designed and operated, and helped to him to adjust to the demands of his new business more easily.

The Dunns knew that they had to create a plan to make the business a thriving and viable one once again, and their first official step was the incorporation of The Heffron Company on March 8, 1946. The Dunns also learned to live frugally through the learning curve, and even with credit from only one supply house in the city, they kept the business going. It was during this time George Dunn realized he had a gift for marketing—and one that began to pay off. He was able to win contracts for several major installation and service accounts including Safeway, Georgetown University, U.S. Chamber of Commerce and White Tower Restaurants.

Jack Kent Cooke Stadium 1995, now FedEx Field.

Potomac Electric Generating Station, Morgantown, Maryland.

The years of struggle and perseverance finally brought Heffron Company, Inc. back to solid ground. By 1967 the growing company moved, first renting offices in Bethesda, Maryland, and a few years later purchasing its own property in Bethesda. While still in high school, George and Eileen's son George Dunn, Jr. was drawn into the business and began to spend his summers working at Heffron, learning the skills that would one day help him to run the company.

Gradually the company took on more and more major accounts and continued to nurture the relationship started by the late Joseph Heffron with Potomac Electric Power, which was now PEPCO. The Heffron Company either built or participated in building several large power plants and generating stations for PEPCO, such as Chalk Point, Morgantown, and Potomac River, which they did along with Stone and Webster, and Bechtel. An outgrowth of this work was the building of 20 major dairies along the East Coast throughout the 1960s, '70s and '80s, including facilities for

Embassy Dairy, Shenandoah Pride, Southland Corporation, Sealtest, and Safeway. Heffron partnered with a specialist to design the sophisticated dairy systems and the company then installed all the process piping used for pasteurization and making by-products such as cottage cheese and sour cream. This was a major new direction for the Heffron Company, and propelled them beyond the average installation of plumbing and heating systems into the birth of a new and highly specialized field.

Knowing that he wanted to be a part of the family business since his youth, George Dunn Jr. set out on a course that would allow him to follow in the footsteps of his father and grandfather before him. He first received his undergraduate degree in business from the University of Notre Dame. He then complemented his degree by studying engineering at the Georgia Institute of Technology, and at his father's suggestion, completed the Small Company Management Program at Harvard University. George, Jr. worked in various capacities in the family company until 1985, when he stepped in as president,

replacing his father, who was retiring after 40 years of dedication and service to the company.

Under the innovative leadership of George Dunn, Jr., the Heffron Company has played an integral role in the development of biotechnology labs and research facilities along Maryland's Route I-270 corridor since the early 1990s. George, Jr. accurately foresaw that this was the direction in which business was moving in the Washington, D.C., Maryland, and Virginia regions, and went about training his staff in this specialized area. This decision marked a new turning point for Heffron Company Inc., and one from which the company would greatly benefit.

George Dunn, Jr. considers the work the company has done for Human Genome Sciences in Rockville, Maryland, to be a major landmark in Heffron's success. Working in a design assist capacity, Heffron partnered with Human Genome Sciences, Gil Bane Building Company and other professionals in the design of their campus. The buildings are unique in design, and often required highly sophisticated ventilation systems, which are extremely critical to controlling pressurization, contamination, and cross-contamination. The design required that each of the labs have an independent supply and exhaust system, isolated from all other adjacent systems in the building. Where most structures have no more than three or four piping systems, Heffron installed more than 30 different piping systems for Human Genome Sciences that included lines for hot and cold water, chill water lines, soft water lines, and all different types of gases such as argon and helium. The Heffron Company had more than 200 full-time employees working on the Human Genome

Sciences project alone and at completion will have installed thirty miles of piping systems, a 4,500 ton central plant and sophisticated auto claves and bioreactors.

In the last decade of the 20th Century, 20 percent of Heffron's business has come from the biotechnology industry. Today, approximately 90 percent of the company's business originates from within Maryland's biotechnology corridor, which includes research and development laboratories and pharmaceutical plants, such as those owned and run by Avalon Pharmaceuticals, Genetic Therapy (Novartis), Genvec and BioReliance.

Heffron also remains committed to serving the needs of new commercial and school markets, as well as the tenant renovations markets. The company has worked on such notable projects as the new seven-building, $100 million Eastern Distribution Center for Safeway, Inc. Heffron was also selected as a member of the design/build team for the conversion and renovation of the Old Tariff Building (built by the government in the 1830s) into the new Hotel Monaco owned by the Kimpton Hotel and Restaurant Group. Heffron was responsible for installing the new plumbing system for the hotel's 184 guest rooms, the kitchen, restaurant, duplex ejector grease interceptors, storm drainage and domestic hot water heater exchangers. They also converted the building's existing steam service for hotel comfort heating and installed chilled water pumps, condenser water pumps, and a cooling tower. Other projects for which Heffron has been part of the design/build team include the corporate headquarters for the American Institute of Architects, the Georgetown Visitation Preparatory School, and the food service concessions at Jack Kent Cooke Stadium.

George Dunn, Jr. credits the company's success to the dedication, commitment, and teamwork of their employees, who to this day follow the core values and goals that his grandfather Joseph Heffron

Genetic therapy, Novartis division, 1998.

Human Genome Science Pilot Expansion Plan.

set for the company back in 1922. Dunn, Jr. specifically credits the management team, consisting of Executive Vice President Frank Weis Jr., Vice Presidents Brian Foster and Tom Sullivan, Chief Financial Officer Leslie Jones and Service Manager Bill Parrish, for the company's continuing success. It is also the company's consistent entrepreneurial spirit which contributes to Heffron's longevity. As George Dunn, Jr. says, "We are not a company that is 83 years old, we are a company that is 83 years young."

Safeway Distribution Center 1994.

HOLY CROSS HOSPITAL OF SILVER SPRING

The pathway to Holy Cross Hospital began nearly 20 years before the first brick was laid. Sailors and solders were returning home from World War II, and the Washington, D.C. suburbs were expanding to accommodate the post-war baby boom. The residents of the greater Silver Spring, Maryland, community wanted a local hospital to support the healthcare needs of a young and growing population.

But raising funds for a hospital was a challenge, and after nearly 10 unsuccessful years, the community approached the Congregation of the Sisters of the Holy Cross about building its dream healthcare facility. The Sisters were well-respected founders and sponsors of hospitals throughout the United States, having first begun their healthcare ministry in 1862 during the Civil War.

And so it happened. With the continuous and steadfast support of the community, and with the dedicated support of a core group of committed citizens, the Sisters of the Holy Cross accepted the

challenge, breaking ground for the new hospital on May 8, 1960. Less than three years later, on January 10, 1963, the first patient was admitted.

Today, Holy Cross Hospital stands as the largest community hospital in Maryland, serving nearly 100,000 patients each year. The hospital is also the largest accredited teaching hospital in Montgomery County with physician residency programs affiliated with George Washington University and Children's National

Dignitaries of the day joined the Sisters of the Holy Cross on May 8, 1960, for the hospital's groundbreaking. Less than three years later, on January 10, 1963, the first patient was admitted to Holy Cross Hospital.

Medical Center. Holy Cross also serves as a training site for 13 area nursing programs, operates its own School of Radiologic Technology, and trains students in other disciplines, including respiratory therapy, laboratory technology, physical therapy, occupational therapy and speech pathology.

From the advanced diagnosis and treatment of cancer to the latest in neonatal and pediatric medicine, Holy Cross offers a full range of inpatient and outpatient specialty care services, including emergent care, cardiac, cancer, seniors, surgery, and women and children services.

The hospital serves a broad geographic region, encompassing two of Maryland's largest counties (Montgomery and Prince George's) with a growing population of 2-million people. Women, infants and children represent a significant percentage of the hospital's patient base, and more than 70 percent of the hospital's inpatient admissions are women. Over the past four decades, the hospital's leadership in maternal-child health

On May 15, 1972, Holy Cross Hospital was thrust into the national spotlight, when former Alabama governor and presidential candidate George Wallace was brought to the hospital after being shot in Laurel, Maryland. A state police helicopter and television news crews sit on the front lawn of the hospital.

Opening the same year as I-495 Capital Beltway—the interstate that encircles Washington, D.C.—Holy Cross Hospital has been a familiar and visible landmark for commuters and visitors alike.

services is best illustrated by the fact that more babies are born at Holy Cross Hospital each year than any other facility in Maryland or the District of Columbia. In addition, Holy Cross Hospital operates the only level III+ NICU referral center.

The community surrounding the hospital is also changing as minority populations continue to grow. Responding to these changing demographics, Holy Cross became the first hospital in the region to create a multicultural office to ensure that the hospital's staff has a better understanding of the cultural and linguistic needs of patients. True to their devotion of caring for the whole person—and reflective of how multicultural their staff has become—nearly 200 employees fluent in more than 50 languages, including American Sign Language, volunteer as interpreters when needed.

New technology is evident throughout the hospital—one of the many reasons why Holy Cross has pioneered and refined some of today's leading surgical techniques and medical procedures. Advances in minimally invasive surgery, medical imaging and obstetrical care, have led to Holy Cross's reputation as a recognized leader in the delivery of quality healthcare services. The hospital was one of the first in the greater Washington metropolitan region to create a center of excellence for teaching and refining minimally invasive surgical techniques. Known as the G.A.T.E. Institute, the center provides quality, comprehensive medical education and training in surgery for physicians and other medical professionals. G.A.T.E. also includes a teleconference center where surgeries are often broadcast live into teaching classrooms of other hospitals throughout the United States.

Holy Cross is one of only six cancer teaching programs in Maryland, and with its partners, operates four radiation treatment clinics located in three counties. The hospital has the largest inpatient cancer program in the Maryland suburbs of Washington, D.C., and offers a full range of in-house and outpatient diagnostic and treatment services, serving more than 1,300 newly diagnosed cancer patients annually. The program offers comprehensive cancer services, including advanced medical imaging, chemo- and radiation therapy, surgical intervention, clinical research and a host of educational and supportive programs. Holy Cross also operates its own hospice and home care program.

Equally important is Holy Cross' commitment to those who lack adequate insurance or financial resources for receiving quality healthcare. Each year, Holy Cross—in keeping with its Catholic health care mission—provides free or reduced-cost services for thousands of individuals and families. The hospital operates two obstetrics and gynecology clinics for uninsured women, demonstrating the hospital's commitment to having a significant role in ensuring a healthy future for its community.

And the future is indeed bright. In 2001 Holy Cross Hospital began an historic $78-million facility expansion and modernization project that will add more than 210,000 square feet in new construction and renovate approximately 155,000 square feet of existing space.

Facility upgrades include two new patient care floors, one of which is home to the Holy Cross Hospital; a new physician specialist building that will house an expanded emergency department and surgical critical care floor; a new women and infants center to include all private rooms; a 520-car garage; and a new professional and community education center.

Holy Cross Hospital is in every sense of the word a *community* hospital and reaches out in a variety of ways to improve the health status of the community it serves. This is accomplished by offering an array of community health activities, by collaborating with more than 140 local groups with like-minded objectives for the community, and by reaching out to the poor and most vulnerable among us.

HUDDLES & JONES, P.C.

Specializing in construction law, Huddles & Jones, P.C., is one of the premier law firms in the Mid-Atlantic region representing contractors and people involved in construction disputes. Founded in 1995, the firm was originally called Huddles, Pollack, & Jones, but shortly after opening, partner Howard Pollack was invited by the Clinton Administration to become a federal judge. The firm then became Huddles & Jones, P.C., named for its founding partners, William M. Huddles and Roger C. Jones, and opened its offices in Columbia, Maryland, halfway between Baltimore and Washington, D.C. The firm began with four attorneys but was not considered in any way a "start-up" firm, since the two partners had already amassed more than two decades of construction law experience.

William Huddles received his bachelor of arts from Pennsylvania State University and attended the Georgetown University Law Center. In 1971

Senior Partner, William M. Huddles, Esq.

Senior Partner, Roger C. Jones, Esq.

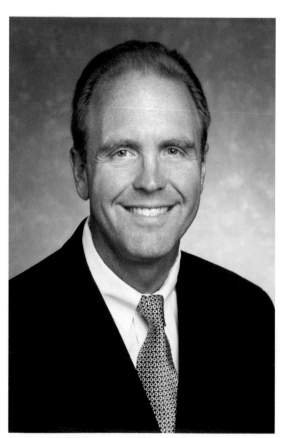

he received his JD with honors from The National Law Center at George Washington University. That year Mr. Huddles began his legal career as a law clerk to Judge Thomas M. Anderson of the Court of Special Appeals of Maryland. His venture into construction law began in 1972, when he was appointed as Assistant Attorney General for the State of Maryland. Mr. Huddles played an integral part in establishing the omnibus Maryland Public Procurement Act, which set forth the procedures for entering into contracts with the state of Maryland. He was also involved in creating procedures for deciding and resolving disputes under those contracts. In addition, he played an instrumental role in creating the Maryland State Board of Contract Appeals, which enabled construction-related cases to be heard by Judges with an expertise in construction law.

From 1975 to 1977, Mr. Huddles was the General Counsel to the Maryland State Aviation Administration. During his tenure as general counsel the state undertook its initial expansion of the Baltimore-Washington Airport, adding to Mr. Huddles' growing experience in the area of construction law. He was named General Counsel to the Maryland State Department of Transportation in 1977 where he advised the state on the construction of the new Baltimore subway system. Mr. Huddles went into private practice in 1979, and in 1981 became a principal partner in the law firm of Braude & Margulies, P.C.

In 2003 Mr. Huddles was appointed by Maryland Governor Robert Erlich as chairman of the Task Force to Study Efficiency in Procurement. This prestigious appointment is a testament to Mr. Huddles' expertise and authority in the areas of government and construction law. The Associated Builders and Contractors also endorsed Mr. Huddles' appointment as chairman. Mr. Huddles sees his appointment as a great opportunity to improve and enhance the procurement and construction system in the state of Maryland.

Roger Jones is a founding partner and the managing director of Huddles & Jones, P.C. Mr. Jones received his Bachelor of Science in Architecture from Catholic University in 1982 (Tau Beta Pi, Engineering Honor Society), with a concentration in construction management. He then received his J.D. from Washington University (Phi Delta Phi, Executive Board, Wiley S. Rutledge Moot Court Society), in 1985. After law school, Mr. Jones joined the firm of Braude & Margulies, P.C., where he became a principal and managing director of the firm. As a construction lawyer, Mr. Jones has been involved in construction projects related to the renovation of Grand Central Station in New York City and the construction of the Universal Islands of Adventure in Orlando, Florida, as well as numerous cases involving the construction of high profile buildings. Some of these include The World Bank Headquarters in Washington, D.C., the EPA Research and Administration Facility in North Carolina and a new National Institutes of Health Laboratory.

Since the firm of Huddles & Jones began, it has seen its business triple. The firm credits its success to a sound business plan, to which it has adhered since its formation. Huddles & Jones believes the plan specifically addresses the needs of contractors and those in the construction field. Part of the plan was recognizing that contractors like to do things economically and efficiently so that they can get on with business as usual. By providing their clients with highly skilled legal advice on construction law that streamlines the legal process in an economic way, Huddles & Jones has

Partner, Kenneth K. Sorteberg, Esq.

proven their plan's effectiveness time after time.

Because the firm limits itself exclusively to construction and government contract law, Huddles & Jones selects attorneys with a high degree of expertise in the field. Mr. Kenneth K. Sorteberg is a perfect example. Mr. Sorteberg came to the firm with both a bachelor's and master's degree in engineering, and worked as a project manager with one of the largest construction companies in Maryland.

Mark S. Dachille, like Mr. Huddles, was an Assistant Attorney General for the state of Maryland and was extensively involved in state construction procurement issues.

Huddles & Jones, P.C., prides itself on its impressive record of resolving 95 percent of the cases it handles, without having to

move into costly litigation. This record does not go unnoticed by other contractors and lawyers who frequently ask the attorneys at Huddles & Jones to serve as mediators or arbitrators.

Though many of their clients are located in the Mid-Atlantic corridor, Huddles & Jones provides legal counsel for clientele across the United States in both the government and the private construction industry. The firm represents general contractors, mechanical, electrical and plumbing subcontractors and numerous specialty subcontractors who perform sheetmetal work, fire protection work, control work, structural steal work, masonary work, grading and excavation work, highway and bridge construction, demolition work and abatement of hazardous materials.

The firm's cases involve contractor, insurance and surety claims on construction projects of virtually every type. Often the cases involve nonpayment, design defects, bid mistakes and protests, labor inefficiency, default terminations, changes, delays and suspension of work.

William Huddles has been admitted to practice law in the state of Maryland, the District of Columbia, the United States Court of Appeals, Fourth Circuit and the D.C. Circuit, as well as the United States Supreme Court. Roger Jones has been admitted to practice law in the state of Virginia, the United States District Court of Virginia, the United States Court of Appeals in the Fourth, Eleventh and Federal Circuits, as well as the United States Court of Federal Claims.

Today Huddles & Jones, P.C. has grown to eight attorneys who are supported by an excellent staff. Their website address is www.constructionlaw.com.

Partner, Mark S. Dachille, Esq.

HUMANIM, INC.

Imagine a 35-year-old woman, institutionalized for the past 25 years, who eats in a restaurant for the first time. A mother of four who leaves public assistance and takes her first job. Or an abused child who tries to take his own life—and finds the courage to get help.

These inspiring stories highlight the difference Humanim, Inc., is making in the lives of thousands of Maryland residents. Since 1972 the Columbia-based nonprofit community rehabilitation agency has offered assistance to individuals with disabilities through vocational, clinical, social and residential services.

A group of Howard County community leaders recognized the need to provide a work-related environment for adults with disabilities through a sheltered workshop, and responded by incorporating the organization in July 1970. Originally known as the Howard County Workshop, the agency opened its first offices in Simpsonville with a staff of five and served less than 10 clients. Initial funding came from the Maryland Division of Rehabilitation Services, the United Way and the Howard County Government.

The organization has undergone two name changes since its founding. In 1983 Howard County Workshop was renamed Developmental Services Group, Inc. (DSG), to reflect the agency's shift from "sheltered" services to a more holistic

Henry Posko, Jr., CEO of Humanim, Inc.

approach of serving disabled individuals. DSG was changed to Humanim, Inc. ("I'm Human" in reverse) in 2001 to give the organization a more recognizable name and reflect the philosophy of its services.

Today Humanim has a staff of 550 professionals serving more than 4,000 individuals in 18 Maryland counties. The organization has over 30 clinical, vocational and residential programs, including programs for children and older adults.

Company President and CEO Henry Posko joined the organization as a vocational evaluator in 1976. He worked

in this capacity for two years, left for a short time, and returned in January 1981 to do contract procurement. In October of that year he became the executive director. Posko succeeded the original director, Roger Newcomb, whose decade-long service helped solidify the agency's presence in the community.

Humanim faced its greatest crisis in the early 1980s, when a crippling recession sparked a dramatic plunge in funding and referrals. Unable to meet financial obligations or pay its nine employees, the board confronted the possibility of closing its doors in late 1981. But Chairman Charles Brehm and other members of the board recommitted themselves—and their wallets—to the future of the organization. Personal checks in the amounts of $500 and $1,000 were written in order to meet that week's payroll. Board members also agreed to hold a series of fundraisers over the next year to pay off debts and regain financial footing.

Once the crisis was over, Humanim began to experience significant growth. The staff moved from its location on Red Branch Road in Columbia to a new building on Gerwig Lane. Several vocational and clinical programs were added, including services to those with chronic mental illness, deafness and transitional school students. In addition, the State of Maryland contracted with the organization to transition to the community individuals who were inappropriately placed in state institutions. This project served individuals who were dually diagnosed with mental illness and developmental disabilities.

The agency undertook a different kind of initiative in 1984 with the opening of a records management division. This optical scanning and microfilming entity provides in-house training and job opportunities for the disabled. Operating under the name Iscan, the division now employs 50 individuals with disabilities and has over $1 million in state, local, and private contracts.

The agency's client list swelled to over

Humanim's current main location as it was when Humanim, Inc. was DSG (Developmental Services Group, Inc.).

Standard for Excellence Class of 2001—December 2001 awards ceremony at Martin's West, Baltimore, Maryland. From left to right: Peter Berns, Maryland Nonprofits executive director; Bob Causer, vice president of human resources; Martina Martin, chair of ethics standards committee; Henry Posko, Jr., CEO; Andrea Paskin, vice president of admissions; and Robert Sharps, immediate past chair of Humanim's Board of Directors.

400 individuals by the mid-1990s. Humanim's staff also grew to more than 100 employees, and operations were transferred to a newly-built facility at Woodside Court. The work center continued to operate at Gerwig Lane until its closing in 1996. At present the Gerwig Lane building houses vocational training programs and a neuro-behavioral unit.

The year 1997 was a time of significant growth for Humanim. The state of Maryland contracted with Humanim to provide behavioral support services for all of Central Maryland. Humanim began their Work Force Solutions program in Towson in order to provide job placement services to Baltimore County's welfare-to-work program. This led to Humanim being recognized as the Small Business Administrations' Welfare to Work Employer of the Year in 2000.

In 1998 Humanim merged with Vantage Place, a large residential program in Howard County. Further growth occurred with the opening of the Woodside Outpatient Mental Health Center. The Center serves over 1,000 individuals annually and is a residency training site for the University of Maryland School of Medicine. Several months later Humanim was asked to manage the in patient psychiatric unit at Howard County General Hospital, a member of Johns Hopkins Medicine. Today Humanim manages all psychiatric services throughout the hospital.

Recognizing the need to provide services to those in Baltimore City, Humanim merged with WorkFirst, Inc., in January 2003. This strong vocational rehabilitation program enabled Humanim to continue focusing on the original cornerstone of their programs, vocational services. Posko says Humanim will continue to move forward with its commitment to community service, "one community at a time." Humanim hopes to offer assistance to an estimated 10,000 individuals by the year 2012.

Today the organization assists people of all ages who have a variety of developmental, psychiatric, physical and neurological disabilities. Through compassion and a commitment to high quality care, Humanim staff strives to live up to their signature phrase "the human spirit of one . . . the compassion of many."

"Staying true to the mission of identifying those in greatest need in our community and providing *uncompromising* human services motivates us," says Posko. "The notion of 'uncompromising human services' says that we will find a way of obtaining the specific services an individual needs regardless of what it takes. Our vision that 'all people in our community will have access to the human services that they require' is bold and challenging. That challenge is rewarding."

Humanim's ribbon-cutting ceremony, 1996. Former Chairman of the Board Charles Brehm and former County Executive Chuck Ecker.

KELLY & ASSOCIATES INSURANCE GROUP

One of the Baltimore area's biggest success stories had its beginnings in the basement of Frank and Janet Kelly's Timonium home in 1976.

It was there that the two started a small health and life insurance agency.

Today, their business has grown into Kelly & Associates Insurance Group (KELLY), the largest group insurance benefits administrator in Maryland and one of the Mid-Atlantic region's largest and fastest-growing administrators, brokers and consultants specializing in healthcare.

With nearly 200 employees and close to $1 billion in insurance premiums administered and under management, KELLY now operates from its 30,000-square-foot headquarters in Hunt Valley and regional satellite offices in Bethesda and Rockville, Maryland; Vienna, Virginia; and Wilmington, Delaware.

Much of this growth has been sparked by the enthusiasm, energy and expertise of Frank and Janet Kelly's four sons, Frank III, John, David and Bryan, who learned the insurance business during summer vacations from college and joined the company full-time after receiving their diplomas.

KELLY's cutting edge technology and state-of-the-art Call Center allows the company to consistently exceed industry service standards.

Kelly & Associates Insurance Group operates from its corporate headquarters in Hunt Valley, Maryland and regional offices in Washington, Virginia and Delaware.

Their focus today is on cutting-edge technology, proven benefit knowledge and personalized administration.

Kelly & Associates' unique *Total Benefits Solution*™ allows employers to create their own customized Benefits Management System and access information 24 hours a day, seven days a week. This advanced technology, and the company's state-of-the-art Call Center, greatly enhance efficiency for employers and brokers of every size.

The company's professional and responsive service team representatives consistently beat industry service standards with an average speed of answer (ASA) of less than 13 seconds, and an abandoned call ratio of less than one percent.

Kelly & Associates' web technology, KTBS*Online*, allows employers and employees to verify coverage, access key benefit information, request ID cards, and more, at any hour of the day. Its other web solution, KAIG*Online*, is an integrated resource for brokers and their clients.

Every aspect of this web technology is guarded by a comprehensive security system that provides multiple lines of assurance.

Through an unwavering dedication to excellence, Kelly & Associates has earned the trust of more than 700 of the region's finest agents and brokers. Its direct sales and marketing division, Kelly Benefit Strategies (KBS), also remains a major area of focus. KBS offers innovative products and services to meet a diverse range of needs for clients as large as MBNA America Bank and as unique as the Baltimore Ravens.

Former State Senator Francis X. Kelly and his wife Janet with their four sons (from left) Bryan, Frank III, John and David.

From sole proprietors to companies with more than 20,000 employees, Kelly & Associates provides the very best personalized service, attention to detail and the most modern tools to manage all human resource needs in one integrated package.

Overseeing corporate affairs as chairman and CEO is former state senator Francis X. Kelly Jr., who represented northern Baltimore County and parts of Carroll and Harford counties in the Maryland General Assembly during a distinguished 12-year political career.

The day-to-day operations of Kelly & Associates are handled by President Frank Kelly III, CLU, RHU, REBC. Since Frank assumed that position in 1994, Kelly & Associates has taken off as a regional powerhouse.

John Kelly, the second of Frank and Janet's sons to join the business, is a veteran of the insurance industry and is president of Kelly Benefit Strategies. John developed the company's *Total Benefit Solution*™ approach, which is unique in the health insurance industry. His primary focus is large employer groups and refining KBS' computer technology.

David Kelly, executive vice president and senior consultant for Kelly Benefit Strategies, supervises marketing and sales for all Kelly & Associates divisions. He also oversees the company's facilities and real estate management. Additionally, David handles the daily operations of Kelly Benefit Strategies' group and association sales team and serves as a benefits consultant.

Bryan Kelly, executive vice president of broker sales and marketing for Kelly Marketing Services (KMS), acts as liaison with insurance carriers and the more than 700 affiliated brokers serviced by Kelly. He manages KMS and maintains the company's presence within the Mid-Atlantic broker community and at industry association meetings.

When Frank and Janet Kelly set up shop, they applied for a $10,000 line of credit and started selling insurance. Within a year, Frank brought in a business partner, Gary Chick, CLU, and changed the name to Kelly-Chick & Associates. They focused on assisting small companies in search of affordable health insurance benefits.

The concept was simple. By pooling small businesses into larger groups through industry, trade or professional associations, they provided better benefits at lower rates for their clients. This innovative response pro-pelled Kelly-Chick into the small group market.

In 1985, Frank Kelly and Gary Chick agreed that the Kelly family eventually would buy the entire business. The buyout began in 1988. A short time later, Gary Chick retired. He remains a close personal friend of the Kelly family.

During the 1990s, the Kelly sons made a significant impact on the enterprise's direction and growth. They set their sights on expanding marketing support and administrative services both to, and through, independent insurance agents and brokers. They also reengineered KELLY's technology so it would become an industry leader.

The results are obvious: KELLY has grown from 1,000 corporate clients in the early 1990s to nearly 10,000 clients today throughout the Mid-Atlantic region, and from approximately $15 million in annual-ized insurance premiums administered and under management to nearly $1 billion today.

Kelly & Associates' mission statement sums up the company modus operandi: a commitment to the pursuit of excellence in an effort to honor and glorify God; always putting "the customer first" through quality insurance products, benefits and services; dealing honestly and professionally with carriers and suppliers; and valuing KELLY employees by treating them with dignity and respect.

Hard work, integrity and strong faith have propelled the Kellys to new heights in the insurance world. What began as Frank and Janet's vision now thrives in reality, thanks to their sons. It is, indeed, a remarkable story of success.

LEXINGTON MARKET

Consume chocolate to your stomach's content. Watch elephants high-step through the streets en route to a feast prepared just for them. Enjoy live music on weekends or simply lose yourself in the maze of food stalls and specialty shops.

Visitors can experience all of this and so much more at Lexington Market, a Baltimore treasure whose colorful history dates back to the founding of our nation.

Renowned for being the oldest continuously operating food market in the U.S., Lexington Market celebrates its 221st anniversary in 2003. And officials are making plans for the market to flourish for at least 200 more.

The marketplace has been a fixture on Lexington Street since 1782 and still occupies the original site, located between Eutaw and Greene Streets. Revolutionary War hero and future Maryland Governor John Eager Howard donated the property

Historic Lexington Market, circa 1920s.

for the market. Formerly a pasture, the tract was part of the Howard family's expansive landholdings that extended north and west to the present locations of George Washington's monument and General Howard's statue. The market was named for the Battle of Lexington, where the famous "shot heard around the world" marked the beginning of the American Revolution.

Now the length of two city blocks, the sprawling food and entertainment complex features 140 vendor stalls, a music stage, a dining area, and a variety of annual festivals that draw an estimated 3.7 million visitors each year. In fact, Lexington Market ranks as the third biggest attraction in the Greater Baltimore area.

That's an accomplishment which makes Casper Genco, the general manager of Lexington Market, feel very proud. "We draw more people than either the Baltimore Orioles or the Baltimore Ravens. I don't think there is anyone who has grown up in and around Baltimore who

hasn't heard of Lexington Market," says Genco. "Not only does it serve the residential community, but the business community as well. Lexington Market also serves as a major tourist attraction. People from Virginia, Pennsylvania, Delaware, and New Jersey come here and visit the market."

Genco spent 32 years in the supermarket industry with the A&P and Super Fresh chains before joining the organization last summer. He fondly remembers coming to the market with his parents when he was a young boy. "If I was well-behaved, I got chocolate," he says.

The experience of traveling to market has greatly changed since the early days when farmers drove their horse-led Conestoga wagons over rough terrain to sell their wares. Roads were poor at best, especially during the rainy seasons. The 20-mile journey from Towson or Reisterstown was tedious and difficult. In many cases, farmers traveled all night long so they could arrive for the

Lexington Market today after $4.2 million renovation. Photo by Hudson Pinckney

opening ringing of the bell at dawn.

Without the luxury of stalls or sheds, farmers displayed their wares on blankets spread out across the field. They sold fresh produce, hams, turkeys, eggs, and butter. The nearby Chesapeake Bay, with its wealth of fish, crabs, and oysters, also presented fishermen with the opportunity to sell seafood at the market. Soon merchants joined farmers and fishermen in establishing a purchase and barter exchange system for grain, livestock, and staple items.

The site remained an open air market until 1803, when a wooden shed was constructed on the corner of Eutaw and Lexington Streets. By 1925, the market expanded over another block to Greene Street and included hundreds of stalls. For 145 years, the familiar clang of the bell could be heard ushering in the start of a new day and signaling its close.

But tragedy struck on March 31, 1949. A six-alarm fire tore through the entire marketplace, destroying the sheds and resulting in a staggering $4 million in damage. Even then, the market did not close down completely. Only hours after the devastation, undaunted merchants found a few unscorched spots where they could set up shop. The market was temporarily reestablished in less than a week.

By late 1951, rebuilding the complex was completed, primarily with financing through revenue bonds. Sturdy buildings made of brick and concrete replaced the wooden sheds. At long last, the new and improved market officially opened for business in 1952.

Lexington Market has continued to evolve from its humble beginnings as an informal gathering of farmers in a donated field to a 400,000-square-foot shopper's paradise. The city of Baltimore owned and operated the market for many years. In 1979 the Lexington Market Authority became Lexington Market, Inc., a quasi-public corporation which leases the property from the city.

Today the marketplace consists of two major buildings, known as the West Market and the East Market, respectively. Located between Greene and Paca Streets, the West Market features about 20 retail stalls inside, 16 outside non-food stalls and six full retail stores, and a parking garage that holds more than 1,000 vehicles. The East Market, situated between Paca and Eutaw Streets, boasts 80 stalls, a sit-down restaurant, a convenience market, the Arcade music stage, a 500-seat dining section overlooking the stage and surrounding shops, and three meeting rooms to cater lunches and business events.

The list of vendor selections will stir even the smallest of appetites. An 8,000-square-foot grocery store sells a cornucopia of foodstuffs. Six meat stalls and five poultry stalls offer fresh beef, pork, veal, lamb, sausage, turkey, and chicken. There are 11 delicatessens, eight bakeries, and 10 fresh produce stands.

Among the four fresh seafood vendors is Faidley's, an institution at Lexington Market since 1886. Faidley's is famous for its jumbo lump blue crab cakes. The company has been featured in prominent publications such as the *New York Times* and *Southern Living*. *GQ* magazine voted Faidley's crab cakes "one of the top 10 dishes in the world" and honored them with the Golden Plate award.

Candy is the specialty at Konstant's, the oldest continuous family-run operation at the market. Konstant's opened up shop here in 1896 and now manages three stalls. From taffy to hard candies to fresh roasted peanuts, the choices are simply irresistible for anyone with a sweet tooth. Konstant's also sells hot dogs and sandwich wraps.

The new and improved Lexington Market in 1952.

Other food shops specialize in salads, ice cream, pretzels, potatoes, fried chicken, and fresh ground coconut. In fact, there are over 40 prepared food stalls at the market, half of which feature dishes with a distinctly international flavor. Baltimore is well-known for its diverse ethnic communities, and nowhere in the city is this more apparent than at Lexington Market. Just as European immigrants opened up stalls at the market in the 19th century, today vendors from a myriad of ethnic and cultural backgrounds serve up their own traditional cuisines. Among the nations represented are Korea, China, India, Greece, Italy, Mexico, and Jamaica.

In addition, there are numerous non-food merchandisers who sell an assortment of jewelry, cosmetics, leather goods, music, and magazines. Two tax service companies and a bank are on-site, as well as a florist shop and a shoe repair business.

Food and general merchandise are not the only offerings at the marketplace, however. Lexington Market also hosts several annual festivals, holds health awareness events, and features live music year-round.

"Lunch with the Elephants" has been a rite of spring in the Baltimore area for the past 18 years. Held in conjunction with the mid-March arrival of the Ringling

Brothers and Barnum and Bailey Circus, the event showcases 10 to 13 elephants who march from the First Mariner Arena, up Eutaw Street to Lexington Market's south parking lot. Here they are greeted by thousands of adoring fans and treated to the world's largest stand-up buffet of vegetables and fruits. Eight-foot-long tables are spread out with mouthwatering delicacies any pachyderm would gladly sink his trunk into. A crew starts chopping up the food at 6 a.m. that day. Servers feed the elephants an astonishing 1,100 oranges, 1,000 apples, 500 heads of lettuce, 700 bananas, 500 carrots, and 400 pears. Live music and authentic circus clowns are also on hand to entertain the crowd. As part of its claim to fame, Baltimore is the only city in the nation to host this celebration on an annual basis.

Mid-May is horseracing season in Maryland, so what better time to hold a Preakness event for…uh, crabs? That's right, now in its 13th year, the Preakness Crab Derby is one of the most ridiculous, absolutely hilarious events one can imagine. Twenty-two crustacean contestants took part in this spring's competition. Local personalities from television, radio, and newspapers race live blue crabs in a series of events. The celebrities get down on their hands and knees, armed only with a spray bottle and a long stick with a whiffle ball attached on a string.

Customers enjoying the market today.

The crab is placed on the ground behind two large circles and is gingerly coaxed to crawl toward the line. The first crab to cross the line wins the race. The celebrity winner of the lap race receives $500 to be given to the charity of choice, and is treated to a bushel of crabs.

For the chocoholic, Lexington Market hosts the Annual Chocolate Festival during the second week of October. Celebrating its 20th anniversary in 2003, the festival lasts for three days and draws about 30,000 people each year. A dozen or more Baltimore chocolatiers and bakeries participate, creating hundreds of delectable confections. Fudge, truffles, chocolate-layered cakes, cookies, pies, and hand-dipped strawberries, apples, and bananas are just a sampling of the many offerings. Cooking demonstrations, children's entertainment, and live music shows add to the fun. The highlight of the festival is the chocolate eating contests. Beginning with small items and moving to the cakes in the grand finale, contestants eat as much chocolate as they can in three minutes with no hands. The grand prize

for this year's winner is a trip to a Caribbean island.

During the month of December, Lexington Market sponsors a number of holiday events. The Christmas Concert series, held at noon on Monday through Saturday, features local school choirs and regional bands performing the sounds of the season. A holiday fashion show gives the Westside merchants an opportunity for added publicity. The models carry platters of sushi, chicken, and other famous dishes made at the market.

Fresh Music at the Market is a year-round event held on the Arcade stage on Fridays and Saturdays from noon to 2 p.m. Local bands perform jazz, rhythm and blues, reggae, country, pop, gospel, and big band music.

Health and Nutrition Day is held in mid-June, offering health screenings, cholesterol and blood pressure checks, and nutritional information. The event is sponsored by the University of Maryland Medicine and Maryland General Hospital. A half-marathon is planned for spring 2004 with proceeds going to charity.

As a focal point of downtown Baltimore for more than two centuries, Lexington Market must continuously reinvent itself to better serve the community. A two-year,

$4.2 million renovation was completed in January 2003 to make the character of the existing buildings more compatible with 19th century structures in the district. New lighting and signage, and larger exterior windows were added to create an open, airy atmosphere. Increased seating and refurbished restrooms also improved comfort and convenience for market patrons.

These are exciting times for Lexington Market and the entire neighborhood it anchors. A major renaissance is underway in the Westside of downtown Baltimore with a mixture of historic preservation projects and new development planned. Next year the $70 million renovation of the historic Hippodrome Theater will be completed, transforming it into a major performing arts center in the city. Across from the theater will be a new residential and commercial development called Centrepoint. The project will include 325 apartments, 50,000 square feet of retail stores, and parking areas. The recently-completed Atrium, located about a block away from the Centrepoint site, added another 174 apartments to the district.

"It is very fulfilling to work on behalf of an institution that has such a long and respected history," says Bernard Berkowitz, president of the Board of Directors of Lexington Market, Inc. "It is a vital part of downtown Baltimore and its economy, and it's especially gratifying to see the changes that have taken place in the last two years."

Standing behind its proud tradition of community service, Lexington Market is committed to lead the way in efforts to revitalize Westside Baltimore. With recent interior and exterior renovations now complete, officials hope to make the market even more of a magnet to residents and tourists. Through festivals, music concerts, and a smorgasbord of great food, Lexington Market plans to welcome patrons through its doors for years to come.

Lexington Market is open Monday through Saturday, from 8:30 a.m. to 6:00 p.m.

...ES OF LEADERSHIP

...APER COMPANY

...athew Chakola ... in India, he ... ...bled notes on his door. ... ...e from fellow students, who mo... ...d his belief that Apollo 11 would really make it to the moon. After the astronauts' first moonwalk, the notes stopped. But that was just the beginning of Chakola's dreams. He felt that if it was possible to walk on the moon, it was possible to do anything.

Today, Chakola—who has wisdom, a wonderful sense of humor and a philanthropist's heart—is the CEO and owner of the Maryland Paper Company, a paper recycling company that is environment-friendly, and is one of the greater Washington D.C. area's leading users of recycled waste paper. His dream for global recycling has been set in motion, with the 2003 addition of Alabama Paper Products in Tuscaloosa, Alabama, and another plant set to open soon in Bakersfield, California. All plants focus on recycling felt paper used in the roofing industry. Customers, who buy the product, then saturate it with asphalt and make tar paper or roof shingles out of it. The Maryland Paper Company's customer base ranges from

all over the Southeastern United States, stretches to California and even has some Canadian clients.

Chakola holds a bachelor of science degree in mechanical engineering from the University of Kerala in India, and a master of engineering degree in engineering mechanics from Widener University, in Chester, Pennsylvania. He believes that we're all here to do something that God would be proud of—to leave this planet better than the way we received it. He credits both his parents for instilling in him the faith and courage to live his beliefs. "I inherited the best of both

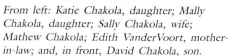

From left: Katie Chakola, daughter; Mally Chakola, daughter; Sally Chakola, wife; Mathew Chakola; Edith VanderVoort, mother-in-law; and, in front, David Chakola, son.

worlds," he says. "My mother was a strong Christian woman, and my father was a self-made man with unlimited dreams." His father passed away in 1982. "He was noble of look and speech." Chakola and his wife, Sally, are the proud parents of Mally, a law student at Pace University; Katie, an architecture student at the University of Maryland; and David, an elementary school student at Mother Seton School.

From 1976 to 1979, he worked as a project engineer for the Fintkote Company in Peachtree City, Georgia. When he first applied for the job, though, he remembers being told that he was overqualified, because of his master's degree. He replied, "Don't hold my education against me; I need to start somewhere." Flintkote then hired him, and Chakola eventually served as general contractor for the design and construction of a new fiberglass mat plant.

By 1979 Chakola was working as the assistant plant manager and plant engineer in Frederick, Maryland, for Tamko Asphalt Products, Inc., and in 1985 he was serving as project manager for Frederick's Morgan-Keller, Inc. He became the vice president of engineering for Laser

Mathew Chakola with son, David, before taking off for Alabama plant.

Maryland Paper Company.

Applications, Inc., in Westminster, Maryland, in 1987.

All of his work experience would prepare him to start the Maryland Paper Company, which broke ground on May 6, 1989, and became fully operational by October 1990. In under a one-year period, he engineered, designed, developed and implemented plans to erect and operate a multi-million dollar, ongoing, full-production capacity dry paper felt manufacturing plant. He purchased a 70-year-old processing machine from Celotex Corporation in Grays Ferry, near Philadelphia, Pennsylvania, and then rebuilt and redesigned it. Today, it has the production capacity of 10,000 tons of paper per month.

What makes this paper plant so unique and successful is that it uses no chemicals in the recycling process. Chakola created a system to recycle old corrugated cardboard, newspaper and office paper without harming the environment. This system, which is odorless, clean, fast and energy-efficient, uses only water, which also gets reused, with nothing going back into the public water system. Also, natural gas is used for heating the water—and, as a result, no pollutants are released.

Chakola challenges everyone to recycle. He once told *The Northport Gazette*: "Ours is the only planet with life, and it is shrinking. Humanity produces more waste than any other living thing, and

what are doing about it? Who will take care of our planet if we don't?"

The Maryland Paper Company started off with only eight workers, and now employs 91, with most having been with him since the beginning. His secretary, Claudia Millhouse, has been with the company for 10 years—after retiring as a paralegal—and another employee, Bill Delouney, retired at the age of 62 with another company before going to work with Chakola. Also vital to the business is Barbara Graff, Chakola's receptionist, who has been with the plant since the beginning. Chakola respects his employees and talks about them as though they were part of his own family. In leadership positions are: George B. Delaplaine III, operations manager; Ronald Baker, production superintendent; Bernard Keefer, safety director; Akbar Lotfi, plant engineer; Debi Dennis, comptroller; and Jeffrey Hooper, manager of shipping and receiving. This group stays current on all new machinery, products and innovative techniques that are indigenous to the recycling industry.

Around the office, Chakola makes sure there is room for laughter in the middle of all the work. He loves that anyone in America can dream big; he loves the United States. "You are as free as an eagle here," he says. "You have no idea—this could never happen in India," he says, referring to the caste system. "In America, I am judged on who I am;

they are interested in my content. This is a beautiful country founded on Christian values, but America has lost those spiritual values. We are the ones that people around the world are trying to copy, and if the whole world is trying to copy us, why do we want to change?"

He is also a believer in children—in their ability to make our planet a better place. But, he sees the need to encourage their potential abilities. "We should educate our children," he says. "They are the dreamers; they are the future." He continues, "Prosperity makes us less productive. Wealth always moves with dreamers. Dreamers become producers. Where are the dreamers? They are random shooting stars; some stay still."

A bit of cherished advice that was given to Chakola was from his uncle, "Dr. Chacko," who had worked for Ghandi and served at the United Nations for 22 years. Right before he died at the age of 89, he told him that "a little bit of conservatism will help you." Chakola explained that conservatism would ask you to evaluate the situation when someone knocks at your front door; to not open the door immediately; but, to look through the window first and then make a decision.

Chakola must have looked through the window on many occasions. The Maryland Paper Company is doing extremely well, with all signs pointing toward a wonderful future, where the sky's the limit.

MARYLAND PAVING, INC. AND GRAY & SON, INC.

In 1942 George Palmer, current company chairman of Gray & Son, Inc., and Maryland Paving, Inc., began his career as a teenager, working as an oiler on a steam shovel for a Maryland construction company. At the age of 19 Palmer joined the Navy Seabees, the Navy's Construction Battalion ("CB") that made a point of recruiting civilians with some construction experience in civilian life. Palmer joined in the Seabees' construction efforts overseas in Okinawa and on the Aleutian Islands, helping to build roads and airports in the Pacific theaters of World War II.

The Maryland Construction Company of Gray & Son, Inc., a leading Baltimore contractor specializing in earthwork, utilities and paving, traces its origins to a trade in 1908 of two mills. Thomas Gray, who owned and operated a large mill in Ashland, Virginia, traded his Virginia mill for a mill and dam in Butler, Maryland. Gray then operated the grist mill there, grinding flour for nearly a decade until he was put out of business by larger area mills. In 1920 Thomas Gray's son, Oscar M. Gray, opened the Butler Stone Quarry, located on the property, where the old mill stands today, along scenic Falls Road in Maryland's Baltimore County. Gray began selling stone

Hot Mix facility, Aberdeen, Maryland.

throughout the state and in Washington. Some of the first stone excavated from the quarry went into the building of Baltimore City College.

In 1925 Oscar Gray leased his quarry to Harry T. Campbell & Son Company. Both Gray and Oscar would work for the Campbell Company until its quarry lease expired in 1939, when the Grays reestablished their own quarrying business. The quarry business survived the war years, and in the post-war years, the Grays began building houses with the superior stone supplied by their quarry. In 1952 the Grays added E-Z Surface, a tennis court building division, to their list of business concerns. The new

company itself dissolved within a few years, but its methods of applying asphalt pavement transferred easily into the road building operations of Oscar Gray & Son. George Palmer, hired by Gray to manage the new tennis court operation, stayed on with him after the division closed in 1953.

The Federal-Aid Highway Act of 1956 called for the designation of a national system of interstate highways to connect metropolitan areas and industrial centers, in part as a way of serving the national defense during the cold war. In 1955 President Eisenhower characterized the growing system of roads as "dynamic elements" uniting "forces of communication and transportation," which would serve to strongly establish a system of "united states" in this country. A good deal of the work accomplished by Oscar Gray's company in the 1950s adhered to Eisenhower's vision: the road building operation of the company obtained contracts for new development roads, as well as contracts with the school board of Baltimore County and the Department of Public Works of the State of Mary-

Left to right: William Ensor, George Palmer and Robert Webbert at mill.

George Palmer in 2002 with a 1962 B-61 Mack truck at an antique truck-and-tractor show.

land. By the mid-1960s, Oscar M. Gray & Son would employ over 100 workers.

In 1966 Oscar P. Gray sold his burgeoning company to George Palmer. The company's new co-owners included Calvin Palmer, Palmer's brother, and Clyde Cofiell, Palmer's brother-in-law. The new owners renamed their company Gray & Son, Inc., keeping the old family name for legal reasons and for established lines of credit, but especially for the good will associated with the company's name. During the 1970s, Gray & Son, Inc., under Palmer's leadership, would grow into one of the largest and most respected construction companies in the state. Today, the company employs 350 people. Its good will continues to thrive, especially in regard to employee relations: Palmer notes that employee Bill Cole retired recently after 44 years with the company. Employee Dave Baer retired after 47 years, and Earl Wolfe after 49 years of employment with Palmer. Many

employees have been with the company for at least 20 years.

In 1964, at Palmer's suggestion, Oscar P. Gray and Harvey Myers founded Maryland Paving, primarily to quickly and economically supply Palmer's company with hot-mix asphalt for construction projects. Gray & Son bought out Myer's share of the company in 1974, and in 1978 Palmer bought out the remaining interest of Oscar Gray in the company. In the spring of 1980, Palmer, now primary owner of Maryland Paving, Inc., brought in his nephew, William Ensor, as his vice president and general manager. The company flourished under the stewardship of both men. Ensor now serves as president of Maryland Paving, which remains on the supply side of the business, continuing to provide asphalt for Gray & Son projects. In 1988 Palmer's son-in-law, Robert Webbert, added his plumbing company to Gray & Son's roster. Webbert now serves as president of Gray & Son, Inc. Palmer's daughter, Barbara Webbert, serves as its treasurer.

Both Gray & Son and Maryland Paving have been honored with

awards of excellence within the industry, with Maryland Paving's plants winning three Maryland With Pride Plant of the Year awards from the State of Maryland within the decade. Both of Palmer and Ensor's companies have received the National Asphalt Association Diamond Achievement Award for exercising exceptional diligence regarding environmental concerns. In 1999 Maryland Paving acquired the Lafarge asphalt paving company, thereby doubling its production capabilities overnight.

Family ties between Ensor and Palmer are especially close: Palmer's wife, Jane, is the twin sister of Ensor's mother. Ensor describes his uncle, an ardent bluegrass guitarist, sportsman, hunter and fisherman, as "one of the old school," whose word is his bond. Palmer, in fact, employs an even more venerated custom of transacting business: all company purchases, including those for trucks and equipment, are made in cash. Both men enjoy antique truck shows, and a photo of Palmer with his hand on the finial of a highly polished Maryland Paving antique truck shows a face filled with vitality and good humor.

In the winter of 2000, Gray and Son, Inc., and Maryland Paving, Inc., resurfaced a portion of Falls Road, a dirt road that Palmer had walked on his way to school many years ago. Speaking recently from his office at Gray & Son at the age of 80, he notes with humor that he "doesn't want to work forever!" Working or retired, he can certainly look back over a long career with pride.

THE MARYLAND PUBLIC LIBRARY

What was once unimaginable is now commonplace: Marylanders can walk into one of the many branches of their public library system and choose from an impressive array of services. They can meet their congressional representative, learn how to plant a fall garden, join a chess club and borrow works of art. They can learn English as a Second Language (ESL), find a repair manual for a 1937 DeSoto, or conduct a comprehensive job search. With a mere click of the mouse, a student struggling with calculus can be connected with live homework help. Fledgling third-grade readers can increase their confidence by reading aloud to therapy dogs, the most non-judgmental audience in existence. And all of this is happening in Maryland's progressive public library. Obviously, a visit to one of its libraries is no longer solely about books.

The day has arrived when libraries such as Maryland's are no longer passive repositories of printed material. Rather, they have changed with the times and with the shifting needs of the people they pledge to serve. Today, Maryland's library serves as an "engine of learning"—a place where a spark is struck for disadvantaged citizens, older Americans and anyone who previously did not enjoy access to the vast stores of knowledge that most of us take for granted.

Uniquely, every citizen of Maryland has access to every volume—millions of books—across the state, thanks to a system of reciprocity that began in the 1950s and which Marylanders easily take for

The Book Buggy, a library on wheels, visits Head Start centers throughout Baltimore City and provides books, cassette tapes and educational toys for thousands of preschoolers.

Enoch Pratt, founder of the Enoch Pratt Free Library in Baltimore City.

granted. If you own a library card in one of Maryland's systems, you can use the same card in the other 23 systems without paying a registration fee. The card catalogue is "online" for all counties, allowing patrons to search all libraries simultaneously. "The amazing thing is that it has worked so well," says Maurice Travillian, a retiree and former Maryland state librarian.

Maryland boasts the first urban public library in the country—the Enoch Pratt Free Library, founded in 1882 in Baltimore City by the merchant banker Enoch Pratt. The Central Library, built in 1933, serves as Maryland's State Library Resource Center (SLRC) and is the hub of SAILOR, the state electronic information network. "We just caught a wave at the right moment," says Travillian. "The Internet came along; we happened to have the funds; and we could move on this initiative right away." The network worked so well that the state began to invest funds in it.

Every library in Maryland—some 200 of them—is connected to the Internet, as are schools and government agencies.

SAILOR has experienced phenomenal growth and a record number of "hits" a year. The state is one of the few in the nation to enjoy computer and Internet penetration to over 65 percent of its population. Its statewide electronic interlibrary loan system, MARINA, boasts over 90,000 public library patrons.

The Maryland State Library Network consists of the SLRC (the Enoch Pratt Free Library in Baltimore); three regional library resource centers (Eastern Shore, Southern Maryland, Western Maryland); four academic libraries lending specialized materials, and more than 125 libraries that fill interlibrary loan requests from their collections.

Although the Maryland Public Library of today is the beneficiary of support from many sources (The Bill & Melinda Gates Foundation recently provided the state's libraries with $700,000 worth of computers, Internet access and technical training through their State Partnership Program), the early years of the system were marked by slow growth and a lack of funding.

According to Travillian, the earliest effort to develop a system of libraries offering books to Marylanders began in 1699, thanks to the then-newly appointed commissary of the Anglican Church, the Reverend Thomas Bray. The Oxford-educated man, who began to recruit clergymen for assignment to Maryland, discovered that many of his recruits were too poor to own books. He decided, therefore, that each of his new parishes should have a library.

Reverend Bray raised money and sought donations of books from not only authors but from people who owned large private libraries. He made the books available to all literate people in the parish and designed a circulation system and a book catalogue—emulating the modern librarian of today. His early writings communicate a desire to develop "lending libraries" to accommodate "persons who must ride some miles to look into a book . . . such journeys being too expensive of time and money."

Enoch Pratt Free Library, Baltimore City.

Fundraising quickly became a problem, so Bray turned to then-Governor Francis Nicholson to "turn swords to books" by diverting revenue normally reserved for arms and ammunition to form a library in Annapolis, Maryland.

In 1882 a wealthy hardware merchant named Enoch Pratt proposed to the Mayor and City Council of Baltimore City that he build a public library on his own lot. He agreed to provide the building, plus an endowment for the operation of the library, if the city would agree to provide $50,000 a year for its support. Voters approved the arrangement by a wide margin that same year.

In 1901 The Washington County Free Library opened for business as one of the first countywide library systems in the nation supported partially by public money. It was this library that introduced the book wagon as a means of getting materials to rural parts of the county, serving as the precursor to the bookmobile that became a major source of library service in the 1950s and 1960s.

In the early 1900s, only three free libraries in Maryland were supported with public funds. A newly formed Maryland Public Library Commission struggled in its attempts to develop public library service for the citizens of the state.

Ironically, the early years of the 20th century witnessed a very rapid development of public library service in many states—though not in Maryland, with the exception of the Enoch Pratt Free Library and a few others. This may have been partly attributable to the lack of an adequate law that provided a legal framework for county government to operate a public library. Another hindrance was the fact that almost 50 percent of the population resided in the City of Baltimore, which was already well served by the Enoch Pratt Free Library.

In 1922 responsibility for the development of libraries was transferred to the state superintendent of schools. Growth in the public library service was very slow in the period before World War II. A 1944 study showed that only 10 libraries were open more than 25 hours a week. Only five libraries circulated more than four books per capita.

These bleak statistics helped lead to a major lobbying effort to secure new legislation to support library service. In 1945 the General Assembly passed a bill that established the Public Library Act of Maryland. This provided for state aid to libraries giving free county-wide services and established the conditions for the organization and management of library systems.

By 1960 circulation in public libraries had increased dramatically. In 1971 a new law named the Central Library of the Enoch Pratt Free Library as the State Library Resource Center. It also created three regional library resource centers, as well as the Maryland Advisory Council on Libraries. By 1980, 545 professional librarians and 2,688 total staff were serving Maryland library patrons.

Thanks to its ability to embrace change, innovation and creativity, Maryland's public library system is in a position to provide its citizens with information anytime, anyplace and anywhere. Throughout its history, it has paid attention to how people are using information, identifying and testing new technologies and services to fit this model.

One such test of new technology was conducted by a committee headed by Scott Reinhart, assistant director for operations at the Carroll Public Library System. Reinhart and his committee have been studying the benefits of a statewide library card capable of storing information about the user, such as name, address and other contact information. This data will allow library patrons to more easily use any public library in the state. The Smart card also provides additional benefits, including debit card capabilities to allow the customer to use the card to pay for

The Grantsville library, Garrett County, moved to the Liberty Trust Bank Building in 1967.

fines, copying fees and other services. The innovation may have an added benefit: it will be capable of identifying whether the customer would like to have information from the Internet filtered, and at what level. The system could be operational by next spring. "The technology is here right now. Previously, we didn't have the mechanism to do this," says Reinhart.

The state's libraries continually seek new ways to support customers wherever they might be. Over the past five years, 24/7 Reference has been delivering customized software tools for the emerging virtual reference market. Maryland is now part of a consortium of libraries nationwide through 24/7 Reference offering round-the-clock online service.

At the Pratt Center for Technology Training, free computer learning courses such as Microsoft® Word, Excel, and PowerPoint® are offered.

Father and son enjoying the Wicomico County Library's Birth to Four family resource area.

After hours, libraries from Massachusetts to California provide service to Maryland residents. Likewise, librarians in Maryland do the same when other areas of the country have gone to bed.

A unique collaboration between Jean Johnson, director of the Somerset County Library, and June Brittingham, a librarian at Maryland's Eastern Correctional Institute (ECI), led to a summer reading program for prison inmates. After hearing Brittingham lament the fact that inmates had little to do over the summer months, Johnson gave the issue some thought. The result was a summer reading program for prison inmates, giving them incentives (often small gifts) to accumulate and read as many books as possible, following up with written book reviews. Now in its second year, the program has been a huge

success. Last year, 68 inmates returned 410 book reviews, and 34 inmates read at least five books. The program has since been expanded and still enjoys state funds and support.

According to George Sands, director, "Thanks to work in progress at the Caroline County Public Library, and a website named myfamilyneeds.info, patrons can access a database of local agencies and organizations which connect people in need to the agencies that can serve them." The local agencies are trained on how to use the database, so it's a two-way street: the patron is brought to the agency and the agency is brought to the patron. The state is also working on digitizing important historical data that patrons can access through something as simple as a key word. This enhanced information referral service is being tested as a model to be used statewide, and its base of local information will continue to grow.

Kathleen Reif, director of the Wicomico County Library, is a living example of another recent innovation in the Maryland Public Library. Not long ago, she and two fellow directors delved into research on the development of a baby's brain from birth through age three. After conducting extensive research on how children learn to read, they discovered that kids require "building blocks of experiences" to best prepare them for school. "We observed an intense interest among Marylanders in this issue, and we didn't want to miss out on public discussion and public funding. We needed to be at the table to set policy," said Reif. The library systems began to network with other agencies in an effort to reach kids from birth to age five. The result was the Birth to Four family resource area. The partnership has created new library programs and handouts to teach parents the most effective practices for helping a child enter school ready to learn to read.

"We felt we had not paid sufficient attention to the outside world in our research on how children become ready to learn," Reif said. "We had taken a

Catonsville Library, Baltimore County, Maryland.

traditional approach instead of introducing stories for kids from birth to 12 months old, and another set of stories for kids 12 to 24 months old.

"The librarian works with the parent, and the parent in turn works with the child," Reif says. "What's so exciting is that we transformed a traditional service (children's story hours) into an innovative one. We reached out to families in need . . . often to teenaged parents. After all, we didn't wish to simply preach to the choir." Results of this emergent literacy project were presented at the national Public Library Association Conference in Seattle, as well as at the American Library Association Conference.

"Maryland is the only state that has done this in such a coordinated, state-wide level," Reif says. "Public libraries are an essential component of the educational system. Many people do not realize that libraries in Maryland come under the Department of Education."

Another innovator—Kathy Coster, marketing and programming manager of the Baltimore County Library—supervises the "Blast Off to Reading!" program. Her goal was to top last year's record-setting 13,000 participants in a program that offers games and incentives for young readers, teens and even adults to expand their minds. In addition, the A+ Partners in Education initiative represents a collaboration of Howard County Library and Howard County Public Schools.

Launched in September 2002, this ground-breaking initiative promotes scholarship, assists with eliminating student achievement gaps and expands the academic opportunities for each of Howard County's 47,000 public school students. It recognizes that the word "education" need not be limited to teaching in schools.

"This is a good model that can work in any system, says Dr. Carla D. Hayden, executive director of the Enoch Pratt Free Library in Baltimore and president of the American Library Association. "Nationally, people will look at Howard County's public library as a model."

With the passage of the No Child Left Behind Act of 2001, this initiative is especially important as all schools strive to improve their students' overall reading and writing skills. A total of 94,000 students, faculty and parents have benefited from an A+ Program activity. "We have developed a comprehensive way to reach all students," said Valerie J. Gross, director of Howard County Library. "It's taking the library into the schools, and taking the schools into the library."

The Division of Library Development and Services, which acts as the central state library agency, provides leadership in developing public library services and statewide resource sharing activities among all types of libraries. Assistant State Superintendent for Libraries, Irene M. Padilla states "Today, libraries have assumed heightened visibility and importance in the areas of educational support, literacy, technology and community partnerships. The leaders of Maryland's public library system look forward to continued partnerships. with other the Maryland State Department of Education and other organizations to advance their common goals of literacy, education for all Maryland residents."

Although free public libraries have come a long way since their modest beginnings in the mid-19th century, Maryland's public library system has continued to represent all that our country embodies: freedom of information, an educated citizenry and an open and enlightened society.

Towson Library, Baltimore County, Maryland.

MATTRESS DISCOUNTERS

Service—to consumers and to community—is the key to building relationships and, in turn, a strong customer base, in highly competitive industries. This is the belief and experience of Mattress Discounters, the pioneer in specialty sleep shops, which dominates the bedding business in Baltimore, Boston, Pittsburgh, Richmond and the Washington, D.C., metropolitan area.

With revenues of $200 million a year, Mattress Discounters has 540 employees and 110 stores in Massachusetts, New Hampshire, Rhode Island, Pennsylvania, Maryland, Washington, D.C., and Virginia. It plans to open additional stores in each of its markets in the coming years. Each store also carries a full line of accessories such as mattress pads, pillows and a large selection of unique and beautiful head- and footboard

Today's Mattress Discounters stores are designed as a comfortable, relaxing shopping environment; from the calming green color palette to the lifestyle photos of people enjoying the cozy comfort of their beds, to their exclusive Discover Your Comfort zone where each customer takes the comfort test. Every care is taken to ensure customers know Mattress Discounters is there to help them find a good night's sleep.

designs, as well as day beds, bunk beds and futons. Prices are guaranteed to be the best and customers are given ample time to try out their new beds with their "60 Night Comfort Guarantee."

Now celebrating 25 years of service, Mattress Discounters was founded in 1978 by three friends, Wally Teitelbaum, Steve Lytell and Sam Katz, in Alexandria, Virginia. Carrying the top brands at the best prices, they soon became known as the resource for people who need a good night's sleep.

The second store opened the same year, and expansion continued. Although its first headquarters were in Alexandria, Virginia, in 1991 Mattress Discounters moved their 100,000-square-foot support center to Upper Marlboro, Maryland.

The same year, the company added manufacturing, establishing Comfort Source®, their own private label, to provide a range of models with quality comparable to other leading brands at exceptional value. By 2000, Factory Direct was the 11th-largest-selling brand of mattresses and the largest manufacturer of private label and house-brand mattresses in the United States. The

Upper Marlboro factory was designed to be fast, efficient and flexible, and is one of the most productive in the industry. It turns out thousands of mattresses weekly, all to the highest quality specifications.

Mattress Discounters prides itself on making mattress buying simple and enjoyable. Sleep consultants encourage each customer to "Discover Your Comfort" by giving each customer a comfort test. Determining whether they prefer a hard, medium or soft comfort level narrows the choices in finding the right mattress for each individual. They can ultimately choose from famous brands such as Sealy Posturepedic®, Stearns and Foster®, Simmons Beauty-rest®, BackCare®—or Mattress Discounters' own brand, Factory Direct Comfort Source®.

Exemplifying its focus on building relationships are Mattress Discounters' employees. The company hires outstanding individuals and empowers them to develop their talent and creativity with a career about which they are passionate. This applies to sleep consultants, delivery teams, support center

Kevin Etheridge, Mattress Discounters regional vice president, and Susan Moscareillo, director of community relations, at Baltimore's Ronald McDonald House.

personnel and administrative staff: each is committed to doing an outstanding job. The company supplements good benefits with excellent training and development programs and a clear career path encouraging growth within the organization.

In addition to outstanding products and staff, Mattress Discounters remains on the competitive edge of technology, with software systems that elevate service by augmenting the ability of sleep consultants to find exactly the right products for each customer.

Mattress Discounters believes in giving back to its communities, supporting both local and national charities. "Mattress Discounters is a real blessing to us," said Susan Moscareillo, director of community relations at Baltimore's Ronald McDonald House, which gives families who have hospitalized children an affordable place to rest.

"We have over 38 bedrooms, and most have more than one bed. Mattress Discounters has replaced the mattresses and boxsprings. For many years families would sleep in chairs or on windowsills," said Moscareillo. "Mattress Discounters

is the first to ever donate beds to us."

Bethlehem Haven in Pittsburgh, Pennsylvania, provides emergency overnight shelter and supportive service programs for homeless, drug-addicted,

A recent graduate of Bethlehem Haven is delighted to receive a new mattress set.

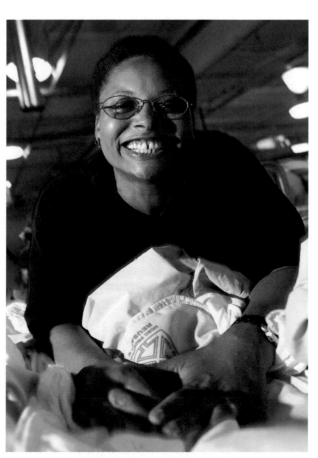

or alcoholic women and men. The women's residential program, in particular, caught the attention of Mattress Discounters, which arranged a promotion: for each game the Pittsburgh Steelers won, Bethlehem Haven was given a complete bed (mattress, boxspring, frame) for a recent graduate of the residential program.

"These are women who have to learn the essential responsibilities we take for granted: finding a job, washing clothes," said Development Assistant Aeren Martinez. "The women have very little; with Mattress Discouters' help, program graduates can begin to furnish their homes—and rest easier."

The company also works with groups of radio stations to designate a charity of the month, effectively donating a portion of its $20-million-a-year advertising budget to delivering charities' messages, including ACTION-Housing, American Express Charge for the Cure, Boston Living Center, the Child ID Campaign, CityTeam Ministries, Jon Ashford Link House, Prince George's County Women's Shelter, the Juvenile Diabetes Research Foundation, Habitat for Humanity and Operation Smile.

Its advertising program, highlighting Mattress Discounters' name and jingle, "Have a Good Night's Sleep on Us," has made the company a household name. It enjoys more than 80 percent customer awareness in key markets.

For more than a quarter century, Mattress Discounters has been working with customers to provide the bedding best suited to each and every one of them. Its goal continues to be providing customers with mattresses that will provide years of comfort, satisfaction and—most important—good sleep.

289

McLEAN CONTRACTING COMPANY

Since it's founding in 1903, the McLean Contracting Company has demonstrated steady adaptation, improvement and growth. For a century McLean has been in the Heavy Construction Industry performing an extensive range of both land based and marine construction. Throughout those 100 years strong traditions of integrity, efficiency, preparedness and excellent employee relations have been evident. These traditions have survived the death of the founder, a brief period as a division of a larger company, the Depression, wars and many other challenges.

An integral part of all of McLean's projects is its commitment to the safety of its own workers and others, the environment and equal employment opportunities. McLean has always been committed to its best asset, its employees, as evident by its many second and third generations of employees dedicated to their work. It is not uncommon in McLean to find many employees with 30 to 50 years of service. Among the benefit programs developed for the employees was a profit sharing plan approved and instituted in 1973.

U.S. Coast Guard Yard, Curtis Bay, Baltimore, Maryland.

Although employees had always owned McLean, the ownership was a select group. In 1989 McLean established an Employee Stock Ownership Plan (ESOP) so all of the then 407 employees would own a piece of their company. Currently, McLean employs over 300 people and operates out of its office

McLean was instrumental in the reconstruction of Baltimore's Inner Harbor, starting with the Pratt Street, Light Street and Key Highway Bulkheads (1971 photo), and continuing with the Constellation Pier, Pier 4, dredging, South Shore Marina and the Rusty Scupper Pier.

in Glen Burnie, Maryland. The company maintains staging and repair yards in the Curtis Bay area of Baltimore, Maryland, and in Chesapeake, Virginia.

Over the years, McLean has worked mostly in Maryland and Virginia, though it has completed jobs throughout the Mid-Atlantic States and most of the Southeast.

The founder, Colin McLean, started the company by incorporating it on April 7, 1903. As a result of the great Baltimore Fire, McLean received a contract to repair Bowley's Wharf, dated April 4, 1904, the contract included the repair of about 250 linear feet of the wharf and platform. In later years, Colin McLean also became involved in the sand and gravel business and the founding of the Arundel Corporation.

In September 1916, after Colin McLean's death, Oscar Coblentz bought controlling interest in the company and became president of the firm. Coblentz, a lawyer, had no formal training as an engineer, but made himself one of the best in the

Choptank River Bridge, Talbot & Dorchester Counties, Maryland.

field. Born in Frederick County, Coblentz prepared for a career as a schoolteacher at St. John's College in Annapolis in 1901. In 1906 Coblentz continued his education, studying law at the University of Maryland. Coblentz' interest in education continued throughout his life. He served as Superintendent of Schools in Frederick County. Beginning in 1924, he served on the Baltimore County Board of Education and was president of that body in 1941. He was also a member of the Board of Trustees of Hood College in Frederick, Maryland.

In 1918 Frank Beasman joined the company and later became president. He had met with success at the beginning of World War I, working with mules and wagons and axes and sweat to clear the land for Fort George Meade. Both Coblentz and Beasman came from well-established Maryland families. Beasman's father, Johnzie E. Beasman, had been a state senator. The family owned land, Liberty Reservoir, which had been granted them by King George.

Beasman left his estate in trust of his wife, Viola, to start a home for the aged. It was to be named for his father, Johnzie, but was actually named for the family land on which its sits, Fairhaven.

During the World War I military buildup era, McLean built docks and railroad yards for the Navy. In 1918 at least half of McLean's jobs were related to the military. McLean was commended for its work in World War I, specifically the naval mine depot project in Yorktown, Virginia.

McLean Contracting Company was an important contributor to the World War II effort. In 1942 the estimated average number of employees stood at 2,163, more than seven times the number currently employed by McLean. In March 1943, McLean was awarded the Army-Navy "E" for its performance. This award, presented by Rear Admiral Gaylord Church,

was given to companies and their subcontractors who produced excellent quality work with an exceptional level of organization and efficiency. The employees decided to forgo the dinner or other entertainment, which came with the award in order to donate $2,500 to the Navy Relief Fund and $2,500 to the Hampton Roads Women's Auxiliary. One year later, 16 McLean employees representing all groups, and officers of the company were cited with the Meritorious Civilian Service Award.

Although most of the work in World War II was for the Navy in the Tidewater area of Virginia a significant project in Maryland was the construction of the auxiliary ship repair facilities for the Coast Guard at Curtis Bay in Baltimore. Also, in Annapolis, McLean built a small training facility for midshipmen.

Innovation and adaptation were essential in the development of McLean. The company developed new techniques wherever someone saw a possible improvement in efficiency or a potential competitive edge. Equipment was invented and assembled and machine parts tooled in-house. The most innovated was through the efforts of William R. Aycock, President of McLean from 1967 to 1983. Aycock designed and had McLean employees build its own floating crane "Cape Fear." The crane has a 200-foot boom with lift capacities

Kent Narrows Bridge, Queens Annes County, Maryland.

Erect 7 container cranes, Sumitomo/NIAC-Seagirt Marine Terminal, Baltimore, Maryland.

Bridge over Chester River, Maryland State Highway Administration, Chestertown, Maryland.

up to 150 tons, the ability to revolve a full 360 degrees and is assembled on four barges.

McLean developed the technology to make pre-stressed concrete on its own. This was used in its building of the Route 90 Bridges leading into Ocean City. From 1986 to 1988, the Seagirt Marine Terminal bulkhead job in Baltimore was the largest prestressed concrete project ever for McLean.

McLean has always, and is still today, committed to its customers, whether public or private, and ready to respond to their needs on a moment's notice with all of it resources. Often McLean, ready with the necessary expertise and equipment, is automatically called to the scene in emergency situations. This readiness and McLean's good reputation was evidenced when the Benjamin Harrison Bridge, near Hopewell, Virginia, was hit by the tanker Marine Floridian in 1977. The authorities, knowing that McLean was prepared for the job, quickly called Aycock, who had workers and equipment to the site within hours. In a similar instance McLean was on site shortly after the collapse of a bridge over the Choptank River, which isolated

Denton, Maryland, in 1972. In 1976 when four container cranes at the Dundalk Marine Terminal in Baltimore were damaged by a sudden storm, McLean immediately began the salvage operation and worked the first 72 hours straight. In 1986 a bridge on I-95 in Baltimore had a structural problem that needed immediate attention. McLean worked around the clock for five straight days.

McLean has built and rehabilitated numerous bridges, piers, bulkheads, pipelines and has performed marine salvage work for both public and private customers in Maryland. With few exceptions, McLean has erected all of the Container Cranes, Coal Stackers/Reclaimers and Loaders in the Port of Baltimore.

Some of McLean's most notable projects in the state of Maryland have been: Cargo Pier at Hawkins Point in 1958, the first major construction project awarded by the newly formed Maryland Port Authority; the United States Coast Guard Yard on Curtis Creek; the Inner Harbor bulkhead from the Rusty Scupper to and including the Constellation Pier; the floating marina in the Inner Harbor; bridges on I-695 over Bear Creek, Curtis Creek, and Back River; bulkheads at

Dundalk Marine Terminal and Seagirt Marine Terminal; bulkhead at South Locust Point Marine Terminal; piers at North Locust Point Marine Terminal; numerous projects for Bethlehem Steel at their Sparrows Point Shipyard; dredging of the Chesapeake Bay tributaries; Russell Street Bridge and both Bridges on Hanover Street in Baltimore; Maryland Avenue and St. Paul Street Bridges over the Railroad in Baltimore; both I-95 and Route 40 Bridges over the Susquehanna River; portions of the Jones Fall Expressway; both the old and new bridges over Kent Narrows; Choptank River Bridge on Route 50; rehabilitated Riva Road Bridge in Annapolis; and salvaged the SS Baltimore for the Museum of Industry.

Most importantly, McLean's largest and best asset is its skilled and loyal work force. The company is proud that not one day of work has been lost to labor strife in its history. This excellent work force combined with excellent leadership has placed McLean at the top of its field.

Built on a solid past, McLean is thoroughly prepared for the future.

Baltimore's skyline is one of the nation's most dramatic, and represents a mixture of architectural styles. Courtesy, Baltimore Area Convention & Visitors Association

MEDSTAR HEALTH VISITING NURSE ASSOCIATION

In 1900 women doctors were not only a rarity, they were looked upon with ridicule and suspicion. One Washington, D.C., female doctor, along with two of her female associates, would not only prove the naysayers wrong, they would go on to be the founders of one of America's greatest agencies, addressing the needs of the sick and poor like few others had done in the past. The Instructive Visiting Nurse Society (IVNS) was founded in 1900 by Dr. Anne A. Wilson, Emily Tuckerman, and Mary W. C. Bayard, wife of then-Secretary of State, Thomas E. Bayard. Emily Tuckerman was a philanthropist active in church causes, and Wilson was a doctor in a time when women could only attend a handful of medical schools.

Created to supplement the functions of hospitals and doctors, the mission of the IVNS was to provide home nursing care and instruction in better health practices to people of all classes, colors and creeds. Within a short time, the IVNS became one of the most recognized institutions in Washington, D.C.

Emily Tuckerman personally paid for the services of the first IVNS nurse to be hired, Ruth E. Mason. In the beginning

Reliable transportation for visiting nurses and therapists is vital to their jobs. VNA's first nurse in 1900 made visits on a bicycle, which limited her travel. Today's VNA visiting staff will drive 1.978 million miles across Maryland, Washington, D.C., and Northern Virginia. Pictured lowered right, Yasmin Maypa, R.N.

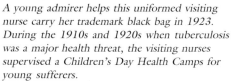

IVNS nurses such as Mason made their visits by foot or on bicycle, mostly to patients in the Southwest section of the District, and were paid five cents per visit. In Mason's first month she made more than 175 visits, averaging seven visits per day during a six-day workweek. The charge to a patient who could pay for a visit was 50 cents, with the actual cost to the IVNS being more than 37 cents.

Mrs. Henry Cabot Lodge, wife of the Massachusetts senator, became the first IVNS president and made fundraising her primary focus. In 1907 a private philanthropist endowed an individual

A young admirer helps this uniformed visiting nurse carry her trademark black bag in 1923. During the 1910s and 1920s when tuberculosis was a major health threat, the visiting nurses supervised a Children's Day Health Camps for young sufferers.

nurse's annual salary of $800. In 1912 five "memorial nurses" were supported by donations in memory of loved ones.

These early years saw no lack of need for IVNS services. One of every seven visits in 1913 was to a person suffering from tuberculosis. That same year, infant mortality had reached its peak. IVNS nurses made more than 15,000 visits to nearly 2,500 infants, almost two-thirds being of African American descent. The IVNS home care services were even more greatly needed as World War I raged in 1918, and when the great influenza epidemic swept through Washington, D.C., in 1919, killing 3,500 citizens and causing the IVNS to lose one of their own nurses to the fatal flu.

The years following the stock market crash of 1929 proved to be challenging for the IVNS. In one month in 1934 the IVNS was unable to visit more than 600 patients, and in 1936 the City Board of Public Welfare refused to pay for nursing care for patients on relief.

Eventually this resulted in higher incidents of disease, which the IVNS had warned the government would happen without proper preventative care. Undaunted, the IVNS continued to serve the community.

During World War II the IVNS functioned with a greatly reduced staff, as nurses were needed elsewhere. Even with minimal staff, in 1945 alone IVNS nurses made more than 99,000 visits to nearly 15,000 patients and expended $167,000.

The post-war years saw tremendous advances in healthcare with the use of penicillin and other "miracle" drugs. This in turn increased the needs for the services offered by the IVNS, but the continuing shortage of nurses created a great challenge in meeting those needs, forcing the IVNS to turn to the federal government for funding.

The Instructive Visiting Nurse Society officially changed its name to the Visiting Nurse Association (VNA) in 1953. The new VNA expanded to include physical therapists, and by 1955 they had added to their staff two practical nurses, two registered physical therapists and a mental health consultant. By the late '50s the VNA created the Broad Spectrum Home Care Program which offered the patient coordinated home healthcare services, including the services of a physician, visiting nurse, social worker and physical therapist.

Tremendous strides were made in healthcare reform during the Kennedy-Johnson era. The Social Security Act amendments of the mid-1960s established Medicare and Medicaid, which eventually include services such as the VNA. Group Hospitalization Inc. (Blue Cross) contracted with the VNA in 1964 to provide home nursing services to participants in its Senior Citizens Program, which also brought VNA nurses to eight senior citizen centers during the 1970s and 1980s. In this same period the VNA created the Terminally Ill Project, in which volunteers befriended the chronically and terminally ill. This

Linda Waite Maurano, RN, MSN, president since 1993, has been responsible for the agency's diversification into home medical equipment and infusion services, and moved the agency from paper-based operations to a technologically advanced, integrated network of streamlined operations.

program resulted in the current holistic hospice programs.

By the 1970s the VNA had broadened its geographic reach to include patients in the Montgomery and Prince George's counties of Maryland. In 1980 the VNA consolidated the Washington branches, while the Maryland services continued to expand. In

The visiting nurse uses a laptop computer to update a patient's medical record and process paperwork immediately, freeing him to spend more time on patient care. VNA has always maintained a patient-first philosophy. Today's technological advances allow nurses to do what they do best: improve quality of life for patients and the families who love and care for them. Pictured: Bernard K. Morris, R.N.

1965, 3,000 of 84,000 visits were to Maryland patients. In 1980, 40,000 VNA visits were made to patients in suburban Maryland.

One of the most significant milestones in the history of the VNA was its merger with Medlantic in 1987. Despite fears that the VNA would lose its identity under the shadow of a large corporation, Medlantic proved to be the association's savior. The VNA almost lost its crucial contracts with Medicare and Medicaid in 1989, but Medlantic led the association through a major modernization that staved off the crisis.

The VNA Board hired Linda Maurano as its new president in 1993. Maurano, a former visiting nurse with extensive experience in home healthcare, brought tremendously positive changes to the VNA. She promoted "one-stop shopping" care to alleviate patient frustration over having to deal with multiple organizations. She also expanded their services to include those suffering from AIDS and created the "Fight the Flu" campaign, the largest flu immunization program in the region.

In 1998 VNA's parent company Medlantic Healthcare Group, merged with Helix Health, which expanded the VNA service area to include Baltimore area, southern Maryland and parts of the Eastern Shore. The merger also helped the agency to successfully meet the growing costs of providing quality healthcare services. In addition, the merger resulted in a name change to MedStar Health Visiting Nurse Association and a move of its headquarters from Washington, D.C., to Calverton, Maryland.

As the 20th century came to a close, the original IVNS had grown from a nurse on a bicycle to one of the largest not-for-profit home healthcare systems on the East Coast, with more than 750 employees. MedStar Health VNA now serves patients in Washington, D.C., northern Virginia and Maryland.

MELE ASSOCIATES, INC.

Mel Chiogioji presides as foundation chairman over the dedication of the National Japanese American Memorial on the Mall in Washington, D.C. in November 2001.

It is the third time he takes his seat at the Maryland Fast 50 awards, the third time that his company has been recognized as one of the fastest growing technology firms in the state, and in the nation. A smile breaks across Mel Chiogioji's tanned face as his name is called. Everyone who knows him, and so many do, calls him "Mel." Neither his doctorate in business administration nor his status as one of only three Japanese Americans to achieve the rank of Admiral in the U.S. Navy Reserve gets in the way of his reputation as "Mel," the warm and enthusiastic businessman from Maryland. He laughs and notes that it's probably also because his last name is so hard to pronounce. You'll find you can't help but laugh, too; his deep voice is contagious. It is 2003: at the age of 64, Mel has a treasure trove of memories to look back on.

Mel's mother was pregnant with him in 1939. Her father took ill that year, so she and her husband—Japanese Americans who had emigrated to the states many years before—took a ship out to Hiroshima, Japan, to be with him in his last few months. And that is where Mel was born. It was an uneasy

time all around the world. With the outbreak of World War II, the family took three months to get back to their home in Hawaii. They lived at Pearl Harbor, and were home on the day that the Japanese attacked. Mel hardly remembers it; he was just two at the time. Because the population of Hawaii was so diverse, (almost one-third Japanese Americans in those days), the hardships encountered by Japanese American families all across the country were not as acute, and soon life returned to normal. Mel graduated from private school in Hawaii with honors, and he won a Naval Reserve Officers Training Corps scholarship to Purdue. From there, he spent five years on active duty and 27 years in the Reserve, reaching two-star status, and commanding the Second Naval Construction Brigade, responsible for all active duty and reserve Seabee Battalions in the U.S. Atlantic Fleet. Years later, in 2002, Purdue University would recognize Mel for his extraordinary accomplishment, and his

lifelong service to his country by inducting him into the ROTC Hall of Fame.

But during those years, Mel did so much more. As a Professional Engineer (Electrical Engineering), he simultaneously pursued a career in federal service, which is ultimately what brought him to Maryland, the state that he and his family have called home since 1969. As the director of the Weapons Evaluation and Engineering Division of the Naval Ordnance Systems Command, he began a quick climb into the Senior Executive Service of the Federal Government at the U.S. Department of Energy, where he held various positions including director of the Office of Transportation Systems, director of the Office of Industrial Waste Management, and construction manager for the New Production Reactors Program. A published author of technical publications on energy efficiency and a lecturing professor, Mel constantly found new ways to challenge himself, and at the same time, make friends.

It was about the time that he began to consider retiring from federal service, that Mel began his first foray into business. Using his federal experience and his strong academic background and combining it with his infectious charm and reputation for honesty, Mel first started an auto body shop in Rockville so he could supplement his income and send his two children to college. Eventually, one of the rooms in the auto body shop became the birthplace of MELE Associates, a small business that broke into management consulting with just three employees. In a record 72 days, MELE Associates had received certification as an 8(a)—or Small Disadvantaged Business—a great way to get a foothold in the booming federal marketplace.

Today, MELE Associates has gradu-

PurdueUniversity inducts Mel Chiogioji into the ROTC Hall of Fame.

Mele Associates' staff at a retreat facilitated by president/CEO Mel Chiogioji at Copper Mountain, Colorado.

ated from the 8(a) program as a $35 million company, and it has started mentoring other small firms. With headquarters in Rockville, Maryland, and offices in Honolulu and six other locations around the country, the company is making a name for itself as a dependable firm with a talented staff that provides management consulting and information technology services to scores of federal clients. Mel is an active

president, traveling constantly and tirelessly building his company. And, as he carries on the business he started in 1993, he continues to dedicate himself to philanthropic endeavors as well.

Mel served as chairman of the National Japanese American Memorial Foundation for seven years, during which time they raised $14 million to build a memorial to the patriotism of Japanese Americans in World War II. In 2001 Mel presided over the dedication of the Memorial, a beautiful park marked by the bronze figure of two cranes entangled in barbed wire. It sits right next to the U.S. Senate in Washington, D.C., and is the only memorial honoring a minority population in the nation's capitol. His childhood memories had come full circle, and Mel was finding ways to give back, and lay down a legacy for others to follow.

The private Mel is humble and vigorous. He can often be seen hard at work on a construction project at his home in Rockville—never afraid to get his hands dirty. He is also often spotted skiing down the black diamond slopes in Colorado—one of his favorite sports— or on the golf course. But what really motivates Mel is a love of life, and a commitment to bringing others along on his great journey. When asked why he continues to work so hard, he says "I've been really lucky. I had great mentors throughout my life. Now it's time for me to give back and build up a company that can provide opportunities for young people in Maryland and in Hawaii, and contribute to the economies of the places that have been so good to me." Everyone who knows him would agree that this man is more than a fellow businessman, or a boss, or an acquaintance. Mel is a trusted friend. And in today's fast-paced faceless world, you can't put enough value on true friends.

MIE PROPERTIES, INC.

Since 1971 MIE Properties, Inc., has executed a simple, yet powerful business plan to near perfection. The bread and butter of MIE Properties is the ability to develop and lease "flexible office space," a term in the real estate industry that has been shortened to "flex/office." MIE is widely regarded as the real estate firm that both invented and perfected this concept. It entails developing single-story flex/office buildings in a campus-like setting that offers total flexibility to match an almost endless array of uses, from sales offices to light manufacturing operations to warehousing. MIE places these projects, which feature 16-foot-high ceilings, rear loading docks and surface parking in strategic locations throughout a metropolitan area, so they are convenient to where people live and work.

MIE has applied this basic formula throughout Maryland, Virginia, Colorado, Louisiana and Wisconsin. The firm currently owns and manages more than 10 million square feet of commercial office space. The total real estate portfolio, which includes flex/office, warehouse, Class A office and retail space has an annual average occupancy of approximately 97 percent. The company has also invested in more than 2,200 apartment units.

The company prefers to sign leases in the 3,000 to 10,000-square-foot range to

The company creates values by transforming raw land into office buildings and mixed-use business communities, with the addition of utilities and infrastructure.

smaller, entrepreneurial-driven businesses that run the gamut from sales offices to dance studios to printing companies. They prefer to leave the larger leases—20,000 square feet and above—and the risks that come with them, to other real estate firms.

Originally named Maryland Industrial Enterprises, the firm was among the first local companies to build industrial and commercial structures in the suburbs of Baltimore. With headquarters off Beltway Exit 15 in Catonsville—chosen for its central location near virtually any location in metropolitan Baltimore—the company has evolved to become among the largest and most prolific commercial real estate developers and property management firms in the region.

888 Bestgate Road is a 135,000-square-foot Class A office building located in historic Annapolis. The lobby is richly appointed with marble flooring and an original sculpture.

Founder and President Edward A. St. John, Jr., grew up in the business of building. The senior St. John was the quintessential entrepreneur as a builder and owner of other companies. "Because of the war," St. John explained, "relatively little had been built in the Baltimore area in the first half of the 1940s. Before my father's first warehouse was half finished, he was offered a profitable price to lease the facility. Within five years, the elder St. John had amassed a portfolio of 50,000 square feet and sowed the seeds for a property development and management empire.

Every aspect of MIE Properties relates to its philosophy of keeping things uncomplicated and repeating what has worked successfully. One tenant summed up MIE Properties' approach to real estate quite succinctly: "Their space was strategically located, built to the highest of standards and matched the exact requirements of my business. When they gave us our lease, it was eighteen pages, compared to the fifty-page document that we were accustomed to. The company keeps it simple, but does it right."

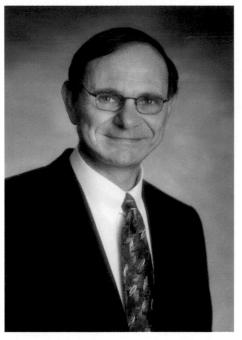

Edward A. St. John founder and president MIE Properties, Inc.

A lease with MIE can be compared to a consumer purchasing a condominium unit. That is, the tenant handles its day-to-day business and MIE oversees the building, mechanical equipment, plumbing, road system, parking and landscaping. MIE takes special pride and attention to the exterior landscaping of all its buildings, believing that an

A dedicated landscaping crew maintains exterior grounds during all four seasons, from snow removal to grass cutting.

attractive curb appeal builds value for its projects, and first impressions are extremely important for the company's tenants.

With no shared costs for hallways, bathrooms and the lobby, businesses get exactly what they rent. They can also park directly in front of their entrance, control the gas and electricity and enjoy 24-hour unrestricted access to their space. Companies can also generally expand—by adding an adjacent bay—or they can downsize without being forced to pay for space they no longer need or can afford.

The backbone of MIE's development activities are its flex/office buildings utilizing a unified architecture approach. The typical MIE flex/office building offers thirty-foot-wide spaces and sixteen-foot-high ceilings for maximum tenant flexibility. Photo by Roger Miller

Although the real estate industry is subject to periodic up and down cycles that mirror the status of the national economy, MIE Properties has gained momentum during its more than 30-year history, by focusing on smaller leases and sticking to its basic business principles. The company has built on its success in the Maryland area by expanding to four other states, and currently has approximately 1,300 tenants in all.

As larger real estate developers have merged with other firms or succumbed during recessionary times, MIE Properties continues to thrive. "There aren't too many of us independently owned developers left," St. John said. The company intends to maintain this independence, and continue with its time-tested formula of developing mixed-use business communities in strategic locations throughout metropolitan areas.

This approach, which has worked to near perfection since 1971, continues to build momentum with each successful year.

MILVETS SYSTEMS TECHNOLOGY, INC.

What started out as a small disadvantaged business with a core of military veterans has grown into an organization with almost 400 employees recognized as a reliable supplier of quality information and technology services to the public and private sectors. Its clients, in the years since its founding in 1986, have included a broad cross section of government agencies and commercial businesses. Today, these clients are located across the country.

Milvets Systems Technology is headquartered in Lanham, Maryland—and also has offices in Kearneysville, West Virginia; Lexington Park, Maryland; Norfolk, Virginia; Orlando, Florida; and San Diego, California. Staff members are also based at numerous client work sites, most in the Washington, D.C., metropolitan area.

Milvets, short for military veterans, was formed as a small business. Its first projects were as a subcontractor for government contractors, augmenting staffs of information technology professionals, often with military veterans having high-level security clearances.

President, chief executive officer and founder, Bob Daniels, drew together talented veterans, many of whom fought in Vietnam. He is himself a veteran who retired after 22 years of service. He joined the Marines in July 1962, shortly after graduating from Weequahic High School in Newark, New Jersey. Daniels served in Vietnam in 1968, as a marine infantry platoon commander. In the mid 1970s, he served as a drill instructor at Parris Island, South Carolina.

Along the way, Daniels went to college, earning his bachelor's degree in business administration from the University of Maryland, a master's degree in personnel administration from Central Michigan University, and a master's in business administration from Golden Gate University.

After leaving his last post, at Cherry Point, North Carolina, in 1984, Sergeant Major Daniels worked as a technical recruiter for American Security Bank

Weekly staff meeting with senior management team.

and for Essex Corporation. Two years later he set out to build his own business. His technical and personnel experience stood him in good stead.

Milvets's first government contract came in 1988. It was an ideal fit. Working for the Department of Labor's Veterans Employment and Training Service, Milvets designed and staffed a career transition program for Marine Corps veterans.

In June 1990, Milvets was accepted into the Small Business Administration's 8(a) business development program as a small disadvantaged business.

This program, created to help qualifying businesses compete in the U.S. market and access the federal procurement market, is open to small businesses owned and controlled by one or more socially and economically disadvantaged U.S. citizen(s) of good character. The law defines social disadvantage in terms of membership in minority groups and economic disadvantage in terms of diminished capital and credit opportunities.

The businesses must also demonstrate potential for success in the nine-year development and transition program.

Milvets's initial projects as a recognized

8(a) government contractor included computer maintenance and help-desk assignments at the Internal Revenue Service and the Library of Congress. As the 1990s continued, the company began realizing its potential. It won major contracts, as well as subcontracts, with several large businesses, including IBM, Booz Allen, Northrup Grumman and Electronic Data Systems (EDS).

As an 8(a) contractor, it distinguished itself in the document management arena, helping government agencies and the defense community move from paper to a digital environment. Prior to graduating from the 8(a) program in June 1999, Milvets won its largest contract with the Department of the Treasury's Bureau of Alcohol, Tobacco and Firearms (BATF). Performed at ATF's National Tracing Center in West Virginia, the contract enabled Milvets to double in size from some 100 employees to more than 200. Growth continued in the years that followed.

In addition to its business success, Milvets was recognized as an exemplary participant in the SBA program. It received the Small Business Administration's Award for Excellence for Contract Performance as a subcontractor to Planning Research Corporation working in information technology at the Department of Commerce's Patent and Trademark Office. The award recognized Milvets for "outstanding contribution and service to the nation by a small business in satisfying the needs of the Federal procurement system."

Milvets specializes in developing and implementing the best business solution for each customer. It lists its core capabilities as facility management and systems operations, maintenance and help desk, temporary professional services, assistive technology, document management and imaging, and electronic enterprise solutions. It also provides software and database engineering, network and

Ms. Crystal Gipson, administrative assistant, helps Mr. Daniels keep track of a busy schedule.

systems security and engineering, business process reengineering and telecommunications.

Founded to offer efficient, cost-effective contract staffing and training services to commercial and government clients, Milvets has realized Daniels' vision through the development of a strong commitment to long-term client satisfaction and corporate expansion.

"Successful application of good business principles and management techniques has been fundamental to our growth, integrity and financial stability," he says, adding, "All our offices are equipped with the latest in automation technology, computers and business tools but—most important—we hire good people."

These people, including many with disabilities, are highly trained professionals, focused on meeting the evolving needs of the company's clients. With 15 years of experience, Milvets now offers support to younger businesses, seeking strategic partners for subcontracting opportunities, including woman-and-disabled-veteran-owned companies.

Daniels, who has been joined in the business by two of his children, has become a spokesman for small business success. He speaks to veterans groups and small business conferences, demonstrating that Milvets is an example of what small business in America is all about.

Congratulations to Mr. Don Perry, whose proposal team led to a recently won Veteran's Administration contract.

MONUMENTAL LIFE INSURANCE COMPANY

Explore the Enoch Pratt Library Archives in Baltimore City and you will find photos of Colonel George P. Kane, Monumental Life Insurance Company's colorful and civic-minded first president.

Following the Confederate attack on Fort Sumter in 1861, which ignited the Civil War, Baltimore was caught in the crossfire between North and South. Colonel Kane, then Baltimore's marshal of police, and Mayor George W. Brown were arrested while trying to restrain a mob of angry Baltimore citizens who had ambushed Union troops. Accused of being Southern sympathizers, both men were imprisoned at Fort McHenry.

Released after a short stay, Kane was later elected mayor of the city of Baltimore. He also helped build the foundation for what is today one of the oldest, largest and most respected life insurance companies in the country.

Like many successful business organizations, Monumental Life grew from humble beginnings. The Maryland

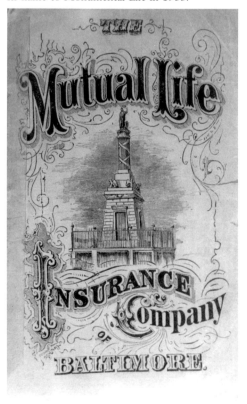

Career agents used premium receipt books like this one for over 100 years to record payments collected in their clients' homes. The Mutual Life Insurance Company of Baltimore changed its name to Monumental Life in 1935.

Colonel George P. Kane was Monumental Life Insurance Company's first president. He was later elected mayor of the city of Baltimore.

General Assembly granted a charter to the Maryland Mutual Life and Fire Insurance Company in 1858. Two years later, the company's Board of Directors held their first organizational meeting at 91 Second Street in Baltimore. The company opened for business using rates adopted from the Mutual Benefit Life Insurance Company of Newark, New Jersey, founded in 1845. The company's first agent was licensed in 1860.

"Owing to the unsettled condition of the country," the young company's directors voted to cease taking risks of life and fire insurance on January 3, 1862. No new policies were written until 1870, when the word "fire" was deleted from the company's name and it resumed operations as the Mutual Life Insurance Company of Baltimore.

As the country pushed westward following the Civil War, industry and commerce grew along with the demand for life insurance. Adapting to European immigration and changing economic and social conditions, the company opened a German Department

and, in 1873, issued what was believed to be the country's first *weekly premium* life insurance policy, to Baltimore resident Valentin Bauscher.

Weekly premium policies—sold and serviced by agents assigned to specific geographic territories—appealed to the city's merchants, manufacturers, small business owners, factory workers, farmers and watermen. As a result, the company's Weekly Premium or "Industrial" Insurance Division grew rapidly. By 1883 insurance in force reached $1 million. Small, paid-weekly policies, with premiums collected by agents, provided the foundation for Monumental Life's business for more than 100 years.

The company survived the Baltimore Fire of 1904 with more than $4.2 million insurance in force, and moved to its current location at the corner of Charles and Chase Streets in 1926. Located midway between Penn Station and Baltimore's Washington Monument—just steps from the famed Owl Bar, frequented by journalist H.L. Mencken—the company's new home was situated on prestigious, prime real estate atop one of the city's highest hills.

Monumental Life moved its home office to Charles and Chase Streets, across from the Belvedere Hotel, in 1926.

In 1928, with $11 million of assets and $147 million of insurance in force, the company converted from a mutual to a stock life insurance company. Then, in another bold move in 1935, it changed its name to reflect its presence and prominence in Baltimore, the "Monumental City."

Following World War II, the company continued to prosper. Returning servicemen married, bought homes and started families. With children's futures to protect, they needed life insurance and Monumental Life had products to meet the demand! By 1957 Monumental Life had 59 field offices in 12 states and $1 billion of insurance in force. Insurance in force doubled again in the next ten years to $2 billion and, in 1967, the company broke ground for a $3.8 million addition to its home office. When completed in 1968, Monumental Life and the newly-incorporated Monumental Corporation occupied the entire 1100 block of Charles Street.

Withstanding a hostile takeover attempt in 1978, Monumental Life headed into the 1980s committed to meeting the final expense and income replacement needs of America's middle-income consumers. Though the last paid-weekly policy was sold in 1973, the company's career agents continued to visit policyholders regularly in their homes to review insurance coverage, meet needs and, if requested, to collect premiums.

In 1986 the AEGON Insurance Group, the second largest insurer in The Netherlands, recognized the company's strength, solid performance and potential. Monumental Life and Monumental General, its sister company in Baltimore, were acquired by AEGON and became members of one of the largest, most respected and successful insurance organizations in the world.

Today, still headquartered in Baltimore, Monumental Life is the oldest and largest life insurance company in the state of Maryland. As of result of acquisitions in 1990, 1992 and 1997, Monumental Life's assets at year-end 2002 totaled $17.4 billion and its insurance in force totaled $65.2 billion. The company paid $319

Baltimore Mayor Martin O'Malley on the left, joins Monumental Life President and CEO Henry Hagan in planting flowers at Charles and Chase Street. Projects like this—a collaboration of business, government and citizens—demonstrate the company's commitment to the community. Hagan serves on the board of Baltimore's Charles Street Development Corporation.

million in benefits to individual policyholders in calendar year 2002 based on coverage provided by 5.6 million in-force individual life and health policies.

Monumental Life's three distinct distribution systems—Career Agency,

Military and PreNeed—market individual life and supplemental health insurance products to individuals and families. With more than 500 home office employees in Baltimore and Durham, North Carolina, and more than 2,900 career agents and field managers serving over 1.5 million families from 180 field offices in 22 states, Monumental Life has become an acknowledged leader in the insurance industry's lower and middle income marketplace.

As it nears its 150th birthday in 2008, Monumental Life, like Baltimore, is a unique "melting pot" of companies, people, cultures and traditions. It has experienced nearly 15 decades of growth and change and served policyholders born in three centuries. It has contributed "monumentally" to the area's economy and continues to support community efforts to help the needy, revitalize our city and bring new businesses into our state. Under the leadership of Henry G. Hagan, president and CEO since 1998, Monumental Life remains focused on the future and strongly committed to its mission to help all American families improve the quality of their lives.

Today's Monumental agents don't go anywhere without their laptop computers. Help Desk reps in the Baltimore Home Office are on call to provide the technical support agents need to serve their clients.

NUTRAMAX LABORATORIES INC.

Founded In 1992, Nutramax Laboratories, Inc. is a private company that researches, develops, manufactures and sells high-quality products for the consumer and veterinary markets. Located in Edgewood, Maryland, Nutramax Laboratories® has dedicated itself to helping animals and humans with joint problems and other problems associated with aging, as well as creating environmentally friendly bio-fertilizers.

Under the direction of Founder, President, and Chief Executive Officer, Pharmacist Robert Henderson along with Executive Vice President, Veterinarian Todd Henderson, the company has become an industry leader in setting high standards in manufacturing, quality control and clinical studies of nutraceuticals. Nutraceuticals are natural, bioactive compounds that have health promoting properties and which provide demonstrated benefits. Dr. Robert Henderson discovered and patented the combination of glucosamine, chondroitin sulfate, and manganese ascorbate, which are the nutraceutical ingredients in both Cosamin®DS for humans and Cosequin® for animals. These ingredients have been scientifically formulated by Nutramax Laboratories to safely support and maintain the health of both human and animal joints. The Hendersons

Nutramax Laboratories, Inc. Edgewood, Maryland.

On the left, Dr. Todd Henderson, executive vice president and Dr. Robert Henderson, president and CEO.

have also been awarded several additional patents on nutraceutical combinations.

The company has nutritional supplements in its product line for both humans and animals. CosaminDS, which was created by Nutramax Laboratories in 1992, is a product primarily geared toward the aging population who have joint problems. Senior Moment®, another Nutramax Laboratories product, is an advanced dietary supplement that contains cerebral phospholipids and docosahexaenoic acid (DHA), nutrients that are important in memory function. These ingredients can be depleted due to factors such as aging, stress, poor diet,

or dietary deficiencies. Both products are available over-the-counter.

Under the direction of Dr. Todd Henderson, the company has also created nutritional supplements for animals, both large and small. Cosequin for Cats and CosequinDS for dogs have the same ingredients as CosaminDS, but have been specially formulated for joint health in animals. These animal supplements help maintain healthy cartilage while slowing the enzymes that break down cartilage. Cosequin Equine has been specially formulated for horses and ponies. Nutramax Laboratories Denosyl® SD4 is used to support hepatic (liver) function in cats and dogs and is the only researched veterinary brand of its kind available. Another Nutramax Laboratories product is Consil®, a bioactive ceramic used by veterinarians for the regeneration of bone loss in animals due to periodontal disease and tooth extraction. Nutramax Laboratories products for animals are only available through veterinary clinics.

Nutramax Agriculture, Inc., one of the Nutramax Laboratories' family of companies, has established itself in the golf course turfgrass industry with its bio-fertilizers, MACRO-SORB® and QUELANT®. These products are based on a combination of L-amino acids, which are essential nutrients to enhance stress tolerance, photosynthesis, water and nutrient efficiency to produce healthier and stronger plants. MACRO-SORB and QUELANT are products supported by university research and environmentally safe.

Good Manufacturing Practices. The Food and Drug Administration (FDA) has authority over supplements sold to the consumer through the "Dietary Supplement Health and Education Act", which was passed by the United States Congress. Nutramax Laboratories cooperates with government agencies and trade organizations to encourage higher quality control and manufacturing standards in the industry. All raw materials and finished products at

Nutramax Laboratories are subjected to strict quality control guidelines, a process that far exceeds requirements. Products go through many stages of quality control including raw material, in-process and finished product analysis. The actual ingredients the company uses in its products are of high purity. Nutramax Manufacturing, Inc. has a state-of-the-art manufacturing facility and is a participant of the USP Dietary Supplement Verification Program. As part of the program, USP conducts a GMP audit of the facility and awards a Seal for products manufactured at such facility which have been submitted to USP for testing.

Nutramax Laboratories has a research facility that conducts on-going research to develop new products. The company hired noted cartilage researcher, Louis Lippiello, Ph.D. Dr. Lippiello conducted cell culture research on the combination of low molecular weight chondroitin sulfate and glucosamine hydrochloride, the results of which were published in *Clinical Orthopedics and Related Research* in 2000. In 2000, Dr. Chuck Filburn, formerly with the National Institute of Health (NIH), joined the company as Director of

Capsules and tablets are tested for consistency during daily quality control procedures.

Research. His expertise is in the aging process.

Nutramax Laboratories believes solid and validated research is of great importance to the consumer because of the wide range of nutritional supplements that are available on the market. The company believes that the clinical studies they have conducted will help consumers make more educated choices on what is best for them and their pets with the guidance of their physicians and veterinary professionals.

Unlike most nutritional supplement manufacturers, Nutramax Laboratories products are based on scientific evidence. The first trial on CosaminDS was conducted and published by the U.S. Department of Defense at the Portsmouth Naval Hospital in February 1999. Other Cosamin research has been conducted at Johns Hopkins University in Baltimore, University of Maryland School of Pharmacy as well as other prestigious research institutions. Through support of physicians and pharmacists, CosaminDS has been credited with setting a standard in

Nutramax Laboratories conducts ongoing research to develop new products.

nutritional excellence. A testament to this fact came from the NIH, when after an exhaustive search for material to use in its multicenter clinical trial of glucosamine and chondroitin sulfate, it chose over other material the researched low molecular weight chondroitin sulfate found in CosaminDS and Cosequin.

Cosequin has been subjected to third party, independent, placebo-blinded controlled studies conducted and published in the U.S. These major studies have been conducted at many leading veterinary schools throughout the country, including Cornell University and Auburn University.

Dr. Henderson credits the success of Nutramax Laboratories to the high standards that it demands of each of its products through every step of the process, from research to market. He also credits the dedication and professionalism of his employees with an equal part of the company's success. Henderson's recipe for the success of Nutramax Laboratories is hard work, research, innovation, the highest standard of quality, and commitment to produce products that are safe and effective in humans and animals, none of which he believes could be possible without the company's superior staff of professionals.

OAO TECHNOLOGY SOLUTIONS

The Passion to Go Beyond: At 2 a.m. on a Saturday morning, a project leader for OAO Technology Solutions, Inc. (OAOT) received an SOS phone call from one of the world's largest IT infrastructure companies. They urgently needed an entire team of sophisticated IT professionals with expertise in fixed assets and general ledger procedures. The hitch? They needed to be on-site in the UK in less than 48 hours. OAOT snapped into action. By Monday morning, a full team arrived in the UK. "We do whatever it takes to meet our clients' needs," the project leader explained, "even if that means dealing with the unexpected in extraordinary ways."

Then again, the extraordinary is the standard operating procedure at OAOT. As a leader in providing managed IT solutions, OAOT embodies the passion to go beyond. The employees of OAOT combine strong IT skills, extensive experience and clarity of vision that has produced a track record of success in both the corporate and government arenas. Working with OAOT, companies around the globe have gained a team of dedicated leaders who push themselves to the max to improve productivity and lower costs. OAOT empowers its people to be strategic thinkers and proactive problem solvers—a philosophy that attracts the brightest minds and the most energetic spirits. OAOT's reliability, leadership and passion to go beyond deliver maximum ROI with minimum risk.

The company traces its roots back to OAO Corporation, which was founded in 1973 by Cecile D. Barker. Initially OAO Corporation supported NASA's Orbiting Astronomical Observatory, hence the acronym OAO. In 1993 OAO Corporation established the Commercial Systems Group to provide services to the private sector. The commercial group spun off as a separate company in 1996 and changed its name to OAO Technology Solutions, or OAOT for short. OAOT then went public in 1997.

From its 1993 origin as a division within OAO Corporation, OAOT has focused

Employees' commitment to excellence is the backbone of OAO Technology Solutions.

on Managed IT solutions, leveraging today's technology for its clients' success. While its initial portfolio provided clients with 24/7 support for management and operations of data centers, OAOT has expanded its managed solutions portfolio to include applications development and maintenance services, network and systems management, desktop management services and professional staffing services to its managed solutions portfolio. By 2003 OAOT became recognized as the "Outsourcer's Outsourcer," partnering with the world's largest and most well-respected IT outsourcing firms to deliver applications management, infrastructure support and professional staffing services to Fortune 500 firms and government agencies worldwide.

Because OAOT continually evaluates its services portfolio against the needs of its clients, the company launched a second line of business in 1997. OAO Healthcare Solutions (OAOHS) was created with the acquisition of MC400, a managed healthcare information management system, from UniHealth Investment Company in Burbank, California. Then, in 2001, OAOHS expanded its product line to include a health benefit administrative system, EZ-CAP, which it acquired from

Quadramed Corporation. EZ-CAP is the world's leader in managed care information solutions for at-risk healthcare organizations. As a result of investing more than $100 million in research and development, OAOHS provides a full range of IT solutions and services that enable HMOs, PPOs, IPAs, TPAs, medical groups, self-funded organizations, employer groups, Medicare and Medicaid plans to automate their business processes, streamline operations and improve their workflow.

In 2001 OAOHS expanded its product line to include a health benefit administrative system, EZ-CAP, which it acquired from Quadramed Corporation. OAOT continually evaluates its services portfolio against the needs of its clients and adds new services and solutions as required.

The bottom line is that OAOT can help bolster any system and streamline any process to improve overall efficiency. And OAOT does it hassle-free. OAOT deploys sophisticated diagnostic and implementation methodologies to tailor its IT solutions to the client's exact needs, with no guesswork involved.

Using repeatable processes, detailed metrics and reporting processes allow for seamless and transparent operating procedures every step of the way. That's why OAOT routinely earns *A*s on balanced scorecards for service delivery, technology, processes and staffing. OAOT is so confident of its ability that it is willing to sign service level agreements (SLAs) with penalty clauses. It's a simple, but effective, formula: The client sets the bar for excellence; OAOT clears it.

More than anything else, it is the OAOT culture of empowerment that motivates its people to be strategic thinkers and proactive problem solvers.

The OAOT work culture includes training, cross-training and certifications to ensure employees meet the highest performance standards and are prepared for all situations.

easy access to the three metro area airports.

OAOT understands its people are the key to its success—people with skill and inspiration who can quickly grasp organizational procedures and consistently go the extra mile to deliver truly exceptional services that go beyond expectations time and again. This passion to go beyond applies to the people at OAOT in tackling the complex IT challenges of multinational companies around the globe, as well as in tackling the challenge of building a strong community at home in Greenbelt, Maryland.

Proactive problem solving, defying perceived limits and achieving the highest levels of customer satisfaction are the foundations of OAOT's continued success.

OAO Technology Solutions is headquartered in Greenbelt, Maryland.

The founders of the original parent company, OAO Corporation, originally chose to locate in Greenbelt, Maryland, because of its close proximity to NASA's Greenbelt facilities. When OAOT spun off as a separate company in 1996, it also established headquarters in Greenbelt, because it was a center point for the company's existing employees and offered

Since 1996 OAOT has sponsored the "Warm Nights Program," which is an annual event run through the churches in Prince George's County to provide housing and an evening meal to the homeless during the winter months. This commitment was inspired in 2001, when OAOT employees donated money toward a family at the homeless shelter—a family of seven who became homeless when the father lost his job at National Airport after September 11, 2001. The money donated by OAOT and its employees provided a hearty Christmas for the family, including food and gifts for all. And there was money enough left over for the INS processing of the mother who had lived in the U.S. for more than 18 years as the wife of an American but had never become a citizen.

The "Warm Summer Nights" program is just one of the ways that the people at OAOT have donated to the Greenbelt community over the last 30 years. Today, OAOT volunteers help with a number of community programs including the Marine's Toys for Tots, the Prince Georges Literacy Council, St. Anne's Children's' Home, the Salvation Army Angels program, and the American Heart Association.

With a team of dedicated leaders willing to push themselves to the max and a responsive core business structure, OAOT has succeeded in becoming a preeminent provider of innovative business solutions, leveraging key technologies to improve customer competitiveness, growth and profitability.

"Jump?" OAOT asks, "How high?"

No matter what the demand for managed IT solutions, the team at OAO Technology Solutions, Inc., has the passion to go beyond.

307

OBA BANK

The sense of community and service that led six German immigrants to found one of the nation's first savings and loan associations remains strong at OBA Bank.

The year was 1861. What banks there were in the Washington area focused largely on commercial accounts, favoring shorter-term business loans. This left small consumers, who wanted longer-term real estate loans, with no place to turn. The answer appeared in mutual savings institutions, whose depositors and borrowers were its owners, and continued around the nation in a range of institutions referred to generally as thrifts.

The founders of the Oriental Bauverein (Building Association) were German immigrants and members of a fraternal

The old OBA building in downtown Washington, D.C. from 1910 until 2003.

group with Oriental Lodge in its name. It is probably from this fraternal order that the name of the association was derived. Each of the six founders put up $250, providing initial assets of $1,500. Leading organizers of the new organization were Conrad Schafer, John Banf, John Walter and Augustus Gersdorff.

The Building Association's goal then, as now, was to help people achieve home ownership and their savings goals. It enabled people to invest money safely and to borrow funds to buy or build homes. It soon had 85 members, and this grew to 3,357 by 1926, its 75th year. Total assets reached $20 million in 1970 and $440 in 2003. Growth has been particularly strong in the last six years, up from $120 million in 1997.

Today, OBA is the oldest thrift in America. It employs 57 people at four locations in Washington, Gaithersburg, Germantown and Bethesda, and offers a full range of banking services. These include telephone banking in English, Spanish and Vietnamese; Internet banking; home personal computer check imaging; credit and debit cards; a large selection of deposit and checking accounts for individuals and businesses, and many home and investment mortgage products all at favorable and competitive interest rates.

OBA's mission is to offer customers excellent value with highest quality financial products while providing superior customer service, and to help customers and employees achieve their financial and professional goals.

Initially, Oriental's programs were on a serial plan, sort of like today's certificates of deposit,

which have a maturity date. Each serial was organized to run five years. However, in 1892, after the fifth serial matured, the association was changed to a permanent plan, known initially as Oriental Building Association Number 6. It was named OBA Federal Savings and Loan Association after changing from a Washington chartered institution to a federally chartered one in 1974, and in 2001 became OBA Federal Savings Bank.

OBA is federally regulated, subject to regular and intensive examinations, which have routinely resulted in a very high "safety and soundness" rating. It is a member of the Federal Home Loan Bank System, America's Community Bankers, the Federal Deposit Insurance Corporation and the Maryland Bankers Association.

In 1894 the association opened its first permanent office. Until then, business was done from the homes of the officers. Customers wishing to withdraw money from their accounts visited the home of the association's secretary to get a voucher, which they took to the treasurer's house to get the money.

General meetings of members and meetings of the board of directors were held in private residences or rented meeting halls.

Until 1917, business at these meetings was conducted in German, and written documents were also in that language. The first effort to change this practice came in 1892, when a director moved to conduct business in English. This was soundly defeated, as were similar suggestions made intermittently until strong anti-German sentiment triggered by World War I swung the balance. The bank faced similar negative sentiment during World War II.

Voting members at meetings were required to be 21 years old, a member for at least six months, and present. No proxies were allowed, nor could trustees vote at general meetings. Both men and women attended. At one meeting in 1892, several ladies asked if elections of Board members could be held during the day so they would not have to be out late in the evening. The secretary noted that

The new OBA building in Germantown, Maryland, surrounded by a greensward and adjacent to I-270.

The community service room with several officers. left to right: back row, Burnett, comptroller, Mallorey, chairman of the board, Hennessy, vice president and CFO; front row, Ludwick, vice president and COO, Low, a president and CEO, and Rosenberger, assistant vice president.

quarters moved to Gaithersburg, in Montgomery County, Maryland, in 1987, and to Germantown in 2002. The Washington branch moved to 700 7th Street NW in 2003.

The county, one of wealthiest in the nation, is a highly competitive market. Average income is high which helps when it comes to making good loans. "We make good loans and have a good reputation," says Warren N. Low, OBA's president. "That gives us a top credit rating."

It's also a diverse area, home to a variety of ethnic groups, the largest of which is Asian.

OBA has retained its structure as a mutual institution, governed by the votes of

the constitution prevented such a motion, and added that earlier meetings were not possible since most of the members worked during the day.

The first permanent office was two rooms at 804 E Street NW. In 1900 the office was moved to 600 F. Street NW. That site remained OBA's headquarters until 1989 and its Washington Branch until 2003, when it was razed to make way for the Shakespeare Theatre. The head-

depositors and loan holders. "As a mutual, rather than a stock company, we just have to cover expenses," says Low. "We're not bottom-line oriented and don't have any SEC (Securities and Exchange Commission) strictures which we'd have if we were publicly traded."

Low, who has been president since 2000 and on the bank's board for 33 years, notes that continuity is important to OBA. He replaced Wendell Tascher, who was in the office for 28 years. Tascher's predecessor, John George Kolb, was president for more than 30 years.

Key to OBA's growth are service, both to customers and to the community; long-term relationships and the latest technology. "We are "Where Customer Service and Technology Meet," Low says, quoting OBA's trademarked tagline. "We receive a lot of compliments on our service, and we support the arts and charitable programs in the area."

OBA also has a community room in its Germantown branch, which is available free for civic and non-profit activities.

"We're still a small community bank," Low says, "and we treat all people with respect."

PDI-SHEETZ CONSTRUCTION CORPORATION

Building bridges isn't just a figure of speech for the Sheetz-Kight family—it's a way of life. In fact, PDI-Sheetz Construction Corporation's three generations of owners have been doing exactly that for more than 50 years.

Barbara Kight, owner and president of the Linthicum, Maryland company, is in an elite group. While other women operate boutiques, beauty salons, or florist shops, she is at the helm of a construction company. In an industry that revolves around male entrepreneurship, Kight has faced—and overcome—the inherent challenges.

"Early on they were taken aback," Kight says of her male colleagues. "They didn't realize they were going to be working with a woman, and then I walked through the door." Usually their initial surprise diminished, however, and "they came around after a while," she says.

Kight's parents, John and Lois Sheetz, started the company in 1950 in Hale-thorpe, Maryland, under the name John D. Sheetz Construction. The two met in 1934 while John was working on the Old Narrows Ferry Bridge at Hoopers Island. Lois' father, William Tolley, was captain of the ferry that transported cars across the waterway during construction. Lois brought her father lunch three times a day so she could catch a glimpse of John.

A self-taught man, John Sheetz started working in bridge construction around 1930. He began his career as a water boy at job sites, later became a crane operator, and learned everything he could about

John D. Sheetz, circa 1953.

the business by listening and doing. Recognizing there were further opportunities for pile driving work as a subcontractor, John and Lois established a second business, Pile Drivers, Inc., in 1954. This company was capitalized with two bulldozers and $3,000 in cash. Lois served as vice president of both companies and managed the office and bookkeeping duties.

Barbara began working in the family business at age 17, handling payroll, banking, and material ordering. She also attended business college and earned a degree. She married Richard Kight, had sons Steven and Todd, and in the early 1970s focused most of her time and energy on taking care of her family. Kight returned to full-time work at the company in the late 1970s. Concerned by a downturn in the industry and what that might entail for the future of the company, Kight got a real estate license as a backup job. She worked at Pile Drivers, Inc. during the day and met with real estate clients in the evenings and on weekends.

When her father retired in 1979 at the age of 70, Barbara

was already groomed for the job. Concerns lingered, however. New construction work was drying up. The economy was unstable. Could a woman succeed in a male-dominated industry, especially during such uncertain times? Barbara was confident that she could.

Changes would be necessary. In order to increase business, Kight diversified the companies' services. Primarily bridge builders in the past, Sheetz Construction, and Pile Drivers, Inc., began to venture into maintaining and rehabilitating bridge structures. Moving the two companies was also in the works. For years, Pile Drivers, Inc. had rented an acre of land for $75 a month in Linthicum Heights to store equipment. In 1979, Kight purchased that acre and its only structure—a ranch house. The very night of the purchase, the old ranch house caught fire. Because of a building moratorium, Kight resurrected the burnt-out building and set up offices there in 1980.

Today the company is headquartered on that same site on Central Avenue, which now covers seven acres. A two-story building was constructed in 1994, with

PDI at Interstate 83 over Big Gunpowder Falls River. The company performed concrete repairs to the piers using a method of pneumatically applied mortar. The crews worked off of the mobile scaffolding platforms seen in this picture, circa 1988.

Baltimore Harbor Outer Tunnel approach structure—in progress, by John D. Sheetz Construction, 1973.

front offices, a 5,000-square-foot warehouse, and inspection bays on the side.

In 1990, Kight merged Pile Drivers, Inc. and John D. Sheetz Construction into one company—PDI-Sheetz Construction Corporation. She also started two new companies: the New Barbet II Corporation, a construction material supplier, in 1986, and Chesapeake Guardrails, a division of PDI-Sheetz, in 1998. Both companies operate out of the Central Avenue location.

John D. Sheetz Construction built Hollins Ferry Road Bridge, part of the original Baltimore Beltway, in 1957. During Barbara's tenure, the company tore it down to the foundation and rebuilt it in 1988. In 1966, Pile Drivers, Inc.

John Sheetz built the Hollins Ferry Road Bridge.

participated in a project for the Chesapeake Bay Maritime Museum to save the Hoopers Strait Light-house. Barbara's grandfather, William Tolley, once worked as a keeper of that lighthouse. The company also built jetties and approach bridges for the Chesapeake Bay bridge and helped build the Harbor tunnel approach bridges. Today the company performs a mixture of new construction, structure rehabilitation, and repairs throughout the state of Maryland.

Several of the company's employees have worked for Kight for 20 years or more. Jerry Sheets is one of these individuals. He came to Sheetz Construction in 1981, and

later became the chief estimator following the death of George J. McClure, Jr. "We're like a little family here," says Kight.

Her eldest son, Steven, has been vice-president since 1996. From an early age, Steven took an interest in the company, particularly the cranes. At first he enjoyed sitting in the cranes with operator Charlie Hawkins; later he learned how to operate them himself. His first responsibility was working as a foreman in the maintenance of traffic and inspection of bridge structures. "I'm probably the only mother in the world who tells her son to go play in the traffic," laughs Kight.

While running the family business is very fulfilling, Kight cherishes her roles as wife, mother, grandmother, and daughter. Her younger son Todd is a computer engineer. Kight's husband Richard is a retired bank vice president—and her constant cheerleader over the years. "He was always worried that I would never get recognition for my hard work. He thought

Barbara S. Kight, Linthicum office

I would always be in my father's shadow," Kight says.

Over the past two decades, Kight has indeed come into her own, demonstrating business savvy and strong leadership that have propelled the company through tough economic times. And she thanks her father, now 93, for having faith in her and entrusting the family business to her care. "I think he let me fall down sometimes and have my own scrapes," she says. "But I know I can always ask him for advice."

PDI-Sheetz has been recognized as one of the largest minority-owned companies by the *Baltimore Business Journal*. The company has also received citations of appreciation from The Department of the Navy and the American Institute of Steel Construction.

PDI-Sheetz setting structural steel for replacement of Dorsey Mill Road Bridge in Howard County, Maryland, 2002.

BOB PORTER COMPANY, INC.

What started in 1979 as a modest acoustical drywall and carpentry contracting company has developed into one of the most widely-respected and dependable general contracting firms in the Washington-Baltimore metropolitan area. With an estimated annual revenue of more than $13 million, Bob Porter Company Incorporated combines superior craftsmanship with personal attention in an industry where builders all too often emphasize profit rather than clients' individual needs.

Its history is simple, but weaves a common thread followed by so many small-town Maryland businesses. Amongst the hustle and bustle of the big-city metropolitan market, Bob Porter Company represents the staying power of a 25-year-old American Dream.

Bob Porter Company, Inc., opened its doors to business in 1979 from the confines of a small home-office in Sandy Spring, Maryland. The company was entirely family-run, with Barbara "Donnie" Porter officiating as secretary and treasurer, while Robert H. "Bob" Porter, Sr., and Robert II. "Bob" Porter, Jr., served as president and vice president, respectively. Both experienced carpentry and general construction veterans, The Porters provided quality craftsmanship with efficient, personalized service that came to be associated with the Porter name and their trademark bulldog logo.

Within its first year of incorporation, Bob Porter Company outgrew its headquarters in Sandy Spring, Maryland, and expanded into a 1,500-square-foot office space on Queenaire Drive in Gaithersburg, Maryland. The new office location set the company in an ideal location for Washington, D.C., metropolitan area projects and in the heart of Montgomery County—a diverse county developing commercially as well as residentially.

As the construction market expanded in the early '80s and beyond, so did Bob Porter Company. Each consecutive year brought new employees and opportunities for business relationships with local gov-

Bob Porter Sr. accepts a plaque from Dr. Helen Tuel, Therapeutic and Recreational Riding Center co-founder and director, at the dedication ceremony for the Donnie Porter Indoor Riding Pavilion. Bob Porter Company has been involved with TRRC, a non-profit organization in Glenwood, Md., since the mid '80s.

ernments, private professionals and national clients. Soon the company had more than 25 full-time employees and had established itself as a firm competitor throughout Maryland, Washington D.C. and Virginia.

In 1987 Bob Porter Company merged into the Northern Virginia construction market fully, opening office space in Manassas, Virginia. Revenue doubled each consecutive year from 1984 to 1988 as the company enjoyed steady growth and increased property development.

The company additionally practiced philanthropy by teaming with the Therapeutic and Recreational Riding Center, now located in Glenwood, Maryland, to sponsor an annual horse show and golf tournament. Throughout the years and even still today, Bob Porter Company and its employees continue to donate to the center. Bob Porter, Jr., serves on TRRC's Board of Directors.

In 1986 Bob Porter Company purchased land on Lindbergh Drive in Gaithersburg and developed a

commercial marketplace to house their newest business enterprise, BPC Supply Corporation. BPC Supply Corporation served primarily as a construction equipment and tools distributor, complete with a tool showroom and retail facilities.

The company's reputation continued to prosper, and Bob Porter, Jr., earned accolades as a nominee for "Entrepreneur of the Year" in 1989 from *Inc.* magazine.

Anxious to become involved in the property management sector of the industry, the Porters bought land adjacent to the existing property on Lindbergh and began construction on a 30,000-square-foot industrial park to replace the space they had since outgrown on Queenaire Drive.

Bob Porter Co. employees moved into their new offices in 1991. The location proved ideal for other construction industry professionals as well, as tenants specializing in construction subtrades populated the building. The facility offered ample office space as well as warehouse storage areas and was officially dedicated in April 1991 to Donnie Porter, who passed away January 31, 1991.

In 1991 the Porter's embarked on their latest business venture, launching

The "construction bulldog," complete with hardhat, is Bob Porter Company's official logo. This rendition was sketched by a friend of the Porter family.

Porter Construction Management, a commercial general contracting company.

Bob Porter, Jr., said the transition from carpentry and drywall into construction management was gradual; as clients began requesting more and more construction management responsibilities from the family-run business, the company evolved into a management corporation for Bob Porter Company. The new organization offered all the benefits Bob Porter Company offered previously, but also provided an increased range of services through the management of subcontractors. Keeping trades such as supply, millwork and general carpentry and drywall in-house, Porter Construction Management continued to provide clients both large and small with the efficiency of a large conglomerate organization coupled with the personal attention accomplished by the locality of the firm.

Bob Porter Company continued its philanthropic efforts with the construction of the Donnie Porter Indoor Riding Pavilion at the TRRC headquarters in 1996.

Over the years Bob Porter, Jr., opened millwork, demolition, glass and glazing, two electrical subcontracting firms and a property-management

Bob Porter, Sr., reviews job progress with a project manager. Since 1979 employees of Bob Porter Co. Inc. have completed thousands of construction projects for a wide variety of clients. The company outgrew its headquarters pictured here in Gaithersburg, Maryland, and moved to a new office and warehouse space in Woodbine, Maryland, in 2001.

corporation, strengthening his industry approach of keeping all trades closely knit and keeping construction projects centrally managed from all angles.

Bob Porter, Sr., died in 1998 after battling cancer. His mark on not only the construction industry but on the community around him is enduring. His professional business skills and generous demeanor allowed Bob Porter Company to grow into the business it is today. Prior to his death, Bob Porter, Sr., was awarded a "One and Only Nine" award from Maryland's WUSA Channel 9 for his volunteer service with TRRC. Dedicated to con-tinuing his father's legacy, Bob Porter, Jr., became president of the organization in 1992.

In June 2001, the companies again outgrew their commercial space in

Gaithersburg and moved to a 23,000-square-foot facility in Woodbine, Maryland, just inside Carroll County, where they operate today. The Woodbine location boasts increased warehouse space for all the Porter companies, and also houses a millwork and cabinet manufacturing shop.

Bob Porter Company has enjoyed success in a variety of construction aspects. Their work remains visible and steadfast throughout Maryland, Washington D.C. and Virginia. In just 24 years of business, the Porter companies have grossed over $250 million dollars in revenue, while staying true to their small business demeanor. The average employee of Bob Porter Company has been there more than 20 years. Bob Porter Company celebrates 25 years of incorporation and superior construction service on January 31, 2004.

Bob Porter Company and its family-based administration epitomize diligent and hard working blue-collar success stories that weave Maryland's economic growth and rich history together; Bob Porter Company is very much a part of that history, and a permeating mainstay in Maryland's future.

The Porter Companies now operate out of this 23,000-square-foot office space and warehouse facility in Woodbine, Maryland.

QUALITY TELECOMMUNICATION SERVICES, INC.

John L. Huggins, Jr., President and CEO of Quality Telecommunication Services, Inc. (QTSI) in Oxon Hill, Maryland, knows what it means to strive for excellence, attain it and encourage others to do the same. Huggins, who grew up in the projects on the west side of Chicago, quickly learned how to create his own opportunities in order to succeed, a habit he acquired early in life and a pattern which continued throughout.

Huggins knew that he had to set goals for himself in order to rise above the low-income neighborhood into which he was born. His first challenge was to gain admittance to Lane Technical High School on the north side of Chicago. Not only was the high school situated in a better neighborhood, which meant a healthier environment, but it also provided a superior education. Acceptance demanded that Huggins score high scholastically to meet the school's admissions criteria. Huggins did so, successfully, and graduated from the school in 1970.

Just a year later, however, Huggins felt his life was going nowhere. He was attending University of Illinois-Circle Campus in Chicago, but felt direction-less. "I was having too much fun partying all the time and wasting my mom's money. She obviously couldn't support that. I knew I had to do something different." says Huggins. He credits his mother for getting him back on track. She convinced him the next decision he made would be an important one. It would determine his life's path for the next 20 years. It was then he took a bold step, literally, into a United States Air Force recruiting office and joined the Air Force.

At that time, Huggins had no idea what the telecommunications industry was all about. It was his high military test scores which guided him into the military's telecommunications arena. He was among the very first and few minorities selected to monitor telecommunications in the Far East. It was there he learned about the

Co-Founder and President/CEO John L. Huggins, Jr., Captain, USAF-Retired. Quality Telecommunication Services, Inc. is headquartered in Oxon Hill, Maryland.

inner workings of the telecommunications industry—design, installation, testing and maintenance.

As Huggins continued making advancements in his military career, he also continued his education. While stationed in Illinois, he received his bachelor of science degree in industrial engineering technology from Southern Illinois University at Carbondale in 1981—the first in his family to earn a college degree. About four years later, he received his master's degree in computer resource management from Webster University in St. Louis, Missouri. Nine years later he completed his MBA from the same university.

His transition into the civilian world happened with the same level of excellence as his other accomplishments. He was one of 27 Air Force officers chosen to take part in a special program called the Education with Industry Assignment, a one-year program permitting officers to work in the commercial world as civilians. He worked for ITT Communication

Services Group in Secaucus, New Jersey. The experience provided insight into the commercial world and the revenue-generating possibilities therein. And it gave him the desire to create a business of his own—a desire that stayed with him along the entrepreneurial road to success.

"I always knew I would do something on my own," Huggins remembers. and just a few years later, he did.

Huggins retired from the Air Force in 1992 and went to work for CACI, a large government contractor. He stayed with the company for over three years, but the aspiration to start his own telecommunications company was always at the forefront of his mind. In March of 1995, his dream became a reality. His friend and now partner, Bennie Davis, retired from the Air Force and joined Huggins in his new business endeavor. With just one other part-time employee, the two began Quality Telecommunication Services Inc. By December of 1995, QTSI had its first two five-year contracts, both with the Air Force, to operate and maintain the telecommunications systems at two military locations.

Presently, QTSI has over 105 employees who provide telecommunication services to departments not only within the Air Force, but also within the Army, the Navy, the U.S. Postal Service, the Veterans Administration, U.S. Department of Commerce and the Federal Bureau of Investigation. Their client list is not limited to government agencies; commercial clients have included the Prince Georges' County Maryland Board of Education, Prince Georges' Community College, Verizon, Sprint, Washington Hospital Center, Guallaudet University and others.

QTSI has grown strong not only because of its employees' technical training and expertise, but also because of Huggins' business philosophy. "Our vision is to deliver superior service and outstanding solutions to our customers, provide fulfilling and rewarding opportunities to our employees and raise the quality of life for the communities in which we operate." Huggins has a very hands-on approach consistent with his statement of vision.

Huggins had the idea to create a training center or school within his company where employees could study to improve their technical skills and advance to higher positions. In 2001 QTSI's Technical Training Center was born. The program was strong, the training thorough, and it was quickly indorsed by Building Industry Consulting Services International (BICSI), a global standards organization for cable installation. Recipients of this certificate were qualified to install cable anywhere in the world where the certification was recognized as standard. The program was so enriching, he decided to afford others, within the community and beyond, with the same opportunity. He opened the training center doors to under-represented groups within the

Ms. Mickens, QTSI Technical Training Center instructor assists Mr. Montgomery, a QTSI cable technician with fiber-optic cable splicing techniques.

Maryland and District of Columbia urban areas. The unemployed, underemployed, veterans, and even the homeless were given opportunities not only to learn new skills, but also to have a career with QTSI. To date, over 200 people have benefited from the program.

Huggins' efforts to give back to the community were recognized when two graduates of QTSI's Technical Training Center were selected as winners of the Rising Star award by the National Workforce Investment Council. Huggins himself was given the prestigious President's Award from the University of the District of Columbia for his involvement in these students' success. Among other awards for his exceptional business skills, Huggins recently received the National Black Chamber of Commerce Entrepreneur of the Year award for 2003.

Huggins learned at an early age that having goals and pushing through obstacles was the only way to create a life for himself. Against tough odds, he was able to do so. His example is an inspiration to others who face those same odds. Huggins takes it upon himself to guide and instruct those individuals, and the Maryland urban communities and surrounding areas benefit greatly.

Hands-on instruction is a vital part of QTSI's training programs. Students are practicing their cable "cut-down" or connectorization skills.

REGIONAL MANAGEMENT/WELSH CONSTRUCTION COMPANY

The story of The Macht Real Estate and Banking Business (1891–1954), Welsh Construction Company (1911–present) and Regional Management Inc. (RMI, 1959–present) began with Ephraim Macht, the family patriarch.

Macht, who was born in 1866 in Kovno, Lithuania, at a time when that small eastern European nation was under Russian control, emigrated to the United States in 1887. His new hometown of Baltimore, Maryland, offered the immigrant the opportunity to flex his entrepreneurial muscles. His legacy now extends into the fourth generation, as his great-great-niece, Amy Macht, president of Regional Management, Inc., presides over a real estate business that has undergone an extensive metamorphosis since Ephraim began his American adventure more than 115 years ago.

What hasn't changed, though, is the company's deep commitment to Baltimore's economic vitality—as evidenced by the restoration of the historic Macht Building at 11 East Fayette Street in downtown Baltimore, and Regional Management's expansion into the neighboring building at 15 East Fayette Street.

Ephraim Macht was 21 when his transatlantic steamer docked in 1887 in Baltimore, which, at the time, ranked second to New York's Ellis Island as the most popular destination for immigrants

Morris Macht, 1890–1954.

Ephraim Macht, 1866–1944.

bound for the hopes and dreams of America. On the journey, he met Annie Marowitz of Riga. They were married that same year. Ephraim arrived with no special skills or crafts. It was his wife Annie's work making and selling hats from a pushcart in Fells Point that gave the couple their economic start. The hats Annie made provided enough capital for her husband to begin buying older homes that he would remodel for rental or resale.

This was the origin of The Macht Real Estate and Banking Business that Ephraim established in the early 1890s as he bought, repaired, sold, rented and traded properties—in addition to providing financing for the customers of his housing. Ephraim did well enough to set up an office in the Equitable Building in downtown Baltimore. Macht is thought to be the first Jewish licensed Real Estate Broker in Baltimore; his 1904 license is still on display at the company's offices.

When Baltimore's central business district was ravaged by fire in 1904, the city's economy was prosperous enough to rebound rather quickly. Macht was one of the city's rebuilders: he purchased a small but prominently located lot in the heart of downtown to build a new office building for his business.

The Macht Building, with a facade of lions' heads, gargoyles and provocative

maidens, reflected the Ephraim's European sensibilities and expansive personality. The building opened in February 1909. Macht's business occupied the entire second floor while he leased the rest of the space to tenants.

In this period Ephraim began large-scale building of new homes. Newspaper reports mention developments in Clifton Park, Virginia Avenue and Irvington. Though a prosperous time for building, it was also a time of harsh anti-Semitism, and Ephraim encountered obstacles, particularly in dealing with suppliers. In response, Ephraim formed a new building company using the name of John Martin Welsh, an Irishman who worked for the company as a salesman, and who was a trusted friend of Ephraim's until Ephraim's death in 1944.

The Welsh Construction Company was formed in 1911, launching nearly a

Architectural Rendering of The Macht Building, 11 E. Fayette Street, circa 1907.

Morton Macht, 1899–1966.

Regional Management, Inc.'s offices in the Macht Building, and its restored neighbor at 11-15 E. Fayette Street.

half century of activity that would see it rise to a position of leadership, producing quality housing for people of all income levels and contributing mightily to the growth of Baltimore. During this period, Ephraim brought his 18-year-old son, Morris, who was born in 1890, into the business. "Morris was an intellectual and wanted to go to college," said Amy Macht, "but his father insisted he join the company and go to work. Morris did as his father wanted, and became a driving force in the business. By 1919 his father had formed a partnership with Morris, which gave him 50% of all the interest in their pursuits going forward from that time." In addition to running the financial aspects of the business, Morris continued his intellectual pursuits and was very well educated despite being denied the opportunity to go to college.

Amy's branch of the family was about to become involved as well. Ephraim's brother had immigrated to the United States, settling in Virginia, where he operated a dry-goods store. Dying at an early age, he left a widow, five children and not too many financial resources.

"The oldest of the five was Morton Macht, who was my grandfather," Amy said. "He was about nine years old when he was sent to Baltimore to live with Uncle Ephraim; Morris was 18. The relationship between Morris and Morton was more than cousins; it was that of a little brother idolizing a big brother. Morton, who professed that he never was sent to school after arriving in Baltimore, grew up in the business, just as Morris did."

As Ephraim, who was referred to by this time as "the king of the homebuilders," phased the operation of Welsh Construction over to his son, Morris came to rely on his cousin, Morton. "They really complemented each other. Morris, the intellectual, concentrated on the financial part of the business," Amy said, "while my grandfather focused on the construction, and on dealing with people."

It was because of their leadership that the company, which could both mass-produce homes in a variety of price ranges and build a customized residence, was solid enough to survive the tough times of the 1930s. In a 1932 brochure, before the depression of the '30s had really taken hold in the real estate market, Welsh Construction Company was advertising homes in 16 different areas of the city, from Ashburton on the west to Chesterfield Avenue on the east. By the mid-1930s there was very little new building going on.

The homebuilding business picked up after World War II. One of the notable Welsh developments of the post-war era was the construction of Academy

Renovated office in the origianl Banking Room of the Macht Building.

Heights in 1950, which consists of 487 neocolonial row houses in Catonsville. The "first-ring" suburb constituted Baltimore's version of the national housebuilding boom and the post-war trend of migration from city living. The GI Bill fueled this phenomenon. It is estimated that Morris and Morton were responsible for constructing over 8,000 homes throughout Baltimore.

When Morris died in November 1954, the company reins passed to Morton. However, Morton, who was very active philanthropically, was

Two of the townhouse apartment developments managed by Regional Management, Inc.: Walden Circle Townhouses and Gardenvillage Apartments and Townhouses.

beginning to wind down his involvement in the day-to-day activity of the business. Fortunately, his son, Philip Macht, who had joined the firm in 1949, was ready to step in.

Philip, who received his engineering degree from the Massachusetts Institute of Technology, was the first of the Macht family to earn college credentials, and in a field that was relevant to what the family business was all about. However, it was not until he tried out a year as a philosophy graduate student at Columbia University that Philip was convinced that the family building business was the career he wanted. During the 1950s Welsh Construction Company's team was comprised of many talented people including, among others, Nathan Abell, Stuart Wilcox, Morris Goodhart, E. Lee Kaufman and H. William Cohen, who was connected to the Macht family by marriage to Ephraim's granddaughter. Along with Philip Macht, they played key roles in the transition in the late 1950s and 1960s from a company that built new homes on sites across Baltimore City and County to one that developed and built rental properties throughout the 1960s, 1970s and early 1980s. It was in 1959 that Regional Management, Inc., was formed to manage this growing rental portfolio.

Pursuing its own version of the three Rs—reasonable, reliable and regional—the properties that Regional Management manages include St. Agnes Apartments, Lothian and Oakridge Apartments, Goodnow Hill and Franconia Apartments, Gardenvillage Apartments and Town-houses, Eastfield Townhouses, Parkside Gardens Apartments and Townhouses, Hollinswood Townhouses, Westland Gardens Apartments and Townhouses, College Gardens Apartments and Townhouses, Melbourne Townhouses and Walden Circle Townhouses.

Ephraim established a philanthropic and civic-minded legacy in his family that lives today. He endowed Baltimore's Sinai Hospital and founded the "Jewish Home for Consumptives." Morris followed in his father's footsteps, serving on Sinai's Board of Directors and helping to guide the Associated Jewish Charities. During World War II, he was appointed by the federal government to serve on a national defense committee that focused on America's housing needs.

Morton, a strong advocate for people who lived on limited incomes, brought his experience as a Sinai Board member to his service on the Provident Hospital Board. Morton was appointed by Mayor McKeldin to be the first chairman of the Baltimore Community Action Committee formed as part of President Lyndon Johnson's "War on Poverty." Because of ill health, he resigned from that post shortly before he died in 1966.

Also shortly before his death, The Maryland Home Builders Association, of which he had twice served as president, presented him with its most prestigious honor, the Trowel Award, for community service. At his funeral, Mayor Mckeldin eulogized Morton with democracy's highest accolade—the rank of "Citizen First Class" for working for the rights of all people.

Philip continued his father's work on the Provident Hospital Building Committee, and went on to many other philanthropic and civic involvements, including serving on the Baltimore City School Board from 1964–1970.

Carrying on that tradition is the Morton and Sophia Macht Foundation, established in 1956, which today focuses on supporting youth programs. The foundation is how Amy Macht found her way to Regional Management.

After graduating with a major in environmental biology from the University of Pennsylvania, she attended the University of Maryland School of Architecture. Her architecture school thesis focused on designing a customized facility to serve nonprofits dealing with women's issues. In her research, she often saw that the Macht Foundation was a supporter of many of the agencies. When she graduated in 1978, Amy then went to work for her sister Carol's architectural firm of Hord, Coplan, and Macht, but she also started to get involved in the operation of the Macht Foundation.

"I really didn't know anything about it until my father explained what the foundation was all about and how it was formed," Amy said. "I began to read the grant proposals sent to the foundation and became very interested. While working at the foundation, I became interested in the business as well. I started at the foundation in 1978 and left my sister's firm in 1981 to join Regional Management."

By 1958 Ephraim's enterprise was occupying the entire building that bears his name. "By 1999," Amy said, "we were really crunched for office space and needed to expand. When the four-floor building next door became available, we jumped at the chance. Now both it, and Ephraim's 1909 building have been restored. I think that shows RMI plans to stay in Baltimore City." And that's good news for Baltimore.

Once home to rotting piers, Baltimore's Inner Harbor is now one of the nation's leading urban tourist destinations. Courtesy, Baltimore Area Convention & Visitors Association

RONKIN CONSTRUCTION, INC.

Jim Barron, founder and president of Ronkin Construction, Inc., in Joppa, Maryland, began his professional life as an advocate, serving as a special education teacher in his native western Pennsylvania. Barron's career path has greatly diverged since then, but his passion for advocacy remains constant.

A few years after college graduation, armed with a degree in education and a minor in psychology, Barron found himself working as a laborer on a pipe crew for Armand Construction company in Roseto, Pennsylvania. His three jobs of teaching, driving a school bus and pumping gas on the Pennsylvania Turnpike proved insufficient for launching a family after marriage to his high school sweetheart, Ginny, a very distantly related "Barron."

Barron's work with Armand brought him to Bel Air, Maryland, when the company took on a project there. The company dissolved shortly thereafter, and Barron went to work for Armand's supervisor in his newly formed Hanks Contracting. The former teacher served at Hanks Contracting as foreman, estimator and superintendent before moving on to Atlantic Precast, a manhole manufacturer. Precast groomed Barron for plant superintendent, but he preferred to work in the field, and instead joined Reeves Construction in

Jim and Ginny Barron of Ronkin Construction, Inc.

the Baltimore area. Jobs with Reeves included construction of the Baltimore subway. After two bounced paychecks from Reeves, and with a second baby on the way, Barron decided that it was time to start his own business. A second mortgage on the couple's home provided startup cash and financing for equipment.

Edmund Jenkins joined forces with Barron to create Jen-Bar in May 1978. The company's founders merged last names to name their new company. In 1981, for accounting reasons, they organized under Ronkin Construction, Inc., keeping Jen-Bar as an equipment company. In the fall of 1986 Barron

bought out Jenkins to become sole owner of Ronkin. The year 1983 saw the company's first million-dollar job, the Market Place development where they laid 98" x 76" elliptical pipe below sea level near the current Port Discovery, an 80,000 square-foot children's museum located where the old fish market used to be. Ronkin workmen laid pipe for Baltimore's "Comfort Link," a system of chilled water used for air conditioning by area hospitals, museums and shopping facilities. Work for the Montebello Filtration Plant, responsible for purifying drinking water for the Baltimore area, included cutting existing pipe installed by the city in the early 1900s to divert water from Maryland's Susquehanna River to Lake Montebello. Ronkin workmen at that site cut into the reservoir's original 18-inch-thick, poured-in-place concrete to install a meter monitoring water flow.

Ronkin workers trace Maryland's history on many jobs, sometimes working with maps of area infrastructure that date back to the 1800s. Workers on a job at Maryland's Fort Meade Army base once discovered what looked like "a coffee can with legs"—which turned out to be an unexploded land mine. Department of Defense workers took the land mine down to the rifle range to detonate it. Jobs in Baltimore's Fells Point area showed sewer lines running through as many as eight different bulk-heads, some filled in with old beer bottles, others with oyster shells from the old canning factory. Geologists came to a site in Howard County to examine petrified wood turned up by a work crew. Excavation work in front of the Hyatt Regency at Baltimore's Inner Harbor turned up a well, hand-lined with brick and still filled with water.

Barron expresses a real regard for his staff, comprised at this time of seven work crews and office staff. Staff exhibit reciprocal loyalty: many are longtime employees. Backhoe operator Willie Ferguson, who "can make a backhoe talk," has been with Ronkin since 1978.

Ronkin Construction, Inc.'s office and shop in Harford County, just east of Baltimore.

Key management employees of Ronkin Construction, Inc. Left to right: Jim Barron, co-founder, owner and president; Wade Jenkins, head estimator; Greg Orzeck, vice president of operations; and Phil Pyle, general superintendent.

Ferguson's current heart condition does not prevent him from showing up for work every day. Barron talks of an "open shop" where everyone "does what it takes" to get the job done. His staff leaned their craft as he did, in the field from the ground up. Wade Jenkins, now chief estimator, joined the staff as a laborer in 1978. Phil Pyle, Barron's general superintendent and a friend from third grade, started as a foreman. Greg Orzeck joined Ronkin in 2001 as vice president of operations, bringing with him a wealth of knowledge in operations that he had gained from em-

polyment with the utility contracting giant, Henkel & McCoy. All staff, including office workers, are taken into "the field" to get a better grasp of the workings of the organization. This attention to detail and emphasis on staff knowledge across the board has proved immensely effective: in an economy where many are struggling, Ronkin is turning away work.

Barron's sense of advocacy again came into play in the 1990s, when the National Utility Contractors Association (NUCA) asked him to attend a meeting. Barron would become chairman of NUCA's damage prevention task force, and would serve on the steering team for the U.S. Department of Transportation's Office of Pipeline Safety "Best Practices" study. These practices are viewed by experts in damage prevention in construction as extremely effective in preventing damage to underground facilities, while protecting excavators

and the public, as well as the environment. Barron now serves as president of the Common Ground Alliance (CGA), a nonprofit organization whose 1999 "Common Ground Study" gathered and assessed information to determine the best facility damage prevention practices, including introducing a "one call" system that would help excavators prevent underground utility damage. Common Ground's "one call" legislation has been approved by Congress, but has not yet been adopted by the FCC. The CGA now functions as an advocate for best practices in the industry, developing and conducting public awareness and education programs and serving as a "clearinghouse" for damage data collection, analysis and dissemination.

Barron's office at Ronkin, a beautiful, modern facility, is decorated throughout with photos of family. His desk includes a "zen garden," a gift from telecommunications cohorts, complete with tiny backhoes, a buried fiber optic cable and a sign warning excavators to "call before you dig." A plaque commemorates NUCA's 2000 "Ditchdigger of the Year" award, presented to Barron for voluntary activities benefiting the national organization. He can only recall his mother's admonition after his father's death: that without a college education, he would end up "as a ditchdigger."

Ronkin Construction, Inc., laying twin 24-inch chilled water mains in Conway Street on the Comfort Link project located between Baltimore's popular Inner Harbor, and the home of the Baltimore Orioles, Camden Yards.

Ronkin Construction, Inc., providing the on-site underground utilities for the Market Place project near the Inner Harbor in East Baltimore in 1983.

ST. JOSEPH MEDICAL CENTER

In the midst of the American Civil War, three courageous and committed nuns of the Third Order of St. Francis of Philadelphia arrived in Baltimore to care for the sick and wounded. In 1864, in a group of row houses on Baltimore's North Caroline Street (donated by Catherine Eberhard), Sister Mary Clara, Sister Crescientia, and Sister Scholastica created what was to become Saint Joseph's Medical Center. Originally called Saint Joseph's German Hospital, Catherine Eberhard had worked closely with the local German parishes of Saint James, Saint Michael's, and Saint Alphonsus in bringing the Franciscan Sisters to Baltimore to begin caring for sick parishioners.

Within a short time of establishing the facility, the health care demands put upon East Baltimore's only Catholic hospital made it clear to the sisters that there was a great need to expand their facilities and services. According to a handwritten history of the hospital, "a temporary building was erected capable of accommodating about 50 patients at a cost of $5,800." More sisters were also assigned to the expanding facility. By 1871 a new wing was under construction which was designed by Dr. Oscar Coskery, who also became the hospital's first chief of staff. Opened in 1872, the new wing was built for $50,000 and could accommodate 72 patients.

In November 1870 the hospital incorporated as Saint Joseph's, and was listed

Entrance to Saint Joseph's Hospital on Caroline Street.

The chapel in Saint Joseph's Hospital on Caroline Street.

in the Catholic Directory as Saint Joseph's General Hospital. A few of the lay trustees prevailed upon the Reverend Mother General to permanently call the hospital "Saint Joseph's German Hospital," but with so few German physicians on a staff that was dominated by a non-German board, the name was not changed.

In 1881 the hospital was designated by the city of Baltimore and the state of Maryland to care for indigent patients. The care of private charity patients represented a sizable percentage of the hospital's work and was very much in keeping with the philosophy behind the sisters' community work. The first nursing students began training at the hospital in 1901, a program that would last 87 years and would eventually graduate more than 2,100 students. A wing was also added in 1901 to house the nursing students.

The hospital's medical board was founded in 1910, which completed the modernization of the hospital.

This modernization included appointing a lay surgical nurse, requiring that resident physicians pass an examination, keeping up patient records, appointing a pathologist and a radiologist, and separating patients suffering from tuberculosis. Within a short time the board also took charge of dispensary operations, separated its staff from the hospital, and designed rules for its governance. Even with modernizing the facility and its operations, the German-American character of the Franciscan community persisted. The primary concerns of the Sisters of St. Francis were to care for the infirm and to respond to the poor, sick, and dying with Christian charity.

The hospital began its long tradition of being a medical teaching hospital in 1912 with the appointment of Dr. Edward S. Johnson as its surgical resident. The hospital once again changed its name in 1918, to Saint Joseph's Hospital. In 1924

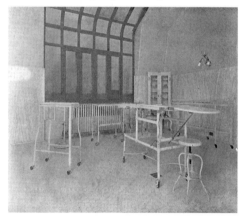

Trimble Operating Room, Saint Joseph's German Hospital, 1911.

ground was broken for a new housing unit for nurses. By 1941, Saint Joseph's was one of the only Baltimore-area hospitals to have an iron lung, the life-saving treatment for polio.

By the 1950s the hospital was the first in Maryland to have a structured coronary/pulmonary resuscitation team. Yet, even with the good work the sisters and the hospital were doing, the hospital building began to deteriorate and was no longer able to meet city safety codes in 1954. By 1956, the Sisters of St. Francis decided to close the hospital, unable to pay for the necessary improvements. However, supporters of the hospital—including friends and physicians—stepped in, and the search for a new home began.

Within two years the future of the hospital was secured with the purchase of the 37-acre Turnbull estate in Towson, Maryland, in 1958. Ground was officially broken on Saint Joseph's Feast Day on March 19, 1963. By 1965 the new hospital was fully operational.

Throughout the decades leading up to the turn of the century, Saint Joseph's Hospital continued to expand the services it offered to the community, as well as improve the quality of its existing services.

Original location of Saint Joseph's Hospital on North Caroline Street in Baltimore.

The first short-term inpatient psychiatric unit in the state; a sleep disorders clinic; state-of-the-art Heart Institute; Orthopaedic Institute; a comprehensive cancer program; a Mother/Baby Unit; and the Digestive Disease Center are now all part of the medical center.

Now called St. Joseph Medical Center, the hospital has received numerous accolades for the quality of its care, including being named by *U.S. News & World Report* magazine as a top orthopaedic facility. St. Joseph also performs more open-heart and interventional heart procedures than any other Maryland facility, and has been named a national Top 100 cardiovascular facility by independent healthcare ranking firm Solucient. And, its nationally recognized Center for Eating Disorders treats patients from across the country. Most recently, St. Joseph has undergone considerable renovation, tripling the size of its Emergency Department and creating a dedicated orthopaedic inpatient unit.

In keeping with its goal of caring for the people of the region, St. Joseph Medical Center offers exceptional

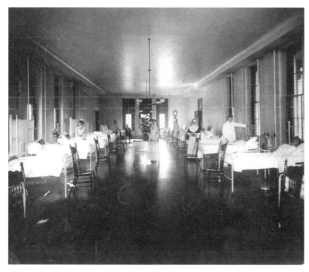

Saint Mary's Hall, Saint Joseph's Hospital on Caroline Street, circa 1924.

Pharmacy, Saint Joseph's Hospital, 1925.

community outreach programs through its St. Clare Medical Outreach and other free health education programs. It also offers free support groups to caregivers, widows and widowers, people suffering from diabetes, and a smoking cessation support group. In addition, the medical center offers free flu immunizations, free screenings for head and neck cancer, hearing, osteoporosis, prostate cancer, skin cancer, and vision.

St. Joseph Medical Center is governed by a set of core values to which it credits its continued success. In brief, they are: Reverence—illuminating profound spirit and awe for all persons around us; Integrity—implying a moral wholeness; Compassion—serving people with limited access; and Excellence—offering the community the best possible medical care.

Today, 140 years after it began, St. Joseph Medical Center, a not-for-profit, 328-bed facility, offers a comprehensive range of inpatient and outpatient health care services The hospital has more than 1,200 affiliated physicians, more than 2,000 employees and is part of Catholic Health Initiatives. It consistently ranks as one of the best in the nation, and is accredited by the Joint Commission on the Accreditation of Healthcare Organizations.

TAYLOR MANOR HOSPITAL

Dr. Irving Taylor was not looking to change the course of modern psychiatric history in 1952 when he went out to dinner in Baltimore with his wife Edith. It just happened by accident. "Outside the restaurant, I met an associate, Dr. Edgar Berman," Dr. Taylor recalls. "Dr. Berman was a surgeon who had just returned from Paris. He had been working with a new drug. The drug was not helpful in surgery, but it had been used on schizophrenic patients for two years, and a number of patients no longer had delusions. Dr. Berman said, 'Irv, I think you'd be interested in this medicine.'"

Irving Taylor was very interested. He knew only too well that at that time there was no medical treatment for major medical illnesses like schizophrenia aside from electro-convulsive therapy.

Irving's Taylor Manor Hospital became the first psychiatric hospital in the United States to administer Thorazine—the first neuroleptic, and the first of a new generation of drugs that today help millions of patients around the world actually recover from mental illness. It was a turning point in modern psychiatry, as well as a revolution in drug therapy for psychiatric patients.

Healing has truly been a family business at Taylor Manor Hospital. "My father, Isaac Taylor, started a jewelry and optometry business in Ellicott City in 1912," Irving recalls. "He was a self-made man who left school in the sixth grade to sell newspapers and help his family out."

Taylor Manor Hospital's main dining room in the 1950s.

Three generations, left to right: Bruce T. Taylor, M.D.; Isaac H. Taylor; and Irving J. Taylor, M.D. Behind them on the wall in Isaac's office are some of his awards for civic service in Maryland and Israel.

Isaac sold everything in Taylor's Furniture Store—glasses, furniture, jewelry, records, washing machines, floor coverings—everything except clothing and groceries. He even operated a Firestone auto supply store. "Our family always lived above the store," Irving recalls. "So I was raised in the business—which was fortunate for a doctor because most doctors do not know all that much about business."

In 1939, Isaac and his son Irving, a first year medical student, went out to look at the Howard County Sanitarium Company, which was established in 1907 and was called Patapsco Manor Sanitarium. It had 10 to 12 patients on an estate of 56 acres. "We looked over the hospital one day, and the next day we bought it," Irving recalls. "My father and I became equal partners in the business."

In the 1940s the facility was renamed the Pinel Clinic, after a French physician renowned for humane treatment of the mentally ill. While Irving completed his medical training and fulfilled his military duty, Isaac served as the hospital's administrator, remaining active in this role until his death in 1978. According to Irving, "My father worked from seven in the morning to 11 at night, seven days a week. He was an inspiration to the entire staff."

Irving J. Taylor, MD, became the medical director of the facility in 1949. "I took a patient's room and lived at the hospital," Irving recalled. "I really started at the bottom there. In fact I always say I knew the hospital from the ground up, because at one time I mowed the lawn . . . so I knew everything about running a hospital."

In 1954 the hospital was given the family name and became Taylor Manor Hospital. In addition to their ground-breaking work with Thorazine, Dr. Irving Taylor went on to work with each new antipsychotic, antidepressant and anti-anxiety medication before it came to market in the '50s and '60s. Dr. Irving Taylor's research included therapeutic benefits, side effects and clinical dose equivalences of the new medications. "Twenty-five years later the table of equivalences for psychiatric drugs I developed was standardized with minor variations," Irving recalled. "That was quite rewarding."

Irving credits much of his success, and the success of Taylor Manor Hospital, to the fact that he studied internal medicine first, before he took up his psychiatric training. "We did not try to put a patient in our own therapeutic rut," he recalls. "We tried to mold the various treatments around the individual. So before the days of individualized treatment programs this is what we did." Irving noted that his daughter Stephanie was an early proponent of utilizing an integrated approach to assessing and caring for each patient, in part due to her interest in holistic health and alternative methods of healing.

In keeping with his eclectic approach to psychiatric treatment, in 1966 Dr. Irving Taylor started the first psychiatric hospital treatment program in Maryland specifically for adolescents. This was followed in the '70s by the development of a Dual-Diagnosis Program for emotionally ill substance abusers called Group 9, and by a specialized Young Adult Treatment Program.

Bruce Taylor completed his psychiatric residency at The Johns Hopkins Hospital and joined the full-time staff in 1979. Almost immediately, Bruce was called on to take over as medical director of the hospital. "Within six months he had the confidence of our staff," says Irving. "He was the youngest doctor there, but they recognized his ability, and respected his position as director. That was an achievement."

In addition to his administrative duties, Dr. Bruce Taylor is actively involved in patient treatment throughout the hospital. Groundbreaking psychiatric work is a tradition in the Taylor family as Dr. Bruce Taylor has also been involved in clinical research, including being the first to use Wellbutrin in adolescent populations in the United

Left to right: Bruce T. Taylor, M.D.; Edith L. Taylor; and Irving J. Taylor, M.D.—September 2003, at the Delta Society fund-raiser.

States. In the 1980s Taylor Manor Hospital offered the nation's only specialized in-patient treatment for compulsive gambling and a specialized program, the Isaac H. Taylor Institute for Psychiatry and Religion was developed.

Both Drs. Bruce and Irving Taylor acknowledge that Irving's wife and Bruce's mother, Edith, played a very significant role in everything in the hospital's success. Ever since Irving married Edith in 1946, she has served as the hospital's executive director, manag-

The hospital rotunda, its trademark, designed by Edith L. Taylor.

ing human resources and marketing for the family hospital. Edith Taylor designed all of the brochures for Taylor Manor Hospital, and won an international prize for one of her hospital publications.

Edith helped design and build a new Center Building which was occupied in 1968, expanding the Hospital's capacity to 176 beds. She was responsible for the facility's distinctive turquoise color scheme and its logo. According to Bruce, "My mother made it part of her effort to make the hospital as homelike an environment as possible even though it was an institution. She sewed different curtains for each patient bedroom and lounge herself and purchased various pieces of artwork to place throughout the hospital." For her artistic efforts, Edith received the Artist's Equity Award in Maryland. Bruce says, "We had, in fact, an art gallery that used to have art shows for the community. It serves to invite people into our facility and make them more familiar with the fact that a psychiatric hospital was a comfortable place and not something that needed to be feared or shunned." These programs along with many others lead to the Hospital recieving the first National

Institute of Mental Health Award for Destigmatizing Mental Illness.

Edith Taylor was also the force behind the Taylor Manor Hospital's Annual Symposium, first held in 1968. Only two years later a major three-day symposium entitled "Discoveries in Biological Psychiatry" highlighted the major advances in psychopharmacology with presentations by 18 of the world's major researchers. "At the time, nobody was doing this," Bruce notes, "and doctors didn't even have continuing education requirements." The educational programs, and the publications that have resulted, have helped to shape the psychiatric education of thousands of professionals throughout the region and the nation.

Beyond the medical field, the Taylor family has been involved with a wide variety of community development work. Isaac Taylor was instrumental in founding the first African American high school in Howard County and the first public library in Ellicott City.

Since the early '70s the Taylor family has also been involved in acquiring and renovating historic properties in the area. In 2003 Dr. Bruce Taylor's efforts were recognized when he was honored

by the Ellicott City Business Association for his family's efforts in assisting the city and the community in rehabilitating property.

The Taylor family has long supported the Jewish National Fund, the American Friends of Hebrew University and the Delta Society. "What they do is just incredible and heartwarming," Bruce explains. "The Delta Society is a group that trains trainers who work with dogs, horses, cats, monkeys and a variety of animals that provide assistance to handicapped individuals. They bring animals

The activity workshop at Taylor Manor Hospital.

into nursing homes and hospitals to assist in caring for patients."

In May 2002 the Taylor family faced the realities of the medical marketplace and signed a binding letter of intent between Sheppard Pratt Health System and Taylor Manor Hospital, leading

The Ruby dining room with a mosaic by artist Betty Wells in the background.

The hosptial rotunda, seen from the inside, is also the reception area.

The pool facilities and the auditorium/gymnasium in the background.

Bicycle riders enjoying the many outside activities on the hospital's park-like grounds.

to Sheppard Pratt's asset acquisition of Taylor Manor's programs on July 1, 2002. "The reimbursement climate for psychiatric services has become increasingly difficult," explains Dr. Bruce Taylor. "After much soul-searching, our family of owners decided that it was preferable to find an organization who could introduce economies of scale as part of its larger organization in order to assure the perpetuation of what we have built over the past 60-plus years. We have seen several other private psychiatric hospitals in our state succumb to bankruptcy over the past decade, and we were determined not to experience that fate."

Dr. Steven S. Sharfstein, president and chief executive officer of Sheppard Pratt Health System, speaking about this arrangement, recently said "This is a marriage of two of Central Maryland's most esteemed providers of psychiatric care. We are delighted that we have been able to craft this agreement, which will preserve the legacy of Taylor Manor and the delivery of services to the community it has served for so many years."

The acquisition of Taylor Manor by Sheppard Pratt Health System has proved thus far to be a stunning success, continuing the tradition of top quality private psychiatric hospital care that stretches back six decades. Today, high quality, cost-effective psychiatric treatment and special programs are provided in a campus setting. Each patient's treatment and length of stay is individualized with a focus on crisis management and stabilization. A treatment plan is developed by a multi-disciplinary team in conjunction with the patient and the referral source. As medical director of the hospital, Dr. Bruce Taylor says "Our mission has always been to provide personal high quality mental health services. Now that we are part of a larger institution, we are still small enough to be like a large family of caring providers assisting patients and their families."

The Sheppard Pratt at Ellicott City hospital is currently licensed for 92 psychiatric beds and also operates the Taylor Residential Treatment center and special education school, as well as the Taylor Respite Service for adolescents. All referrals are welcome, and patients return to their referring professionals. Referrals may also be made by a patient, friend, employer, family or other health professional. Admission is usually voluntary, but may be by court recommendation or with physicians' certificates. Programs include adolescent, adult, respite and residential treatment.

Dr. Bruce Taylor's grandfather, Isaac Taylor, took as his motto the words "Live, let live and help others live." Working today as part of Sheppard Pratt at Ellicott City, the Taylor family and their dedicated coworkers continue that tradition of helping others to live well. "Our hospital strives to provide the very best mental healthcare in an efficient, respectful and cost-effective manner," Bruce says. "Our vision is to be the health system of choice for mental health services, and to be the preeminent mental health provider in the region."

Sculpture, Humanity in Harmony, *by Wasyl Palijczuk on hospital lawn.*

UNIVERSITY OF MARYLAND, COLLEGE PARK

Back in 1856, in rural Prince George's County, Maryland, Charles Benedict Calvert saw the need to offer young men the chance to get an education in agriculture. A wealthy and well-known individual, Calvert was a congressman, planter, and philanthropist. Calvert was a leader in the United States Agricultural Society, and sold his Rossborough Farm to the Maryland Agricultural College for $21,400. Known as the father of what is now the University of Maryland, Calvert was the acting president of the college in 1859 and 1860, and was also the president of the Board of Trustees.

The college actually received its charter from the Maryland General Assembly on March 6, 1856, but it wasn't until March 22, 1858, when Calvert sold the land to the college, that the school and campus began to take shape. The land was made up of parcels with names such as "Arthur's Stamp," "Original Buck Lodge," "God-father's Gift," and "New Look Out," and consisted of 428 acres. At the same time Calvert issued stock certificates to help launch the school.

Benjamin Hallowell was the college's first president and opened the school to its first students. October 6, 1859, marked the day of the formal dedication of the

Historic Rossborough Inn has served many purposes: as a resting spot for weary travelers, the Agricultural Experiment Station and, today, home of the Maryland Alumni Association.

This portrait of Charles Benedict Calvert, founder, benefactor and trustee of Maryland Agricultural College, is based on a Matthew Brody photograph.

college with Joseph Henry, then head of the Smithsonian Institution, as the main speaker. Thirty-four male students made up the first class. Military training was required of all students, who were called Cadets. The first professors at the college included George C. Shaeffer, a professor of the science of agriculture; Hugh Dorsey Gough, a professor of the exact sciences; and Battista Lorino, a professor of ancient and modern languages.

Under Calvert's brief administration enrollment increased from its original 34 to 68 students. He established a non-

credit preparatory program for applicants who could not meet the college's academic requirements, and was also responsible for hiring the prominent Washington scientist Townend Glover as professor of botany and entomology.

The first class graduated from the Maryland Agricultural College on July 11, 1862. That same year President Lincoln signed the Morrill Land Grant Act, providing federal support for state colleges to teach agriculture, mechanical arts and military tactics. By February 1864, the Maryland legislature voted to accept the Morrill Grant, which was a boon for the small college.

During the Civil War both the Union and Confederate Armies used the campus. Union General Ambrose Burnside camped his 6,000 men on the grounds en route to General Grant in Virginia, and General Bradley Johnson camped Confederate troops there before they joined Jubal Early's raid on Washington.

In that same period the college failed to open, but within a short time the Maryland legislature appropriated money and the college became partly a state institution, with an emphasis on military training. In 1867 the college reopened, enrolling 16 students.

The Hatch Act of the late 1880s provided federal funding for agriculture experiment stations, which in turn helped the floundering college grow. At this time the college began to attract students from many parts of the globe. Pastor A. Cooke made the journey from Panama to study at the college, while A. P. Menocal came from Cuba. Of two students from Korea, Min Chow Ho and Pyon Su, the latter was the first Korean to graduate from any American college, in 1888. That year also marked the college's first recorded intercollegiate athletic competitions, which were baseball games against the Naval Academy and St. John's College.

Phi Sigma Kappa, the first fraternity on campus, was founded on January 8, 1897. Shortly after, Morrill Hall was built for $24,000. It is still in use today, the

Aerial view of the University of Maryland.

oldest existing academic building on the university's campus.

During the early years of the 20th century the college continued to grow. New buildings were constructed as college enrollment continued to rise,

The university's rising quality is combined with diversity. Students of color represent a third of enrollment, and Maryland is among the nation's top 20 research universities for African American graduates with doctorates and the top five for master's degrees in engineering, according to Black Issues in Higher Education.

but the college experienced a major setback to its growth on November 29, 1912. A fire, which began during a Thanksgiving dance, destroyed all of the school's dormitories, half of its classrooms and offices and most of the college records. The loss was appraised at $250,000. No deaths or injuries occurred.

Between 1916 and 1920 the college was known as the Maryland State College of Agriculture. It was during this period that the first female students attended the college. Emma S. Jacobs, the first woman graduate, received her master's of science degree in 1917. Jacobs was followed by Grace B. Holmes, Charlotte Vaux, and Elizabeth Hook. Shortly afterwards the college brought in its first female faculty member. Agnes Saunders became acting dean and professor of home economics in 1919. The next year the college reorganized in response to its continuing growth by dividing the college into six schools, each with its own dean: Agriculture, Engineering, Liberal Arts, Chemistry, Education and Home Economics.

The college officially became the University of Maryland in 1920, with Albert F. Woods as its president. The first sorority, Sigma Delta, was formed, and the graduate school awarded its first doctoral degrees. Charles E. Sando was the first to receive his Ph.D. from the new university, with a degree in botany. Enrollment had reached 517, of which 20 were women. By 1925 the university had been accredited by the Association of American Universities.

From the 1920s through the 1940s the school experienced unprecedented growth in all areas. Many new buildings were added, including residence halls and classrooms, and additional acreage was acquired. By 1945 more than 4,000 students were attending the university. After WWII, enrollment increased to more than 11,000 under the GI Bill.

Hiram Whittle, Parren James Mitchell, and Elaine Johnson became the first African American students to attend the university in the 1950s. Mitchell was the first African American to receive a graduate degree at the school, with a master of arts in Sociology. Some years later, the university welcomed its first African American faculty member: M. Lucia James was a full professor in the College of Education beginning in 1965.

Athletics were also growing at a tremendous rate. By the 1960s the school had teams in baseball, football, basketball, golf, lacrosse, field hockey, and in 1967 formed its first men's rugby team.

The university continued to build its outreach to the African American community by chartering the first collegiate chapter in Maryland of the National Association for the Advancement of Colored People (NAACP) on July 7, 1975.

Enrollment at the College Park campus

McKeldin Mall, anchored by the Main Administration and McKeldin Library, is a hub of activity for the more than 34,000 undergraduate and graduate students.

In 1858, landowner Charles Benedict Calvert issued stock certificates to help launch the Maryland Agricultural College, the forerunner of the University of Maryland.

reached its highest level in history in 1985, with more than 38,000 students attending classes. The five university campuses were joined with the six Board of Trustees' institutions in 1988, forming the University of Maryland system, with the College Park campus designated as its flagship. This legislation legally opened the door for the university to be funded at the same level as its peers: UCLA; University of Michigan; University of California, Berkeley; University of North Carolina and the University of Illinois, with the University of Maryland funded at the 75th percentile of all the schools

Baseball was the earliest known sport played competitively, beginning about the time of the Civil War. By 1898 the team had won its first state championship.

combined. This law also allowed a tremendous infusion of funds to be allocated to the school. The state's commitment has significantly helped build the University of Maryland into one of the top public research universities in the country.

With this momentum, the university excelled in academic areas across a broad spectrum. New programs were introduced that enriched the undergraduate experience. Today, more than 40 percent of first-year students participate in special living/learning programs, including a dozen College Park Scholars programs, considered one of the most innovative programs in the country. Students with areas of mutual interest, not necessarily based on their major field of study, join faculty directors within special residence halls and take their classroom learning experience into the community.

Gemstone is a four-year interdisciplinary research program that brings students from the sciences and technology together with students from the humanities and social sciences to closely study a specific societal problem or issue that might be solved through the use of technology.

Of the 13 colleges and schools within the structure of the university, seven of the units—the Smith School of Business; the College of Education; the Clark

School of Engineering; the Philip Merrill College of Journalism; the College of Computer, Mathematical and Physical Sciences; the College of Information Studies and the School of Public Affairs —have been recognized by their peers and in various rankings as among the 25 best in the nation.

Two philanthropists, both alumni of the Class of 1950, acknowledged the university's great strides by making generous gifts to their respective schools. In 1994, A. James Clark gave $15 million to the engineering school and, in 1998, Robert H. Smith gave $15 million to the business school. The university renamed both schools in their honor.

The sciences are another of the many areas in which the school is rapidly growing. Recently, Assistant Biology Professor Sarah Tishkoff was named as one of *Popular Science* magazine's "Brilliant 10."

The university is especially proud of its connection with NASA/Goddard. In a joint project called Deep Impact, the university, in partnership with NASA, will be sending up a space probe on July 4, 2005. The probe, the first of its kind, will impact into the core of a passing comet. Information gathered by the probe will provide both the students and NASA with the ability to research and analyze the exact makeup of a comet. Another aspect of the NASA partnership allows university students to go out into the neighboring communities to teach schoolchildren about science and the basic principles of aerospace, one of the many community outreach programs conducted by the university.

On September 11, 2001, the University of Maryland lost 11 students, employees, and alumni in the tragic events that occurred both at the Pentagon and the World Trade Center. On September 24th of that same year a devastating tornado ripped through the university campus, killing two students who were also sisters. The twister damaged several

The Clarice Smith Performing Arts Center, opened in 2001, is the home to the Departments of Dance and Theatre and the School of Music.

buildings, including the President's House.

Despite the tragedies and hardships that marked the start of the 2001–2002 academic year, there were high points as well. The school's football team won the ACC championship and played in the Orange Bowl, and the men's basketball team brought home the NCAA National Championship title.

One of the other great additions to

The Robert H. Smith School of Business is ranked among the nation's and world's best by Business Week, The Wall Street Journal, Financial Times of London *and* U.S. News & World Report.

the university in the 21st century has been the 318,000-square-foot Clarice Smith Performing Arts Center, the largest performing arts center on any university campus in the country, and the largest building ever constructed in the state of Maryland. The Center, dedicated on September 29, 2001, was named after alumnus and benefactor Clarice Smith, wife of Robert Smith, and a well-known artist in her own right. The state-of-the-art performing arts "village" consists of 10 interconnected structures, which include a 1,100-seat concert hall, performance and recital spaces, practice studios and office spaces. Each year, more than 210,000 people attend the Center's more than 1,000 performances in the areas of dance, theatre, and music. The Smiths are the largest private donors to the University of Maryland.

Above: The A. James Clark School of Engineering, ranked by U.S. News & World Report *in the top 25, has been a cornerstone of Maryland education since 1894.*

The University of Maryland has been ranked by *U.S. News & World Report* as one of the top 20 public universities in the country in both 2002 and 2003. The same source also placed 68 University of Maryland programs in the top 25 in the nation. Far exceeding its market share of talented students, the school continually lists high school valedictorians and high-achievers among its incoming student body.

Employing more than 12,000 people on its 1200-plus acres of campus and nearby facilities, the school contains more than 10,000 residence hall spaces, and currently educates approximately 25,000 undergraduate and 9,500 graduate students. For every dollar of state funding the University receives, it is estimated it returns about $6 to the state's economy.

Among the University of Maryland's illustrious faculty and alumni are four Nobel Laureates—including physics faculty member William Phillips, two Rhodes Scholars, nine Pulitzer Prize winners, three MacArthur Fellows, one Academy and four Emmy Award winners, two Grammy winners, a National Humanities Medal recipient and three astronauts. Included among notable alumni are actress Dianne Wiest, reporter Connie Chung, National Football League quarterback Boomer Esiason, *Washington Post* reporter Carl Bernstein and the beloved late puppeteer Jim Henson. While a student in textiles at the University of Maryland, Jim Henson is said to have created "Kermit" from an old piece of clothing belonging to his mother.

THE WARD FAMILY

"We were just a couple of old farm boys who had a dream that we could make it," said the self-effacing R. Walter Ward, the late pioneer of Harford County's land development industry, reflecting upon his, and his brother's, careers. The story of his family's origins in Appalachia, as well as the Depression-era hardship that inspired his father to relocate to Harford County, lays the foundation for a compelling story.

It's the story of a farmer's quest to see his large family survive and work its way out of hardscrabble existence in the mountains of western North Carolina. The story ends with the dramatic transformation of Harford County, Maryland, from a rural, agricultural community into the thriving suburban county it is today.

It all began in 1930, when brothers Frederick and R. Walter Ward, at the tender ages of 2 and 5, along with their four older brothers and a sister, said good-bye to the hard mountain life of Watauga County, North Carolina. Although their late grandfather, Thomas Ward, had successfully farmed the largest parcel of flat land in the county, his death in 1900 had resulted in a period of family dissension. Soon the farm was divided into four tracts, one of which was managed by R. Walter and Frederick's father, Walter Lucky Ward. But sometime during the '20s, Walter Lucky found it necessary to borrow money against the farm and

Front row, left to right: R. Walter Ward, Julius (John) Ward and Frederick Ward. Back row is Walter Lucky Ward with daughter Mary Helen, in 1934.

Left to right: Mary Helen Ward Cooper, Betty Ward, Fred Ward, R. Walter Ward and Joan Ward in 2002.

general store. With the onset of the Depression came financial difficulties. His failure to repay the loan resulted in the foreclosure of the property.

Although Walter Lucky's first wife, Lillian, had died in 1920, leaving him solely responsible for raising their four children, he married Eliza Yates in 1922, and soon the family grew by three more children (two others died in infancy). The family included seven children (ages 2 to 20) when Walter Lucky and Eliza moved the family to Harford County, Maryland. An eighth child, Mary Helen, was born in 1933. Initially, the family moved to the Scarff Farm in Upper Cross Road, working as tenant farmers. This reflected the times, which were characterized by a large migration of families from Appalachia in North Carolina, Tennessee and Southern Virginia to the rural areas surrounding Baltimore, Maryland. A farmer and his family would typically live on a landowner's property and work on the farm in exchange for lodging and a portion of the crop or a small salary.

Walter and his family lived this tenant farmer life from 1930 to 1940, initially at the Scarff Farm and later at Rock Run on Lapidum Road near Havre de Grace, the Mahoney Farm near Bel Air and the Skillman Farm on Singer Road at Winters Run. Interestingly, the Mahoney Farm, and its manor house, Tudor Hall, is famous as the boyhood home of John Wilkes Booth,

President Abraham Lincoln's assassin.

In the late 1930s, Eliza and her son Fred contracted tuberculosis and were sent to a sanatorium in Baltimore. Fred recovered and returned home in 1940 but Eliza did not survive her illness. At about the same time, Walter Lucky decided to forego farming for building and other carpentry jobs, and remarried yet again to Gertrude Trivette in 1943. The family moved several times over the ensuing years before settling in the town of Bel Air in 1944. Walter Lucky stopped building homes in the mid-1950s but continued to take on odd carpentry jobs. The tough, hard-driven man, who had never asked for anything he hadn't earned, died of bone cancer in 1961 at the age of 76. What he left his children was a legacy of hard work, self-discipline and a sense of pride in one's family.

While brothers R. Walter and Fred shared a country boyhood of farming and tight means growing up around Bel Air, their lives after high school took distinctly separate paths, though each eventually returned to Harford County. Unlike R. Walter, Fred maintained little of his country roots and became the first of the seven siblings to complete college. He entered the army in 1945 and served in the Pacific. Following the war, he took advantage of the GI Bill, graduating second in his class in civil engineering at the University of Maryland in 1954.

Less than 6 months out of college, Fred married Joan Eccles and founded a land surveying firm in Bel Air that would become Frederick Ward Associates, Inc. The business quickly progressed from its modest beginnings to become a regional engineering, architecture and surveying design firm. FWA lead the way in development design as Harford County grew through the 1960s, 1970s and beyond. In the mid-1970s Fred also lead the redevelopment of Downtown Bel Air after the old retail area declined, by purchasing and renovating numerous old properties along Main Street when no one else would risk the investment. Professionally, Fred's career always focused on Land Surveying and he became an industry leader, serving on the State of Maryland's Licensing Board for Professional Surveyors for many years and receiving the Lifetime Achievement Award from the Maryland Society of Surveyors in 2000. Fred and Joan also created a scholarship fund for surveyors at Towson University, the largest single contribution ever made to the institution.

Having sustained injuries in an automobile accident, R. Walter was ineligible for the armed services following high school. Instead, he farmed for a while before venturing out west for a few years with his friend Melvin Bosely. The two

R. Walter Ward at his office, at Office Street, Bel Air, Maryland.

Gertrude and Walter Lucky Ward, 1960.

friends eventually reached Denver, where R. Walter found a job at a supermarket from which he was subsequently laid off. Years later, he would say the experience of losing a job was humiliating enough to cause him to vow never to work for someone else again. He honored his promise. In 1945, the same year Fred went to war, Walter began selling real estate under the license of an Elkton broker, making $50 a week. Together with Melvin, the two became the youngest licensed brokers (at ages 21 and 22) in the state. They set up shop in the home of R. Walter's parents in Bel Air and formed their building company in 1950. R. Walter married Beatrice (Betty) Lauterbach in 1952, the company grew, and he soon became a pillar of building and development in Harford County, finding time to mentor other developers even as he succeeded on his own.

Through their Ward & Bosely Realtors and Art Builders, Inc., Walter and Bosely developed and built homes in residential communities around Maryland. They started out in Howard Park on Bel Air's west side, moved into Edgewood where a demand for civilian housing grew in the late 1950s and early 1960s, and then staked out much of the territory along Route 24, which they developed in the '60s, '70s and '80s. Walter and his partner bought farmland when it was relatively cheap, hedging their bets that the county would eventually install public water and sewer lines. Their prediction proved correct, and the face of Harford County was to change forever. Over his

career, R. Walter's companies built several thousand homes in dozens of projects as Harford County grew from a population of 50,000 in 1950 to over 200,000 in the 1990s.

"He was a good friend, a really decent guy who tried to treat everybody right," said Edwin Hess, a close friend who often accompanied Ward on trips to the Eastern Shore and Pennsylvania until Walter's health began to fail, resulting in his death in early 2003.

Frederick, who survives his brother today, says of Walter, "He wasn't just a brother; he was a friend who was very helpful to me when I was in college and in my career. He also helped my wife and me with our first house purchase. And he loved gardening."

The logic and symmetry of a tenant farmer's son—a successful land developer—retiring to his garden is no surprise to Betty Ward, R. Walter's widow, who also speaks glowingly of her husband. "He was always fair, and you could count on what he said," she commented recently from her home. "He saw opportunities that others missed, and he loved to make a deal."

R. Walter was also generous in his community support. He and Betty donated land in the Box Hill Corporate Center for the future site of the Walter and Betty Ward YMCA. In addition, they have financially supported the community's new hospital, The Upper Chesapeake Medical Center and Harford Community College.

Today, the companies that R. Walter and Frederick founded and grew remain successful and vigorous under the leadership of their respective sons, Bob and Craig Ward. Bob Ward Homes is one of the largest builders in the Baltimore area and the Ward Development Group handles the development side of the business. Frederick Ward Associates now has three offices in Maryland and Northern Virginia and continues to grow. Bob and Craig also continue their fathers' legacies of community support and leadership in Harford County and the region.

R. J. WILSON & ASSOCIATES, LTD.

Ron Wilson is no different from any other entrepreneur. He wants to profit from his labors, provide employment opportunities for people, help his community make progress, and enjoy life.

But there is more to his blueprint: Wilson is energized by finding creative solutions for ticklish, seemingly-insurmountable problems involving risk management and insurance-related issues. That's the ideology with which he formed R. J. Wilson and Associates, Ltd., in 1980 in Abingdon, Maryland.

"A client's problem presents an opportunity for the Wilson affiliate companies," he said. "Finding a prospect with a knotty, complex problem is primary. If the client does not have a problem, the prospect of obtaining new business is nil because they're satisfied with the status quo."

Wilson has crafted a systematic approach to obtaining new business. It starts with finding a company or institution with an insurance-related problem, then finding out who's responsible for dealing with the problem, which sometimes can be the most complicated phase of the process. "There are a lot of people who can say 'No,' but normally only one who can say 'Yes,'" Wilson said. "You have to think like the person who is writing the check. Once we get a commitment from that person, we will invest the time needed to solve the problem."

Canton House is at 300 Water Street in Baltimore, Maryland, where the Canton Agency began.

Ronald J. Wilson, founder of R. J. Wilson & Associates, Ltd.

Next, the appropriate Wilson affiliate(s) offer to assemble a risk-management program that solves the problem with the understanding that if the program does in fact solve it, the client will let the Wilson companies have the business. They complete an exhaustive survey of the prospect's operation to determine exactly what the problems are, a step Wilson calls "tearing down the problem," and it's similar to how nanotechnology workers reach into the atomic stratum as a base for analysis. They research the industry, the tax situation, its regulatory situation, and whatever else it takes to come up with a program to solve the problems.

Two crucial components are involving the client in every step of the problem-solving process, and presenting the solution in a way that makes it clear the recommendation handles each aspect of the predicament.

Putting the solutions in place is the final phase, which Wilson labels as the simplest step. "The public is looking for problem-solvers," he said, "not peddlers of insurance policies. We are willing to make a com-

mitment to solve difficult problems." This time-honored procedure is the calling card of a company deeply rooted in Baltimore's past.

R. J. Wilson & Associates, Ltd., traces its origins to the Canton Company of Baltimore, one of the state's oldest enterprises, which was chartered by the Maryland Legislature in 1828 as a trading company doing business with the port city on the South China Sea that is now known as Guangzhou.

Closely linked with the shipping industry, the company founded Canton Railroad, Canton Packing and Warehousing, and a stevedoring business called the Cottman Company to service the Baltimore harbor. In addition to dealing in commercial real estate, in1969 the charter company formed Canton Agency Inc., a commercial insurance entity that would eventually specialize in assisting railroads and nonprofit hospitals, as well as its sister companies.

Wilson, born in Wyandotte, Michigan (near Detroit) to a Wesleyan minister, grew up in the Midwest. After majoring in history and religion in college, he initially worked in the space industry before entering the insurance business. In 1974 he moved from the Hartford Insurance Group to join the Canton Agency in 1974 as the benefits manager for the Canton Company and its subsidiaries. By then, the family of companies was owned by the International Mining Company.

Wilson was on board when International Mining and its related entities were purchased by Pacific Holding's David H. Murdock. During this period the Canton Agency also underwent expansion, adding to its holdings such businesses as the Baltimore-based Werner Insurance Agency. In 1978 Wilson was advanced to the agency's presidency.

Woven into America's legacy is the dream of one's own business, which Wilson realized in February of 1980, while the Canton Agency continued as a part of Murdock's operations. This was the beginning of R. J. Wilson & Associates, Ltd.,

R. J. Wilson & Associates, Ltd. officers from left to right: Keith Rambo, assistant vice president; R. Jeffery Wilson, vice president; Laura Chenworth, assistant vice president; Richard Chaney, Sr., vice president; Kim Kasson, vice president and controller; Joseph Scheide, vice president; Erin Bennett, chief financial officer; and Ronald J. Wilson, president.

launched as a general insurance agency specializing in cash-flow plans for workers compensation and a new, self-funded, workers-compensation trust program developed for more than 40 nonprofit hospitals in the District of Columbia and in the Mid-Atlantic states, and a similar venture for sheetmetal workers.

Equally innovative approaches were formulated for the Good Samaritan Employer Association (evangelical churches and related entities), the Small Railroad Business Owners Association (operators of small interstate freight lines), and the American Shortline Railroad Association (owners of both small and large freight railroads, and their suppliers).

R. J. Wilson & Associates, Ltd., prospered into a respected regional agency, absorbing six smaller firms. Establishing a working relationship with Lloyd's of London, the company broadened its operations, including a surplus lines division providing coverage for non-standard and difficult risks.

When Murdock decided to move his in-house insurance operations to his headquarters in California, some of his holdings in Maryland went on the block, including the Canton Agency. Wilson bought his old firm on July 1, 1983. With a new national railroad property and casualty program, the Canton Agency continues to be recognized as a leading wholesaler of railroad insurance throughout the United States.

The Wilson family of companies has grown to include Medical Benefits Administrators of Maryland, Inc., a full-service benefit-administration firm established in 1987 that manages benefit plans for two national associations. There are two real estate investment companies and five active insurance providers.

"We have 45 employees," Wilson said, "who are among the brightest, most experienced risk-management talent in the industry. They are experienced insurance financial people, accountants, compliance specialists, actuarial consult-ants, and marketing specialists.

"Our skillful employees have an uncanny knack for turning innovative ideas into practical, proven risk-management solutions. That allows us to provide a 'one-stop shop' that can put together an entire risk-management solution in-house at the lowest possible cost."

The Wilson companies' motto is: "Insurance is nothing more than a prom-ise, and a promise is only as good as the people who make it." In keeping with this spirit, Wilson said, "We seek out employees who are looking to top themselves every day. People who will not stop doing their jobs until the customer is completely satisfied. Our customers don't have to be risk-manage-ment experts to deal with us. But we do."

Canton Railroad Pier 11 is one of the early Canton Railroad facilities still in existence today.

WINDERMERE

Known in 2003 to be one of the fastest growing information technology (IT) companies in the country, The Windermere Group (Windermere) is a one-stop provider of innovative technology solutions that are both practical and responsive.

Windermere is an employee-owned business that has successfully merged a 50-year legacy of resolving communication security issues at the national level with cutting-edge technology in order to deliver a broad spectrum of inventive products and services.

Headquartered on a private 36-acre campus in Annapolis, Maryland, Windermere also maintains a full-service operation in Reston, Virginia, along with field offices in Columbia, Maryland; Washington, D.C.; Eatontown, New Jersey; and Tampa, Florida.

"We are proud to support our country" is far more than a slogan—it is Windermere's way of life and business. On September 11, 2001, when four planes were hijacked by terrorists who attacked the World Trade Center in New York City and the Pentagon in Washington, D.C., Windermere found that their niche expertise in personnel, products and services offered ideal solutions for new national security efforts being funded by the federal government.

Windermere's CEO and President, Raymond T. Tate and Robert G. Pozgar.

Growing tenfold in only six years, Windermere has grown to over 400 employees, has gross revenue in excess of $50 million, and has a customer base of more than 15 federal agencies and 100 commercial companies.

Even more important is their sense of being a family, their sense of accomplishment, and their sense of doing something positive for their country and humanity. Windermere's total commitment to employee equity, profit sharing and personal development has been instrumental in their ability to attract and retain dedicated and talented professionals.

Because they deal with issues that affect our nation's security, Windermere has developed a unique set of in-house skills and resources that allows for the rapid design, prototyping, qualification testing, and deployment of operational systems. Through the effective utilization of complimentary Delivery Teams that are servicing various national interests, Windermere takes pride in offering first-pass success in the delivery of operational systems. As such, they have become very unique in being able to offer each customer a one-stop company for innovative technology solutions to their operational needs.

Windermere products and services satisfy the full spectrum of IT requirements, including world class information assurance, software development, and advanced engineering design along with an established wireless video/audio product line. They offer rapid prototyping of digital, analog and radio frequency (RF) products along with medium-volume turnkey custom manufacturing. An area of specialization includes structured data integrity analysis and integration of customized-security solutions into legacy systems, that is coupled to comprehensive legal and technical support to detect, prevent and respond to cyber crimes.

An example of Windermere's product line includes a family of transmitters and receivers that are employed by robots, which disarm bombs and land mines.

Windermere's Columbia field office.

Another example is a custom communications device that currently flies on all B-2 bombers in the Middle East and elsewhere. Additionally, they have redesigned computer equipment and radios—"ruggedized" them—allowing them to be dropped from aircraft to troops on the ground without damage to the equipment—all crucial assets for the U.S. military currently deployed in Iraq and Afghanistan.

Windermere's CEO is Raymond T. Tate —an 80-year-old patriot who is also a workaholic. Tate worked with the National Security Agency (NSA) from 1952 until 1978, where he rose to being responsible for communications security for the U.S. government and NATO. When he left NSA in 1978 as its deputy director, he became deputy assistant secretary of the U.S. Navy, responsible for technical and financial oversight of research and development of all Navy communications, navigation, electronic warfare, tactical computers, space programs, intelligence-related activities and other classified operations.

Such a career path did not leave much time to be home with his family or to enjoy his favorite activity, fishing. So when Tate founded Ashton Technology Group in 1994, a commercial company that developed a security system for large commercial investors to trade securities directly with certain stock exchanges, he asked two of his children (Susan Burrowbridge and Elizabeth Winters) to come to work for him. They liked the arrangement!

After selling Ashton in 1996, Tate sought another opportunity for them to work together. Tate had enjoyed a long working relationship with Alliant Technisystems, who announced they were closing their Signal Analysis Center in Annapolis, Maryland. The Tates needed a partner with strong leadership skills, so they asked Robert G. Pozgar to join them. Tate had been a friend and mentor to Pozgar for over 20 years. Pozgar, who specializes in design engineering, has over 30 years experience developing telecommunication and information

processing systems. Together they went forward, and on February 12, 1998, they purchased Alliant's assets in Annapolis, Maryland (100,000 square feet of fully equipped engineering and manufacturing buildings, 38 acres, 49 Alliant employees and $500,000 in existing contract backlog).

The name Windermere comes from a small village in the Lake Country of southern Scotland. During World War II Raymond Tate was a member of a B-24 bomber crew with the 8th Air Force. On his 24th combat mission he was wounded and needed months of recuperation. He spent much of the time in Windermere, where the people were unbelievably friendly. As he grew strong enough to hike the hills and fish the lakes, he found a peace that took his mind away from the war and "the destruction we were in the process of bringing to most of the European continent." Though the war's destruction was necessary in the name of world peace,

Windermere's Corporate Training Center.

Windermere itself "was good luck and a happy time in my life and a tradition I wanted to pass on to others in hopes that the positive good fortune would continue," Tate said.

Windermere's mission is to establish collaborative environments that focus staff expertise on technology issues of critical importance to their customers. Their business model is designed to recruit and retain creative employees along with facilitating the robust marketing of their innovative talents. The key element of the model is an equity and bonus program that is unique since it is the direct opposite of a traditional venture model—employee equity can never be diluted, and it grows proportionately with the growth of individual business units.

Windermere's Annapolis headquarters.

ATTRANSCO

Attransco Ship Management Company of Annapolis, Maryland, owns three ocean-going tank ships that were constructed in San Diego, California, in 1982–1983. The 50,000 dead-weight ton tankers are the *Delaware Trader*, *Chesapeake Trader* and *Potomac Trader*. Now called the *Sr. Galena Bay* and the *Sr. Puget Sound*, the *Chesapeake Trader* and *Potomac Trader* are, respectively, still assets of Attransco while under long-term leases with Exxon. The *Delaware Trader* trades in the U.S. coastwise spot market. Crewing and other technical management services for this ship are outsourced to Keystone Shipping of Philadelphia.

Patrick Johnsen, president and CEO of Attransco since 1996, is part of a six-member Board of Directors who reports regularly to approximately 29 shareholders, mostly individuals, in this privately held company. As president, Johnsen markets, services and consolidates expenses generated by ship managers with revenue. He is responsible for the overall performance of Attransco with his main interest being in maximizing the shareholder's return on their investment. Each member of the Board of Directors was chosen based on the individual's expertise, which ultimately benefits the daily operations. Membership of the Board of Directors includes a prominent local attorney, and a former manager of Exxon's Marine Department.

Delaware Trader *delivers to Arco Marine under a bareboat charter in 1999.*

The tanker Chesapeake Trader *prior to being renamed the* SR Galena Bay.

Johnsen himself comes from a life-time career and interest in sailing and shipping. He started out attending a three-year program conducted by the California Maritime Academy, which trained him to be a deck officer. Immediately after completing the program, he entered the U.S. Army, where he worked as harbor-master in South East Asia during the Vietnam War. He worked on his first commercial ship with Mobil Oil and has been employed by a variety of maritime companies.

After 15 years, however, Johson grew tired of going out to sea, and was eventually offered a shore assignment by Mobil Oil in New York in the mid-1980s. Over the next ten-plus years his duties included oversight of commercial contract execution, responsibility for pollution prevention and safety, marketing, financial management and labor relations. In 1996 he accepted the position of president and CEO of Attransco.

The Attransco shipping operation was originally a part of ATAPCO (American Trading and Production Company), a larger family of companies. Louis Blaustein, a Lithuanian immigrant, came to America, worked as a peddler and eventually became an oilman and businessman. For many years he worked for Standard Oil before founding his own company, American Oil. He and his son Jacob Blaustein worked together in their first office in Baltimore, which was a converted stable. Together, they accomplished much in the field of gas and oil transportation as well as usage. They started the first drive-in gas station and the first gasoline pump that made it possible for the motorist to see how much gas he was actually getting. Their greatest contribution was anti-knock gasoline, which in turn enabled the automobile industry to develop high-compression engines. It was this type of fuel that Charles Lindbergh used in the *Spirit of St. Louis* flying across the Atlantic Ocean.

In addition to Blaustein's contributions to the oil industry, he was an accomplished diplomat. He advised and assisted both Presidents Franklin D. Roosevelt and Harry S. Truman, and in 1955 was appointed a member of the U.S. delegation to the United Nations by then President Dwight D. Eisenhower. Jacob insisted that West Germany pay reparations to the victims of Hitler, and he was one of two people who negotiated that agreement.

ATAPCO was formed in 1931 to consolidate, diversify and expand the Blaustein's family business. ATAPCO set up Attransco, the marine transportation division, in 1938 and was headquartered in New York City. The company's first ship was the tanker, *Crown Trader*, used primarily to service the transportation requirements of the family-owned Crown Central Petroleum. It grew to operate over a dozen ships and was a significant profit center within ATAPCO. For 60 years, from 1937 to 1997, the company remained entirely devoted to U.S. flag shipping, expanding to become independent of its sister

Attransco has joint ventures with the Norden Group in Denmark.

company, Crown Central Petroleum. The high point of the company's history occurred from 1982 to 1983, when the only new ships in the company's history were built by what is now Attransco.

Since then, the shipping industry has gone through some dramatic changes. The greatest change was how petroleum products reached their market. The use of pipelines changed the role of shipping from the primary, to the secondary supplier of petroleum products, and the construction of refineries to supply local petroleum needs. The number of U.S. flagged ships in the industry has declined steadily. In 1982 the fleet numbered between 400 and 500 tankers. Now, there are about 60 ships in the market. In addition, the grounding of, and immense pollution caused by the *Exxon Valdez* largely impacted the industry. The Oil Pollution Act

Launch of the Nordholm, *a joint venture bulk carrier with Norden.*

of 1990 mandated retirement dates for tankers. In response to these developements the active management of ships was outsourced, resulting in the downsizing of Attransco from 40 employees in New York to two in Annapolis, Maryland.

Attransco continues to change with ebbs and flows of the shipping industry. The three U.S. flagged ships owned by Attransco will be forced to retire in 2012. Even so, the company refuses to take environmental risks if the tankers are unable to complete their mission safely. Johnsen says, "We equate profitability with environmental stewardship. We may lose money with our ships before they are forced to retire, but we will do that, rather than lower our operating standards."

Besides owning and marketing the three ships, Attransco also owns an airplane that is leased to Continental Express. The once solely American-owned-and-operated marine transportation company is now an international company with offshore subsidiaries and joint ventures in worldwide shipping with Germans and Danes.

DE LA SALLE CHRISTIAN BROTHERS

John Baptist De La Salle was born in Rheims, France, on April 30, 1651, in a time of upheaval known as the Fronde during the reign of King Louis XIV. The rebellion did not encourage France's "Sun King," a teenaged monarch at the time of the uprising, to embrace reformist measures. His Palace at Versailles stands today as the symbol of his reign.

Privilege also characterized De La Salle's childhood. Early in life, he made known his intention to enter the priesthood, and as a teenager was made canon in the cathedral at Rheims, a position of great honor and financial benefit, and one that would place him directly on course for high ecclesiastical power within France's Catholic Church hierarchy. A chance encounter in 1679, when a layman encouraged De La Salle to assist in the opening of a parish school for poor boys, would alter his future irrevocably.

De La Salle complied with the stranger's request, and in so doing launched his own ideological revolution. Over the next 40 years, he would establish throughout France a wide array of institutions to meet the needs of the poor, ranging from primary schools to boarding schools to teacher training centers and homes for runaways. He insisted that students be taught practical subjects as well as religion, and that they be taught in their native French, not in the Latin language of scholars. De La Salle instituted the simultaneous method of instruction, as opposed to private tutorials, which allowed instructors to reach many more pupils. In 1680 he founded a religious community of lay teachers, whom he called Brothers of the Christian Schools, advising them that their greatest miracle would be to touch the hearts of their students.

The first forays of the Christian Brothers to the New World proved ill-fated. In 1817 Bishop Dubourg of New Orleans, with missionary zeal, sent out three Brothers separately, to New Orleans and to two different sites in Missouri, circumventing the rule of the Order, which

The Ammendale Motherhouse is 13 miles from Washington, D.C. It is situated far back from the main highway, so that the bustle of the world does not disturb the peace and tranquility of Saint Joseph's Normal Institute, its official title. The wing on the left housed the Novices, and the Ancients once resided in the opposite wing. Today, the community for retired Brothers is located elsewhere on the property.

called for at least two or three brothers within each house. These early religious followers returned to secular life. In 1837 the Christian Brothers' efforts to establish themselves in the Western Hemisphere proved successful, when four Brothers of the Christian Schools under the leadership of Brother Aidant sailed from Le Havre, France. They touched land in Montreal one month later, where they founded the Christian Brothers School of St. Laurent.

It would require the efforts of Samuel Eccleston, fifth Archbishop of Baltimore, to bring De La Salle's Christian Brothers to the United States. In 1842 Archbishop Eccleston, along with two Baltimore priests, sent five young men as novices to Montreal for their training there by Brother Aidant. Distant provinces were learning of Brother Aidant's gifts as an educator and as a religious leader. Of the quintet of novices who arrived from Baltimore, only one, John McMullen, would endure the rigors of Montreal's weather and the sacrifices endemic to religious life. He returned to Baltimore in ill health as Brother Francis, without

having taken his final vows. At the age of 18, Brother Francis went on to found the first De La Salle Christian Brothers School within the United States.

The Cathedral Parish School opened its doors at the intersection of Saratoga Street and what was then known as Little Sharp Street in Baltimore on September 15, 1845. One hundred pupils were in attendance, many more having been turned away due to lack of space and a shortage of teachers. Old annals record that a ceremonial Mass of the Holy Ghost marked the occasion. Brother Francis did not live to teach long within the new school. One year later, he again fell ill, and on the advice of superiors and his physician, traveled with his mother to Florida for the winter. He died in St. Augustine, Florida, on March 7, 1847, at the age of 20. The Order continues to honor Brother Francis' memory.

Cathedral Parish School soon became Calvert Hall College, which took its name from the founder of the colony of Maryland. The recently rebuilt school, an institution for secondary education, would also become the site of the first novitiate in this country. In 1880 the novitiate moved to Ammendale in Prince George's County, Maryland, to a site donated to the Order by the Catholic convert Admiral Ammen. In 1890 Calvert Hall College moved again to Cathedral and Mulberry Streets in Baltimore. In the early 1960s, educators followed a national trend, moving Calvert Hall College High School, a college preparatory high school for boys, to its current location on La Salle Road in suburban Towson, Maryland. The McMullen Scholars Program for gifted students commemorates the name of the school's founder, as its street name honors the founder of the Order. The school's mission includes preparing its students "for a life dedicated to achievement, leadership and service to the church and community."

In 1987 Christian Brothers from Baltimore aligned themselves closely with their founder's principles when they joined the Oblate Sisters on the teaching staff of St. Frances Academy, located on Chase Street in East Baltimore, within view of a prison located there. St. Frances Academy, founded to teach children of slaves to read the Bible, represents the country's longest continuously operating school serving African American children.

The Christian Brothers' Rule, to educate "the economically deprived victims of social injustice" and "those neglected by the rest of society" is effectively borne out in the Order's court adjudicated programs, directed toward youths who have been convicted of crimes. The Brothers' San Miguel School, located in Camden, New Jersey, within

St. John Baptist de La Salle (1651–1719), founder of the Christian Brothers and patron saint of teachers. The original statue is located in St. Peter's Basilica in Rome.

the Order's Baltimore District, is characteristic of the Christian Brothers' San Miguel schools. It is named for South American educator Saint Miguel Febres Codero and dedicated to the education of at-risk youths in inner-city neighborhoods. By September 2003 the Order will include almost 20 such schools among its educational facilities.

The Catholic Church canonized De La Salle in 1900, and in 1950 declared him the patron saint of teachers of youth. The saint's chance encounter with a layman in 1679 has had far-reaching effects. Today, 6,700 Brothers of the Christian Schools and over 60 thousand Lasallian lay teachers serve over 800 thousand students in 84 countries worldwide, in areas as far ranging as La Salle Petaling in Jaya, Malaysia, and St. Joseph School in Addis Ababa, Ethiopia. All of these schools continue to honor their founder's enlightened mission.

Calvert Hall College was located in this building at Cathedral and Mulberry Streets from 1890 to 1960. Today the offices of the Baltimore Archdiocese are located on this site.

GROCO

The inventive spirit runs deep in the blood of Groco owner and CEO Don Gross. For the past 85 years, this Hanover, Maryland, company has applied the principles of innovation and fine craftsmanship in the production of hardware for the marine industry.

Gross is a third-generation owner of the family business. Groco specializes in the manufacture of more than 400 marine products, including raw water strainers, toilets and wastewater treatment systems, pumps and seacocks. Many of its applications are also used in the automotive and industrial sectors.

Don's grandfather, Angus Roy Gross, Sr., was a born inventor whose mind raced with ideas of gadgets he wanted to design. In fact, he has over 20 patents to his credit, some of which are familiar household names.

His first invention was the carbonating faucet, which was patented in 1913. Several years later, he invented the automotive taillight. Now the stuff of family legend, the story goes that Angus, Sr., bought a car in the 1920s and parked it at his house, delighted with his new treasure. To his great dismay, he discovered the following day that someone had plowed into his car overnight. So Angus, like any masterful inventor, came up with a plan. He designed a glass reflector to serve as a taillight on his car. He received nine patents for

Packaging label for an early GROCO® automobile parking light design provides collision insurance for cars that are struck after nightfall while equipped with the light.

GROCO® founder Angus Roy Gross is shown by one of his beloved yachts, circa 1952.

various taillight innovations between 1917 and 1925.

And his inventions didn't stop there. Angus, Sr., also developed the original blow torch, patented in 1918, and the ice shaver, patented in 1951.

In 1918 he decided to start his own business selling heat exchangers he designed himself. Groco's first office was located in the basement of a rat-infested downtown Baltimore rowhouse. He later received patents in 1930 and 1932 for refinements to his product.

Eventually the business grew, and Angus, Sr., moved into a 5,000-square-foot manufacturing plant. He enjoyed moderate success, but it wasn't until World War II that his fortunes changed

dramatically. The beach-landing crafts used by the U.S. Navy suffered engine problems due to clogging of sand and debris. Angus, Sr., devised a filtering system containing a two-chamber strainer that filtered the debris out of the engines. He received three patents for this device in 1942. Soon he was making several thousand filters a week. He was later awarded the "Navy 'E' for Excellence" award by the U.S. Navy for his contribution to the war effort. Those same filters, with some modifications, are still sold today to the Navy, Coast Guard and Marines.

Once the economy rebounded following the end of World War II, the marine industry turned its focus to recreational boating. The need arose for a better filtering system in private boat engines. As a boater himself, Angus liked to tinker with the equipment, always looking for ways to improve the parts or find new applications. Among Groco's biggest selling product lines today are several versions of engine strainers that evolved from the early military designs from the WWII years.

Marine toilets, patented in 1936 and 1950, were another product line, which the elder Angus designed and sold. Currently Groco manufactures a household-size toilet and a smaller economy model.

In the 1950s, Angus, Sr., developed a series of valves, called seacocks, which were used to shut off the incoming flow of water when the need arose. Although the design has been greatly altered from the original, Groco continues to sell seacocks. The company also manufactures seacock strainers, a combination of seacocks and raw water strainers that were made as a single unit and patented by Angus, Sr., in 1963.

Don's father, Angus Roy Gross, Jr., grew up under the shadow of this creative master. Though not as inventive as Angus, Sr., he had the business savvy to maintain Groco's place in the marine marketplace for many years to come.

"My grandfather was a creative genius, but it was my father who taught me how

Landing craft such as this one were able to complete their mission, thanks in part to the strainer designs of A.R. Gross, and to the manufacturing efforts of GROCO®.

to navigate the increasingly complex world of running the family business," says Don.

Don began helping out at the family business around age 12. At first he swept floors and loaded trucks, but his responsibilities increased as he matured. Don graduated from the University of Baltimore in 1970 with a degree in industrial management. He was drafted into the Army shortly thereafter, and spent two years overseas. When he returned home, he had a job waiting for him.

With his father's initial guidance, Don gradually took over operation of Groco. "My dad gave me free rein in the decision-making as I got older. I made lots of mistakes but that's how I learned."

Don's father died in 1983, leaving him with the sole responsibility of overseeing the future of the company. Gross recognized the need to tap into the vast overseas markets in Asia, Australia and Europe. His perseverance has paid huge dividends for Groco, whose clients now include distributors and boat builders the world over. "We are wherever there is water," says Gross.

Half of the company's business is derived from distributors such as the widely-known company West Marine and many other traditional two-step

distributors. The remainder is drawn from boat-builders, like Grand Banks, S-2, Sea Ray, Bertram, and Chris Craft, and from the military.

Gross sees advantages to keeping Groco a small family-run operation. Now 60 employees strong, the company has thus far maintained its competitive edge without losing its sense of identity.

"I don't want to be a big company. You sacrifice your eye for quality and innovation with efforts to achieve greater sales. That's not our goal," asserts Gross. "Our driving force is to build a better mousetrap, not more mouse-traps. We have to find our niche and be good at it." The tradition continues with

Don's patent efforts in 1992, 1995, 1998, 2000, 2001 and 2003, and several more in the patent application process.

For Gross, one of the most rewarding aspects of running a family business has been the relationships he has developed over time. Invaluable to the success of Groco are employees like Earl Smith, who worked for 56 years in the machine shop, and John Foster, who worked in the assembly plant for 48 years. Charles Schadle, the first employee Don hired, has been with the company for over 30 years. Such longevity and loyalty, almost unheard of in modern corporate America, testify to the truth of Gross' business philosophy. Others with whom Groco could not have carried on are Gertrude Bush, Bob Rehbein, Mike Mullin, Mel Jourdain, Quintin Nore, Patrick Scanlon and Simon Shkolnikov.

"Forget computers and the technology of today. We need people to keep it all running smoothly," says Gross. "I am so proud of our employees and of my grandfather and father for the opportunity they've given me to carry on. But we can't sit on our laurels. We have to keep innovating and coming up with new products."

During World War II, GROCO® produced thousands of duplex raw water strainers for U.S. Navy beach landing craft.

J.J. HAINES & COMPANY, INC.

At the outbreak of the Civil War, Virginian John James Haines joined the Confederate Army. He fought under Stonewall Jackson at Manassas and was wounded in Winchester, Virginia. Captured in the spring of 1863, he spent the rest of the war in Union prison camps. As he awaited the inevitable collapse of the Confederacy in the early spring of 1865, Yankee guards and Rebel prisoners found a peaceable way to make the time pass by playing poker. With consideration and reluctance, Captain Haines joined the games. He won nearly $800 in gold coins, of which $100 was won in one hand the day before being released. John Haines sewed his winnings into a cloth belt, which he wore around his waist and headed home.

Returning to Upperville, Virginia, Haines rebuilt his life and his business. He worked from dawn to dusk, making a success of his general store. In the process, he saw new opportunities in supplying stores such as his own. The place to do that was in Baltimore, the new wholesale center of the South. There, in 1874, he established a wholesale business selling a diversity of goods, including woodenware, rope, seed, wicker ware and even fishing tackle.

The Haines executive team.

In the 1890s, Haines's future son-in-law, Casper T. Marston, joined the firm. An astute businessman, Marston saw the potential in carpeting and soon headed the company's new floor covering department. China matting, a best-seller at the time, was brought from the Orient aboard Haines's fleet of swift clipper ships.

J.J. Haines & Company was selected as one of Armstrong Cork Company's first 12 distributors of linoleum in 1909. At that time, Haines also carried carpets and rush matting, selling and shipping by train and boat to stores from Pennsylvania to Florida, and as far west as Ohio and Texas.

John Haines Marston, Casper's son, took the helm during the Great Depression, determined not to "let the company go under." His concern for his employees, customers and suppliers kept J.J. Haines

in business. By the end of World War II, the company was stronger than before the Depression.

Growing with changing times and technologies, Haines strengthened its partnership with Armstrong, handling everything from linoleum to carpets, wood and ceramic. In the 1970s, Haines was an industry leader by computerizing its operations, and the innovations continued under the leadership of John Marston's nephew, Lee, now retired as

Order acknowledgement from 1898.

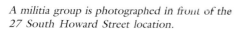

A militia group is photographed in front of the 27 South Howard Street location.

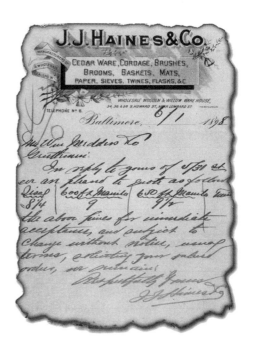

chairman emeritus. During his many years as president, Lee maintained the continuity of successful policies and traditions forged by his uncle, grandfather and great-grandfather. That, as he says, meant following in his uncle's footsteps, "doing the same tried and true things: servicing our customers, taking care of people and keeping our employees and suppliers satisfied."

By the 1990s, with the acquisition of Landis & Company, Raymond Rosen Company and Peerless Company, Haines was one of the nation's largest wholesalers. The Haines fleet of "Big Red" trucks crisscrosses an area encompassing thirteen states, from New Jersey to Georgia, from

Corporate office located in Glen Burnie, Maryland.

John James Haines in Confederate uniform circa 1861.

Delaware to Ohio, Tennessee, Kentucky and all the states in between. Among the products Haines now carries are Armstrong resilient flooring; ShawMark and Milliken Carpets; Bruce, Robbins Eterna, BR 111, Sheoga and Award hardwood flooring; American Olean, Azuvi, Interceramic, American Marazzi, TEC ceramic and mastics. Haines also carries Armstrong Laminate flooring, which was introduced in 1996.

Tradition and continuity are evident in the home office near BWI Airport, where a fifth generation is coming along in the person of Lee's daughter, Anne Minor Kurtz, presently managing the FLASH team responsible for the transition of the corporate software to the J.D. Edwards ERP system.

At the September 2002 Board meeting, Robert H. Thompson was elected CEO; the first non-family executive to run J.J. Haines. Bob's executive team is comprised of Bruce Zwicker, president; Rosana Chaidez, chief information officer; Fred Reitz, vice president, ceramic division; Christina Lightner, vice president, finance; and Kevin Rowley, vice president, operations. All are experienced, talented and capable managers with diverse backgrounds. The Haines Board of Directors, which is recognized by suppliers as the most outstanding board in the industry, includes Phil Adams, Toby Gordon,

A view inside the main distribution center located in Glen Burnie, Maryland.

Dave Griffith, Bruce Lindsay, Lee Marston, Tom Mitchell, Bob Thompson and Mort Creech, a great grandson of J.J. Haines, who has been an important part of the Haines management team for over 40 years and was CEO from 2000 to 2002. He is now Chairman of the Board.

Although much has changed since J.J. Haines arrived in Baltimore in 1874, there remains an appreciation for the legacy of a company born in the days of clipper ships. J.J. Haines management is dedicated to preserving and protecting the culture and heritage of the company and the region in which the company does business. Many of the company's associates are actively participating in various civic and charitable activities; plus, through the J.J. Haines Foundation, the company is able to further contribute to needy causes.

To grow all aspects of J.J. Haines and make the company the very best distributor in the world has been a stated goal that drives the management and associates daily and yearly. Over 130 years ago, John James Haines gave his customers the vision of having a "tradition of service"—and that vision, which turned into reality, is still true today.

KRA CORPORATION

He may not be a politician, but KRA Corporation President and CEO Knowlton R. Atterbeary has found a way to help shape social and economic programs in America.

For the past 22 years, Atterbeary's company has provided professional and technical services to federal, state and local governments in the areas of workforce development, information operations and management consulting. KRA's tremendous success has been recognized by *Inc.* magazine, which listed the firm as "One of America's Fastest-Growing Companies" for four consecutive years.

The Philadelphia native understood the importance of education and hard work as prerequisites for future success. He received his M.B.A. degree in management and finance from Michigan State University in 1970. While there, he served as the graduate student director of the

KRA headquarters, 8757 Georgia Avenue, Silver Spring, Maryland.

President and CEO Knowlton Atterbeary with President Bill Clinton.

Computer Institute for Social Science Research.

Atterbeary's interest in promoting minority businesses began early on in his career, when he was hired as a consultant for the Black Economic Union of Greater Kansas City. He also worked as a management instructor for the Business Institute Training Center in conjunction with the University of Missouri in Kansas City. His consulting expertise later led to a position as corporate vice president and senior partner at Macro International, Inc., a management consulting firm in Maryland.

He started KRA in the den of his Howard County home in 1981, driven by a desire to build an enterprise involved in solving complex social issues.

"Too often federal policy makers relied on academic analysis of everyday problems as guidance for federal policy formulation," says Atterbeary. "I believed a blend of

academic rigor and real-life experiences could result in practical policy recommendations that could change the country for the better."

Atterbeary set out to establish a company that would assist government agencies in the research and implementation of programs promoting causes he cared deeply about, such as youth work development and advocacy for small businesses.

In its first year, the company employed six part-time workers. All of them were deployed to the U.S. Naval Academy in Annapolis, Maryland, where KRA started and staffed the Academy's Family Service Center. The center provided counseling assistance to active and retired military personnel.

The corporation prospered, and in 1988 KRA moved to a high-rise building in Town Center Columbia. However, many of the firm's clients were located in the federal headquarters offices in Washington, D.C. Three years later Atterbeary relocated KRA to Silver Spring in Montgomery County. Here, they would be based in close proximity to their Washington, D.C., and suburban Maryland customers and would have easy access to the Metro public transportation system.

Currently KRA employs over 400 people located in eight states and foreign countries. Atterbeary attributes much of the company's growth to its dedicated workforce.

"We have an employee culture that is based on a sense of shared mission with our customers—a mission to improve our nation, its communities and the quality of life of millions of people," he says. "It's what motivates us to deliver the highest quality of work with integrity and purpose."

KRA offers customized business solutions in three distinct areas: workforce development, information operations, and management consulting. Its extensive list of government clients includes the Department of Education, the Department of Housing and Urban Development, the Department of Labor, the State of Maryland and the government of Washington, D.C.

The Workforce Development Division assists clients in the design and implementation of employment programs through educational enrichment, training and career development. Employers, labor and educational organizations, and community groups each play a vital role in the facilitation of these programs.

The Information Operations Division provides technical support through document management, records processing, and information retrieval and dissemination for government and industry clients.

Two distinct service groups make up the Management Consulting Division— Research and Evaluation (R&E) and Communications and Management (C&M). The R&E group supports federal, state and local agencies as well as private companies in the development and evaluation of their programs. KRA offers analysis, research, technical support and training to help organizations increase

Governor Parris N. Glendenning of Maryland (left) talks with KRA President Knowlton R. Atterbeary in downtown Silver Spring, January 26, 1998.

President and CEO Knowlton R. Atterbeary.

the social and economic impacts of their programs and to devise cost-effective solutions. The C&M group provides clients with administrative, conference and travel management support services, as well as systems development, publications development, production and distribution.

To remain competitive in the marketplace, Atterbeary says KRA is committed to refining its services to meet the needs

of its clients. "We will continue to succeed by making a difference every day for our customers," he says.

KRA has already been honored with numerous public and private awards over the past decade. But Atterbeary says his greatest source of pride is found in his employees. "I am always humbled to receive accolades and awards for their exemplary performance. I am indebted to each of them for their hard work and loyalty to KRA," he says. "They make my job far easier than it should be."

KRA is actively involved on both the state and federal levels in advocating small businesses, particularly minority-owned and women-owned enterprises. The corporation also participates in the Boys & Girls Club of Greater Washington, HIV/AIDS Prevention, youth empowerment programs and economic revitalization of downtown Silver Spring.

Atterbeary has participated in South African Trade and Outreach Missions, sponsored by the Corporate Council on Africa, the U.S. Small Business Administration and the Maryland Governor's Office, to develop strategic contacts for expanding KRA's in-country business. KRA has conducted business in the Caribbean basin and in Turkey, and deems South Africa a strategic target in its international business objectives.

Through a business and education partnership, Atterbeary is seeking to expand the capacity of selected historically black colleges and universities. He also actively supports the Dr. Ronald E. McNair Youth Leadership Development Program, which encourages minority students to pursue careers in engineering and science.

Atterbeary's high esteem for education is a value shared by his family. His son, Knowlton Atterbeary III, is currently working on his M.B.A. degree and is employed as a network administrator at KRA. His daughter, Vanessa, is an attorney with Bulman, Dunie, Burke, & Feld in Bethesda, Maryland. Atterbeary's wife, Rosalynne, is an educator in the Howard County Public Schools system.

TAKOMA PARK SILVER SPRING CO-OP

For over 20 years the Takoma Park Silver Spring (TPSS) Food Co-op has been providing natural foods to neighboring Maryland communities. Area residents banded together to "offer an alternative food distribution center that is responsive to human and community needs." With their first storefront opening in January 1981, the Co-op has gone through many incarnations and trials that today have made it both a successful business and an asset to the community.

The TPSS Food Co-op is owned and operated by community members. Co-ops (cooperatives) are a form of economic democracy with each member having equal ownership and equal voice in the operation of the store. The TPSS Co-op began, like many others in the United States, when the members of the community were not finding the foods they wanted in the retail stores in their area. During the 1970s the "health food" movement spurred many of the nation's co-ops into existence. The TPSS Food Co-op came about for many of the same reasons. The Takoma Park/Silver Spring suburb of Washington, D.C., is known for its counterculture community. Additionally, the Seventh-day Adventists, who are practicing vegetar-

Current location of TTSS Co-op, 201 Ethan Allen Avenue.

ians and very conscientious about food, have a large headquarters in this same community. This community was a nexus of people looking for food alternatives.

The first store in Silver Spring was 1,000 square feet. The store operated with no financial losses for many years. Because the store was growing at a steady rate, it was clear to the members that they needed more space to accommodate the growing number of customers and to provide the selection of foods people wanted. By the 1990s the natural food market was becoming more mainstream, and soon the Co-op

wasn't the only store in town offering natural and vegetarian foods. Large natural food retailers were moving into the community, and for the first time they had serious competition.

The Co-op moved to a larger space, and immediately the store doubled its business. Jim Johnson, president of the Co-op Board from 2000 to 2002, was present during this great transition. The store tripled its product selection, purchased shopping carts, doubled the size of the staff and changed to a computerized checkout system. "It was a herculean effort," Johnson says. Many people helped and volunteered their time and abilities. But soon it became clear that those involved in running the Co-op were overwhelmed and unable to keep up with the huge growth of the store. Besides the management crisis the Co-op faced, they also had a financial crisis.

In the early '80s there were about 1,000 co-ops nationwide. Now only about 300 exist. Seventy percent of the food co-ops closed at a time when the natural foods industry was growing. "What kills co-ops is the people who run them don't think like a business," Johnson explains. Even though the TPSS Co-op is for the

The beautiful produce department offers a large variety of choices.

community and run by the community, it needed to be a store that could compete with the retailers in town, who were offering many of the same food items as the Co-op. The Co-op voted to change the management structure before it collapsed under its own weight.

Changing to a management structure was a difficult transition for the Co-op. For much of the past 20 years major decisions were handled by the workers present at the store—and not according to a hierarchical and managerial system. More accountability was needed to insure better customer service and quality control of the food. A general manager was needed, and it took nearly a year for the TPSS Co-op to find Bob Atwood.

Atwood personified the reorganization of the Co-op upon his arrival in late 1999. The Co-op was overstaffed and morale was low. "It was emotionally difficult," Atwood admits. "It took a lot of work." In a year and a half he was able to take the Co-op out of the red and open a second store in Takoma Park. Since Atwood's arrival, the Co-op has made tremendous strides in the direction of a well-run and viable business. The Co-op has had more opportunities to get involved in the activities of the communities by participating in the town's local celebrations, folk festivals and parades. Because their main source of advertisement is word-of-mouth, they have to rely on the community to support their business—and also make it a business worth supporting. As evidence, they have customers who drive from Washington, D.C., and Virginia.

With the addition of a second store and the growth of the natural foods industry, the growing pains for the Co-op have not subsided. The Takoma Park store's customer base was requesting natural meat products. Since its incarnation, the Co-op had been primarily a vegetarian operation. Now, with the market shifts and more customers to serve, the Co-op had to address this difficult issue. "People were very passionate about this issue," says Johnson. It was a big philosophical

The front end staff cheerfully greets customers.

debate as well. So, in the winter of 2003, a vote was made. Seventy percent of the membership voted that the store staff should have the discretion to sell meat products. Once again, another huge change for the Co-op.

The Co-op has approximately 2,800 members; however, about 45 percent of those who shop at the store are not members. Membership to the Co-op not only gives individuals a say in the business, it also allows members to receive discounts based on the number of hours they volunteer at the store. The store has several departments including bulk foods, grocery, produce and health and beauty. TPSS buys the bulk of their produce

Satisfied customers make their choices from a large variety within the produce department.

from local vendors and is supplied with a variety of breads by local bakers as well. But besides its variety of natural food options, the Co-op is a friendly community store. Jim Johnson describes it as a "warm place to shop." With such a diverse membership and customer base, he enjoys the shopping atmosphere. "It's a neighborhood general store first," he says. Every time he shops at the Co-op he ends up having a conversation with a stranger. The store provides that sort of comfort and atmosphere—alive, friendly and helpful, all dressed in earth tones. More details about the TPSS Co-op food store, membership and events can be found on their website: www.tpss.coop.

As the TPSS Co-op faces the challenges of being a successful business while at the same time operating under the ethical standards for which it was founded, there may be more growing pains. The balance of idealism and actually making it work in the community is clearly quite difficult. The strength of the TPSS Co-op lies in its community: Takoma Park and Silver Spring Co-op is the beating heart of their community.

A TIMELINE OF MARYLAND'S HISTORY

1608   Captain John Smith explores the Chesapeake Bay.

1629   George Calvert, 1st Lord of Baltimore, sails from Newfoundland to Virginia.

1631   Kent Island trading post and farming settlement established by William Claiborne, member of the Virginia Council.

1633   English setters on *Ark* and *Dove* set sail from Cowes, England for Maryland.

1634, March 25   Landing of settlers at St. Clement's Island (Maryland Day). Calvert party eventually purchases Indian land and constructs "Fort at St. Mary's City."

1637   St. Mary's County first cited in provincial records.

1639   First elections in province for delegates to Assembly ordered by Governor Calvert on Kent Island.

1646–47   Leonard Calvert, governor.

1647–48   Margaret Brent denied right to vote in General Assembly.

1649–52   William Stone, governor.

1649   Governor Stone invites Virginia Puritans to settle in Maryland.

1649   An Act concerning Religion

Prince George's County – Court House, Upper Marlboro. The fourth Court House, built in 1880. Courtesy, Enoch Pratt Free Library

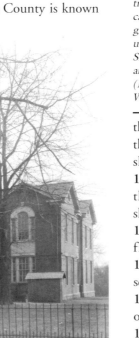

(Religious Toleration Law) enacted.

1650   Anne Arundel County created.

1650   General Assembly is divided into an upper house and a lower house.

1654   Patuxent County (now Calvert County) formed by order of council.

1658   Charles County created by order of council.

1659–60   Baltimore County is known

Construction began on the building of Homewood by Charles Carroll of Carrollton for his son, Charles Carroll between 1798 and 1800, completed about 1808, on a 155-acre tract purchased in 1795 from Thomas Homewood, after whom it was named. In 1840 it was bought by Samuel Wyman. From 1897 until 1910, Homewood was the home of the Country School for Boys (which later became the Gilman Country School. Offered to the trustees of the Johns Hopkins University for its campus, the property was accepted in 1902 as a gift from William Wyman, and the house was used as the faculty club from 1916 to 1928. Since then it has been restored and refurnished, and was opened as a permanent museum in 1932. (Hughes Company, 1939. Gift of D. Stuart Webb.) Courtesy, Enoch Pratt Free Library

throughout to have been established by this date due to a writ issued to county sheriff.

1661–62   Talbot County established by this date. Writ was issued to county sheriff.

1663   Augustine Herrman is the first naturalized citizen of Maryland.

1664   Slavery is sanctioned by law; to serve for life.

1666   Somerset County established by order in council.

1667   St. Mary's City incorporated.

1668–69   Dorchester County is known to have been established by this date.

Writ issued to county sheriff.

1670 Authoritative map of Maryland completed by Augustine Herrman (engraved in London, 1673).

1670 Voting restricted by governor to planters with 50-acre freehold or property worth 40 pounds. Further, officeholding is restricted to owners of 1,000 acres.

1672 Cecil County created from Baltimore and Kent counties by governor's proclamation.

1676 Brick state house completed at St. Mary's City.

1679–84 Charles Calvert, 3rd Lord Baltimore, governor.

1683 Assembly passes Act for Advancement of Trade.

1684 Cambridge on the Choptank River is laid out by commissioners.

1684 Presbyterians under Francis Makemie construct a church at Snow Hill, the first in the colonies.

1692–1715 William and Mary declare Maryland a royal colony and appoint Sir Lionel Copley as governor. Maryland is now governed as a royal colony rather than a proprietary province.

1692 The Church of England is now the established church.

1694 Anne Arundel Town renamed Annapolis.

1695 Prince George's County created from Charles and Calvert counties.

1696 King William's School (now St. John's College) founded in Annapolis.

1704 Construction completed on new state house and St. Anne's Church, Annapolis.

1704 In October, State House burned.

1706 Queen Anne's County formed.

1715 Principio Iron Works, Cecil County, financed by English capital.

1718 Catholics disenfranchised by Assembly.

1720–27 Charles Calvert, governor.

1727–34 *Maryland Gazette*, the first newspaper in the Chesapeake, is published by William Parks at Annapolis.

1727–31 Benedict Leonard Calvert, governor.

1729 Baltimore Town established by charter.

B & O Railroad Tobacco Warehouse. (C. M. Kepner. 1885–1902.) Courtesy, Enoch Pratt Free Library

1731 Baltimore Company begins ironmaking on Patapsco River.

1732 Salisbury Town laid out by commissioners.

1732 Establishment of state's boundary line with three lower counties of Pennsylvania, later Delaware.

1732–33 Charles Calvert, governor.

1733–34 Samuel Ogle, governor.

1742 First Baptist Church in Maryland established at Chestnut Ridge, Baltimore County.

1742 Worcester County erected from Somerset County.

1743 First Lutheran church in Maryland constructed under David Candler, Monocacy River.

1744 Native American chiefs of the Six Nations relinquish all claims to land in the colony by treaty. Assembly purchases last Indian land claims in Maryland.

1745 Daniel Dulany the Elder lays out Frederick Town and invites German settlement.

1745 Assembly combines Jones Town and Baltimore Town.

1748 Frederick County established from Baltimore and Prince George's counties.

1750 John Stevenson ships cargo of flour to Ireland, the first in an export trade that will spur development of Baltimore.

1755 French-speaking Catholics arrive in Baltimore from Nova Scotia.

1762 Elizabeth Town (later Hagerstown) laid out by Jonathan Hager.

1765 Stamp Act resistance at Frederick.

1767 Annapolis merchants sent Charles Willson Peale to London to study painting with Benjamin West.

1769 Maryland merchants adopt policy of British good nonimportation.

1769 First smallpox hospital in the colonies established by Henry Stevenson, Baltimore.

1771 First brick theater in America opens in Annapolis.

1772 Ellicott brothers erect largest flour mill in Maryland on Patapsco River.

1772, March 28 Cornerstone laid for new State House in Annapolis.

1773 Assembly unites Baltimore Town and Fells Point.

1773   Caroline County created from Dorchester and Queen Anne's counties.

1773   Harford County formed from Baltimore County.

1774   First Provincial Convention, an extralegal body, meets in Annapolis and sends delegates to First Continental Congress.

1774   Mob burns tea-laden *Peggy Stewart* in Annapolis harbor over violating nonimportation agreement.

1775, July 18   Rifle companies under Thomas Price and Michael Cresap leave Frederick Town to join Washington's army at Boston.

1776   Montgomery County created from Frederick County.

1776   Washington County created from Frederick County.

1776, July 4   Declaration of Independence is adopted in Philadelphia. Engrossed copy signed by Marylanders William Paca, Charles Carroll of Carrollton, Thomas Stone and Samuel Chase.

1776, July 6   Maryland Convention declares independence from Great Britain.

1776   Maryland's Bill of Rights adopted by Ninth Provincial Convention. Church of England disestablished.

1776, November 8   First State Constitution adopted by Ninth Provincial Convention.

1776–77   Continental Congress meets in Baltimore.

1777, February 5   First General Assembly elected under State Constitution of 1776 meets in Annapolis.

1778   Count Casimir Pulaski raises independent troops in Baltimore.

1780, August 16   Maryland soldiers fight at Battle of Camden in South Carolina.

1781, January 17   Maryland soldiers fight under John Eager Howard and play a critical and decisive role at the Battle of Cowpens in South Carolina.

1781   Property of Loyalists and British subjects confiscated.

1781, March 1   Maryland ratifies and makes effective the Articles of Confed-

Enoch Pratt Free Library, completed in 1933. (Leopold. My Maryland) Courtesy, Enoch Pratt Free Library

eration.

1782   Washington College established at Chestertown.

1782–85   William Paca, governor.

1783, November 26 – June 3, 1784   Annapolis serves as nation's capital.

1783, December 23   George Washington resigns commission as commander-in-chief of Continental Army at State House in Annapolis.

1784, January 14   Treaty of Paris, ending Revolutionary War, ratified by Congress at Annapolis.

1785   Trade with China begins with John O'Donnell's arrival in Baltimore with cargo from Canton, China.

1787   General Assembly authorizes toll roads connecting Baltimore with Frederick, Westminster, Hanover, and York.

1789   Allegany County created from Washington County.

1789   Georgetown College chartered.

1789   Maryland ratifies federal Bill of Rights.

1791, December 19   Maryland cedes land for federal District of Columbia.

1792   African Americans form Sharp Street Methodist Church in Baltimore.

1793   Refugees from Haitian slave uprising arrive in Baltimore.

1794   Baltimore Equitable Society, the first fire insurance company in Maryland, is formed.

1795   Bank of Baltimore established.

1796   Maryland law prohibits import of slaves for sale and permits voluntary slave emancipation.

1796   Baltimore City incorporated.

1797   Harris Creek, David Stodder's shipyard, launches frigate USS *Constellation*.

1806   Construction initiated for Basilica of the Assumption, America's first Roman Catholic cathedral. The Basilica was designed by Benjamin Henry Latrobe.

1807   University of Maryland chartered at Baltimore as the College of Medicine of Maryland.

1811   Alexander Brown & Sons opens as investment banking firm in Baltimore.

1812   Thomas Kemp of Fells Point launches the Baltimore Clipper *Chasseur*, made famous under the command of Thomas Boyle.

1813 The *Chesapeake* appears, the first steamboat on the Chesapeake Bay.
1813 British conduct raids on Chesapeake targets, including Havre de Grace.
1813 Hagerstown is incorporated.
1814, August 24 Battle of Bladensburg.
1814, September 12 British repelled by local militia at Battle of North Point.
1814, September 13 Francis Scott Key is inspired by the bombardment of Fort McHenry to write the "Star-Spangled Banner."
1816 Daniel Coker and other African American church leaders form independent African Methodist Episcopal Church.
1817 Gas Light Company incorporated to provide streetlights in Baltimore, the first such firm in the nation.
1824–29 Chesapeake and Delaware Canal constructed through Cecil County to link the Chesapeake Bay with Delaware River.
1827, February 28 Baltimore and Ohio (B & O) Railroad chartered.
1828 Maryland and Virginia Steam Boat Company offers regular Baltimore to Norfolk service.
1828, July 4 First earth turned for construction of B & O Railorad and Chesapeake and Ohio (C & O) Canal.
1828–48 C & O Canal constructed to Cumberland.
1829 Work begun on Baltimore and Susquehanna Railroad (completed to Pennsylvania line 1832).
1830 B & O Railroad Station at Mount Clare, the first in the U.S.
1832 In the aftermath of the Nat Turner rebellion in Virginia, Maryland enacts laws to restrict free blacks.
1834 B & O Railroad reaches Harpers Ferry.
1837 Chief Justice Roger Brooke Taney writes majority opinion in the *Charles River v. Warren Bridge* case.
1837 Carroll County formed from Baltimore and Frederick counties.
1837 *The Baltimore Sun* begins publication under Arunah S. Abell.
1838 Frederick Douglass escapes from slavery in Baltimore.

1842 B & O Railroad reaches Cumberland.
1849 Harriet Tubman escapes slavery in Dorchester County.
1850 Sun Iron Building constructed, Baltimore's first all-iron structure.
1852 Loyola College founded in Baltimore.

An early view of Gay Street. Courtesy, Enoch Pratt Free Library

American Oil Company. Filling trucks, which deliver gas, at the plant at Curtis Bay in 1931. Courtesy, Enoch Pratt Free Library

1852 B & O Railroad lines reach Wheeling, Virginia.

1854 Baltimore County seat moved to Towson Town.

1855 Baltimore-built clipper ship *Mary Whitridge* sets transatlantic sailing record.

1857 Chief Justice Taney writes majority opinion in *Dred Scott v. Sanford*.

1857 Peabody Institute founded in Baltimore.

1859, October 16 John Brown launches raid from Maryland on federal arsenal in Harpers Ferry, West Virginia.

1860 Druid Hill Park opens in Baltimore.

1861, April James Ryder Randall writes "Maryland, My Maryland".

1861, April 19 Sixth Massachusetts Regiment attacked by a Baltimore mob.

1861, April 27 President Lincoln suspends writ of habeas corpus between Washington and Philadelphia.

1861, June Military arrests Baltimore police board members.

1862, May 23 Marylanders combat one another at Battle of Front Royal.

1862, June 16 Confederate cavalry enters Cumberland.

1862, September 17 Battle of Antietam (or Sharpsburg), 4,800 dead, 18,000 wounded.

1864, November 1 Maryland slaves emancipated by state constitution of 1864.

1865 Chesapeake Marine Railway and Dry Dock Company, the first black-owned business in the state, established by Isaac Myers.

1865 General Assembly permits oyster dredging, but only under sail.

1865, April John Wilkes Booth assassinates President Abraham Lincoln and escapes through Prince George's and Charles counties.

1867 Centenary Biblical Institute chartered under the auspices of the Methodist Episcopal Church; later becomes Morgan State University.

1867 Wicomico County created from Somerset and Worcester counties.

1868 Western Maryland College (now

Views of Baltimore: 1933–1934. From Emerson Tower Building. The taller structures, left to right, are the Fidelity Building, Lord Baltimore Hotel, B & O Building, Munsey, Baltimore Trust, Southern Hotel and First National Bank Buildings. In the center is the six-story Rouse Building, temporary home of the Pratt Library while the new library was under construction. (Morris G. Westerkan. 1933/34). Courtesy, Enoch Pratt Free Library

McDaniel College) chartered by Methodists.

1870 Maryland Jockey Club sponsors racing at Pimlico track.

1872 Garrett County formed from Allegany County.

1873 School Sisters of Notre Dame establish College of Notre Dame of Maryland in Baltimore, the first Catholic women's college in the U.S.

1875 Ceremonies dedicate Baltimore City Hall, a George Frederick design.

1875 Atlantic Hotel is built, the first hotel in Ocean City.

1878 Young men return from Newport, Rhode Island with lacrosse sticks.

1883 Chesapeake and Potomac (C & P) Telephone Company formed.

1885 Women's College of Baltimore is chartered by Methodists, later Goucher College.

1885 Bryn Mawr School founded by M. Carey Thomas in Baltimore.

1885 Baltimore-Union Passenger Railway Company established, the first commercial electric street railway in the country.

1886 Enoch Pratt Free Library opens in Baltimore.

1887 Pennsylvania Steel builds blast furnace at Sparrows Point.

1889, May 7 The Johns Hopkins Hospital dedicated in Baltimore.

1892 *Baltimore Afro-American* founded by John H. Murphy Sr.

1893 Women's College of Frederick founded, later Hood College.

1893, October The Johns Hopkins University School of Medicine opens in Baltimore, accepting women.

1894 Baltimore Orioles win their first professional baseball championship.

1895 Maryland Bar Association holds its first convention.

1895 Charles County seat relocated from Port Tobacco to La Plata.

1897 Frederick Law Olmsted Jr. plans west side of Roland Park.

1904, February 7–8 Baltimore fire.

Seventy blocks in the heart of the business district ravaged.

1908 H. L. Mencken becomes literary editor of *Smart Set*.

1909, April 6 Matthew Henson of Charles County reaches the North Pole with Robert Peary.

1910, August 30 First statewide primary election in Maryland.

1911 Baltimore completes sewerage system.

1914 Babe Ruth pitches for International League Orioles.

1916 The Johns Hopkins University moves to Homewood in Baltimore.

1916, February Gustav Strube organizes the Baltimore Symphony Orchestra.

1917 The federal government establishes Camp Meade, now Fort Meade.

1917 U.S. Army establishes Aberdeen Proving Ground as its first testing center.

1920, November 2 Women voted for first time in Maryland.

1920–35 Albert C. Ritchie (Democrat), governor.

1924 Albert C. Ritchie campaigns for Democratic presidential nomination.

1924 Floods destroy much of the C & O Canal.

1925 Maryland and Virginia pass legislation protecting the blue crab from extinction.

1926 Baltimore equalizes pay for black and white teachers.

1929 Baltimore Trust Building constructed, the tallest structure in Baltimore.

1929 Baltimore Museum of Art opens.

1931, March 3 "Star-Spangled Banner" adopted as national anthem.

1932, June Albert C. Ritchie loses second bid for presidency.

1933 Billie Holliday auditions with Benny Goodman orchestra.

1934 The Walters Art Gallery opens in Baltimore.

1935 Hall of Records opens in Annapolis.

1937 Pan American Airways inaugurates Baltimore to Bermuda service.

1938 Federal government begins relocating National Institutes of Health to site near Bethesda.

1938 Silver Spring Shopping Center opens.

1939 Ritchie Highway connects Baltimore and Annapolis.

1941, December 7 USS *Maryland* among naval ships attacked at Pearl Harbor.

1942 Patuxent Air Station opens in St. Mary's County.

1944 Blue baby operation is developed at Johns Hopkins Hospital, setting the stage for the heart surgery era.

1944 New Baltimore municipal airport in Anne Arundel County recommended by Baltimore mayoral commission.

1947 Commercial television stations broadcast from Baltimore and Washington, DC.

1950 Lawsuit opens University of Maryland School of Nursing to African-Americans.

1950 Friendship International Airport (now Baltimore/Washington International Airport, BWI) begins service.

1951 University of Maryland graduate school is integrated.

1951–59 Theodore R. McKeldin (Republican), governor.

1952 **July 30.** The Chesapeake Bay Bridge opens.

1954 St. Louis Browns move to Baltimore, and become American League Orioles.

1955 Greater Baltimore Committee organized by business leaders.

1956 Maryland Port Authority established.

1956 Baltimore Regional Planning Council (now Baltimore Metropolitan Council) formed.

1956 I-70 connects Frederick and Baltimore.

1956 James W. Rouse opens Mondawmin Mall in Baltimore.

1958 James W. Rouse builds Harundale Mall, Anne Arundel County, the first enclosed shopping center in the state.

Ice in Baltimore harbor during severe weather January–February 1936. In the foreground is the steamer Allegany, at the Merchants and Miners Transportation Company pier (Pier 3) on Pratt Street at the end of Gay Street (right). At left are the News-Post buildings and the Arundel Corporation pier (Pier 2). At upper right is the U.S. Appraiser's Store. The large building between this and the City Hall Tower is the U.S. Customs House. (Enoch Pratt Free Library. February 1936) Courtesy, Enoch Pratt Free Library

1958, March Greater Baltimore Committee unveils plans for Charles Center to reinvigorate Baltimore's central business district.

1958 Baltimore Colts are National Football League Champions.

1959 Baltimore Colts repeat.

1962 Jones Falls Expressway opens.

1963 I-95 connects Baltimore and Wilmington.

1964 Eastern Shore leaders establish Wye Institute, Queen Anne's County.

1964 Dundalk Marine Terminal begins handling containerized cargoes.

1966 University of Maryland campus at Baltimore County opens.

1966 Baltimore Orioles win World Series.

1967 Morris A. Mechanic Theater opens in Baltimore.

1967–69 Spiro T. Agnew (Republican), governor.

1969, April Riots in Baltimore and Washington, D.C., follow the assassination of Dr. Martin Luther King.

Ocean City beach. (Blackstone Studios, Inc., New York, 1937. Gift of Photolyte Studio, Salisbury.) Courtesy, Enoch Pratt Free Library

Chesapeake and Ohio (C & O) Canal – Keeper's House, 1937. (Negative loaned by Sloan.) Courtesy, Enoch Pratt Free Library

1969–77 Marvin Mandel (Democrat), governor.

1969 Maryland Public Broadcasting airs.

1969 USS *Constellation*, the last surviving ship of the Civil War, moored permanently at Pier 1 in Baltimore.

1969 Baltimore Gas and Electric Company begins construction of Calvert Cliffs Nuclear Power Plant.

1970, September Baltimore stages first city fair.

1970, October Baltimore Orioles win World Series.

1971 Baltimore Colts win Super Bowl.

1971 First high-rise condominium in Ocean City.

1971 I-95 opens between Baltimore and Washington, D.C.

1973 The second (parallel) Chesapeake Bay Bridge opens.

1973 State adopts lottery.

1973, September Urban "homesteading" begins in Baltimore. City sells abandoned homes for $1 to encourage renovation.

1973 Spiro T. Agnew resigns vice-presidency, pleads no contest to felony charge.

1975   Mother Elizabeth Seton canonized by Pope Paul VI.

1976   Maryland Science Center opens in Baltimore.

1977   World Trade Center opens in Baltimore.

1977, **August**   Governor Marvin Mandel found guilty of mail fraud charges. Succeeded by Lt. Governor Blair Lee III.

1978, **September 5–17**   Camp David Accords negotiated at Camp David in Frederick County between President Jimmy Carter, President Anwar Sadat of Egypt, and Prime Minister Menachem Begin of Israel. Signed in Washington, D.C., March 26, 1979.

1979   Daniel Nathans and Hamilton Smith of Johns Hopkins Hospital win Nobel Prizes for medicine.

1979   Baltimore Convention Center opens.

1979–87   Harry Hughes (Democrat), governor.

1980   Maryland and Virginia establish Chesapeake Bay Commission to coordinate interstate legislative planning and programs to help restore Bay resources.

1981   The National Aquarium opens in Baltimore.

1983   Behind second-year sensation Cal Ripken, Jr., the Baltimore Orioles defeat the Philadelphia Phillies in five games to win the World Series.

1986   William Donald Schaefer (Democrat), former mayor of Baltimore, is elected governor. He will serve from 1987–1995.

1987   Kurt L. Schmoke (Democrat) becomes the first elected African American mayor of Baltimore. He will serve until 1999.

1992, **April 6**   Orioles Park at Camden Yards, a stadium for the Baltimore Orioles, opens in downtown Baltimore to rave reviews.

1993   The Chesapeake Bay Partnership Agreement to reduce pollution in the Bay's tributaries by the year 2000 is signed by the Governor and Maryland's 24 jurisdictions.

1995–2003   Parris N. Glendening (Democrat), governor.

1998   Ravens Stadium, home to the Baltimore Ravens National Football League team, opens in Camden Yards, Baltimore.

1998   Wye Summit. Middle East Peace Talks between Israel and the Palestine Liberation Organization held at Aspen Institute's Wye River Conference Center in Queen Anne's County. The Wye River Memorandum is the result, and is signed in Washington, D.C., on October 23, 1998.

2001   The Baltimore Ravens rout the New York Giants to win Super Bowl XXXV.

2002   The Maryland Terrapins defeat Indiana to win the NCAA men's basketball championship.

2003   Robert L. Ehrlich Jr. (Republican) is elected Maryland's 60th governor, and is the first Republican elected since 1966 (Agnew).

Source:
Maryland State Archives, *Maryland Historical Chronology*

Robert L. Ehrlich Jr. (Republican) is elected Maryland's 60th governor,

BIBLIOGRAPHY

GENERAL WORKS:

Dilisio, James E. *Maryland: A Geography.* Boulder, Colorado: Westview Press, 1983.

Dozer, Donald M. *Portrait of the Free State.* Centreville, Maryland: Tidewater Publishers, 1976.

Hall, Clayton C. *Baltimore: Its History and Its People.* New York: Lewis Historical Publishing Company, 1912.

Olson, Sherry H. *Baltimore: The Building of An American City.* Baltimore: The Johns Hopkins University Press, 1980.

Radoff, Morris L. *The Old Line State: A History of Maryland.* Annapolis, Maryland: Hall of Records Commission, 1971.

Walsh, Richard and Fox, William Lloyd. *Maryland: A History 1632-1974.* Baltimore: Maryland Historical Society, 1974.

CHAPTER ONE

Clemens, Paul G. *The Atlantic Economy and Colonial Maryland's Eastern Shore: From Tobacco to Grain.* Ithaca, New York: Cornell University Press, 1980.

Earle, Carville V. *The Evolution of a Tidewater Settlement: All Hallows Parish, Maryland, 1650-1783.* Chicago, Illinois: University of Chicago Press, 1975.

Land, Aubrey C. *Colonial Maryland: A History.* Millwood, New Jersey: Kraus-Thompson Limited, 1981.

Land, Aubrey C. Law, ed. *Society and Politics in Early Maryland.* Baltimore: The Johns Hopkins University Press, 1977.

Main, Gloria. *Tobacco Colony: Life in Early Maryland, 1650-1720.* Princeton, New Jersey: Princeton University Press, 1982.

Price, Jacob M. *Capital and Credit in British Overseas Trade: The View From the Chesapeake, 1700-1776.* Cambridge, Massachusetts: Harvard University Press, 1980.

Quinn, David B., ed. *Early Maryland in A Wider World.* Detroit, Michigan: Wayne State University Press, 1982.

Tate, Thad W. and Ammerman, David L., eds. *The Chesapeake in the Seventeenth Century: Essays on Anglo-American Society.* Chapel Hill, North Carolina: University of North Carolina Press, 1979.

CHAPTER TWO

Barker, Charles A. *The Background of the Revolution in Maryland.* New York: Archon Books, 1967.

Gould, Clarence P. *Money and Transportation in Maryland, 1720-1765.* Baltimore: The Johns Hopkins University Press, 1915.

Hoffman, Ronald H. *A Spirit of Dissension: Economics, Politics and the Revolution in Maryland.* Baltimore: The Johns Hopkins University Press, 1974.

Middleton, Arthur Pierce. *Tobacco Coast: A Maritime History of Chesapeake Bay in the Colonial Era.* Newport News, Virginia: The Mariners Museum, 1953.

Papenfuse, Edward. *In Pursuit of Profit: The Annapolis Merchants in the Era of the American Revolution, 1763-1805.* Baltimore: The Johns Hopkins University Press, 1975.

Skaggs, David C. *Roots of Maryland Democracy.* Westport, Connecticut: Greenwood Press, 1973.

CHAPTER THREE

Brown, Alexander B. *Steam Packets on the Chesapeake: A History the Old Bay Line.* Cambridge, Maryland: Cornell Maritime Press, 1961.

Browne, Gary L. *Baltimore in the Nation, 1789-1861.* Chapel Hill, North Carolina: University of North Carolina Press, 1980.

Cassell, Frank A. *Merchant Congressman in the Young Republic: Samuel Smith of Maryland 1752-1839.* Madison, Wisconsin: University of Wisconsin Press, 1971.

Chapelle, Howard I. *The Baltimore Clipper: Its Origin Development.* Hatboro, Pennsylvania: Tradition Press, 1965.

Gray, Ralph D. *The National Waterway: A History of the Chesapeake and Delaware Canal, 1769-1965.* Urbana, Illinois: University of Illinois Press, 1967.

Hungerford, Edward. *The Story of the Baltimore and Ohio Railroad, 1827-1927.* 2 Vols. New York: G. P. Putnam's Sons, 1928.

CHAPTER FOUR

Marks, Bayly Ellen. "Economics and Society in a Staple Plantation System: St. Mary's County, Maryland, 1790-1840." Ph.D. Dissertation, University of Maryland, 1979.

Wiser, Vivian. "The Movement for Agricultural Improvement in Maryland, 1785-1865." Ph.D. Dissertation, University of Maryland, 1963.

Bruchey, Eleanor S. "The Business Elite in Baltimore, 1880-1914." Ph.D. Dissertation, The Johns Hopkins University, 1967.

Crooks, James B. *Politics and Progress: The Rise of Urban Progressivism in Baltimore, 1895-1911.* Baton Rouge, Louisiana: Louisiana State University Press, 1966.

Harvey, Katherine A. *The Best Dressed Miners Life and Labor in the Maryland Coal Region, 1835-1910.* Ithaca, New York: Cornell University Press, 1969.

Hayman, John. *Rails Along the Chesapeake: A History of Railroading on the Demarva Peninsula, 1827-1978.* Unpublished: Marvadel Publishers, 1979.

Hirschfeld, Charles. *Baltimore, 1870-1900: Studies in Social History.* Baltimore: The Johns Hopkins University Press, 1941.

Johnson, Arthur N. "The Present Condition of Maryland Highways," and Sioussat, St. George L. "Highway Legislation in Maryland: Its Influence on the Economic Development of the State," in Maryland Geological Survey Commission, *Maryland Geological Survey, Vol. 3.* Baltimore: The Johns Hopkins Press, 1899.

Kennedy, Victor S. and Breisch, Linda L. *Maryland's Oysters: Research and Management.* College Park: University of Maryland, 1981.

Maryland Board of World's Fair Managers. *Maryland, Its Resources, Industries and Institutions.* Baltimore: Board of World's Fair Managers, 1893.

Maryland Bureau of Industrial Statistics and Information. *Biennial Reports* (1884-1891), *Annual Reports,* 1894-1916.

Preston, Dickson J. *Talbot County: A History.* Centreville, Maryland: Tidewater Publishers, 1983.

Stegmaier, Harry, et al. *Allegany County: A History.* Parsons, West Virginia: McClain Printing Company, 1976.

Williams, Thomas J. C. *History of Frederick County Maryland.* Baltimore: Regional Publishing Company, 1967 (1910)

CHAPTER FIVE

Anderson, Karen. *Wartime Women: Sex Roles, Family Relations and The Status of Women During World II.* Westport, Connecticut: Greenwood Press, 1981.

Argersinger, JoAnne. *"Baltimore: The Depression Years."* Ph.D. Dissertation, The George Washington University, 1980.

Baltimore Association of Commerce. *Baltimore,* 1920-1950.

Consolidated Gas, Electric Light and Power Company of Baltimore. *Industrial Survey of Baltimore.* Baltimore: Consolidated of Baltimore, 1914.

Hamill, W. S. *The Agricultural Industry of Maryland.* Baltimore: Maryland Development Bureau, 1934.

Consolidated Gas, Electric and Power Company of Baltimore. *Second Industrial Survey of Baltimore.* Baltimore: Consolidated of Baltimore, 1939.

Del-Mar-Va Association. *Del-Mar-Va Takes Inventory: Conference Proceedings.* The Del-Mar-Va Association, 1927.

Fairbanks, W. L. and Hamill, W. S. *The Manufacturing Industry of Maryland.* Baltimore: Maryland Development Bureau, 1932.

Kimberly, Charles M. *"The Depression and New Deal in Maryland."* Ph.D. Dissertation, American University, 1974.

Hiebert, Ray E. and MacMaster, Richard K. *A Grateful Remembrance: The Story of Montgomery County, Maryland.* Rockville, Maryland: Montgomery County Historical Society, 1976.

Maryland Commission on Post-War Reconstruction and Development. *Maryland Post-War Employment and Programs.* Baltimore: The Commission, 1944.

Maryland Historical Society, War Records Division. *Maryland In World War II,* Vol. 2, *Industry and Agriculture.* Baltimore: Maryland Historical Society, 1951.

Maryland State Roads Commission. *A History of Road Building in Maryland.* Baltimore: The State Roads Commission of Maryland, 1958.

CHAPTER SIX

Baltimore County Economic Development Commission. *Baltimore County Economic Adjustment Strategies Conference.* Towson, Maryland: Baltimore County Economic Development Commission.

Baltimore Magazine, 1950-1984.

Brooks, Neal A. and Rockel, Eric G. *A History of Baltimore County.* Towson, Maryland: Friends of the Towson Library, Inc., 1979.

Lyall, Katherine. "A Bicycle Built for Two: Public-Private Partnership in Baltimore," *National Civic Review.* Vol. 72 (November, 1983), pp. 531-571.

Maryland Department of Economic and Community Development. *Maryland Statistical Abstract, 1984-85.* Annapolis, Maryland: Department of Economic and Community Development, 1984.

Maryland Department of Economic and Community Development. *A Comparison of High-Technology Centers in the United States.* Annapolis, Maryland: Maryland

Department of Economic and Community Development, 1983.

Maryland Department of Economic and Community Development. *Maryland.* Annapolis, Maryland: Department of Economic and Community Development, 1983.

Maryland Department of Employment and Training, Research and Analysis Division. *Employment and Unemployment: 1970-1983. United States, Maryland and Baltimore Metropolitan Area.* Baltimore: Maryland Department of Employment and Training, 1984.

Maryland Department of Employment and Training. *Maryland Labor Market Analysis* (1982-1990). Baltimore: Maryland Department of Employment and Training, 1983.

Maryland Port Authority. *Port of Baltimore,* 1955-1984.

Nast, Lenora H. N., et al. *Baltimore: A Living Renaissance.* Baltimore: Historic Baltimore Society, Inc., 1982.

Washington/Baltimore Regional Association. *The Baltimore-Washington Common Market: An Economic Profile.* Baltimore: Washington/Baltimore Regional Association, 1982.

CHAPTER SEVEN

U.S. Census Bureau, annual Consolidated Federal Funds Reports 1986—2001.

Rusk, David, *Baltimore Unbound: A Strategy for Regional Renewal,* Abell Foundation & John Hopkins University Press, 1996.

Maryland Economic Quarterly, RESI, Towson University, winter 2001.

Baltimore Economic Digest, RESI, Towson University, as published in the Baltimore Business Journal, summer 1999.

State of Maryland, Fiscal Facts, February 1993.

Wasserman, David and Womersley, Mick, *Preserving the Watermen's Way of Life,* fall 1997.

TIMELINE

Maryland State Archives, *Maryland Historical Chronology*

INDEX

Before downtown Rockville went through urban renewal, East Montgomery Avenue had "The Triangle," pictured here on a 1910 postcard. Courtesy, Montgomery County Historical Society

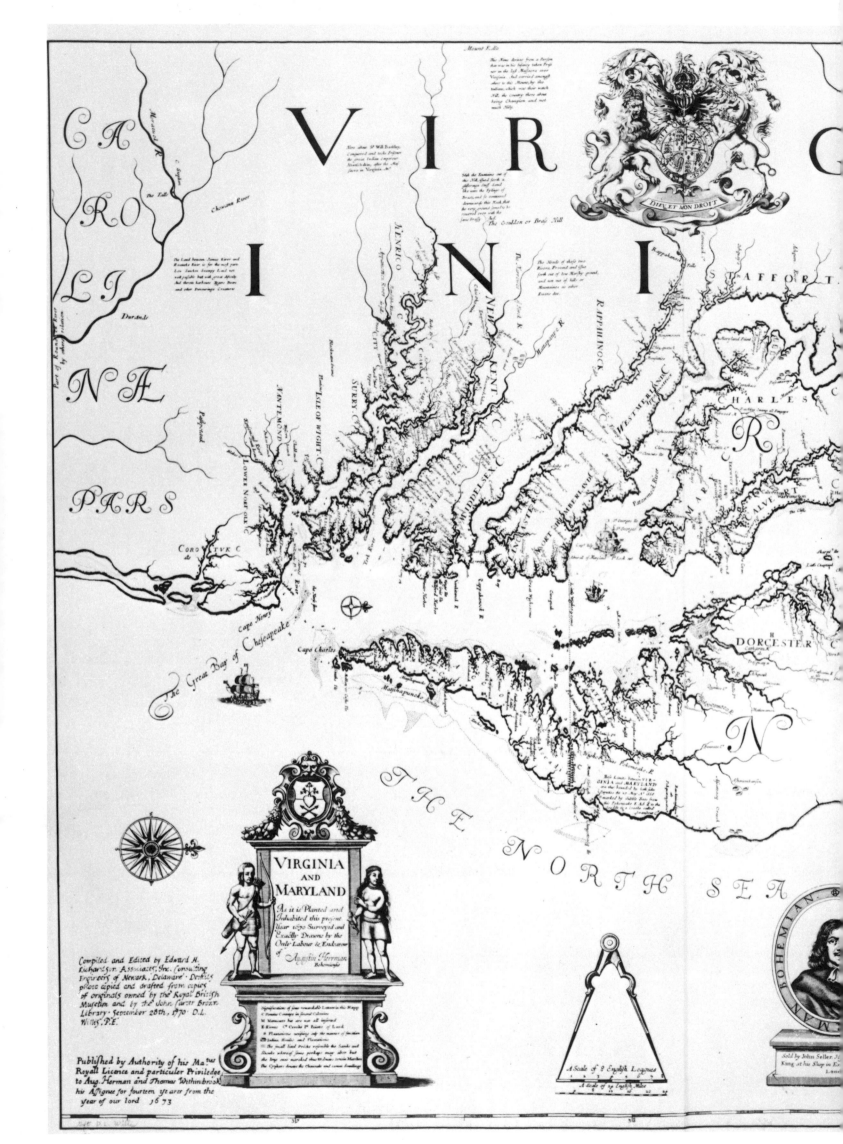